CONSISTENCY IN SOCIAL BEHAVIOR
The Ontario Symposium
Volume 2

CONSISTENCY IN SOCIAL BEHAVIOR
The Ontario Symposium
Volume 2

Edited by

Mark P. Zanna
University of Waterloo

E. Tory Higgins
University of Western Ontario

C. Peter Herman
University of Toronto

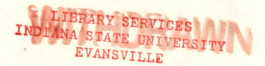
LEA LAWRENCE ERLBAUM ASSOCIATES, PUBLISHERS
1982 Hillsdale, New Jersey   London

Lawrence Erlbaum Associates, Inc., Publishers
365 Broadway
Hillsdale, New Jersey 07642

Library of Congress Cataloging in Publication Data

Ontario Symposium on Personality and Social
   Psychology (2nd : 1979 : University of
   Waterloo)
   Consistency in social behavior.

   Bibliography: p.
   Includes index.

   1. Social perception—Congresses.
2. Cognition—Congresses. 3. Attitude
(Psychology)—Congresses. I. Zanna, Mark P.
II. Higgins, Edward Tory, 1946–
III. Herman, C. Peter. IV. Title.
HM251.0585 1982   153.7′5   82-11489
ISBN 0-89859-221-6

Printed in the United States of America

To our graduate students, and to all the graduate students in personality and social psychology in Canada without whom our jobs would be less rewarding and certainly less enjoyable.

Contents

PART III: COMMENTARY

Preface

This volume presents papers from the second Ontario Symposium on Personality and Social Psychology, held at the University of Waterloo over the 3-day period, October 19 to 21, 1979. The general theme of the second Ontario Symposium was "variability and consistency in social behavior." Participants were selected to present various perspectives on the attitude-behavior and/or the personality-behavior relation. We were fortunate to be able to bring together a distinguished group of personality and social psychologists who have made, and, as this volume will attest, continue to make, major theoretical and empirical contributions to the problem of consistency in social behavior. When taken together, we believe that the chapters of this volume have the effect of, once again, placing this problem on center stage of personality and social psychology. We also believe the contributors have benefited significantly both from the interchange and discussion at the conference, and from the comments that they provided one another on earlier drafts of their chapters. As editors of the volume, we would like to thank the individual authors for their editorial contributions.

The 12 chapters contained in this volume have been grouped into two major parts. Chapters one through six focus on the attitude-behavior relation. Chapters seven through eleven focus on the personality-behavior relation. Chapter twelve comments on the perspectives taken in the previous chapters and suggests new directions for future research.

The purpose of the symposium and the resultant volume was three-fold: first, we sought to report on current research programs and critically review research on the attitude-behavior relation; second, we sought to report on current research programs and critically review research on the personality-behavior relation; and third, as a consequence of the first two purposes, we sought to compare and contrast these two conceptually similar, yet at present relatively independent areas of research. We hope that this volume will generate new ideas and inspire new research in what we continue to believe to be a resurgent field of inquiry.

The symposium on consistency in behavior represented in this volume was the second of, to date, three Ontario Symposia on Personality and Social Psychology. The first Ontario Symposium, held in Fall, 1978, dealt with social cognition (see Higgins, E. T., Herman, C. P. and Zanna, M. P. (Eds.), *Social cognition: The Ontario Symposium*. Vol. 1. Hillsdale, N.J.: Lawrence Erlbaum Associates, 1981). The third Ontario Symposium, held in spring, 1981 was concerned with the social psychology of appearance. The Ontario Symposium on Personality and Social Psychology was initiated for a number of reasons. We felt that an annual, or at least biennial, conference in personality and social psychology was called for. Such a conference would provide a forum in which scholars concerned with the same issue might meet to discuss common concerns and attempt to integrate their findings into a unified picture. The volume that derives from each conference is intended to provide the most up-to-date source book in the particular area being considered. By providing an opportunity for psychologists and non-psychologists actively working in an important, evolving (or resurging) area to meet, exchange ideas, and, hopefully, arrive at some common conclusions, the conference could further our understanding of the issue concerned and guide further research.

We would like to express our sincere gratitude to the Social Sciences and Humanities Research Council of Canada, to the Faculty of Arts of the University of Waterloo, and to the Department of Psychology of the University of Waterloo for their financial support for this second Ontario Symposium. We are indebted to Michel Alain, Alec Lumsden, and, especially, Shelagh Towson for doing everything that had to be done to make the conference, attended by more than 70 graduate students and faculty from over 20 universities, run smoothly. We continue to owe a particular debt to Larry Erlbaum for his enthusiastic response to our idea of an Ontario Symposium as well as for his editorial guidance. Finally, we wish to thank, once again, Janet Polivy and Betsy Zanna for their helpful suggestions and continuous support throughout the project.

Mark P. Zanna

E. Tory Higgins

C. Peter Herman

Note—In response to the questions of some of our colleagues, the colors of volumes 1 and 2, red and white, signify the colors of Canada and the Trillium is the symbol of Ontario.

CONSISTENCY IN SOCIAL BEHAVIOR
The Ontario Symposium
Volume 2

THE ATTITUDE-BEHAVIOR RELATION

1

On Behaving in Accordance With One's Attitudes

Icek Ajzen
University of Massachusetts at Amherst

It has often been asserted that people fail to act in accordance with their attitudes. Reservations concerning the attitude concept are in large part due to the disappointing results of studies conducted in the 1950s and 1960s that attempted to predict overt behavior from verbal measures of attitude. Although these attempts were occasionally successful, most revealed rather low and nonsignificant attitude-behavior relations (see Ajzen & Fishbein, 1977; Wicker, 1969). As a result, some social psychologists have concluded that measures of attitude have little value for the prediction of overt behavior, but most seem to have adopted the view that the effect of attitude is moderated or overshadowed by the presence of such variables as motives, values, habits, experience, norms, and expectations. Recent research has therefore turned to the task of identifying some of the important factors that moderate the attitude-behavior relationship (e.g., Fazio & Zanna, 1978; Liska, 1974; Norman, 1975; Snyder & Swann, 1976; Warland & Sample, 1973).

To state my position at the outset, I take issue with the argument that attitudes have no utility for the prediction of behavior as well as with the suggestion that low attitude-behavior relations are due to the moderating effects of other factors. To be sure, variables other than attitude may influence any given behavior, but the conclusion that there is no direct relation between attitude and behavior is, in my opinion, unwarranted. In this chapter I try to show that people do in fact behave in accordance with their attitudes.

GLOBAL ATTITUDES AND OVERT BEHAVIOR

Let us first examine how behavior relates to global measures of attitude. Although definitions vary, most social psychologists view attitude as a predisposition to

3

respond in a generally favorable or unfavorable manner with respect to the object of the attitude. Standard scaling procedures, such as the semantic differential, are typically used to infer these predispositions from verbal responses to questionnaire items. In marked contrast to the efforts invested in developing valid attitude measures, investigators have been rather cavalier in their approach to the measurement of behavior. They have been willing to accept virtually any operationally defined measure as a valid assessment of the behavioral domain in question.

Single-act Measures

Imagine, for example, that we are interested in the attitudes and behavior of college professors with regard to their students. On the attitudinal side we might use a Likert scale or the semantic differential to assess each professor's evaluation of his or her students. As to the behavioral side, however, no clear guidelines for measurement appear to be available. Suppose we observe whether the professor complies with a student's request to borrow a book or a journal. One might argue that professors who hold favorable attitudes toward their students should be more willing to lend them their books than should professors whose attitudes are more negative.

Closer examination reveals, however, that this behavior is unlikely to possess a high degree of construct validity. Clearly, lending your books or journals is only one of many behaviors you can perform with respect to your students, and a measure of this behavior is thus unlikely to be representative of the general behavioral domain under consideration. I am in complete agreement with those who would argue that the particular behavior of lending books may be influenced by various factors other than general attitude toward students. Professors with relatively positive attitudes toward their students may refuse to lend them their books if they expect to need the books in the near future or if they have found it difficult to keep track of books and journals they have made available in the past. Conversely, professors who hold relatively unfavorable attitudes toward their students may be concerned about their public image and, for this reason, may agree to lend them their books and journals.

In fact, the same arguments apply to any single behavior, be it lending one's books, inviting students to a party, or agreeing to postpone a scheduled exam. In each case, various factors may interfere with the relationship between the professor's attitude toward his or her students and the behavior in question. The particular combination of factors involved will of course differ from one behavior to another, but the result will usually be a weak relation between the global attitude and any single action. The reviews published by Wicker (1969) and by Ajzen and Fishbein (1977) provide many examples of this situation.

On rare occasions, though, only a few factors may interfere with the effect of the general attitude on a particular behavior. A good case in point is the relation, at least in the United States, between attitudes and voting with respect to political candidates. For most people, voting is the only behavior they are asked to perform in relation to a candidate. Moreover, the privacy of the voting context is deliberately designed to prevent interference by other factors. As a result, investigators typically report correlation coefficients in the range of .50 to .70 between attitudes toward competing candidates and voting for or against those candidates (e.g., Campbell, Converse, Miller, & Stokes, 1960; Fishbein & Coombs, 1974).

In conclusion, we can probably agree that—with a few exceptions—global measures of attitude do not predict single-act criteria. But then, we really should not expect a strong relationship of this kind. As early as 1931, Thurstone pointed out that two persons may hold the same attitude toward some object but that "their overt actions (may) take quite different forms which have one thing in common, namely, that they are about equally favorable toward the object" (p. 262). Just as "attitude toward an object" refers to a general evaluative predisposition, "behavior toward the object" stands for a general behavioral tendency. Any single action will typically be a poor representative, and hence an imperfect indicant, of this general behavioral trend.

Multiple-act Measures

The foregoing discussion implies that although we cannot expect a global measure of attitude to predict any single action, such a measure should predict a more general index of behavior based on a representative sample of actions within the domain under consideration. A multiple-act measure of this kind will tend to eliminate the influence of unique factors associated with any given action. That is, we can score each behavior in terms of its evaluative implication for the attitude object and then sum across the total set of behaviors. In this fashion we obtain a relatively uncontaminated measure of the extent to which a person is acting in a favorable or unfavorable manner with respect to the object. In fact, it is possible to use standard scaling methods, such as Likert or Thurstone scaling, to select appropriate behaviors and compute the behavioral index.

A few years ago Fishbein and Ajzen (1974) provided some empirical support for these arguments. Sixty-two undergraduate college students were given a list of 100 behaviors dealing with matters of religion and were asked to check the behaviors they had performed. These behaviors included praying before and after meals, taking a religious course for credit, and dating a person against parents' wishes. Each response constituted a single-act criterion. In addition, four multiple-act criteria were constructed. The first was simply the sum of the total set of 100 behaviors, taking into account the evaluation implied by each action. A second index was a Guttman scale of a subset of eight behaviors. The third and fourth indices were Likert and Thurstone scales based on 20 and 13 behaviors, respectively.

Attitudes toward religion were assessed by means of five scales that were highly intercorrelated. The measures were a self-report of religiosity, a semantic differential evaluation of "being religious," and three standard scales measuring religiosity: a Likert scale, a Guttman scale, and a Thurstone scale.[1]

Correlations were computed between each of the five global measures of attitude toward religion and the various single- and multiple-act measures of behavior. As in most previous investigations, prediction of single actions was largely unsuccessful. Although a few attitude-behavior correlations were as high as .40, most were rather low and not significant. The average correlation between attitudes toward religion and single behaviors was about .14. In marked contrast, correlations of global attitudes with the behavioral indices were high and significant, ranging from .45 to .75 with an average correlation of .63.

It has been argued that one weakness of this investigation is its reliance on self-reports of behavior (cf. Schuman & Johnson, 1976). A subsequent study by Weigel and Newman (1976), however, showed the same pattern of results for observations of actual behavior. These investigators used a 16-item Likert scale to measure attitudes toward protecting environmental quality. A total of 14 behavioral observations were obtained 3 to 8 months later. The behaviors involved signing and circulating three different petitions concerning environmental issues, participating in a litter pick-up program, and participating in a recycling program on eight separate occasions. In addition to these 14 single-act criteria, Weigel and Newman constructed four multiple-act indices: one based on petition-signing behaviors, one on litter pick-ups, one on recycling, and one overall index based on all 14 single behaviors.

Prediction of single actions from the general attitude measure was again very weak. The average correlation between attitude and the 14 single behaviors was only .29 and not significant. By way of comparison, the average correlation with the three behavioral indices of intermediate generality was .42, and the correlation with the index based on all 14 behaviors was .62, both highly significant.

Finally, in a recent study, Werner (1978) demonstrated the predictability of a multiple-act behavioral measure in the area of activism concerning abortion. He assessed general attitudes toward abortion on demand among 488 male and female respondents. In addition, the respondents were asked to report the extent to which they had performed each of 83 activities related to abortion. Among these activities were "trying to convince a friend or acquaintance that abortion should be greatly restricted or prohibited," "encouraging a woman with an

---

[1]Using confirmatory factor analysis, Bagozzi and Burnkrant (1979) have shown that these five scales tend to form two clusters: the self-report and the semantic differential versus the remaining three scales. They interpreted the first cluster as assessing the "affective component" of religiosity and the second as assessing its "cognitive component." Given the strong correlations between the two types of scales, however, the results of their reanalysis may be more parsimoniously attributed to method variance. That is, the self-report and the evaluative semantic differential relied on relatively direct expressions of religiosity, whereas the Likert, Thurstone, and Guttman scales inferred religiosity from a variety of different beliefs.

unwanted pregnancy to have an abortion,'' and ''circulating an anti-abortion petition.'' Consistent with the arguments presented above, attitude toward abortion was found to be a highly accurate predictor of a general behavior index based on all 83 activities. For the total sample of respondents, the attitude-behavior correlation was .78 ($p < .001$).

The studies described thus far demonstrate quite clearly that people do behave in accordance with their attitudes, provided that we obtain appropriate measures of behavior. Any particular action is multiply determined and cannot be predicted on the basis of general attitudes. The overall behavioral trend, however, is consistent with the person's attitude.

In a review of research dealing with the attitude-behavior relationship, Ajzen and Fishbein (1977) argued that it is useful to define a behavioral measure in terms of four facets or elements: the action involved, the target at which the action is directed, the context in which it occurs, and the time of its occurrence. A multiple-act measure involves many different actions performed in different contexts and at different points in time. It thus generalizes across the action, context, and time elements; the only element that remains constant is the target. There is a parallel in this respect between a multiple-act criterion and a global measure of attitude. Like multiple-act criteria, global attitudes involve no specific action, context, or time elements. They represent evaluative responses to the target irrespective of particular actions, contexts, or times. This correspondence in the elements that make up global attitudes and multiple-act criteria ensures a strong attitude-behavior relationship.

Personality Traits and Behavior

The same logic may be applied to an analysis of the relationship between personality traits and overt behavior. As in the case of attitudes, personality traits are said to have little predictive validity. But again we must distinguish between single actions and more general behavioral tendencies.

Traits have been defined in different ways, but they are widely assumed to represent relatively enduring predispositions that exert fairly generalized effects on behavior. In terms of the present analysis, traits may be viewed as predisposing the person to behaviors of a certain kind, across a variety of targets, contexts, and points in time. Thus, people are said to possess traits which predispose them to behave cautiously, to display aggressive behaviors, or to be generally dominant. Whereas in the case of attitudes, all behaviors with evaluative implications for the attitude object are relevant; in the case of traits, only actions falling within a certain category are involved in the behavioral predisposition. That is, a personality trait corresponds to a measure of behavior which generalizes across context, target, and time elements and which involves a set of behaviors within a given class, such as dominance or aggression. There is, by definition, no expectation that a measure of a personality trait will correlate with any particular action, even if that action is part of the behavioral category in question. However, we may expect traits to predict a behavioral criterion that is representative of the category as a whole.

In a conceptual replication of the Fishbein and Ajzen (1974) study mentioned earlier, Jaccard (1974) provided some support for these arguments. He examined the relationship between the personality trait of dominance and self-reports of dominant behavior. Forty-five female undergraduates completed two personality scales designed to measure dominance and were asked to indicate which of 40 behaviors in the domain of dominance they had performed. Among the behaviors were, "I have argued with a teacher," "I have initiated a discussion in class," and "I have let my boyfriend beat me at something I could really beat him in." A multiple-act measure was obtained by summing over the 40 behaviors.

As in previous studies of the relation between personality and behavior, prediction of single actions was rather poor. On the average, the correlation between the personality measures of dominance and the various dominant or submissive behaviors was about .20. Much greater success, however, was achieved in predicting the general tendency to behave in a dominant manner; the two personality measures correlated .58 and .64 (p < .001) with the multiple-act criterion.

In sum, we can see that people's behavior is really quite consistent with their attitudes and personalities. To be sure, this consistency emerges only when we look at global behavioral trends rather than at single actions. But to expect a strong relation between a global measure of attitude and any particular behavior would be naive. In fact, such an expectation contradicts our definitions of attitude and personality trait as general behavioral predispositions.

Validity Versus Reliability of Behavioral Measures

Before continuing I would like to emphasize that the issue addressed thus far is related to the *validity* of our behavioral measures, not their reliability. It would seem possible to argue that multiple-act measures are superior to measures of single actions because, being based on a greater number of observations, they are more reliable. This point is well taken and some of the improvement in predictability may in fact derive from increased reliability. However, I would argue that even if we had perfectly reliable measures of single actions, we would in most instances still obtain only very low correlations with global attitude measures. Single actions are simply not representative of the total set of behaviors a person may perform with respect to the attitude object. They can thus not be considered valid measures of a person's "behavior" in relation to the object under consideration.

Unfortunately, I know of no research that has compared the predictability of single-act and multiple-act criteria assessed on the basis of an equal number of observations. Such a comparison might demonstrate the superiority of multiple-act criteria perhaps most convincingly. However, there is evidence to show that the difficulty in predicting single actions from global measures of attitude cannot be attributed solely to the low reliability of such behavioral measures. Let us thus turn to the prediction of single actions.

PREDICTION OF SINGLE ACTIONS

It should be clear by now that attitudes (as well as personality traits) are useful constructs, at least when it comes to the prediction of overall behavioral trends. This, in itself, is not a trivial matter. As social psychologists we are quite frequently interested in general behavioral patterns rather than any particular action. Discrimination against members of a minority group, for example, cannot be validly assessed by observing a single action. Assessment of discrimination requires consideration of a wide range of behaviors with respect to members of the minority group and selection of a representative set for observation. A multiple-act measure obtained in this fashion should correlate with the general attitude toward the minority group under consideration. Failures to obtain strong relations between prejudice and discrimination have typically been due to the use of only one or two particular actions as measures of behavior.

By the same token, pressing a button to administer an electric shock may be quite reliably assessed, but it would be difficult to argue that this single action, performed in a unique context, is representative of the broad concept of "aggression." In contrast, a multiple-act measure of aggressive behavior would provide us with a more valid assessment of this construct and would correlate better with a verbal aggressiveness scale than can be expected of any single action.

Nevertheless, the discussion up to this point may appear to imply that attitudes and personality traits are in fact quite useless when it comes to the prediction of particular behaviors; that when we consider single actions, people do not behave in accordance with their attitudes or personalities. Since we are often interested in understanding and predicting single actions, concepts which are related only to general behavioral tendencies must appear of rather limited utility.

Consider, for example, the issue of attendance at class lectures. My analysis suggests that students' attitudes toward their instructors in a given course may have little to do with their attending the lectures. But there is really no need to assess general attitudes toward the instructor if we want to predict a specific behavior of this kind. We can obtain a measure of attitude that corresponds much more closely to the behavior in its action, target, context, and time elements. It is possible to assess attitudes toward virtually any concept, including a behavior. In fact, various scales have been developed to measure attitudes toward such behaviors as smoking marijuana, drinking alcohol, having an abortion, or participating in psychological research. By the same token, we can assess students' attitudes toward attending the lectures of a course instructor. Such a measure reflects a rather narrow behavioral predisposition and it should allow us to predict the corresponding overt behavior.

It is worth noting that this attitude toward a behavior is part of a more general theory developed over the last 10 or 12 years (see Fishbein & Ajzen, 1975). In a recent book (Ajzen & Fishbein, 1980) we have termed our approach a *theory of reasoned action*. According to the theory, attitude toward a behavior—together with perceived normative pressures or subjective norms—determines a person's intention and thus his actual performance of the behavior. Research conducted over the years to test the theory of reasoned action has, among other things, provided evidence concerning the relation between attitude toward a behavior and actual performance of that behavior. Generally speaking, this relation has been strong and highly significant.

Some of our early experiments were conducted in the laboratory. For example, Ajzen and Fishbein (1970) and Ajzen (1971) attempted to predict cooperative behavior in Prisoner's Dilemma games. The subjects in the two studies were pairs of same-sex college students who played three Prisoner's Dilemma games that varied in their payoff matrices. Following a few practice trials, the players were asked to complete a questionnaire that included two semantic-differential measures of attitude, each comprised of four or five bipolar evaluative scales. These scales were used to obtain measures of attitude toward choosing the cooperative strategy and of attitude toward the other player. The proportion of cooperative strategy choices following completion of the questionnaire served as the behavioral criterion.

Looking at the three games played in the two experiments, actual choice of cooperative moves correlated .63, .70, and .65 ($p < .001$ in each case) with attitude toward choosing the cooperative strategy. In contrast, the correlations between attitude toward the other player (a global attitude) and cooperative game behavior were very low and inconsistent ($r = .26$, p $< .05; r = .09$, *ns; r* $= .27$, p $< .05$, respectively).

In more recent years, a number of studies have tested the theory of reasoned action in field settings. Many of these investigations are described in Ajzen and Fishbein (1980). As in the laboratory, attitude toward a behavior is typically found to be an excellent predictor of the behavior in question. Consider, for example, a study conducted by Fishbein, Thomas, and Jaccard (1976) in the 1974 general election in Great Britain. Voters were interviewed prior to the election and their attitudes toward voting for each candidate in their constituency were assessed by means of an evaluative semantic differential. The average correlation between these attitude measures and actual voting behavior was .85 (p $< .001$). Parenthetically, more general attitudes toward the candidates themselves also predicted voting behavior, but here the average correlation was only .51, significantly lower than the correlation obtained by using attitudes toward the act of voting.

Other investigators have also provided evidence for a strong relation between attitude toward a behavior and actual performance of that behavior (Janis & Hoffman, 1970; Kothandapani, 1971; Veevers, 1971). For example, Kothandapani investigated birth control practices among 452 married black women. Attitudes toward personal use of birth control methods were measured by means of 12 attitude scales: 3 Thurstone scales, 3 Guttman scales, 3 Likert scales, and 3 self-report scales. The criterion was the self-reported use or nonuse of birth control methods. All 12 attitude-behavior correlations were significant and generally quite high. One correlation was .36 and the remaining correlations ranged from .54 to .82, with an average correlation of .69.

These and other studies demonstrate quite clearly that attitudes can be used to predict not only general behavioral tendencies but single actions as well, provided we assess attitudes toward the particular behaviors under consideration. The behavioral measures employed have occasionally involved repeated observations, as in the case of the number of cooperative moves in the Prisoner's Dilemma games. At other times, the behavioral measure referred to performance of a unique act at a given point in time, such as voting for a candidate in an election. Note also that in these studies attitudes toward the behaviors succeeded in predicting performance of the behaviors, while more general attitudes toward the targets of the behaviors either failed completely or produced much weaker results.

In light of these findings, it would seem difficult to argue that the failure of general attitudes to predict single actions is attributable to low reliability of the behavioral measures. Instead, the empirical evidence discussed up to this point suggests two conclusions: (1) global measures of attitude are appropriate for the prediction of global behavioral tendencies, but not of single actions; and (2) single actions can best be predicted from measures of attitude that represent an evaluative predisposition to perform or not to perform the particular behavior under consideration.

Personality and Single Actions

An issue closely related to the reliability of behavioral measures has been of major concern in the area of personality. Recent disenchantment with the concept of personality trait can be traced to the finding that people fail to exhibit consistency in their behavior. Across different situations and occasions, a person may sometimes behave cautiously and other times be rash; he may be happy or sad, dominant or submissive, optimistic or pessimistic. In his influential book on personality and assessment, Mischel (1968) concluded that, "With the possible exception of intelligence, highly generalized behavioral consistencies have not been demonstrated, and the concept of personality traits as broad response dispositions is thus untenable" (p. 146).

I have argued, however, that a single action cannot be assumed to represent a person's general response tendency. A person who behaves honestly on one occasion but cheats on another may, overall, be relatively honest. To see this personality trait reflected in overt behavior, however, we would have to observe many different actions reflecting honesty or dishonesty, performed under a variety of conditions, and at different points in time.

An action performed on a given occasion is multiply determined and may not be repeated under different circumstances or at a different point in time. Therefore, as Epstein (1979) has recently made clear, single observations of behavior are unreliable in the sense that they lack stability. Epstein provided strong evidence showing that stability, and hence internal consistency, of behavior can be greatly increased by basing our measures on repeated observations of a single action.

For example, the respondents in one of Epstein's experiments recorded, among other things, some of their behaviors on each day of a 14-day period. The behaviors recorded were the number of telephone calls made, the number of letters written, the number of social contacts initiated, the number of hours slept, and the number of hours studied. Consistency of behavior on any 2 days chosen at random was relatively low, ranging from a reliability coefficient of .26 for the number of telephone calls made to .63 for the number of social contacts initiated. Behavioral stability increased dramatically when the behavioral indices were based on more than one observation. For example, comparison of average behavioral scores on the 7 odd days with average behavioral scores on the 7 even days produced correlations of .81 and .94 for number of phone calls and number of social contacts, respectively.

Clearly, then, by considering more than one occasion, it is possible to obtain highly reliable and internally consistent measures of single actions. The question of greater interest for present purposes, however, is the extent to which such measures of single actions, generalizing across context and time, can be predicted from general measures of personality. Prior to recording their behaviors, respondents in Epstein's experiment completed a battery of personality inventories assessing, among other variables, such traits as anxiety, hostility, sociability, and extroversion. The resulting measures of these traits were correlated with indices of behavior based on the total 14-day period.

For anybody attempting to predict single actions from personality, the results were quite disappointing. The great majority of trait-behavior correlations were not significant despite the high reliability of the behavioral measures. Only for social contacts initiated and number of hours studied were significant correlations obtained with some of the personality traits, ranging from .31 to .52. Moreover, it was found that the predictability of behavioral measures across 14 days was only slightly better than that of single behavioral observations (Epstein, 1979, footnote 3).

In short, general personality traits, like global attitudes, are poor predictors of specific actions. Although more reliable and stable measures of single behaviors obtained by means of repeated observations may improve prediction to some extent, correlations are typically quite low and not significant. As Epstein noted, "It should not be expected, of course, that the relationships will be very high, given the different ranges of generalization encompassed by the recording of specific kinds of behavior and the broad personality dimensions measured by the personality inventories" (p. 1119).

This statement is consistent with my argument that the behavioral predisposition addressed by the concept of personality trait is a general behavioral tendency rather than any specific action. The study by Jaccard (1974) cited earlier showed, in fact, that general personality traits are closely related to indices of behavior based on a variety of different actions relevant to the trait in question. It is interesting to note in this context that in Epstein's (1979) study, the behavior best predicted from personality was the number of social contacts initiated. This behavior correlated .40 with a measure of sociability and .52 with extroversion. Clearly, initiating social contacts involves different kinds of behaviors, such as attending a party or approaching a stranger in the classroom. As such, this behavioral measure actually represents a behavioral category that corresponds reasonably well to the personality trait with which it was found to correlate.

CONCLUSION

In contrast to the currently accepted view that there is no close link between attitude and behavior, I have taken the position that people do act in accordance with their attitudes. Like Thurstone (1931) and other theorists (Campbell, 1963; Doob, 1947) I have argued that global attitudes toward an object (or personality traits) predict only the overall pattern of behavior; they are of little value if we are interested in predicting a particular action with respect to the object. To predict a single behavior we have to assess the person's attitude toward the behavior in question.

The objection has often been raised that this conclusion puts severe limitations on the utility of the attitude concept. If, for every behavior, we have to assess a different attitude, we appear to have gained very little. This objection fails to realize that my argument is not so much with the use of attitude measures that are too general but with measures of behavior that are too specific. Rarely, if ever, are we interested in predicting and understanding the performance of a specific action, in a given context, and at a precise point in time. However, if the investigator chooses to define his or her behavioral criterion at such a low level of generality, then the attitude measure has to be equally specific.

To be sure, it would be very convenient if we could measure a general attitude (or personality trait) and use it to predict any behavior with respect to the attitude object, in any context, and at any point in time. Unfortunately, both theory and empirical research negate this possibility. In fact, there seem to be few other concepts in psychology of which it is expected that they allow us to predict a variety of different behaviors from a measure of a global underlying disposition. The concept of attitude toward a behavior is in this sense similar to such concepts as "habit" in learning theory, "subjective expected utility" in decision theory, and "script, scriptal path, or scriptal track" in script theory. Nobody would demand that subjective expected utilities associated with the options in one decision situation also permit us to predict the decision involving a different set of alternatives. Similarly, knowledge of a person's script concerning one type of behavior cannot be expected to permit prediction of a different behavior; each behavior is assumed to be executed according to its own script. By the same token, attitudes help us predict and explain only those behaviors for which they are relevant. If we are interested in a general pattern of behavior, we can assess attitude toward their common target. To predict more specific actions, however, we must rely on attitudes toward the particular behaviors in question. This is not to say that global attitudes are always unrelated to specific behaviors. It is possible to establish conditions that will improve prediction of single actions from general measures of attitude (see Salancik; Schlegel & diTecco; Snyder; Wicklund; and Zanna & Olson in this volume). However, the best predictor of behavior will usually be a measure of attitude that, in its essential elements, corresponds to the behavioral criterion.

ACKNOWLEDGMENTS

The comments of Seymour Epstein, Mark Snyder, and Mark P. Zanna on an earlier draft of this chapter are gratefully acknowledged.

REFERENCES

Ajzen, I. Attitudinal vs. normative messages: An investigation of the differential effects of persuasive communications on behavior. *Sociometry*, 1971, *34*, 263–280.

Ajzen, I., & Fishbein, M. The prediction of behavior from attitudinal and normative variables. *Journal of Experimental Social Psychology*, 1970, *6*, 466–487.

Ajzen, I., & Fishbein, M. Attitude-behavior relations: A theoretical analysis and review of empirical research. *Psychological Bulletin*, 1977, *84*, 888–918.

Ajzen, I., & Fishbein, M. *Understanding attitudes and predicting social behavior*. Englewood-Cliffs, N.J.: Prentice-Hall, 1980.

Bagozzi, R. P., & Burnkrant, R. E. Attitude organization and the attitude-behavior relationship. *Journal of Personality and Social Psychology*, 1979, *37*, 913–929.

Campbell, A., Converse, P. E., Miller, W. E., & Stokes, D. E. *The American voter*. New York: Wiley, 1960.

Campbell, D. T. Social attitudes and other acquired behavioral dispositions. In S. Koch (Ed.), *Psychology: A study of a science*, (Vol. 6). New York: McGraw-Hill, 1963.

Doob, L. W. The behavior of attitudes. *Psychological Review*, 1947, *54*, 135–156.

Epstein, S. The stability of behavior: I. On predicting most of the people much of the time. *Journal of Personality and Social Psychology*, 1979, *37*, 1097–1126.

Fazio, R. H., & Zanna, M. Attitudinal qualities relating to the strength of the attitude-behavior relationship. *Journal of Experimental Social Psychology*, 1978, *14*, 398–408.

Fishbein, M., & Ajzen, I. Attitudes toward objects as predictors of single and multiple behavioral criteria. *Psychological Review*, 1974, *81*, 59–74.

Fishbein, M., & Ajzen, I. *Belief, attitude, intention, and behavior: An introduction to theory and research*. Reading, Mass.: Addison-Wesley, 1975.

Fishbein, M., & Coombs, F. S. Basis for decision: An attitudinal analysis of voting behavior. *Journal of Applied Social Psychology*, 1974, *4*, 95–124.

Fishbein, M., Thomas, K., & Jaccard, J. J. Voting behavior in Britain: An attitudinal analysis. *Occasional Papers in Survey Research*, 1976, *7*, SSRC Survey Unit, London, England.

Jaccard, J. J. Predicting social behavior from personality traits. *Journal of Research in Personality*, 1974, *7*, 358–367.

Janis, I. L., & Hoffman, D. Facilitating effects of daily contact between partners who make a decision to cut down on smoking. *Journal of Personality and Social Psychology*, 1970, *17*, 25–35.

Kothandapani, V. Validation of feeling, belief, and intention to act as three components of attitude and their contribution to prediction of contraceptive behavior. *Journal of Personality and Social Psychology*, 1971, *19*, 321–333.

Liska, A. E. The impact of attitude on behavior: Attitude-social support interaction. *Pacific Sociological Review*, 1974, *17*, 83–97.

Mischel, W. *Personality and assessment*. New York: Wiley, 1968.

Norman, R. Affective-cognitive consistency: Attitudes, conformity and behavior. *Journal of Personality and Social Psychology*, 1975, *32*, 83–91.

Schuman, H., & Johnson, M. P. Attitudes and behavior. *Annual Review of Sociology*, 1976, *2*, 161–207.

Snyder, M., & Swann, W. B. Jr. When actions reflect attitudes: The politics of impression management. *Journal of Personality and Social Psychology*, 1976, *34*, 1034–1042.

Thurstone, L. L. The measurement of attitudes. *Journal of Abnormal and Social Psychology*, 1931, *26*, 249–269.

Veevers, J. E. Drinking attitudes and drinking behavior: An exploratory study. *Journal of Social Psychology*, 1971, *85*, 103–109.

Warland, R. H., & Sample, J. Response certainty as a moderator variable in attitude measurement. *Rural Sociology*, 1973, *38*, 174–186.

Weigel, R. H., & Newman, L. S. Increasing attitude-behavior correspondence by broadening the scope of the behavioral measure. *Journal of Personality and Social Psychology*, 1976, *33*, 793–802.

Werner, P. D. Personality and attitude-activism correspondence. *Journal of Personality and Social Psychology*, 1978, *36*, 1375–1390.

Wicker, A. W. Attitudes vs. actions: The relationship of verbal and overt behavioral responses to attitude objects. *Journal of Social Issues*, 1969, *25*, 41–78.

2 Attitudinal Structures and the Attitude-Behavior Relation

Ronald P. Schlegel
Don DiTecco
University of Waterloo

INTRODUCTION

A variety of critical reviews (e.g. Wicker, 1969; Kelman, 1974) now prevail in the literature concerning the attitude-behavior relation that point to various factors and conditions which may weaken or strengthen this association. Amongst the suggestions to improve the relation between attitudes and behavior has been the notion that attitudes need to be viewed in multidimensional terms. That is, it is presumed that attitudes are comprised of a multicomponent structure with these various components having a differential validity for external criteria, including behavior. A common view found in the literature defines attitudes as existing in terms of three response classes to some stimulus, namely, affect, cognition, and behavior (Rosenberg & Hovland, 1960).

This general structure of attitude organization has been studied from both convergent and divergent validity perspectives. The investigations pertaining to convergence have addressed the effects of changes in one component on the remaining ones in order to achieve an acceptable level of internal organization. Insko and Schopler (1967) have attempted to outline some conditions under which consistency between affect, cognition, and conation is to be expected, both as affective-cognitive change follows behavior change and as behavior change follows affective-cognitive change. Rosenberg (1960) posited that changes in attitudinal cognition would tend to generate consistent change in the affective response toward the attitude object, and conversely, that direct alteration of the affective component would result in cognitive reorganization in order to achieve appropriate levels of consistency in the internal organization of social attitudes. Norman (1975) hypothesized that persons with high affective-cognitive

17

consistency would be more likely to behave in accord with their attitude than those with low intra-attitudinal consistency since the dispositional attitude would be less stable in the latter case. His data confirmed this prediction.

In contrast to these efforts to document the consistency or convergent validity of the tripartite view of attitudes, a few studies have investigated the divergent validity of these three components. Ostrom (1969), studying attitudes toward the church, concluded that the tripartite distinction is tenable in that the verbal responses within each component share a unique set of determinants distinct from those for the other components. However, while the components could be distinguished on the basis of statistical significance, the magnitude of the uniqueness was small. He also argued that behavioral intentions (conation) should correspond more with actual behavior since these represent verbal and nonverbal responses respectively from the same component. Again, the hypothesis was supported but the magnitude of effect was small. Kothandapani (1971) essentially replicated the Ostrom study with another attitude topic, birth control, for which a less homogeneous view existed and consequently a greater diversity of opinion (vis-à-vis Ostrom's attitude topic, the church). Kothandapani's results confirmed the affective, cognitive, and conative classification of attitude structure more clearly, and in a stepwise discriminant function analysis designed to discriminate users from nonusers of birth control, he found intention-to-act to be the best predictor of behavior. He stated that "performance of an act may be considered a function of learned intentions, beliefs, and feelings in combination with current stimulus conditions" (p. 332), and that the affective or feeling component primarily serves to facilitate but not initiate behavior. The unidimensional affective view of attitudes, he suggested, may be too simplified to be helpful in prediction of actual behavior and thus explains why earlier attitude studies failed to predict behavior.

Although considerable evidence is now available to substantiate both the convergent and divergent validity of the cognitive, affective, and behavioral components of attitude, researchers have persisted in measuring attitudes in a variety of ways and seldom have studies completely assessed this comprehensive definition even though many attitude researchers and theorists appear to agree with such a classification. This has permitted a considerable amount of conceptual confusion where, for instance, one researcher may assess attitudes in terms of beliefs, another as feelings, and still another as intentions. Still another may consider beliefs and feelings as assessments of attitudes, which in turn are used to predict intentions, presumably exogenous to the attitude construct in this case. These varying approaches and definitions have contributed at least in part to the inconsistencies and ambiguities often apparent in the literature (cf. fear arousal literature).

In order to achieve a better level of conceptual clarity, Fishbein and Ajzen (1975) have proposed that clear distinctions be made between the various concepts of beliefs, attitude, intentions, and behavior. Their definition of "attitude" is delimited to the affective (i.e. feeling) response by an individual for or against some psychological object or action. This definition is consistent with that proposed originally by Thurstone (1931). "Belief" refers to the information one has about the object, that is the subjective probability that a given attribute or outcome (e.g. lung cancer) is associated with the attitude object or action (e.g. cigarette smoking). "Behavioral intention" is the person's perceived likelihood that he or she will perform a particular behavior and the term "behavior" is used to refer to observable acts that are studied in their own right. These distinctions have received considerable empirical support, and Fishbein and Ajzen have shown that salient beliefs about an object underlie the formation of attitudes and that attitudes predict intentions (under specified conditions) which in turn predict behavior (under appropriate circumstances). The crucial point, for present purposes, is that they view attitudes solely as the individual's affective response, that is feelings for or against a psychological object. This view is in contrast to the multidimensional view where attitude is considered to be a more complex construct comprised of an affective (i.e. feeling) component, a cognitive (i.e. belief or knowledge) component, and a conative (i.e. behavioral tendency or intentions) component (Rosenberg & Hovland, 1960; Krech, Crutchfield, & Ballachey, 1962). Another way of viewing this difference is that Rosenberg and others place these three components into a "horizontal" relationship (as part of the same construct) whereas Fishbein and Ajzen relate cognition, affect, and intentions in a more "vertical" way in that each are separate and distinct constructs that are formed from (i.e. built upon) each other in theoretically meaningful and often predictable ways.

Bagozzi and Burnkrant (1979) have proposed an intermediate position where attitude is conceptualized as a complex construct comprised of cognitive and affective components, which in turn simultaneously account for intentions and/or actual behavior. This two-component view has been supported by others (Katz & Stotland, 1959; Rosenberg, 1968). Bagozzi and Burnkrant reanalyzed Fishbein and Ajzen (1974) data by means of confirmatory factor analytic techniques which tested whether a one- or two-component model fitted the attitudinal data best. Using this rigorous model-testing procedure, they found significant departures (p < .01) from the data for the one-component but not two-component model thereby supporting the latter model of attitude organization. It was also found that both cognitive and affective components gave a more complete accounting of the attitude-behavior relation although the "... affective component was approximately three times as powerful as the cognitive component" (p. 926).

While Bagozzi and Burnkrant set up a direct confrontation between the one factor (affect only) and two factor (affect plus cognition) models, their results need not be interpreted as being in conflict with the conceptual distinctions and theoretical framework proposed by Fishbein and Ajzen (1975). Their results do suggest, however, that further refinement of Fishbein and Ajzen's conceptualizations is warranted. Fishbein and Ajzen view attitude formation in information processing terms where the affective response towards some object is the integrative result of an underlying set of salient beliefs held by the individual. Theoretically, they have postulated (and documented empirically) that attitudes are approximately equivalent to the summation of subjective estimates of beliefs each weighted by the value (i.e. evaluation) one ascribes to the attribute associated with that particular belief (i.e. $A_o = \sum_{i=1}^{n} b_i e_i$). Bagozzi and Burnkrant's analyses suggest that this process of cognitive integration is inexact in that the affective response does not necessarily "capture" the complete information contained by the underlying belief set. That is, Bagozzi and Burnkrant's results indicate that an affective response alone is not always able to adequately represent the universe of beliefs related to a given attitude object. Furthermore, some of the underlying beliefs that missed capture were related to the external criteria—intentions and behavior. Thus when the question is one of explaining attitude-behavior relations, this inexact information integration process may assume a substantial importance. However, this argument does not negate the conceptual distinctions that Fishbein and Ajzen have carefully outlined for beliefs, attitudes, intentions, and behavior. We believe their definitions should be consistently followed in social psychological research in order to achieve greater uniformity; however, their theoretical specifications (although perhaps sufficient for many purposes) should be refined even further in order to accommodate a cognitive structure that may exist independent of the affective response.

Consistent with Bagozzi and Burnkrant's model testing results, Sheth (1973a) empirically tested a theory of attitude structure and the attitude-behavior relation in which a set of evaluative beliefs was uniquely related (from both a conceptual and an empirical viewpoint) to affect and intentions respectively. That is, affect did not mediate entirely the relationship between beliefs and intentions (and subsequently behavior). Sheth (1973b) further argued that the arithmetical summation of this set of distinct beliefs may provide us with little more than a statistical artifact, particularly if these beliefs should vary significantly in terms of their strength and direction of relationship to a given criterion variable. Thus a differentiated profile of beliefs may often exist in a person's thinking, although this profile may be affectively integrated to a greater or lesser degree. This profile of beliefs can be characterized as a cognitive structure which underlies the attitudinal (i.e. affective) response, but which may not be fully captured by this affective response.

The question that one is then led to is whether various dimensions of this belief structure can be defined and be related differentially and in meaningful ways to various external criteria (including behavior). In this regard, Riger and Gordon (1979) factor analyzed independent dimensions of rape prevention attitudes and demonstrated their differential operation in subpopulations that varied in the likelihood of victimization. Beliefs about measures calling for restrictions in women's behavior were rated as more helpful by black females, the group with the highest risk of rape, whereas groups with lower risks of victimization rates more highly beliefs about measures involving changes in the environment or assertive actions by women. Other studies (e.g. Field, 1978) have also supported the multidimensional structure of rape-prevention beliefs.

It would also be important to develop indices that could describe such structures in order to help delineate conditions under which a single affective response is sufficient for optimal association with external criteria as compared to when a cognitive component is required in addition. However, few attempts have been made to develop indices to describe such belief structures. One of the more notable efforts has been by Scott (1966, 1969) who developed various indices for the structural properties of natural cognition, that is, how people characteristically interrelate ideas about objects in the absence of experimental intervention. "A 'structural property' refers to the manner in which elements of cognition (ideas) are interrelated" (Scott, 1966, p. 391). He defined such structural properties as dimensionality, attribute articulation, attribute centrality, evaluative centrality, centralization, image comparability, affective-evaluative consistency, affective balance, and image ambivalence. Various of these properties were intercorrelated as measured within four domains of cognition—nations, celebrities, acquaintances, and self. Dimensionality was defined as the degree to which a subject distinguishes among the elements in a given cognitive domain (e.g. nations), and affective-evaluative consistency referred to a mode of cognitive integration in which objects are liked to the extent that they are seen as possessing desirable characteristics. Affective-evaluative consistency is essentially equivalent to an expectancy-value notion of attitude.

Of particular interest for present purposes, Scott (1969) found that affective-evaluative consistency tended to be found in structures of low dimensionality. Scott cites several studies concerning the effect of information upon the structure of cognitions and these have shown consistently that information tends to increase dimensionality. This finding suggests the hypothesis that with increased knowledge (perhaps gained from experience) belief structures are increasingly differentiated, and these multidimensional structures are less capably summarized or captured (i.e. integrated) by a single affective response. These suggestions would argue for further work in order to provide more detailed assessments of attitude structures.

All of Scott's indices pertain to defining how a class of objects (e.g. nations) are arranged in psychological space rather than defining the cognitive space of one particular object (e.g. Russia). Zajonc (1960), however, did determine the cognitive structure pertaining to a single attitude object (namely a person writing a given letter). He defined cognitive structure "... as an organized subset of the given cognitive universe in terms of which the individual identifies and discriminates a particular object or event" (p. 159). That is, structures represent organized systems whereby the interrelations of the universe elements are expressed. Conversely, some elements are more or less isolated and therefore fall within the complement of this "organized subset." Zajonc defined four morphological properties of cognitive structures—differentiation, complexity, unity, and organization. These indices were employed as dependent variables in comparing persons expecting to transmit information with those expecting to receive information, in order to investigate a process he referred to as cognitive tuning. His results indicated that cognitive structures are activated in ways instrumental to a person's task at hand; for example, persons expecting to transmit information required greater detail and specificity of information and thus activated more differentiated and complex structures than did receivers.

Finally, another development of structural indices has been suggested by Fishbein and Ajzen (1975). Based on responses of belief strength and evaluations of the associated attributes, they proposed indices for cognitive differentiation, belief intensity, total affect, ambivalence, and consistency. However, these indices have only been developed in a preliminary and rather tangential way to their overall theoretical framework for behavior prediction, and have not been considered in relation to other external criteria or phenomena.

It is readily apparent that a limited number of attempts has been made to delineate and describe belief structures, and more particularly, none has attempted to relate these to the question of attitude-behavior consistency. The purpose of this chapter is to outline a method for describing attitude structures and elaborate a theoretical analysis that qualifies the attitude-behavior relation in terms of certain parameters of this structure. The chapter proceeds by presenting some descriptive indices of attitude structure and describing their theoretical implications for the association between attitudes and behavior. Empirical data is then presented to illustrate how attitude-behavior correlations are increased or decreased depending on certain characteristics of these structures. Potential mechanisms which may explain these varying associations are then explored, especially in relation to reorganizational processes of these structures. Finally, recent research evidence relating direct experience to attitude-behavior consistency is discussed in terms of our attitude structures theory.

A DESCRIPTIVE AND THEORETICAL ANALYSIS OF ATTITUDE STRUCTURES

A large number of cognitions or beliefs may exist in relation to any given attribute object or action and these are usually organized more parsimoniously into classes of equivalent meanings. The dimensionality of this universe of beliefs may depend to a large extent on an individual's knowledge and experience relevant to that domain (Friendly & Glucksberg, 1970; Marsh, 1977). One way of examining the organization of a large set of beliefs is by use of factor analysis. This technique has been used most frequently to determine the dimensionality of a set of beliefs, and indeed, it has been demonstrated (Osgood, Suci,

& Tannenbaum, 1957; Fishbein & Ajzen, 1975) that the first factor to emerge can usually be viewed as a general evaluative response factor, provided of course that some of the factored beliefs contain an affective component. While factor analysis provides a group level of analysis (as opposed to individual levels in the case of Scott and Zajonc), it allows for a description of belief structures from both morphological and substantive viewpoints. Morphologically, one would wish to define various properties that describe the form of the structure and examine the various theoretical implications of these forms for external phenomena such as behavior. From a substantive viewpoint one can examine the content of the structure for its psychological meaning and consequently derive various theoretical and applied implications for attitude formation and change.

A more advanced factor analytic technique, hierarchical factor analysis developed by Wherry (1959), has been employed to investigate psychological space and related structures. For example, Roach and Wherry (1972) factor analyzed attitude statements related to corporate image for multiline insurance companies, and then, they attempted to interpret substantively the relationships of the dimensions that emerged across levels in the hierarchical structure. This technique has also been used as an aid in interpreting other multidimensional psychological areas such as morale (Wherry, 1958). However, in none of these investigations was an attempt made to define morphological indices whereby structures per se could be described.

Briefly, the Wherry hierarchical factor analytic computer program employs both principal factor and minres methods to extract basic factors which are then subjected to varimax rotation (Harmon, 1967). The varimax factors are then further analyzed to yield a hierarchical factor structure (i.e. consisting of lower- and higher-order factors) which maximizes simple structure over the entire factor solution (Wherry, 1959). A transformation matrix is derived so that the original varimax solution is transformed into a higher-order factor space in order to find more abstract dimensions which are linear combinations of the original varimax solution.[1] A typical hierarchical solution, then, consists of a general factor, subgeneral factors, and more specific factors (the latter not to be confused with uniqueness or specificity in terms of measurement theory since all factors here are part of the common factor space). Figure 2.1 illustrates two hierarchical factor solutions (for nonusers and regular users of marijuana) where first-order

---

[1]Actually a correlation matrix is recreated from the varimax solution which is of course entirely explained by this factor solution. This "theoretical" correlation matrix is then analyzed in a way to obtain intercorrelations among clusters of correlated items. A transformation matrix is then derived from the intercorrelations of these clusters, and then the original varimax solution is multiplied by this transformation matrix so that this original solution is orthogonally repartitioned into hierarchical levels. This hierarchical factor solution containing both first- and higher-order factors remains orthogonal both within levels and across levels of the hierarchy. See Schlegel and Crawford (1976) for a more mathematical description of this hierarchical transformation.

								Variance at Each Level
Nonusers								
		III (64.3%)						64.3%
	II (7.8%)			II (3.6%)				11.4%
I (4.6%)	I (10.4%)		I (5.7%)		I (3.6%)			24.3%
Regular Users								
		IV (21.2%)						21.2%
	III (9.2%)			III (5.7%)				14.9%
II (3.4%)	II (4.4%)		II (3.2%)		II (3.9%)			14.9%
I (6.7%)	I (17.2%)	I (6.6%)	I (3.2%)	I (7.0%)	I (4.7%)	I (2.1%)	I (1.5%)	49.0%

FIG. 2.1.   Hierarchical factor solutions for nonusers and regular marijuana smokers illustrating differential attitude structures.

Note: I represents a first-order factor, II a second-order factor, III a third-order factor, and IV a fourth-order factor. The variance of the common factor space is orthogonally partitioned both within and across hierarchical levels.

and higher-order factors have been derived from an initial varimax solution. The common factor space variance of the hierarchical solution equals that of the original varimax solution, and the loadings of the items that were factor analyzed initially are examined directly with respect to first-, second-, and higher-order factors in the hierarchical solution. In summary, then, the original varimax solution can be orthogonally repartitioned into hierarchical space in order to determine the extent to which more general or abstract factors can subsume the original (and more specific) varimax factors. That is, since the variance of each item is orthogonally repartitioned within the hierarchical space, one can examine the size of the item's factor loadings on first- versus higher-order factors. If the loadings of most items are highest on a general factor, then one can conclude that this general factor largely subsumes the initial, first-order varimax factors.

Conceptually, the lower-order factors are interpreted in relatively more concrete and content-specific terms whereas higher-order factors are more abstract in nature. The most general factor was derived by the hierarchical transformation procedure to estimate the extent to which one factor is able to mathematically optimize the explained variance across items. Thus, by mathematical definition, this is a general factor and is parallel geometrically to extracting the first factor in a regular factor analysis, which Osgood et al. (1957) have found to be evaluative in nature. Second, the face validity of the most general factor in the hierarchical solution has been examined across a variety of topics such as marijuana smoking (Schlegel, 1973), religion (Schlegel & Sanborn, 1979), and locus of control (Schlegel & Crawford, 1976) and the item content has typically reflected a general "favorable-unfavorable" latent dimension.[2] Third, items loading highest on the general factor correlate substantially higher with a relatively direct (i.e. semantic differential) measure of affect. Thus the most general factor can be viewed as a general evaluative factor that reflects a predominantly affective response toward the target object. Subgeneral and more specific factors represent more specific belief dimensions that reflect relationships between the target object and attribute classes. Thus it can be suggested that the hierarchical factor solution parallels an attitude structure in that the most general factor represents the evaluative affective response and all remaining factors represent the belief structure underlying this response. In some solutions, most of the variance of these belief dimensions is "captured" by the general evaluative factor and thus the item loadings will be high on this general factor as compared to the lower-order factors. This represents the attitudinal structure case where an affective response has integrated more or less completely its underlying belief structure (i.e. affective-evaluative consistency mode of integration as described by Scott, 1969). While this integration process may have occurred rather completely, there existed of course an initial belief set that may have been differentiated in varying degrees (i.e. the original varimax solution). For example, a group of persons may hold many distinct beliefs about a country that would be described as multidimensional by a first-order factor solution. Yet this belief profile could be integrated such that a singular, affective response (e.g. patriotism) would effectively represent the entire profile as this profile may be related to other phenomena and external criteria, say behavior. In contrast to this well-integrated solution, another situation may occur where this general affective factor "captures" only a small portion of the underlying belief structure variance and thus a more complex attitude structure persists. In this case, a general evaluative dimension will be inadequate in representing the cognitive component and consequently the affective and cognitive components may relate independently to external criteria, such as intentions or behavior (as indicated by Bagozzi and Burnkrant's test of the two-component model of attitude organization). Further, the cognitive component that exists residually to the affective dimension may remain as a multidimensional structure in the more complex case. The various belief elements in this multidimensional structure may also be related in their separate ways to external criteria. In summary, then, the term *attitude* refers to the affective response while *attitude structure* is more inclusive, encompassing

---

[2]Examples of items pertaining to marijuana smoking which loaded highly on the general factor were: Smoking marijuana is a good way to have fun. I should smoke marijuana if it makes me feel good. Beauty can be captured more fully while high on marijuana. Smoking marijuana is bad. Smoking marijuana is a sign of moral weakness.

both the affective response and the belief structure underlying this affective response. Conceptually, these distinctions are consistent with those by Fishbein and Ajzen (1975) as summarized by their algebraic equation, $A_o = \sum_{i=1}^{n} b_i e_i$. However, our approach qualifies their definitions to allow for the case where this integration process is completed to varying degrees, and to the extent it is less than complete, allows for a multidimensional belief structure (independent of the affective response) to be related in meaningful ways to external criteria. Thus hierarchical factor analysis provides a useful technique for identifying, describing, and analyzing attitude structures.

Various indices can be developed to define some morphological properties of these attitude structures. These indices can provide us with summary statistics in order to compare attitude structures across various groups of persons with respect to some attitude object. Second, various theoretical deductions that elaborate an attitude structures theory can be made from these indices. Four morphological type indices[3] can be defined and operationalized as follows:

1. *Differentiation*—the extent to which groups of elements associated with the attitude object are perceived and discriminated with the attitude object are perceived and discriminated on the basis of a lesser or greater number of factors. The index (for the kth group) can be measured by the number of primary order (varimax) factors (M_i) extracted by the principal axes and minres methods.

$$D_k = M_i$$

2. *Organization*—the extent to which elements in the attitude space are related to each other. This index can be measured by the total communality ($\sum_{j=1}^{m} h_j^2$) of the factor solution divided by the total (normalized) variance.

$O_k = \sum_{j=1}^{m} h_j^2/n$ (where n is the number of variables being factored).

3. *Centrality*—the importance of a single general dimension for explaining elements within that organized subset of the attitude space. This can be measured by the variance explained by the most general factor divided by the total communality of the solution.

$$C_k = G^2/\sum_{j=1}^{m} h_j^2$$

---

[3]The four indices described herein are virtually identical to those defined by Zajonc. He defined differentiation as the number of attributes that constitute a given cognitive structure; complexity as the way in which these attributes may be grouped and the occurrence of further subdivisions within these groups; unity as the extent to which the attributes are interrelated or depend on each other; and organization as the extent to which one part dominates the whole thereby indicating the role of a central guiding force. As indicated, our definitions are similar except that we prefer to label his definition of unity as organization, and his definition of organization as centrality. These two differences are simply a matter of our semantic preferences.

4. *Complexity*—the extent to which belief discrimination occurs over hierarchical levels of generalization within the organized subset of the attitude space. This can be measured by the number of factors at each level (M_i) in the hierarchical solution weighted by the variance at that particular level (σ_i^2), multiplied by the number of hierarchical levels (r), and divided by the degree of organization for the k th group (O_k).

$$CX_k = \left(\sum_{i=1}^{n} M_i\, \sigma_i^2 \right) r_k / O_k$$

An Empirical Validation of Attitude Structures

In order to document empirically that these structural indices vary in meaningful ways, we needed to study a population that could be divided into groups for which there was some a priori reason to expect differential structures. The attitude object, smoking marijuana, was selected since some suggestive evidence was available that beliefs pertaining to marijuana are viewed multidimensionally and may or may not be integrated into a single affective response. The United States National Commission on Marijuana and Drug Abuse (Appendix II, 1972) found that older persons appeared to respond to items concerning marijuana in terms of an overall favorable-unfavorable disposition, whereas younger adults discriminated more precisely among the opinion statements on the basis of content. Also, research by Sadava (1972) and Goode (1970) has indicated that with increased marijuana involvement, there appeared (a) an increased sense of commitment to future drug use, (b) increased levels of social support for drug use (e.g. available models for drug use, social reinforcement, and absence of sanctions for drug-using behavior), (c) increased reasons or functions such behavior held for the user and the elaboration of justifications for use, (d) intensified social interaction with other marijuana users and marijuana-related activities, (e) greater likelihood of taking other non-medical drugs in addition to marijuana, (f) increased probabilities of buying and selling marijuana as well as attempted proselytization of a nonuser. This and other evidence (Becker, 1953) suggests, in the case of marijuana smoking at least, that a person's behavioral repertoire relevant to an object becomes elaborated with increased exposure. Because of this and the (highly probable) increase in exposure to the drug attitudes, values, and experiences of others, the individual becomes more "sophisticated" and knowledgeable in his thinking about the drug. Thus, an increasing complexity of attitude structure may be required to represent this expanded cognitive activity whether obtained by direct behavioral experience or otherwise.

A second reason for selecting marijuana smoking was that a classification system was available that categorized marijuana users along a continuum pertaining to the extent of their experience with marijuana. Sadava (1972) defined the following five stages of marijuana use: (a) non-users—persons who have never tried marijuana; (b) initial users—persons who have smoked marijuana but have not experienced a ''high'' more than once; (c) casual users—persons who have experienced a ''high'' more than once; (d) occasional users—persons who have experienced a ''high'' more than once and maintain access to a supply of marijuana; and (e) regular users—persons who smoke marijuana or use some other-psychedelic drug nearly every day.

In order to investigate the attitude structures of these groups, extensive psychometric work was completed by Schlegel (1975) to develop a 20-subscale inventory which assessed 20 belief dimensions pertaining to smoking marijuana. Prior to this psychometric development, a strategy was adopted to isolate and identify salient dimensions of the ''attitude towards smoking marijuana'' space that would permit a maximum description of this attitude space, whether for groups with simple or complex attitude structures. Thus subscale construction (essentially a Likert procedure) was based on the following 20 attitude continua: morality, hedonism, euphoric sensory-perceptual effects, dysphoric sensory-perceptual effects, instrumental to philosophic outcomes, instrumental to self-actualization, harm to physical health, benefits to physical health, harm to personality and mental health, harm to intellectual and cognitive functioning, enhances-inhibits motivation, benefits to personality and mental health, social order, public safety, pro-anti legalization, marijuana smokers, control of actions, drug abuse potential, dependency-no dependency, instrumental to social interaction. Subscale reliabilities ranged from .87 to .97 with a mean value of .93 using the Kuder-Richardson $r8$ formula. This 20-dimensional inventory thus enables a more precise mapping of the attitude space and provides the measurement capabilities for detecting more complex and differentiated cognitive structures. For many persons, a one or two or three dimensional inventory will be sufficient to describe their attitudes. Theoretically, however, many more dimensions might be necessary for a complete representation of the salient beliefs held by an individual.

A total of 382 undergraduate college students then participated in a study by responding to 100 opinion statements, which were subsequently assigned to their respective subscale (with 5 items per subscale). The subjects were classified into one of the five Sadava stages of marijuana use. The 20 subscale scores were then factor analyzed by the Wherry hierarchical factor analysis computer program for each of the five user groups separately. Figure 2.1 provides a graphic illustration of attitude structures comparing the two extreme groups, nonusers and regular users. This figure clearly illustrates the greater complexity and hierarchical arrangement for the regular user group. Three levels of factors are obtained in the nonuser group solution whereas four levels result for the regular users. The proportion of variance accounted for by each factor in the common factor space is also indicated. The initial, casual, and occasional user groups yield attitude structures that fall in systematic fashion between these two extreme groups. A result of particular importance was that the proportion of the common factor

TABLE 2.1
A Comparison of Attitude Structures Across the Stages of Marijuana
Use

| User Group | Structural Index | | | |
	Differentiation	Organization	Centrality	Complexity
Nonuser	4	.688	.643	8.036
Initial User	5	.723	.570	8.959
Casual User	5	.728	.508	8.777
Occasional User	6	.619	.262	17.816
Regular User	8	.755	.212	26.628

space explained by the most general factor progressively decreased across the five stages while the proportion accounted for by more specific factors tended to increase. Thus the importance of a single, general factor declined as a response determinant of beliefs for the five successive stages.

Table 2.1 indicates the morphological properties of the five respective attitude structures. The various structural indices suggest systematic trends across the groups. With increased stage of use, greater attitudinal differentiation was apparent. In other words, with increased familiarity and association with the attitude object (i.e., marijuana smoking), "finer" perceptions and discriminations occurred; therefore a greater number of relatively stable equivalence classes (i.e., first-order varimax factors) resulted. The complexity index indicates that this increased discrimination occurred not only at a primary level, but also over levels of abstraction.

The complexity index is lowest (maximum = 1.000) when a single, general factor is sufficient as a response basis. It is next lowest when all of the variance is explained by the primary order, varimax factors. In a truly orthogonal factor solution then, this value would not exceed the degree of differentiation. Relatively simplex structures, therefore, occur where the primary factors are largely explained by a single, underlying dimension, or second, the varimax factors are mutually independent (and consequently there exists no hierarchical structure). A complex structure occurs where primary dimensions are related to each other in the common factor space in ways requiring more inclusive higher-order categories, yet leaving residual variance in the lower order factors. Therefore, attitudinal responses toward smoking marijuana are complexly determined from various levels of the hierarchical structure. As compared to the nonuser, initial user, and casual user, Table 2.1 illustrates that the occasional and regular groups had elaborated their structures in somewhat more complex ways.

Concomitant with differentiation and complexity differences across the five stages of marijuana use, decreased centrality in the structures was apparent. For nonusers, a single general evaluative dimension explained 64.3% of the common factor space. By contrast, only 21.2% of the common space variability was accounted for by the most general factor for the regular group. Nonusers (as well as initial and casual users to a somewhat lesser extent), therefore, appeared to hold a more generalized "set" to respond and evaluate marijuana-related stimuli.

There is an alternative explanation to the finding that groups with more marijuana-related experience hold more complex attitude structures. It may be argued that individual differences variables in general cognitive style (e.g. cognitive complexity) may predispose one to a certain level of behavioral involvement rather than the amount of experience with the attitude object determining the level of attitude complexity. However, the plausibility of this rival hypothesis is considerably weakened by some summarizing evidence by Marsh (1977) who concluded that cognitive complexity is not a general trait, but rather is domain specific. Further the degree of within-domain complexity is a function of knowledge and experience pertaining to that specific area. This conclusion is consistent with the data by Scott (1969) cited in this chapter.

The degree of organization of the universal attitude space was reasonably constant across the five stages of marijuana use. The occasional group appeared least organized with 61.9% of the total attitude space explained by the common factor solution. Therefore, for the occasional group, the role of specific factors (within the context of the Hotelling principal factor model for factor analytic solutions, Harmon, 1967) in determining responses was somewhat more prominent.

While the differentiation, centrality, and complexity indices suggested the occurrence of structural revisions across the five user groups, these changes appeared to result in a considerable degree of consistency among the elements. That is, structural change did not necessarily result in greater inconsistency and less structure (as can be noted in Table 2.1 where the index of organization is rather consistent across the five groups). The present data, however, demonstrate that morphological changes in attitude structure did occur over the five groups. Of course, the reasons and substantive interpretations for this change are not provided by these indices. An analysis of a more substantive orientation is given in a later section of this chapter which investigates some limiting conditions of the unidimensional approach to attitudes.

The data just examined indicate that attitude structures can vary in systematic and meaningful ways across different populations. Although the amount of organization or inter-relatedness of belief elements in the attitude space appears to remain relatively constant, we have seen that attitude structures can become considerably more differentiated and complex and also less central in their morphology. Most crucially, it is readily apparent that viewing attitude towards some referent in terms of a more or less well-defined single, generalized evaluative dimension varies in its adequacy for representing the complete attitudinal space.

The theoretical and empirical implications of this phenomenon will be explored rather extensively for the question of attitude-behavior consistency.

Theoretical Implications of Varying Structures for Attitude-Behavior Consistency

The index of centrality (reflecting the importance of a single, evaluative dimension within the common factor space) assumes a critical importance for the attitude-behavior relation. To the extent that a highly differentiated structure cannot be sufficiently integrated by a unidimensional, affective type of response, and second, belief elements critical to behavior prediction remain nonintegrated, it is hypothesized that the relation between attitude (i.e. the affective component) and behavior will be reduced correspondingly. In the hierarchical factor analytic representation of attitude structure, common factor space variance that cannot be explained by the general factor will remain with the lower order factors, thus indicating some specific beliefs which could not be empirically encompassed by a more general, evaluative factor. If these lower-order (nonintegrated) beliefs are not related to behavior, then a general evaluative measure of attitudes will still describe in full the relation between attitude and behavior. However, if some of these nonintegrated beliefs are related to behavior, then the general measure will describe the true relationship only partially. Our structural specification of attitudes, then, identifies certain parameters where a general measure of affect will be inadequate to fully describe the attitude-behavior relation.

The question that may now be posed is what are the conditions that are likely to yield a highly differentiated structure, and most crucially, one that cannot be sufficiently integrated by a unidimensional, affective type of response. It would appear reasonable to assume that as one becomes more extensively involved with an object and an elaborated behavioral repertoire is developed, an increasingly differentiated and complex attitude structure is required to represent on a cognitive level this behavioral activity. Or more generally, any experience (whether direct behavioral involvement or otherwise) leading to new and more information about the attitude object is likely to result in more complex cognitive activity and attitude structure. Scott (1969) demonstrated that increased differentiation (i.e. dimensionality) resulted from exposure to new information and that dimensionality correlated negatively (range $-.26$ to $-.52$, mean correlation $-.42$) with affective-evaluative consistency. Thus, with increased cognitive dimensionality there was a tendency to have a lower overall affective integration (i.e. affective-evaluative consistency). At the same time, however, the magnitude of these correlations would indicate that increased dimensionality need not result necessarily in less affective integration. One could think of several illustrations where a highly differentiated conceptualization has been developed but which can be effectively represented by an affective response. For instance, it may be possible that one can have extensive knowledge of the various strengths and weaknesses of one's spouse (i.e. beliefs of spouse) and yet demonstrate strong feelings of love (i.e. affect) that capture the more detailed cognitive appraisal. Similarly, one might be extremely well informed about a country but yet be able to synthesize this knowledge into an overall feeling of strong patriotism. As suggested, it appears reasonable to expect that increased cognitive differentiation occurs with more knowledge and experience that links the target object with various attributes, but it is not clear precisely what conditions lead to an attitudinal structure that can be integrated by a single, general response versus a structure that is not integrated as adequately. At this time one can only speculate on some potential reasons. One of these reasons may pertain to the nature of the experience one has with the attitude object and the expected utility of the information derived from this experience. For example, Zajonc (1960) found that persons expecting to transmit information required a higher level of specificity of the cognitive structure (i.e. greater perception of the distinct attributes associated with an object) but there existed a high degree of organization (in his terms, the extent to which the cognitive structure is organized around one specific aspect) in order to focus one's attention for effective communication. However, imagine a politician in an election campaign during which he must face audiences varying in their views on a topic. This person would need to continually adapt and refocus the specific terms of his cognitive structure in order to appear as similar as possible to the position of the audience, leaving behind feelings of liking and hopefully (for the candidate) votes. The structure of this person's response to the issue would be multifocused or multidimensional in nature. All of this is very speculative, however, and much more work is required to identify those conditions that would tend to yield relatively nonintegrated attitude structures.

AN EMPIRICAL DEMONSTRATION OF THE FAILURE
OF THE UNIDIMENSIONAL APPROACH

Although the conditions for nonintegration are not specified very well at the present time, it has been demonstrated that the topic "marijuana smoking" does yield attitude structures that vary in differentiation and affective integration across subgroups of persons depending upon their degree of experience with marijuana. Earlier in the chapter, five stages of marijuana use were described that reflected progressively varying degrees of socialization into the marijuana experience. Considerable evidence (Becker, 1953; Goode, 1970; Sadava, 1972) exists to suggest that in the case of marijuana smoking a person's behavioral repertoire relevant to an object becomes elaborated with increased exposure and this expanded behavioral repertoire leads to additional cognitive representation. Thus, an increasing complexity of attitude structure is required to represent on a cognitive level this behavioral activity. To the extent this highly differentiated and complex structure cannot be sufficiently integrated by a unidimensional, affective type of attitudinal response, then, it is predicted that an attitudinal measure assessing this generalized response will show considerably attenuated predictions of behavior.

A large longitudinal field study pertaining to the social psychology of non-medical drug use has been conducted by Schlegel and DiTecco (Schlegel, 1974) in order to investigate a variety of hypotheses relating to drug-taking behavior for nonmedical purposes. One of the objectives pertained specifically to the structure of attitude space for the object, marijuana smoking. Subjects (N = 1630) consist-ed of male and female high school students selected from two Ontario school boards, one being predominantly urban and the other predominantly rural and small town. In February, 1975 and again 1 year later, subjects were administered a questionnaire containing a variety of personality, social environmental, at-titudinal and behavioral measures. Of particular interest for present purposes were the following measures: (a) 20 ''attitude toward smoking marijuana'' sub-scales (Schlegel, 1975); (b) a semantic differential evaluative measure of attitude toward smoking marijuana assessed by four bipolar adjectives; (c) an intentions to smoke marijuana measure; (d) the Sadava stages of use (Sadava, 1972); and (e) a self-report of actual marijuana use. The latter behavioral measure asked subjects to indicate how often they had used marijuana in the last year and was coded on a 6-point scale ranging from never (0) to nearly every day (5).

Consistent with the results cited previously for college students (Schlegel, 1973), it was presumed for this new sample that occasional and regular mari-juana users would have a substantially more elaborate and complex attitude structure surrounding marijuana use than those at earlier stages, and most cru-cially, that a general evaluative dimension would explain substantially less of the total attitudinal space variance for marijuana smokers at the advanced stages of use as compared to those involved at the more elementary levels of the behavior. Thus, the general (semantic differential) evaluative measure would be unable to adequately represent a complex, multidimensional attitude found in those from a population with a far greater familiarity with an activity (e.g. regular marijuana users) than is normal.

First, we investigated by way of the hierarchical factor analytic technique the attitude structures of the five user stages respectively. Table 2.2 indicates the morphological properties of these attitude structures. Although the structural changes across the progressive stages are not quite as orderly as those for the college sample (Table 2.1), the high school data also indicate greater differentia-tion and complexity, and less centrality for those groups with greater marijuana experience as compared to those with less. In order to simplify the test of our hypothesis, subjects were further grouped so that persons classified as nonusers and initial users were considered to be at a ''simple level'' of marijuana use whereas occasional and regular users were obviously at a more advanced stage of marijuana use. The average centrality for nonusers and initial users (i.e. simple

TABLE 2.2
A Comparison of Attitude Structures Across the Stages of Marijuana
Use for High School Students

User Group	Structural Index			
	Differentiation	Organization	Centrality	Complexity
Nonuser	3	.667	.662	5.022
Initial User	3	.660	.581	5.550
Casual User	4	.625	.380	7.777
Occasional User	5	.654	.405	10.653
Regular User	5	.674	.479	10.036

stage of use) is . 622 as contrasted with . 442 for occasional and regular users (i.e. advanced stage of use). Thus, for persons at a simple stage of use, 62.2% of common factor space variance is explained by a general factor. In terms of attitude structure, this means that 62.2% of the underlying belief structure can be explained by a general, affective type of response, and conversely, 37.8% of the total attitude space variance remains with specific beliefs that have not been affectively integrated. In comparison, for persons at an advanced stage of use, 55.8% of the underlying belief structures variance cannot be explained by a unidimensional affective response. Thus a considerably larger portion of the attitude space is unaccounted for by a general measure in this case, and to the extent that belief elements in the "unaccounted for space" are related to behavior, the attitude (i.e. affective response)—behavior relation will be underestimated. One would expect, then, that a more complete assessment of the attitude structure would provide for a fuller accounting of the relationship.

In order to test these expectations, the adequacy of a unidimensional approach was investigated by correlating the general semantic differential measure of attitude with a concurrent 7-point intentions measure and a behavioral frequency measure obtained 1 year later. A two-step hierarchical regression procedure was used which entered the semantic differential measure first and then entered the first four subscales[4] from the Schlegel multidimensional model in the second inclusion level. By this method, effects of the unidimensional evaluative measure are partialed out in the first step so the unique portion of variance accounted for by the additional belief elements can be estimated. If there exists little

---

[4]In order to minimize capitalization on chance in the stepwise regression procedure, only the first four subscales in terms of step-wise selection were allowed to enter into the equation that tested our hypothesis. In each of the four samples (see below) for which this hypothesis was tested, at least four subscales contributed statistically significant increments in unique variance after the multiple correlations had been adjusted for shrinkage.

additional unique variance, then a general measure[5] can be considered to adequately represent the attitude space for purposes of behavior prediction. On the other hand, a substantial amount of unique variance would indicate that belief elements nonintegrated by the general evaluation response need to be taken into account to explain more completely the relationship between the entire attitude space and behavior.

Table 2.3 indicates the results of these analyses replicated over four samples—rural male, urban male, rural female, and urban female. The unidimensional assessment (i.e. semantic differential scale) was compared to a multidimensional assessment (i.e. four belief subscales) in the prediction of both marijuana intentions and behavior for persons at a simple (i.e. nonusers and initial users) versus complex stage of use (i.e. occasional and regular users). An examination of the rural male sample indicates that both intentions and behavior for the simple stage group can be predicted relatively adequately by a unidimensional measure as compared to the complex stage group, where a multidimensional mapping of attitude structure demonstrates a substantial increment in explained variance. More specifically, it can be observed that the general measure correlates .50 with intentions for the simple group while the additional effect of four subscales yields a multiple R of .53, adding 3.1% unique variance. In contrast to this group, the complex group's correlation between the general measure and intentions was .15 and the multiple R was .54, thereby indicating the four subscales added 22% unique variance beyond that explained by a general measure.[6] Further observation of the data shows that the primary reason for the larger increment in unique variance for the complex group is the substantial drop in the correlation of the general measure of attitude and intentions from the simple to the complex group. This depreciation in the relationship, however, is "recaptured" by the addition of the four belief subscales.

A similar pattern of results is obtained when actual behavior is the criterion for prediction from attitudes. That is, the general, unidimensional measure correlates at a considerably lower level for the complex as compared with the simple group. Thus it is apparent that a general affective type of response for attitude is

---

[5]The semantic differential scale was tested for its convergent validity as a measure of affect in both simple and complex stages. A hierarchical factor analysis was completed for both groups respectively and the semantic differential loaded predominantly on the most general factor of the hierarchical solution in each case.

[6]The possibility of restricted variance being an explanation for these results was examined. However, the variances for attitudes, intentions and behavior were not statistically different when the simple versus complex groups were compared. This restricted variance explanation was similarly ruled out for the other analyses reported in Table 2.3. Notwithstanding these statistical comparisons, it might be noted that differential restricted variance for intentions and behavior would not be particularly troublesome in any event since it is the two models (unidimensional vs. multidimensional) which are being compared at each stage for their predictive efficacy of a common dependent variable.

adequate for prediction of intentions and behavior at simple levels but not at complex levels of attitude structure. Also, it is empirically demonstrated that beliefs exist in the attitude space that are salient to behavior prediction yet remain nonintegrated by a general affective response. Thus the more comprehensive assessment of attitude space provided by the four subscales (representing the multidimensionality of the attitude space) was able to obtain a fuller accounting

TABLE 2.3
Prediction of Marijuana Intentions (BI) and Behavior (B) from
Unidimensional vs. Multidimensional Assessments of Attitude
Structure

Rural Male	Simple Stage		Complex Stage	
	BI (N=268)	B (N=246)	BI (N=47)	B (N=37)
Unidimensional	.50[a]	.39	.15	.02
Multidimensional	.53	.52	.54	.63
ΔR^2	.03	.12	.22	.39

Urban Male	Simple Stage		Complex Stage	
	BI (N=196)	B (N=183)	BI (N=85)	B (N=72)
Unidimensional	.61	.35	.23	.25
Multidimensional	.69	.43	.51	.52
ΔR^2	.11	.06	.20	.21

Rural Female	Simple Stage		Complex Stage	
	BI (N=396)	B (N=383)	BI (N=28)	B (N=22)
Unidimensional	.54	.29	.26	.14
Multidimensional	.59	.36	.64	.67
ΔR^2	.07	.04	.34	.42

Urban Female	Simple Stage		Complex Stage	
	BI (N=299)	B (N=233)	BI (N=49)	B (N=41)
Unidimensional	.60	.39	.57	.30
Multidimensional	.72	.46	.68	.60
ΔR^2	.16	.06	.13	.28

[a]Multiple correlations adjusted for shrinkage.

of the relationship. Considerable consistency of this finding is evident across all four samples, for both intentions measured concurrently and behavior assessed 1 year later as the criteria. Prediction of intentions for urban females is the only exception; thus, seven out of eight analyses are supportive of this finding.

In summary, there exists considerable support for the notion that the observed attitude-behavior relation is qualified by the nature of the attitude structure pertaining to the target object. In cases where the attitude structure is not well integrated, a general evaluative measure may underestimate or even misrepresent this relationship to the extent that there remain nonintegrated beliefs salient to behavior prediction. More generally, for any complex attitude structure, a general evaluative measure may not adequately represent all aspects of the underlying belief structure relevant to any given phenomenon or criterion external to attitudes.

REORGANIZATIONAL PROCESSES OF ATTITUDE STRUCTURES

The differences in attitude structure across groups varying in the extensiveness of their experience with the attitude object suggests that a considerable amount of structural revision must occur as one's experience and behavioral repertoire expands. This revision can be viewed in terms of both disorganizing processes (breakdown) and reorganizing processes (reconstruction). In general, the amount of attitude structure (i.e. degree of organization) will decrease if breakdown exceeds reconstruction and increase if reconstruction exceeds breakdown. The Venn diagrams in Figure 2.2 depict possible organizational changes in attitude structure. In case "a", the emergence of the new structure in the second solution entirely offsets the breakdown of factors from the first solution. Therefore, the size of the organized space in the attitude universe remains constant. Case "b" illustrates that the total organization will be less for the second solution if the breakdown of factors from the first solution is not balanced by additionally organized subspace. Finally, in case "c", the emergence of the new structure in the second solution exceeds the extent of factor breakdown from the first solution. Therefore, a net positive change occurs in that subset area reflecting organization.

In order to gain some appreciation of the amount of such structural change, the hierarchical factor solutions for the five user groups for the college sample (described earlier in the chapter) were compared for similarity of factors by Tucker's factor comparison method (Harmon, 1967). The factors for each pairwise solution (i.e. nonusers vs. initial users, nonusers vs. casual, initial users vs. casual, initial users vs. occasional, occasional users vs. regular) were compared to determine the extent of their congruence between the respective solutions. By comparing a preceding group's (e.g. nonusers) factor solution with that of a

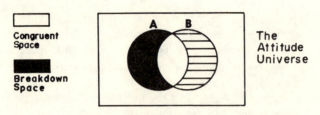

Congruent
Space

Breakdown
Space

The
Attitude
Universe

Case A: Breakdown = Reconstruction
Total Organization remains constant

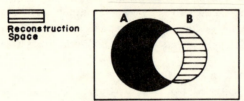

Reconstruction
Space

Case B: Breakdown > Reconstruction
Total organization of solution B decreases

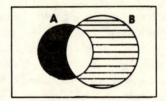

Case C: Breakdown < Reconstruction
Total organization of solution B increases

FIG. 2.2.   Venn Diagram Illustrating Attitude Organization

subsequent group (e.g. initial users), it was possible to assess the extent to which factors were retained in their original form across the five groups (or conversely, the extent of original factor breakdown). Similarly, the emergence of new structure (or reconstruction) could be assessed by comparing the congruence of new factors that emerged in subsequent groups with the existing factors in the preceding groups.[7]

The results indicated that factors in the nonuser solution were broken down by approximately 20% for the initial and casual user groups and by 30% for the

[7]The reader is referred to Schlegel (1973) for a more detailed and technical description of how the respective factor solutions for the five groups were compared using Tucker's coefficient of congruence in order to assess the amount of factor breakdown and reconstruction across the five successive groups.

occasional and regular groups. Generally, the occasional and regular groups had the greatest amount of structural breakdown when their factorial congruence was compared to the preceding groups. Upon examining for reconstruction, there was clear evidence for systematic reorganizational revisions across the five successive stages. For example, when comparing the nonuser and initial groups' factor solutions, it was apparent that reconstruction exceeded breakdown thereby yielding a slightly more organized structure for the initial group. (This is supported by the index of organization in Table 2.1.) When comparing the regular user group to nonusers, the net structural change resulted in the regular group having the highest degree of organization (75.5% of the attitude universe). While the regular group had substantial factor breakdown, its solution also included the greatest reconstructionism. This situation reflects case "c" in the Venn diagrams of Figure 2.2. In contrast, the occasional group's structure indicated breakdown processes were dominant and reconstruction (while being present) was too minimal to permit the emergence of a net positive balance in structural organization. This situation reflects case "b" in the Venn diagrams.

Comparisons of factors across the five hierarchical solutions then clearly indicated that considerable disorganizing and reorganizing dynamics occurred. Despite these substantial structural revisions, however, it is interesting to note the fairly narrow band in which total degree of organization ranged (cf. Table 2.1). That is, a certain consistency tolerance appeared to be maintained in spite of some substantial structural revisions; this effect would appear to lend strong support for cognitive consistency theories.

Of further interest is a substantive interpretation of the factors as they break down and subsequently reconstruct. This more substantively oriented examination may provide further insight into the question of how attitude structures can qualify the attitude-behavior relation. The hierarchical factor structures were substantively interpreted for both college and high school samples in order to provide an actual description of the attitude structures and how the nature of factors appeared to change from one group to another. Since the attitude structure is less complicated for the high school sample, it will be described (at least in part) to explore these questions. At the nonuser stage, there appear three basic dimensions along which high school students evaluate marijuana use. One dimension is "Moral Judgement" (is marijuana good or bad?) and it appears to pertain to society in general (is marijuana deleterious to social order? should it be legalized?). The other two factors are concerned with the effects of marijuana use on the individual, one pertaining mainly to benefits and the other to harms. The "Benefits" factor concerns the potential for marijuana use to positively affect an individual's personal growth (aiding self-awareness, self-actualization and social interactions). The "Harms" factor relates to the potential for marijuana use to harm an individual's personality and intellectual and cognitive functioning.

One can then examine the extent to which these factors are retained or changed in their meaning across the four subsequent user stages. The second factor, Benefits, is the most durable and maintains its composition throughout all five levels of marijuana use. The Moral Judgment dimension, although showing some fluctuations in composition, remains present at each of the five stages. A new factor appears to emerge from this dimension for the occasional group and this factor takes on a predominant meaning of hedonism. The Harms factor is not very stable across the groups and appears to differentiate at different stages in ways that reflect some degree of face validity. At the initial and casual user stages, an inhibition of motivation meaning becomes salient to this factor. The first new actual factor to emerge occurs at the casual stage where individuals have enough experience with marijuana to begin to appreciate its mood-altering effect. This "Loss of Control" factor concerns such issues as the ability of marijuana users to control their actions and concerns about public safety effects of marijuana smoking. This same factor seems to take on some additional meaning for occasional users with respect to beliefs pertaining to drug abuse potential of marijuana smoking and the dysphoric sensory-perceptual effects of the marijuana "high." The transition of occasional use represents a significant step for the individual since at this stage he or she has secured a supply of marijuana for personal use. Recall also that a Hedonism factor emerged at this stage which may reflect the inculcation of a drug culture norm of liberated hedonism, or may perhaps serve a dissonance reduction or rationalization function for the individual since personal commitment to marijuana use is substantial at this point. At the level of regular use (i.e. nearly every day), the original Harms factor has evolved into three dimensions of meaning. The first pertains to perceived harms to self, especially physical health; the second remains more or less the loss of control factor while the third factor may be labeled, "Addictive Syndrome." Addictive Syndrome is a new factor combining elements relating to drug dependency potential of marijuana smoking, inhibition of motivation and drug abuse potential. It would appear reasonable that these dimensions would become salient for persons at a regular stage of use.

These changes in meanings related to attitude structure occur also for the college sample, although there exists greater complexity at every stage. For instance, at the regular level of use, drug dependency, inhibition of motivation and drug abuse potential are strong components of three separate factors instead of being found within a simpler addictive syndrome factor. These results offer further evidence for differential attitude structures dependent upon the degree of experience an individual has with the attitude object. Differences in amount of structure between high school and college samples may be a function of the experience variable or may possibly reflect a maturational difference in cognitive ability. In any event, there appears considerable substantive meaningfulness in the way attitude structures change across levels of use, which demonstrates a certain degree of face validity with the nature of the experience at that stage. Also, the differential attitude structures across the five stages suggest that attitudes used as behavior predictors must also be differentiated according to the experience and cognitive sophistication of the target population.

In the last section of the chapter which examined the sufficiency of the unidimensional affective approach versus a multidimensional mapping of the attitude space, it was empirically demonstrated that an affective response representation was inadequate for cases of complex attitude structure. The present substantive description of attitude structures across the five groups hints at some of the belief dimensions that may not be integrated by an overall affective response at different stages of complex attitudinal structure yet are critical to behavior prediction. These specific belief elements eluding affective integration can be identified directly by examining those subscales that emerged as significant predictors of behavior, after having partialed out the effects of the general evaluative factor.

As indicated in Table 2.3, the additional four belief dimensions added little variance of a psychologically meaningful magnitude to the variance which could be accounted for by the evaluative measure alone in the case of the "simple behavior" groups. When the additional belief subscales were examined individually for their unique variance contribution, few accounted for more than 1% additional variance to the prediction of behavior 1 year later. Also, when the Schlegel subscales alone were entered in a step-wise regression, the first subscale inevitably accounted for most of the explained variance. The relationship between this subscale and behavior was almost entirely accounted for by the general evaluative measure, however, as indicated by the large drop in correlation when the effects of the general measure were partialed out. Thus the beliefs in the attitude space most relevant to behavior prediction were almost completely integrated by a general affective type of response. This analysis held consistently for all four samples—male and female, urban and rural.

A similar analysis in the case of the "complex behavior" groups, however, revealed that specific belief elements existed (in the attitude space) that were most pertinent to behavior prediction yet remained almost totally nonintegrated by a general affective response. In this case, for example, when behavior was regressed on the belief subscales the first predictor selected in the step-wise regression was not at all attenuated in a subsequent analysis when the effects of the general evaluative measure were partialed out. This was consistently apparent for all four samples. In each case, a specific set of unique and statistically significant belief subscales was identified, with considerable unique variance being contributed to behavior prediction by each belief dimension. The specific set of beliefs pertinent to predicting behavior over a subsequent 1-year period was quite idiosyncratic to the particular sample. For instance, beliefs pertaining to marijuana smokers, drug dependency potential, public safety aspects, benefits to personality and mental health, and morality were most salient for the rural males; whereas beliefs involving legalization of marijuana use, self-actualization, social order, philosophical outcomes, harms to physical health and public safety were most salient for the urban male sample. While the belief profile was idiosyncratic to the particular sample, as might be anticipated, the crucial point is that in each case a set of beliefs emerged that was most predictive of behavior yet was not integrated by a general affective type of response, as assessed by the evaluative semantic differential measure in this study.

These analyses then provide us with a further insight into some of the underlying dynamics for those circumstances where a unidimensional view will be insufficient (or even totally inadequate) for describing the true relation between attitudes and behavior. Earlier in this section of the chapter, we presented evidence indicating that considerable disorganizing and reorganizing processes occurred across the five stages of marijuana use. The latter analyses reveal on a more substantive level the nature of beliefs that emerge with increased experience and an expanded behavioral repertoire pertaining to this particular attitude object. These beliefs can be viewed as meaningful cognitive representations of behavior at the complex stage that lie outside the realm of adequate affective integration. Thus the reorganizational process of attitude structure qualify in a substantial and psychologically meaningful way the attitude-behavior relation.

DOES DIRECT EXPERIENCE INCREASE OR DECREASE
ATTITUDE-BEHAVIOR CONSISTENCY?

A recent literature has developed which suggests that people who form their attitudes on the basis of direct experience with the attitude object demonstrate greater attitude-behavior consistency than individuals whose attitudes are formed by other means. Evidence indicates that direct behavioral experience produces an attitude which is more clearly, confidently and stably maintained and hence creates greater consistency between attitudes and behavior (Regan & Fazio, 1977; Fazio & Zanna, 1981). This literature would appear at first reading to be contradictory with the attitude structures approach described in this chapter and the data relating attitude (i.e. the affective response) to behavior for simple versus complex groups. As can be noted from Table 2.3, the correlations drop substantially when comparing simple stage versus complex stage users of marijuana for predicting both intentions and behavior from the unidimensionally based measure of attitudes. Recall that persons at the complex stage are occasional and regular users who have considerably more direct experience with the attitude object than simple stage persons (i.e., nonusers and initial users). Thus, in our case, attitude-behavior consistency would appear to decrease with more direct experience, rather than increase as would be predicted by Fazio and Zanna.

A further analysis of our data would tend to suggest that the two theoretical approaches are not necessarily incompatible. An analysis was completed whereby the simple group (with the relatively integrated attitude structure) was divided up again into nonuser and initial user groups. Then, for each group separately, the semantic differential attitude measure was correlated with the concurrent intentions measure and actual behavior 1 year later. (An examination of variance indicated that enough persons in the nonuser group started to smoke marijuana over the subsequent year to permit the analysis with actual behavior as well.) This analysis was replicated for each of the four samples as previously defined. In three out of the four samples for intentions as the criterion and in all four samples for behavior, the correlation increased from a stage of no direct experience (nonuse) to a stage of direct (albeit initial) experience. This suggests that the effect of direct experience on attitude-behavior consistency may be curvilinear in nature. That is, at the initial stages of behavior acquisition (involving novel tasks) greater attitude-behavior consistency is obtained with increased experience whereas at the advanced stages of behavioral involvement the reverse finding is obtained (cf. Table 2.3).

The theoretical analysis of attitude structures outlined in this chapter provides a potential explanation for this finding. The nonuser and initial user groups, it may be recalled, had relatively well-integrated attitude structures that could be represented by a general evaluative measure. Thus at the early stages of behavioral involvement a unidimensional affective response was an adequate representation of the attitude space regarding smoking marijuana, and with increased direct experience the relationship between this general affective response and behavior became more consistent. But as behavior moves beyond these relatively elementary levels, an elaborated behavioral repertoire develops for marijuana smoking and more complex cognitive representations for this increased experience are required. Thus a multidimensional view of attitude structure is required in this case as compared to the earlier and simpler unidimensional affective response. Since the complete nature of the more complex attitude structure is not adequately captured by this simpler response, the Fazio and Zanna effect is not obtained in this case. However, if the attitude space were to be assessed (more appropriately) multidimensionally, then one might again anticipate the Fazio and Zanna effect. Examining the data in Table 2.3 again, it can be observed that indeed this is the case for each of the four samples for the criterion of behavior (although not for intentions). If one is mainly concerned with the relation between attitudes and behavior, then, one could conclude that even at more advanced stages of behavioral involvement there exists greater attitude-behavior consistency with more direct experience. This increased consistency, however, will be detected only if an adequately sensitive assessment of the entire attitude space is made. Thus, at least for marijuana use as investigated in our study, the Fazio and Zanna effect is obtained provided that the nature of the attitude structure that has developed in relation to a given stage of behavior is appropriately taken into account.[8]

SUMMARY AND DISCUSSION

It was suggested that a large number of cognitions or beliefs may exist in relation to any given attitude object. These beliefs can have a relatively simple organization wherein a general affective dimension is able to integrate them more or less into a single response. Evidence was presented, however, that in some cases a single affective response is not capable of fully representing this profile of beliefs and a person retains a more complex, multidimensional belief structure in one's thought pattern. It was proposed that the term *attitude* refer to the affective response whereas *attitude structure* be more inclusive to include also the belief structure underlying the affective response. It was then shown that hierarchical factor analysis provides a useful technique for identifying, describing, and analyzing attitude structures. This technique permits both a morphological and substantive analysis of these structures.

It has been demonstrated that increased information and experience with an attitude object increases belief dimensionality and that increased dimensionality is negatively correlated with the capability of a general evaluative response subsuming (or integrating) the underlying set of beliefs. Consequently, it was argued that if there exist specific beliefs as part of the attitude structure that cannot be integrated by a general affective response and if some of these beliefs

---

[8]Some initial analyses in our study involving beer drinking, however, clearly show that with increased direct experience, attitude-behavior consistency is systematically reduced. The correlations between a general measure of attitude and concurrent beer drinking intentions depending upon previous beer experience were: nonuser, .61; one to two times per year, .54; three to ten times per year, .29; one to two times per month, .21; and one time or more per week, .17. In line with the theoretical approach outlined in this chapter, one might again posit that a complex profile of underlying beliefs exists for beer use that has not been integrated affectively such that a general semantic differential measure is able to describe the true relationship. Unfortunately, our investigation did not include a multidimensional assessment for beer drinking beliefs as it did for marijuana use, the thus this potential explanation could not be tested. Since the observed attitude-behavior correlation is limited by the nature of the attitude structure at each stage of behavioral involvement, one should first ensure that the entire attitude space is represented in the correlation with behavior before accepting at face value these decreasing correlations (as amount of direct past experience with drinking increases). Nonetheless, it would be premature to rule out the possibility of a curvilinear effect. That is, direct experience may increase attitude-behavior consistency at the initial stages of behavioral involvement, but at advanced stages, more direct experience may decrease attitude-behavior consistency (for example as situational and other factors may assume an increased importance).

are related to behavior, then the general measure will describe the true attitude-behavior relation only partially.

In order to examine empirically how attitude structures may qualify the observed magnitude of the attitude-behavior relation, high school and college students were classified into five sequential stages of behavioral involvement with marijuana. It was found that the groups with more experience with the attitude topic had more complex attitude structures, and most crucially, there remained a number of discrete beliefs within the attitude universe that could not be accounted for (in terms of variance explained) by a general evaluative response factor. It was then empirically documented that the attitude-behavior relation was substantially underestimated for those groups with advanced experience and complex attitude structures. When a multidimensional assessment of the attitude space was made, however, a greatly improved attitude-behavior correlation was observed.

Further analyses were completed that illustrated how the relatively simple structures of groups with less experience with marijuana were broken up and reconstructed into more complex structures by groups with more experience. These analyses revealed on a substantive level the nature of beliefs that emerged with increased experience and an expanded behavioral repertoire pertaining to this particular attitude object. Thus, some further insight was obtained into some of the underlying dynamics for those circumstances where a unidimensional view will be insufficient (or even totally inadequate) for describing the true relation between attitudes and behavior. Finally, we discussed the role of direct experience in mediating the attitude-behavior relation since the observed relationship is limited by the nature of the attitude structure at each stage of behavioral involvement. It was demonstrated that even at more advanced stages of behavioral involvement (with marijuana at least) there exists greater attitude-behavior consistency with more direct experience, provided a comprehensive assessment of the entire attitude space is made.

In addition to attitude structures qualifying the attitude-behavior relation, there exist some further implications which may be briefly discussed. One implication pertains to how knowledge of the attitude structure can guide one in designing effective persuasive communications. Research can determine which dimensions of the attitude structure are most susceptible to change and which are most resistant or perhaps even prone to reactance effects. While a particular dimension may be dominant in the attitude structure and may be especially relevant to external criteria (e.g. behavior) for which change is ultimately desired, it may be more efficacious to direct change attempts to less salient dimensions that are more susceptible to influence while being empirically related to the criterion of interest. Two experimental studies by Schlegel and Norris (1980) provide preliminary support for this strategy. Another implication may involve the situation where a very undifferentiated cognitive structure exists and the total attitudinal response is determined from the affective dimension. For instance, persons strongly opposed to drinking (alcohol) may perceive the issue in simple and categorical "black or white" terms. A strategy for attitude change could involve creating new categories of thought such that a more differentiated attitude structure would result. This increased differentiation would allow belief change along new dimensions while allowing the person to remain opposed to the attitude object on "old" dimensions of the attitude structure. Another implication of an attitude structure orientation for attitude change pertains to measurement sensitivity. A unidimensional general measure will be sufficiently sensitive for a highly centralized, well-integrated structure but will be insufficient where a differentiated set of distinct belief elements in the attitude space are not well integrated by a general, affective response. Thus the results of an experimental manipulation directed towards particular belief arguments not affectively integrated by the attitude structure would not be captured by a general measure, and thus lead to a potentially erroneous conclusion of an ineffectual persuasive communication.

Another issue in social psychology for which our attitude structures approach may have relevance is the ordering of attitude versus behavior change. The theoretical notions of information processing theory suggest that attitudes precede and determine behavior (Hovland, Janis, & Kelly, 1953; McGuire, 1970; Fishbein & Ajzen, 1975). Alternatively, dissonance (Festinger, 1957), self-perception (Bem, 1972), or attribution theories (Kelly, 1967) argue that attitudes follow behavior change. This ordering question is particularly critical in the case of field interventions where the "natural history" of attitude versus behavior change must be understood. Research may find, for example, that some belief elements of the attitude structure establish a general predisposition to the behavior (which may influence, for example, the choice of a membership group with particular attitudes and values pertinent to the behavior), while others function as precipitating factors or triggering mechanisms and still others change after the behavior to justify the act or to establish internal structural consistency. A further and special complication may exist in those circumstances where these underlying beliefs have a differential ordering relationship with behavior (e.g., some preceding and others following behavior) *and these beliefs can be integrated affectively*. These differential relationships could very well cancel each other out if a general "summed" measure of attitude was investigated in relationship to behavior. Another complicating factor with complex attitude structures is that a belief element may follow behavior at an initial level of behavioral involvement but precede behavior at a more advanced stage. Some preliminary work has been completed by Schlegel and DiTecco (1978) that has explored some of these considerations in the area of drug attitudes and behaviors. These results suggest that the complexity of attitude structure also has a bearing on the ordering of attitudes and behavior as well as identifying the magnitude of the relation itself.

The theoretical arguments and empirical evidence presented in this chapter clearly show the need to consider the nature of attitude structures when examining the issue of attitude-behavior consistency. The work on attitude structures is still in its very early stages, however, and needs to be studied more vigorously and extensively. For instance, different methodologies for mapping out structures and different attitude topics should be investigated. Also, the implications of attitude structure complexity should be explored with respect to other major topics in social psychology.

REFERENCES

Bagozzi, R. P., & Burnkrant, R. E. Attitude organization and the attitude-behavior relationship. *Journal of Personality and Social Psychology, 1979, 37,* 913–929.

Becker, H. S. Becoming a marijuana user. *The American Journal of Sociology, 1953, 59,* 235–242.

Bem, D. J. Self-perception theory. In L. Berkowitz (Ed.), *Advances in experimental social psychology* (Vol. 6). NewYork: Academic Press, 1972.

Fazio, R. H., & Zanna, M. P. Direct experience and attitude-behavior consistency. In L. Berkowitz (Ed.), *Advances in experimental social psychology,* (Vol. 14), New York: Academic Press, 1981.

Festinger, L. *A theory of cognitive dissonance.* Illinois: Row, Peterson, 1957.

Field, H. S. Attitudes toward rape: A comparative analysis of police, rapists, crisis counselors, and citizens. *Journal of Personality and Social Psychology, 1978, 36,* 156–179.

Fishbein, M., & Ajzen, I. Attitudes towards objects as predictors of single and multiple behavioral criteria. *Psychological Review, 1974, 81,* 59–74.

Fishbein, M., & Ajzen, I. *Belief, attitude, intention and behavior: An introduction to theory and research.* Don Mills: Addison-Wesley, 1975.

Friendly, M. L., & Glucksberg, S. On the description of subcultural lexicons: A multidimensional scaling approach. *Journal of Personality and Social Psychology, 1970, 14,* 55–65.

Goode, E. *The marijuana smokers.* New York: Basic Books, Inc., 1970.

Harmon, H. H. *Modern factor analysis,* Chicago: The University of Chicago Press, 1967.

Hovland, C. I., Janis, I. I., & Kelly, H. H. *Communication and persuasion.* New Haven: Yale University Press, 1953.

Insko, C. A., & Schopler, J. Triadic consistency: A statement of affective-cognitive-conative consistency. *Psychological Review, 1967, 74,* 361–376.

Katz, D., & Stotland, E. A preliminary statement to a theory of attitude structure and change. In S. Koch (Ed.), *Psychology: A study of a science* (Vol. 3). New York: McGraw-Hill, 1959.

Kelly, H. H. Attribution theory in social psychology. In D. Levine (Ed.), *Nebraska Symposium on Motivation* (Vol. 15). Lincoln: University of Nebraska Press, 1967.

Kelman, H. Attitudes are alive and well and gainfully employed in the sphere of action. *American Psychologist, 1974, 29,* 310–324.

Krech, D., Crutchfield, R. S., & Ballachey, E. L. *Individual in society.* New York: McGraw-Hill, 1962.

Kothandapani, V. Validation of feeling, belief, and intention to act as three components of attitude and their contribution to prediction of contraceptive behavior. *Journal of Personality and Social Psychology, 1971, 19,* 321–333.

Marsh, R. K. *A reptest study on domain specificity of cognitive complexity.* Paper presented at the annual meeting of the American Psychological Association, San Francisco, 1977.

McGuire, W. J. Designing communications to change attitudes regarding drug abuse. In J. R. Wittenborn et al. (Eds.) *Communication and drug abuse.* Springfield, ILL.: Charles C. Thomas, 1970.

Norman, R. Affective-cognitive consistency, attitudes, conformity, and behavior. *Journal of Personality and Social Psychology,* 1975, *32,* 83–91.

Osgood, C. E., Suci, G. J., & Tannenbaum, P. H. *The measurement of meaning.* Urbana: University of Illinois Press, 1957.

Ostrom, T. M. The relationship between the affective, behavioral, and cognitive components of attitude. *Journal of Experimental Social Psychology,* 1969, *5,* 12–30.

Regan, D. T., & Fazio, R. On the consistency between attitudes and behavior: Look to the method of attitude formation. *Journal of Experimental Social Psychology,* 1977, *13,* 28–45.

Riger, S., & Gordon, M. T. The structure of rape prevention beliefs. *Personality and Social Psychology Bulletin,* 1979, *5,* 186–190.

Roach, D. E., & Wherry, R. J. The use of hierarchical factor analysis in the determination of corporate image dimensions. *Educational and Psychological Measurement,* 1972, *32,* 31–44.

Rosenberg, M. J. An analysis of affective-cognitive consistency. In C. I. Hovland & M. J. Rosenberg (Eds.), *Attitude, organization and change.* New Haven: Yale University Press, 1960.

Rosenberg, M. J. Hedonism, inauthenticity and other goods toward expansion of a consistency theory. In R. B. Abelson et al. (Eds.), *Theories of cognitive-consistency: A source-book.* Chicago: Rand McNally, 1968.

Rosenberg, M. J., & Hovland, C. I. Cognitive, affective, and behavioral components of attitudes. In C. I. Hovland & M. J. Rosenberg (Eds.), *Attitude organization and change.* New Haven: Yale University Press, 1960.

Sadava, S. W. Stages of college student drug use: A methodological contribution to cross-sectional study. *Journal of Consulting and Clinical Psychology,* 1972, *38,* 298.

Schlegel, R. P. *Multidimensional measurement and structure of attitudes toward smoking marijuana with prediction of marijuana use.* Unpublished doctoral dissertation, Ohio State University, 1973.

Schlegel, R. P. *A social psychological study of non-medical drug use.* Grant No. 1212-5-105, Health & Welfare Canada/Medical Research Council of Canada, 1974.

Schlegel, R. P. Multidimensional measurement of attitude towards smoking marijuana. *Canadian Journal of Behavioral Science,* 1975, *7,* 387–396.

Schlegel, R. P., & Crawford, C. A. Multidimensionality of internal-external locus of control: Some additional data bearing on the validity of self-control as a third dimension. *Canadian Journal of Behavioral Science,* 1976, *8,* 375–387.

Schlegel, R. P., & DiTecco, D. A. *Drug attitudes and behavior: An application of cross-lagged panel correlation analysis.* Paper presented at the 86th Annual Convention of the American Psychological Association, Toronto, Canada, 1978.

Schlegel, R. P., & Norris, J. E. Effects of attitude change on behavior for highly involving issues: The case of marijuana smoking. *Addictive Behaviors,* 1980, *5,* 113–124.

Schlegel, R. P., & Sanborn, M. D. *Religious affiliation and adolescent drinking: Mediating effects of five religiosity dimensions.* Unpublished manuscript, University of Waterloo, 1979.

Scott, W. A. Brief report: Measures of cognitive structure. *Multivariate Behavior Research,* 1966, *1,* 391–395.

Scott, W. A. Structure of natural cognitions. *Journal of Personality and Social Psychology,* 1969, *12,* 261–278.

Sheth, J. N. *A field study of attitude structure and the attitude-behavior relationship.* Unpublished manuscript, University of Illinois, 1973. (a)

Sheth, J. N. Brand profiles from beliefs and importance. *Journal of Advertising Research,* 1973, *13,* 37–42. (b)

Thurstone, L. L. The measurement of attitudes. *Journal of Abnormal and Social Psychology,* 1931, *26,* 249–269.

United States, National Commission on Marihuana and Drug Abuse. *Marihuana: A signal of misunderstanding.* Washington, D.C.: U.S. Government Printing Office, 1972.

Wherry, R. J. Factor analysis of morale data: Reliability and validity. *Personnel Psychology,* 1958, *11,* 78–88.

Wherry, R. J. Hierarchical factor solutions without rotation. *Psychometrika,* 1959, *18,* 161–179.

Wicker, A. Attitudes versus actions: The relationship of verbal and overt behavioral responses to attitude objects. *Journal of Social Issues,* 1969, *25,* 41–78.

Zajonc, R. B. The process of cognitive tuning in communication. *Journal of Abnormal and Social Psychology,* 1960, *61,* 159–167.

3 Attitude-Behavior Consistencies as Social Logics

Gerald R. Salancik
University of Illinois at Urbana–Champaign

I began this chapter while sitting in West Side Park in Champaign watching a construction worker in his thirties on a picnic lunch with his wife. Like many picnics, theirs was invaded by ants. Watching the man, I tried to understand his attitude toward ants only from his behavior. When one bold ant hoisted itself upon his plate, it appeared as if he would crush it between his fingers in disgust. He appeared enraged at the ant, perhaps thinking of its affront to his food, and brushed it aside. And when the ant returned he seemed to grow in his anger, pushing it more brusquely, muttering something about "these damn pests," infuriated at the ant's obstinancy. And the ant, though stunned for a few moments, returned again. The man, having finished with his food, now simply watched the creature and seemed not at all concerned about the footprints it deposited on his potato salad. Perhaps he was wondering at the ant's hunger, or its fortitude and courage. The food appeared to fade from focus. Perhaps he thought of the familiar creature as an individual and noticed the crook to its walk, and worried that he had put it there. And the man appeared now to think well of the ant, pushing some of his food in its direction, then noting to his wife, "God, look at that strength," as the ant lifted a stray fragment of chicken. Yet, only moments later, when his wife's plate was infested by several ants, he brushed them to the ground and stepped on them. And so it went with this man and these ants moving for twenty minutes through each other's world. And when it was over, I wondered what, in truth, could we ever hope to say about his attitude towards ants at picnics.

Although it is common for social and behavioral scientists to think of attitudes as coherence of behavior (Allport, 1935; Campbell, 1950), we would be hard put to so represent this person's reactions; they change with each experience. Yet, we could be almost certain that were we to ask this man whether he liked or disliked ants at picnics he would answer the latter consistently. Such reactions as these do havoc to our typical concept of attitude-behavior consistency. The havoc would come because some of the man's behaviors suggest a negative orientation to ants and others suggest a positive orientation. Yet each behavior is understandable and sensible. What sense then can be made of the seeming inconsistency? We think none, for our own expectations about consistency may be unwarranted.

It is the purpose of this chapter to argue that the central problem with our theories of attitude-behavior consistency is with the concept of consistency itself. Our theories and our operationalizations of them lead us to expect particular consistencies between particular behaviors. These expectations, however, seem unwarranted. The concept of consistency is deficient because it does not specify how one behavior implies another behavior. This deficiency is a logical deficiency that comes from attitude's directive function over other behaviors (Allport, 1935). What is wrong in this notion is that although it may be true that an attitude directs behavior, the particular behaviors that it directs are not deducible from the attitude itself.

The problem lies in the simple fact that it is not logically or theoretically possible to deduce one behavior from another. One particular behavior does not in itself imply any other particular behavior. It is thus not possible to predict one attitudinally relevant behavior on the basis of other attitudinally relevant behaviors alone.

A second point to this chapter is to argue that the consistencies that arise among a set of behaviors are part of the social logic of a human action. The implications of behaviors are part of the social meanings of those behaviors. The question of whether a particular behavior is consistent with another particular behavior then reduces to the question of whether a particular implication is part of the social meaning of those behaviors and within the psychological domain of the person.

A third purpose of this chapter is to present several unpublished studies which demonstrate that one can create covariations between attitudes and behaviors, or between attitudinally relevant behaviors, by altering the implicational context of behaviors. These studies were all conducted at the University of Illinois during the period 1973–78 by myself and several undergraduates, including Mary Conway, Donna McGreal, and Sue Trieber. These studies together suggest that attitude-behavior consistencies arise from the implications attached to behaviors and suggest that theories of consistency may be theories of how implications attach to behavior. We conclude by noting that such theories cannot be solely cognitive or affective but must include the social uses of human action.

EXPECTATION FOR CONSISTENCY

The notion that attitudes and behaviors should be consistent with one another was widely believed by theorists of the past (Abelson, Aronson, McGuire, New-comb, Rosenberg & Tannenbaum, 1968; Allport, 1935; Doob, 1947; Campbell, 1950), and increasingly under attack by current theorists (Calder & Ross, 1973; Wicker, 1969). However, the latter base their attack more on empirical grounds than any particular forceful argument. While the evidence for attitude-behavior consistency is scant (DeFleur & Westie, 1958; Wicker, 1969), the problem might lie more with our expectations for consistency than with the nature of attitudes.

The expectation for consistency between attitude and behavior, it seems to me, arises from our notion of an attitude as having a directive function. As Allport (1935) asserted nearly 50 years ago, an attitude is a "mental . . . state of readiness, organized through experiences, exerting a directive or dynamic influence upon the individual's response to all objects and situations with which it is related."

This directive function implies necessarily that attitudes in some fashion be related to behaviors. It invites propositions of the following sort, "A person who likes a particular thing will behave in other positive ways toward that thing." Thus we might expect a person who likes a particular food to choose that food when given an opportunity, and in general we certainly would not expect that a person will consistently choose foods that he says he does not like.

This notion of directive function quickly evolves to one of consistency. Thus, Campbell (1963) virtually defines an attitude as the response consistency among a set of attitudinally relevant behaviors. And Bem (1967), from a very different theoretical origin, notes that we infer attitudes from responses, such that if a person behaves in a particular way we might say he has a particular attitude. These two points of view converge on a notion of consistency. Indeed, consistency is the measurement model implicit in constructing an attitude questionnaire. Every question is a proposition, "If a person has a certain attitude, then he will respond in a particular manner to this question." The consistency among these responses then is the evidential base for the existence of attitude.

The notion of consistency implied by attitude's directive function, however, is not without its problems. For an attitude to have a directive role over behavior, two conditions must be met. First, the attitude must be motivating. And second, it must imply a particular behavior. Unfortunately, these two conditions are often tested together and easily become confused.

The motivational aspect of attitude's directive function is a straightforward proposition about individual behavior. A person who prefers a particular thing and seeks to satisfy his preferences might be quite motivated to choose in ways that do satisfy his preferences. Thus we might expect attitudes to inform or guide us in our choices.

It is less straightforward, however, to make meaningful propositions about the implicational relationships that might exist between attitudes and behaviors. It is not clear that any particular attitude has, as one of its defining properties, any particular implication for any particular behavior. It does not follow from a motivational property alone that a particular attitude implies a particular behavior. Propositions of the form, ''If a person has a particular attitude, then he will behave in a particular way,'' make sense as defining statements for identifying when a person does or does not have a particular attitude. Such propositions also make sense as testable empirical assertions about the behavioral relationships. They do not, however, make sense as a logical or theoretical basis for determining whether attitude and behavior are consistent. Thus it makes sense to define a person as religious if and only if he says he is religious *and* he attends religious ceremonies regularly. It also makes sense to ask if a person who says he is religious *also* attends religious services regularly. However, it makes much less sense to say that a person is behaving inconsistently with his attitude when he says he is religious but does not attend services regularly. The reason is because either we are defining ''being religious'' as the co-occurrence of the two behaviors, in which case we would have to say the person is not religious, or we are asking the empirical question, ''do the behaviors co-occur?'' in which case we would have to conclude that they do not. But, then, why should they?

Although it is possible to answer the empirical question, ''If a person says he is religious, does he also attend services?'' it is not clear that an answer of ''no'' can tell one much about whether the person behaves consistently with *his* attitude. The reason is because the implicational relation is not an assertion about the psychological make-up of an individual but an assertion about our own expectations for an individual's behavior. Such assertions may be quite misinformed, or they may be only our own impositions as to how we would like individuals to behave.

The implications of attitudes for behavior are very much like the implications of other personal constructs, such as those about personality. We might say, ''A decent person doesn't do that,'' referring to some particular behavior. But when we do so, we are doing nothing more than asserting our definition of a decent person. A person who sought the status of ''decency'' might be motivated to conform to such a definition, but it is by no means psychologically necessary for him to do so in order to have a coherent personality. For it is conceivable, and frequently the case, that this definition of decency is not itself coherent. Thus, another person might as easily say, ''No, no, you have it wrong. A decent person does do that.'' In the same manner, the behavioral implications of attitudes can vary. We might get advice from friends of a sort, ''If you really think that is important to you, then you should do this about it,'' and find to our dismay that the ''this'' recommended by one friend is completely opposite to that recommended by another. And no matter what we do, one friend would respect our determination and the other consider us a hypocrite.

That implications between attitudes and behaviors are expectations does not of course rule out the notion that attitudes direct behavior. Indeed, it may place that notion on a firmer footing. For if that notion is correct, if attitudes do exert a directive influence upon an individual's response to objects, as Allport (1935) argued, then we might be in a better position to test this notion if we were more explicit about the implicational structure of an attitude. If a person is faced with a particular choice situation and the implications of his attitudes for those choices are made explicit, we might find just such a directive function, as Kiesler, Nisbett and Zanna (1969) demonstrated some years ago. These authors asked several Yale students to solicit petition signatures, and found that when it was made explicit that soliciting implied a belief in the petition's resolve, the students later reported beliefs consistent with the petition.

For this chapter, then, we take seriously the notion that attitude-behavior consistencies are only expectations, and conclude that an attitude (or any behavior used to infer an attitude) has no necessary implications for behavior, at least for any particular behavior. Such a proposition is logically more defensible, and certainly accords better with the empirical findings regarding relations between sets of particular behaviors. This is not to say that relations between attitude and behavior do not exist, but only that particular relations are not necessary. Thus we should not be surprised when they are not found. Indeed, we probably should be more surprised when correlations are found. Such a correlation implies that a set of individuals are deriving very similar implications about their behaviors even though many potentially different implications are possible. So powerful constraint on human potential should not be taken lightly, as incidents such as the mass devotional suicide at Jonestown remind us.

THE SOCIAL LOGIC OF INDIVIDUAL ACTION

By expecting no necessary relation between attitude and behavior, we are forced to explain one when it exists. We are also led to believe that it might be possible for any kind of relationship that we can imagine to exist between attitude and behavior. Consider, for example, a situation that has occurred to me at times in my life. At one point in my relationship with a woman, I have heard the woman say, "If you love me, you would pay more attention to me and take your nose out of those books." At another time, I have heard this same woman say something of this sort, "If you loved me, you would leave me alone and let me do my work." Now it certainly appears on the surface that these two sentences are contradictory. And yet, neither one seems particularly unusual or strange. Nor are they necessarily inconsistent; a simple linguistic transformation can be used to make the two appear compatible, since both are from a subset of behaviors under the rubric "do what I ask." Yet, it seems to me that the possibility of fitting the two into a single set does not imply the necessity of doing so, for the clause ''do what I ask,'' is itself not a necessary implication of loving some one.

Fitting the two clauses into one class also leads one away from the simple elegance of this situation. In this illustration, the consistency that might come about does so not because of any necessary relationship between a given attitude and a given behavior but because of the social implications of human action. We might call this a kind of ''social logic,'' in that we expect that any relation that exists between two behaviors, or an attitude and a behavior, exists in the social definitions of those behaviors and the demands that people place upon one another for behavior from each other.

''Consistency'' among behaviors is a social concept more than a formally logical concept. Whether two things are consistent with one another is a matter of opinion. Some of this opinion is general and well distributed within particular social groups. Thus, for instance, it is not unusual for us all to believe that a person will buy the products that he or she reports liking. Such situations are comprehendible to us who share this culture. We expect to observe the consistency then because it conforms to our cultural understandings of one another and the general expectations which we have for each other's behaviors.

Making these prefatory assumptions, it becomes less meaningful to suggest that a person is or is not behaving consistently. Hidden within the statement is our own imposition of our expectations for how his behavior should cohere at that moment or under those circumstances. We might wonder why we expect of each other that behaviors be consistent. Why, for instance, do we expect a Christian who says he is religious to go to church regularly? Quite possibly because we expect a person who espouses his faith to adhere to the dictates of his church, one of which is going to services. One simple answer is that if is useful for us to have others behave in ways consistent with our expectations. Suppose they did not. Suppose that somebody said to us that they loved us, then behaved in a way that was outside of our own general cultural expectations for the concept of ''loving''? What sense could we make of such behavior, or of such a person? Certainly it would be confusing, and such a person would present a real challenge for our understanding nature. Interactions would be unpredictable and unstable.

But the fact that people expect certain behavioral consistencies should not lead us as scientists to think people will necessarily conform to them, or that conformance is solely a psychological process. Social enforcement of consistency would also seem necessary. Thus, when one person agrees to sell a good and another to buy it, it is necessary to their exchange that each expects the other to fulfill his agreement. That is, there must be something present which enables enforcement of the agreements. For this reason, some economists (e.g., Commons, 1924) have suggested that the minimally defining conditions for exchange require at least one additional person who is capable of enforcing the agreements between buyers and sellers.

It is suggested, then, that expectations for consistencies among behaviors are a necessary by-product of the need to interact with one another and gain predictability and stability in regard to one another. However, our ordinary observations would not suggest that consistencies be consistent. Rather, there may be conflict and disagreement about what attitudes imply. There is a political aspect to our expectations. Thus, to return to our example of the lovers on the couch. When one says, "If you loved me, you would leave me alone," the other might reply, "But I do love you and that is why I am bothering you." Both sentences make perfectly good sense. What is the difference then? Simply that the implications being derived from the attitude of "loving" reflect the particular interests of the individuals involved. What is being observed is a simple conflict of interests as to the proper implication of a person's attitude. Such conflicts are not uncommon. They take place in most of the relationships we have with others. Thus a supervisor might suggest that if an employee really cared about his job he would work harder and faster. The same employee might instead hold to the belief that he can best show his concern by doing a more careful job and thus work slowly and not as hard.

We might add that conflicts follow directly from a notion about social implications that attitudes do have motivational or directive properties. It is to other people's advantage to direct our attitudes into the service of the behaviors they seek from us. Thus a friend might say, "You like slapstick, don't you?" as a preface to asking if we wish to go to a movie to which the friend would like to go, but not alone. And if a particular action is very important to another person, we might suspect that person would attempt to attach any of a number of our attitudes to it. If a particular attitude is so important to one person that he is willing to base choices on it, and at the same time a particular action is so important to another individual, it is certainly within the interests of the latter to attach the first individual's powerful drive to the action he seeks.

But for such political uses of each other's behavior to be possible, it must also be the case that the implications of attitudes are not fixed by the attitude but by the social context of action. It must be the case that attitudes are capable of being linked to a wide variety of actions. We have argued in another place that the linkages between attitudinally relevant behaviors are loosely coupled rather than tightly coupled, and that the correlations are shaped and formed from the social pressures surrounding human action (Salancik, 1976).

Implications then are not logical necessities but vary with the social logic of action, reflecting both the stability and the context of social exchange.

Yet, if attitude-behavior relations reflect prevailing social logics and social uses of behavior, a very different theory of attitudes is needed. It would seem appropriate to consider the explicit implications salient in a situation, rather than assume that they exist because we expect them. Since many implications of an attitude are possible, some of which are contradictory, studies which directly manipulate them might have more success in demonstrating, or testing, whether attitudes play a directive function.

We now turn to some of our own attempts to do this.

DIRECT MANIPULATIONS OF ATTITUDE-BEHAVIOR RELATIONS

In the present section, we examine some implications of this point of view about attitude and behavior and present research that illustrates them.

Altering Social Context: Getting Course Recommendations

One implication is that the consistency observed between attitude and behavior, or different attitudinally relevant behaviors, should occur more when behavior is public than when it is private. This appears to be the case from reviews of attitude-behavior correlations (Tittle & Hill, 1967; Warner & DeFleur, 1969). The reason for this effect according to the present argument is that a person made aware of the public context of his actions may also be made more aware of the commonly held social implications which attach to those actions.

In experimental studies it is found that when you commit a person to a position by having the person take a public action favoring it, the person will subsequently report attitudes more consistent with the position (Kiesler, 1971; Salancik, 1977). A critical factor to this effect appears to be that the behavior is placed into a social context, beyond the mere fact of public exposure. In one demonstration, a student research assistant (Mary Conway) made phone calls to undergraduates at the University of Illinois, interviewing them about a particular course taken in the previous semester.[1] The undergraduates were telephoned about what they did in the course and whether in general they enjoyed it or not, and then whether they would recommend it to another student. For all subjects, the inquiry into the person's general behavior in the course and the person's general evaluation of the course (enjoy it/not enjoy it; thinking it to be a good/bad course) was done under the context of a survey for a ''sociology project'' by the research assistant, also an undergraduate. However, for the recommendation measure, this survey context was either continued or changed to a context in which the research assistant was seeking practical advice about whether to take the course herself. In the first case, the subject was told ''Now, as part of the survey, I'd like to ask you one further question: Would you recommend this

---

[1]This study was conducted by Gerald R. Salancik and Mary Conway in 1974, under the working title, ''Recommending Enjoyable Courses.''

course to other undergraduates such as myself or not?'' For other subjects, the changed context was marked by the statement, "Well, that's the end of the survey. (Pause). But I'd like to ask you a personal question if I may. (Pause). Well, I was thinking of taking this course myself next semester. I'd like to learn about this topic. I don't have to take it, as I have another requirement to get out of the way; but since you had it maybe you could tell me whether you would recommend it or not?''

The correlation between enjoying the course and recommending it was greater when the context was changed from a sociology project to that of practical advice, with coefficients of .27 and .62 (p < .05) respectively.

Because both contexts were public the greater attitude behavior consistency, we suspect, arises because the social implications of the person's evaluation are more salient when giving practical advice. A further variation of this study was done in which the research assistant interviewed undergraduates who either were in her social set or were strangers. All respondents were selected by Ms. Conway asking her sorority housemates for the names of persons from their clasess. These individuals were then telephoned as before and Ms. Conway either revealed or did not reveal that she had gotten their names from the mutual friend. As before, a survey context was used in collecting information about behavior and attitudes for the course. Three contexts for the recommendation question were run: (1) survey context; (2) practical advice to a stranger; (3) practical advice to a potential acquaintance. The covariation of attitude (enjoying) and behavior (recommending) was least in the first condition and greatest in the last condition, with correlations of .19 (13), .53 (15) and .73 (16), respectively (n per condition are parenthesized).

These two studies demonstrate that consistency varies with the context of the student's action. The students were more likely to recommend a course that they enjoyed when they thought they were speaking with a peer than when they were reporting for a survey. But why might such a result occur? One simple possibility is that there are certain implications of enjoying a course which differ with contexts. For instance, one implication about enjoying a course is that you thought it worthwhile. Such an implication is obviously very relevant to recommending it, and in this study was made salient by the experimenter noting, "I'd like to learn something about this." Such an implication is particularly critical when recommending a course to a peer.

But such an implication is not a necessary deduction, as other implications may also be drawn. For instance, one might enjoy a course as a reflection of one's own taste, in which case the relevance of recommending the course to another is less clear-cut.

Suppose the above situation were altered slightly, so that the interviewer communicates an interest in a course which suits her personal taste rather than her thirst for knowledge. Would the respondent's attitude bear the same implication for his behavior of recommending the course? We suspected not and ran just such a comparison at the end of the next semester. The procedures were the same as for the "advice to a stranger" condition in the previous study, with the sociology project as a control. Two "advice to a stranger" conditions were run. One which left the sentence "I'd like to learn about this" as above, and another which replaced it with "I'd like to take something that I could enjoy for a change." The correlations of the respondent's evaluations with recommending the course were, .68 (19) and .32 (16) for the two conditions and .21 (13) for the sociology project control condition.

The above studies suggest that attitude-behavior consistencies can vary with the context of behavior. Specifically it suggests a particular implication may be salient and relevant in one context but not in another. Such a result is similar to that found in Kelly's (1955) study of the resistance of Catholic girls to anti-religious propaganda. When reminded of their status, they were more resistant to the propaganda. In general, one might expect that the implication a person derives from his or her behavior is fitting to the social situation within which that attitude is being expressed. The consistencies with particular behaviors might then similarly vary, a notion not unlike Abelson's (1976) notion of scripts. The La Piere (1934) study certainly makes more sense with such a notion. A person who is being asked about the availability of rooms is certainly in a very different situation from one being asked to respond to a query from an unknown source with unknown intentions.

Multiple Implications: Liking and Helping Friends or Strangers

But actions have a potentially infinite set of implications. That we tend to view them in one way more than another may be more because of the relevance of the action to ourselves than because of the actions. And a second suggestion from this viewpoint of considering consistency as part of a social logic is that different implications for behavior may arise in different social contexts. As a dean, I might think of a professor's attendance at a conference in regard to intellectual stimulation. As a close colleague, I might think the same attendance as an enviable opportunity for renewing old acquaintances. As a spouse, I might think of it still differently, perhaps as a threat, perhaps as a disappointment with my spouse's priorities. The action itself bears no particular meaning outside of the context in which it is regarded. And one would suspect that the meaning or the implications of a statement, "That was a good conference," would vary with the same contexts. The implications which are drawn in terms of subsequent behavior might similarly vary.

I have done a number of studies attempting to demonstrate that the implications which derive from a particular behavior or a particular attitude can be directly varied by varying the context. Such studies are difficult to execute, however, because it requires understanding beforehand the social logic of different social contexts. There is thus a certain uncomfortable hit or miss quality to the research. There is also the feeling that one is creating the cognitive worlds that subjects report. Thus, in one attempt, undergraduate students were asked to report on an incident from their recent past.[2] The incidents were characterized as situations in which the subject had acted intentionally (or unintentionally) in some manner that led to favorable (or unfavorable) consequences for a person known (or unknown) to the subject. The subjects were asked to describe the incident in detail so as to remind them of the particulars. The subjects were also asked to indicate the extent of liking the person. Independent raters rated the favorability or unfavorability of the consequences of the act.

The idea behind this study was that the correlation between the subject's reported attitude towards the person and the coded favorability of his act would vary with the context of the act. If context has no effect, and there is some degree of consistency between a person's action towards another and his expressed attitude towards another, we might expect to find a positive correlation. If the intention of the subject or the subject's relationship to the person affect the implicational relationship between attitude and act, then such a general positive correlation should not be expected. However, beyond this expectation that there should be a difference in the correlation depending on the contexts, no specific hypotheses can be drawn.

As it turned out, significant differences were found. The correlation of liking for the person and doing positive things to the person was .07 when the act was intended and the person was known, .60 when the act was intended but the person was unknown. When the person was unknown and the act unintended, the correlation was −.36, but it was .17 when the intended act was committed upon a person known by the subject. The two larger correlations are both significant and are significantly different from each other and from the two smaller correlations. Although it is possible to make sense of these differences, the important point is that the context of action affected its relation to attitude.

Attaching Implications to Behaviors: Giving Reason to Energy Conservation

A third implication to be drawn from the notion that attitude behavior relationships are loose sets of implications is that one should be able to directly attach implications to attitudes or behaviors and affect their relationships to one another. The basic methodology for achieving such effects was developed from earlier work on the saliency of behavior in affecting the expression of attitude (Salancik, 1974; Salancik and Conway, 1975). In those studies, subjects were

---

[2]This study was conducted by Gerald R. Salancik in 1972 at the University of Illinois and is otherwise undrafted.

primed to think about particular aspects of their behavior so as to effect attitudes directly. The priming is done by placing the subject in a situation that requires him or her to answer questions; the underlying assumption of the procedure is that in the process of answering questions of a certain form the subject recollects episodic or semantic information that may be relevant to his or her attitude or other attitudinally relevant behavior.

To use the methodology, the investigator has to make certain assumptions as to the nature of the relationship which might exist between certain recollected information and subsequent attitudinally relevant behavior. We interpret this now as the investigator using his own store of knowledge about the social implications of attitudes and behaviors. Thus, for instance, in asking a person about how hard she might have worked for a course at a university, it is reasonable to presume that such behavior reflects a positive orientation towards the course more than a negative orientation. Knowledge of one's hard work would better support a judgment of liking than of disliking. However, the "reasonableness" of this presumption is based solely on the fact that the investigator shares in the cultural meaning of hard work and its associations with other behavioral indicators of actors. It makes little sense to us if people were to say they worked hard because they did not like something. Such a sentence violates our cultural understanding of motivation.

The theoretical disadvantage of this methodology is that one is left somewhat with the feeling that all that has been achieved is a demonstration that when you make a person more aware of his personal orientations, he exhibits other personal orientations which are more reliably measured, i.e., which are more consistent with one another. Such a demonstration, however, does not necessarily suggest that different implicational relations vary on attitudes relevant to behaviors. Rather, it only demonstrates that cognitive processes mediate the covariations.

A more convincing demonstration would come from showing that it is possible to attach implications to a particular behavior or class of behaviors, and on that basis affect the direction of a person's subsequent behavior or attitude. The first attempt to do this was made in the spring of 1974 in a study of the energy conservation efforts of 60 Illinois residents interviewed in their homes after the energy crisis of the winter of 1973–74.[3]

The subjects were asked if they did each of 27 energy conserving efforts since the crisis became apparent in late Fall, 1973. Efforts included such activities as lowering thermostats below 70 degrees, driving 55 mph or less, turning lights off when not in use, taking fewer baths, and so on. If the implications among these behaviors derive directly from the behavior itself or speak of some underlying

---

[3]This study was conducted by Gerald R. Salancik and Mary Conway and was previously described in "The effect of retrospective attribution and commitment to past behaviors: consumers and the conservation of energy," 1974 an unpublished manuscript, no longer available.

fundamental orientation of the person, then one would expect to find a similar behavioral orientation in the future.

If, on the other hand, one assumes, as we do, that the behaviors do not reflect a fixed underlying orientation, then it should be possible to lead the residents to develop certain implications and direct their subsequent behavior accordingly. The method used to affect the implications was that of forcing the individuals to attribute their behaviors either to external motivational forces or internal motivational forces. The presumption was that a person would generate implications about his or her behavior consistent with the attributions he makes about them.

One implication derivable about a behavior is that one will behave in similar ways in the future. If a person considers his behavior to be externally motivated, then he might expect to behave in a similar way when external circumstances are similar to those which he believes generated the behavior in the first place. If a person constructs his behavior to be internally motivated, he might expect to behave in a similar way regardless of external conditions.

To examine these possibilities, two manipulations were made. Subjects were induced to generate internal or external attributions; and from each group they were induced to believe that external circumstances demanded or did not demand the behavior. To induce attributions, residents were asked to sort among a set of seven reasons for saving energy. Two sets of statements were prepared, one that listed only internal reasons, and one that listed only external reasons. Individuals were given only one set or the other and were asked to rank each reason according to its appropriateness as a description of themselves. Examples of external reasons are: "The general rising costs of living due to inflation made it necessary to reduce my energy consumption in order to stay within my budget," and "The difficulties of getting sufficient home or automobile fuel made it necessary to cut down." Examples of internal reasons are: "I wanted to explore new ways of running my life without being dependent on consuming a lot of energy and fuel," and "When the energy shortages came, I began to realize that I didn't need as much energy as I had previously thought."

The rationale for this method is similar to that for the saliency manipulations of earlier studies. We assumed that when a person attempts to rank a set of reasons, he is forced to read and consider the meanings and implications of those reasons. By structuring which reasons he is exposed to, we assume one can structure the set of possible thoughts that he might generate. In this way, only certain thoughts about his behavior and its meaning will be salient to him when he considers that behavior in a subsequent context. Our presumption is that the person is primed to construct his behavior according to the implications and meanings made salient to him. An obvious necessary condition is that the behavior is capable of multiple implications, and particularly the implications primed. Conservation behaviors are such behaviors, since they may be construed as motivated by many personal or circumstantial factors.

After the attributions were generated, subjects were asked to report on their plans in the coming year for reducing energy usage in five areas (driving; personal electrical applicances; household electrical appliances; clothes washing; basic household utilities). They specified a percentage reduction for each area. The average of the five estimated each resident's orientation towards energy conservation.

Before asking for future plans, subjects were induced to think of the energy crisis as either lessening or worsening in the coming year (1974). By suggesting that the crisis would continue in the future, it was assumed that persons who believed their behavior to be demanded by circumstances would make plans for conserving only then. To introduce this idea, respondents were told, "We would now like to ask you about your plans for the coming year. As you know, the U.S. experienced many shortages last winter. Some say the extent of the crisis was overstated, but one thing experts agree on is that in the future the availability of cheap plentiful energy..." followed by will "improve" or "get worse." The "crisis worsening" communication pointed out that the Arab control of oil, the unsafe and slow development of nuclear power, and the environmental restrictions on coal fuel, etc., would all contribute to a continuation of the shortage. The "crisis lessening" communication pointed out that new technologies, new oil discoveries, and the improved relations with Arabs, etc., would all contribute to lessening shortages. Newspaper stories supporting the same were waved in front of the person.

The effects of these manipulations were as expected. For the "crisis lessening" conditions, subjects induced to make intrinsic attributions for their past conservations reported plans for reductions of about 26.1 percent while those induced to make extrinsic attributions reported plans for reduction of only about 7.27 percent, a significant mean difference ($t(28) = 4.33$; $p < .01$). For the "crisis worsening" condition, the planned reductions were 20.93 for the intrinsically motivated residents and 15.93 for the extrinsically motivated, which do not differ ($t(28) = 1.01$). Moreover, the extrinsic subjects planned on greater reductions more when the crisis was said to continue than when it was said to lessen (15.93 vs. 7.27; $p < .03$).

The results appear as we expected then, given our assumptions that the implications of behavior can be manipulated and are not fixed aspects of the behavior of the individual attitudes. Moreover, the consistencies among the behaviors varied directly with these implications and their relevance to a particular context.

Two other studies have since been done by colleagues using this direct method of manipulating a person's interpretation of his or her behavior. Seligman, Fazio and Zanna (1980) had young couples sort among a set of either all extrinsic reasons or all intrinsic reasons for their romantic involvements with each other. Subjects were thus induced to believe that they went out with each other because of social and cultural demands or because of personal motivations. When subsequently asked about their plans for future involvement, the subjects for whom personal motivations were induced were more likely to report that they planned on continuing their romantic commitment.

A third use of the sorting technique was made in a study of the traditional "overjustification paradigm," by Porac and Meindl (in press). University of Illinois undergraduates were given opportunities to solve various Soma configurations for money (up to $6.00) or no money. Following this, they answered questions which sought to prime them to construct the task as intrinsically or extrinsically motivating. The questionnaire was not directly related to the Soma puzzles but referred to participation in experiments in general, and asked subjects to rank several expressed thoughts and feelings. An example of an extrinsic item is, "Experiments are physically confusing," and of an intrinsic item, "Experimental tasks are fun and enjoyable." The theoretical purpose of these manipulations was to examine if the saliency of extrinsic or intrinsic ideas about experimental tasks was sufficient to "undermine" free choice play on Soma puzzles. The researchers replicated the typical overjustification effect and found that subjects paid money during the experimental session played less during the free period than subjects not paid money. However, subjects paid money and induced to consider intrinsic thoughts engaged in *more* free play than subjects either paid money and induced to consider extrinsic thoughts, or paid without any specific priming. On the other hand, students extrinsically primed who were not paid money did not play significantly less during the free period than did unprimed no-money subjects.

Taken together, the results of these three studies suggest that the constructions that individuals develop about their behavior are subject to considerable alteration. They demonstrate that it is possible to induce an individual to construct his or her behavior as being either personally motivated or motivated by external demands or forces. For such to be the case, it must be true that there are no necessary implications that derive from behaviors, and hence there are no particular consistencies to be expected generally among a set of behaviors.

The last point, that there are no general consistencies, is theoretically important. For it means that we, as investigators, must specify much more fully how consistencies do arise. Let us consider this question by reference to two other studies we have done. We start, again, by assuming that behavior is capable of a wide range of interpretation, and that this interpretation takes place, for the most part, within a cultural and linguistic community with characteristic modes of construction, or sense-making.

Absenteeism and Attitudes

A fourth study that was done using this methodology was conducted in the spring of 1977 and 1978.[4] Its purpose was to determine if it was possible to create

[4]This study was conducted by Gerald R. Salancik and Susan Trieber, and described under "Absenteeism and attribution," an unpublished manuscript no longer available.

within individuals a characteristic way of interpreting their behavior. The behavior studied was a person's absenteeism from a job. The subjects were clerical employees in various offices at a university; all were women and all held their positions for about two years. Some were part time workers, though most (80 percent) were full time. The design of the study called for interviewing the workers on four separate occasions, starting in the spring of 1977, then again in the summer and fall of 1977, and making a final evaluation in the early spring of 1978. On the first three interviews, the respondents were interviewed in detail, in their homes, about their absences from work. Specifically they were asked to report on their absences, report on the lengths of their breaks during work, report on the number of sick days they used during the past month and the number of times they were late or not late.

The point of this study was to examine the relationship of the clerks' absenteeism with attitudes toward their jobs. Much argument in industrial psychology takes a person's absenteeism to be a behavioral expression of his attitude toward work, and many studies report negative correlations suggesting some implicational relation between the two (Porter & Steers, 1973). But these relations are not strong or stable, leading some writers to question the consistency of attitude and behavior (Smith, 1977). Yet the point of our argument is that if the two are consistent—if saying ''I like my job'' relates to being at a job on time and when required—it is because explicit implications are being drawn between them. That is, it is part of the social meaning of the behaviors.

But absenteeism, like every behavior, is capable of multiple meanings. The research question then was whether we could get individuals to disassociate the implications of one behavior from another. Specifically, we sought to develop an interpretation about absenteeism that would lead clerks not to draw any implications about their attitudes. As with the previous studies, we presented reasons to individuals for interpreting their behavior. Throughout the year when individuals were interviewed about their absences from work, they were also asked to discuss those absences in regard to these reasons. Two sets of reasons were constructed. In one set were six reasons that suggested absences were *work-related*. Another set had six reasons that suggested absences were *circumstantial*. Examples of the work-related reasons are:

    (a) I needed a break.

    (b) I wanted to go out of town.

Examples of circumstantial reasons are:

    (a) Extreme weather conditions

    (b) Sickness in my family (or myself)

In making these distinctions, our assumption was that over time the individuals would construct their behavior as characterized by the reasons of each set. We assume the behavior is capable of each interpretation. A person might easily conclude that he couldn't get to work because the weather made it impossible, and his superiors might just as easily argue that if he wanted to he would have braved every obstacle. Finally, we assume that the two beliefs imply different things for attitudes. If you think your absences were forced by conditions then it should not appear relevant to your evaluation of your job. If, on the other hand, you construct your absences to be reflecting of your attitude, then they are relevant and should be used in evaluating it.

The 20 women clerks in this study were interviewed during the months of March 1977, May–June 1977, and September–October 1977. They were interviewed in their homes by phone the first and last time and at work the second time. The interviewer was an undergraduate at the University of Illinois, Sue Trieber. During each interview, subjects were asked to report on liking their job and then their absences and other time off work, such as lengthy coffee breaks and late arrivals and early departures. Following these reports, the clerks were given a list of reasons for the absences and asked to discuss each and decide which seemed to apply best to them. The interviewer encouraged them to think out loud and used probes such as "could you elaborate," or "why do you think that?" Ten women were presented with the work-related reasons; the others, with the circumstantial reasons.

Several empirical implications follow from our argument and the manipulations. Over time, we should expect that the attitudes for work-related subjects to correlate more with their absences. This occurred. The correlation of the attitudes reported during the spring of 1977 (March–June) with absences reported in this period was $-.143$, and the correlation between similar reports for the period of fall, 1977 was $-.663$, the latter correlation being significant ($t(8) = 2.50$). In contrast, attitudes were uncorrelated with the absences of subjects making circumstantial interpretations with correlations of $-.196$ and $+.118$. It thus appears as if only the subjects given work-related interpretations developed negative attitudes from their absences. Another indicator of this is that the attitudes of the subjects with work-related absences were uncorrelated from period one to period two, while those of the other group were correlated, with correlations of .273 (n.s.) and .688 ($p < .05$), respectively. This is as one would expect if clerks in the former group were using their absences to infer their attitudes in the second period while the latter were developing attitudes only on the basis of other presumably stable aspects of their jobs.

One stable aspect of a job which has been found to relate to attitudes is that of a person's freedom (Hackman & Oldham, 1980). Generally, individuals who experience more freedom in determining how they do their jobs report more favorable attitudes towards those jobs. If the absences of the subjects who were induced to attribute them to work were having an increasing impact on their attitudes, we would expect the correlation of their attitudes with job freedom to decrease over time. Such appears to have happened. For these subjects, attitudes in period 1 correlated .921 with job freedom, but their attitudes in period 2 correlated only .503, a significant difference ($t(7) = 4.49$). No such difference occurred with the subjects induced to attribute absences to circumstances, the correlations being about .7 each period. No effects of the manipulations were found for the actual absenteeism of workers; the whole sample tended to drop in absences and to increase in the amount of time taken for breaks and extended lunching. The changes are understandable as related to the change from winter to summer.

A final difference was found between the two groups when a final interview was attempted in the Spring of 1978, one year after the beginning of the study. In May of 1978, the interviewer attempted to visit each respondent in her office for a final assessment of attitudes. Unfortunately, seven of the women had left the organization and two others had changed departments. Two of these were from the group induced to make work-related attributions, and seven were from the group induced to make circumstantial attributions, a significant difference ($X^2 =$ 5.56 with 1 degree of freedom). Reasons for the difference are not apparent for there were no differences between the groups in terms of attitudes, job freedom, absences, distances of home to work, or anything else that had been measured. However, those leaving from the ''work-related'' group were also those who had the highest number of absences; the departures of the other group were unrelated to absences, although three of the seven had part time jobs, and the two part-timers remained in their jobs. Although it is possible that those leaving from the ''work-related'' group did so because they became more dissatisfied as expressed both in their attitude and their absences, it is hard to imagine that the manipulation of external attributions for absences would have led subjects to become more dissatisfied, and the attitude data do not suggest they were. Indeed, the attitudes of subjects with more absences became more favorable over time for subjects in the circumstantial condition.

Regardless of any interpretation for the job departures, it would appear from this study that one can induce individuals to make characteristic interpretations of their behaviors over time and develop different implications for their attitudes as a result. The next question to address is whether it is possible to take a characteristic interpretation and direct it into a seemingly opposite position.

Reversing Implications: Impeaching Nixon

A final attempt to illustrate how manipulable the implications of behaviors are was made during the public debate on the Watergate incident of the Nixon White House in 1973. The purpose of the study was to show that it is possible to derive completely opposite implications from the same behavior. The behavior chosen for this illustration was that of voting for Richard Milhaus Nixon in the 1972 election. The study was conducted at the height of disclosures about the Watergate break-in and the involvement of Mr. Nixon in that and several other questionable acts. Talk about impeachment was just beginning to be raised in the newspapers and the United States Senate, but the extent of Mr. Nixon's involvement in misdeeds and their cover-up were not at the time known widely.

The idea behind the study was that one could induce a person to derive seemingly opposite implications from his act of voting for Mr. Nixon. One implication, consistent with our knowledge of commitment phenomena (Kiesler, 1971), is that a vote is a declaration of support even in the face of attack. If the vote is public, or made public by asking a person how he voted, then a person should show similar support on future occasions if that implication is salient.

However, another implication of voting someone into office is that one places a certain trust in the person, a public trust as it were. This later implication, unlike the former, does not necessarily imply that a person will support the elected official unconditionally. Rather, the support is directly contingent on the official's trustworthiness. For the Nixon situation, then, a person induced to think he voted for Mr. Nixon out of trust might recant support on that same basis and seek an impeachment. The author interviewed individuals on the University of Illinois campus in late spring, 1973. Individuals were approached in public areas and asked if they had voted in the last election. Those answering yes were asked if they felt uncomfortable discussing politics. They were then asked if they minded discussing how they voted in November; those answering no were asked how they voted. Only those reporting a vote for Nixon were pursued further, with "Good, I'm particularly interested in talking with Nixon supporters. You see I'm part of a group called 'Nixon Supporters for the Impeachment of Nixon' (no pause). Are you a member of the group? (pause) Oh, good." The general issue of Watergate was then brought up and I intimated that I was very distressed by the news and had formed the Nix-SIN group for this reason. The various articles about the "alleged Nixon misdeeds" were alluded to as well as the Senate Watergate hearings. Subjects were then shown plastic covered newspaper clippings reporting on Mr. Nixon's possible misdeeds and each was introduced with a short verbal summary. They were then told, "Obviously these are serious charges against a president who was only voted in by us a few months ago. My group, the 'Nixon Supporters for the Impeachment of Nixon', doesn't believe he deserves our continued support, so we have organized and are asking other Nixon supporters to join us by signing this petition...." Subjects were then given a petition that asked for the impeachment of Nixon.

Of the thirteen subjects who were given the above introduction to the petition, not one agreed to sign it. This contrasts with two out of ten students who were sampled by convenience from the same campus a week earlier without any prior interview or knowledge of their vote. However, another group of 13 subjects was also asked to sign the petition with a slight addition to the above description. Prior to presenting the newspaper clippings, these Nixon voters were told the following: "As you are yourself undoubtedly aware, there are many Nixon voters who are distressed by the recent allegations being brought against President Nixon. Many of the people who voted for him in November of 1972 did so because of the trust he established in his previous term by bringing about an end to the war [Vietnam War], bringing peace with honor to the country, and the way he kept the country from going bankrupt with his difficult but necessary price controls. (pause, reflective, reminiscent) You know, to trust him with all that it was hard not to put your faith in him in 1972. It was reasonable to vote for him. But that was 1972, and in 1972 we didn't know everything about Nixon. At least I didn't. We didn't know about the Watergate thing, and the way he kept what was going on from his voters.'' After this, the subjects were shown the same newspaper clippings with the same brief introductions. Eight of the 13 subjects given this introduction signed the petition. The difference between this and the first condition is significant ($X^2 = 8.33$, corrected for continuity).

CONCLUSION

The purpose of this chapter was to argue that attitude-behavior consistencies arise when the motivational properties of attitude direct a person's behavior according to particular implications. In making this argument, we found it necessary to point out that the implication of one behavior for another is part of the social logic of human action. As such, implications are social expectations that give meaning to a person and his action, are separable from the action itself, and can be attached to attitudes or behaviors so as to shape either in multiple directions. Attitude and act were thus said to be loosely coupled (Salancik, 1976) and held together by social demands and the social uses of human behavior.

Theoretically, this argument is important because it implies that no particular consistencies need ever be found for attitudes to be quite consistent with behavior. If different and even contrary implications can be suggested for any attitude, the lack of regularity between a particular attitude and a particular behavior is not surprising. More importantly, the lack of consistent relationships across individuals may say nothing about whether the individuals' behaviors are consistent with their attitudes. It may only suggest that our expectations about these relations are misinformed.

The results of the studies presented in this chapter do seem to suggest that the manner in which an attitude might direct other behaviors can vary. When specific implications are made salient to a person, attitude-behavior relationships tend to develop according to those implications. These occurred when the announced context of a person's behavior was varied, resulting, we presume, in different implications becoming salient. Such appeared to be the case when a person's behavior was fitted into a context of giving advice compared to the context of a survey. Recommendations were more likely to be consistent with evaluations of a course when giving advice than when responding to a survey. Such also appeared when students indicated their attitudes towards friends or strangers whom they had affected by their behavior. More pointed demonstrations of the same idea, however, were shown in those studies that attempted to implicate attitudes and behaviors directly. Such attempts appeared successful; Illinois residents planned future conservations consistent with their past conservations and the directed implications of their past conservations for the future. And university employees directed to construct meanings for their absences, over time came to develop attitudes consistent with both their behavior and its directed meaning.

The results, as such, are quite consistent with the point of view offered in this chapter. We interpret them as fitting with the idea that particular implications are not necessary between particular attitudes and behavior. We would interpret the behavior of all the subjects in all the conditions of the experiments as being "consistent," in the sense that all seemed to be acting in accordance with some implications. Although the idea has not been tested with these particular experiments, we can consider them to be consistent with the notion that the implications drawn between attitudes and behaviors are part of the social expectations shared with the subjects. The investigator's knowledge of the possible meanings that can be given to behaviors was not an unimportant element in the design of the experiments. And the experimenter's role in reminding subjects of certain of those meanings should be recognized in interpreting the results. We might summarize the findings in the form of a very general proposition about attitude-behavior consistency: *When attitudes and their credible implications are made salient to a person facing a relevant choice, the person should behave consistently with those attitudes and implications.* The terms "credible" and "relevant" are of course the most difficult to define and are themselves social concepts. They become defined in social contexts.

These studies are consistent with a number of other interpretations for attitude-behavior relationships. For one, they are consistent with the notion of "scripts" reported in this volume, if we interpret a script to be a program for action within a particular context. However, we would prefer to go beyond such a notion with our arguments about the "social logic and social use of human action." We would like to suggest that there is a manipulable quality to the linkings of individual action and attitude. A "script" notion hints at a rigidity to social action which loses a lot of what may be involved in social life. A script notion intimates that within a particular context (e.g., the restaurant script), certain implications of an attitude are salient. Thus when one is in the restaurant script, one's attitudes towards food certainly are relevant. And therefore, one would expect that attitude and behavior relations are rather prominent in this context. But a script is not specific in its implications. One could ask not whether menu choices are guided by tastes in food, but which particular choices will be implicated by which particular attitudes. Thus a charming waiter might interject at the dining table, "Ah, I see from what you say that you have adventurous tastes. Certainly, you will attempt the salmon then." Noting that the implications vary with the context of behavior, it seems to us, is not enough to understand the ways which attitudes unfold into behaviors. Thinking back to the construction worker with whom we began this chapter, we can note that the fluidity of his reactions is the striking character of the situation. Watching him, it was as if his behavior and attitudes were shaped with every turn of his attention. Focused on his food, the ants were invaders. Focused on the ant lifting the food, the ants were tiny Samsons. And yet there was a sensible coherence to the flow, as implications shifted with attention.

Somehow, our models of attitude do not capture this malleable and fluid character of a person's reactions to the objects in his world. And the studies in this chapter do not do so either. They merely suggest it is possible to shape a person in many directions when you have his full attention. What is yet needed in the way of theories of attitude, however, are explicit statements as to how the implications which can exist between attitudes and behaviors actually come to exist, how certain implications develop in certain social contexts, and how they become salient in certain choice situations. Without such expectations, tests of whether attitudes are consistent with behavior are meaningless. The scant findings are certainly no basis for rejecting the notion, and might be considered to offer it strong support.

REFERENCES

Abelson, R. P. A script theory of understanding, attitude and behavior. In J. Carroll, & T. Payne (Eds.), *Cognition and social behavior*. Potomac, Md.: Erlbaum, 1976.

Abelson, R. P., Aronson, E., McGuire, W. J., Newcomb, T. M., Rosenberg, M. J. & P. H. Tannenbaum (Eds.), *Theories of cognitive consistency: a sourcebook*. Skokie, Ill.: Rand-McNally, 1968.

Allport, G. W. Attitudes. In C. Murchison (Ed.). *Handbook of social psychology*. Worcester, Mass.: Clark University Press, 1935.

Bem, D. J. Self-perception: An alternative interpretation of cognitive dissonance phenomena. *Psychological Review*, 1967, *74*, 183–200.

Calder, B. J., & Ross, M. *Attitudes and behavior*. Morristown, N.J.: General Learning Press, 1973.

Campbell, D. T. The indirect assessment of social attitudes, *Psychological Bulletin*, 1950, *47*, 15–38.

Campbell, D. T. Social attitudes and other acquired behavioral dispositions. In S. Koch (Eds.), *Psychology: a study of science*. New York: McGraw-Hill, 1963.

Commons, J. R. *Institutional Economics*. Madison, Wisc.: University of Wisconsin Press, 1924.

DeFleur, M. L., & Westie, F. R. Verbal attitudes and overt acts: An experiment on the salience of attitudes. *American Sociological Review*, 1958, *23*, 667–673.

Doob, L. W. The behavior of attitudes. *Psychological Review*, 1947, *54*, 135–156.

Hackman, J. R., & Oldham, G. *Work redesign*. Reading, Mass.: Addison-Wesley, 1980.

Kelly, H. H. Salience of membership and resistance to change group-anchored attitudes. *Human Relations*, 1955, *8*, 275–290.

Kiesler, C. A. *The psychology of commitment*. New York: Academic Press, 1971.

Kiesler, C. A., Nisbett, R. E., & Zanna, M. P. On inferring one's belief from one's behavior. *Journal of Personality and Social Psychology*, 1969, *11*, 321–327.

La Piere, R. T. Attitudes vs. actions. *Social Forces*, 1934, *13*, 230–237.

Porac, J., & Meindl, J. Undermining overjustification: Inducing intrinsic and extrinsic representations. *Journal of Organizational Behavior and Human Performance*, (In press).

Porter, L., & Steers, R. Organizational work and personal factors in employee turnover and absenteeism. *Psychological Bulletin*, 1973, *80*, 151–176.

Salancik, G. R. Inference of one's attitude from behavior recalled under linguistically manipulated cognitive sets. *Journal of Experimental Social Psychology,* 1974, *10,* 415–427.

Salancik, G. R. *Notes on loose-coupling.* Conference on loose-coupling in educational organizations. Washington, D.C.: National Institute of Education, 1976.

Salancik, G. R. Commitment and the control of organizational behavior and belief. In B. Staw & G. R. Salancik (Eds.), *New directions in organizational behavior.* Chicago: St. Clair Press, 1977. Now New York: John Wiley.

Salancik, G. R., & Conway, M. Attitude inferences from salient and relevant cognitive content about behavior. *Journal of Personality and Social Psychology,* 1975, *32,* 829–840.

Seligman, C., Fazio, R. H., & Zanna, M. P. Consequences of extrinsic rewards for impressions of liking and loving. *Journal of Personality and Social Psychology,* 1980, *38,* 453–460.

Smith, F. J. Work attitudes as predictors of attendance on a specific day. *Journal of Applied Psychology,* 1977, *62,* 16–19.

Tittle, C. R., & Hill, R. J. Attitude measurement and prediction of behavior: An evaluation of conditions and measurement techniques. *Sociometry,* 1967, *30,* 199–213.

Warner, L. G., & DeFleur, M. L. Attitudes as an interactional concept: Social constraints and social distance as intervening variables between attitude and action. *American Sociological Review,* 1969, *34,* 153–169.

Wicker, A. Attitudes versus actions: The relationship of verbal and overt behavioral responses to attitude objects. *Journal of Social Issues,* 1969, *25,* 41–78.

4 Individual Differences in Attitudinal Relations

Mark P. Zanna
University of Waterloo

James M. Olson
University of Western Ontario

INTRODUCTION

Social psychologists and personality researchers alike have long believed that although there is great behavioral variation across people within a particular situation, there is also great consistency within a particular person across situations. To account for this assumed, though rarely documented, pattern of behavior in their own domains of inquiry, each group of psychologists turned to an individual difference construct. For the personality researcher, the trait construct was invented to capture the notion of differences among and consistencies within people; for the social psychologist, the concept of attitude was invented to perform essentially the same function.

Numerous and varied definitions of attitude have been offered over the years. For example, in an early and comprehensive definition, Allport (1935) defined an attitude as "a mental and neural state of readiness, organized through experience, exerting a directive or dynamic influence upon the individual's response to all objects and situations with which it is related." Although more recent definitions have stressed the evaluative aspects of attitudes, primarily characterizing attitudes as the evaluative feelings evoked by a given object, the concept has remained an ambitious one. Not only are attitudes expected to influence overt behavior, they also are assumed to influence information processing and memory. That is, in addition to being expected to behave in ways that are consistent with their attitudes, individuals are assumed to learn and remember information that supports their attitudes better than material that challenges their attitudes.

Historically, research support for these two assumed effects of attitudes, on behavior and on memory, has seemed "out-of-phase." Whereas researchers tended to accept the attitude-memory relation early on (e.g., Watson & Hartmann, 1939), the attitude-behavior relation was challenged vigorously from the beginning (e.g., LaPiere, 1934). More recently, researchers have questioned the impact of attitudes on memory (e.g., Greenwald & Sakumura, 1967), while accepting the notion of attitude-behavior consistency, at least under certain conditions (see Ajzen, this volume).

After four decades of work on these problems, it is surprising that little attention has been given to possible personality trait moderators of the effects of attitudes on memory and behavior. Although the notion of individual differences in the effects of attitudes may seem complex, we believe that this perspective can enhance our understanding of the psychological mechanisms that underlie attitudinal phenomena.

In the present chapter, we present data from a program of research that has taken this perspective. Our aim in this research was to explore the effects of theoretically relevant, individual difference dimensions on either the attitude-memory or the attitude-behavior relation. In each case, we treat the attitudinal relation as we would treat any other dependent variable. We are not, therefore, interested in determining the absolute magnitude of the relation, but instead are interested in determining those variables (in the present instance, individual difference constructs) that influence the magnitude of the relation. Our hope is that we may be able to identify subpopulations for whom attitudes do substantially influence memory or behavior, and thereby increase our understanding of the mechanisms which produce that particular effect of attitudes.

It should be noted, of course, that this personality approach to studying the effects of attitudes is quite compatible with the more common, nomothetic perspective. Each approach potentially can identify the mechanisms that underlie attitudinal phenomena. Starting from a hypothesis about a psychological state that mediates the attitude-memory or attitude-behavior relation, researchers can proceed by studying the impact of personality variables that reflect chronic differences in the relevant state or by designing experimental manipulations that vary the state directly. A research program that combines these two methods is probably most desirable. This chapter reports research that employed the personality approach exclusively. It is important to emphasize, however, that the two methods are complementary rather than competing.

In the next section, we present our analysis of the attitude-memory relation. After a brief review of the attitude-memory literature, we report a recent study that was designed, in part, to discover potential personality trait moderators of the effects of attitudes on memory. Next, we present our analysis of the attitude-behavior relation. We review recent work showing that attitudes are more predictive of an individual's future behaviors if they represent summaries of the individual's prior behaviors toward the attitude objects than if they are based on nonbehavioral information. We then report two studies that examined the implications of this finding for potential personality trait moderators of the attitude-behavior relation.

ATTITUDES AND MEMORY: THE SELECTIVE
LEARNING HYPOTHESIS

The role that attitudes play in the learning and retention of attitude-relevant information has become an issue of controversy in recent years. The *selective learning hypothesis* asserts that an individual "notes and remembers material which supports his social attitudes better than material which conflicts with these attitudes" (Levine & Murphy, 1943, p. 515). This notion has intuitive appeal and a long history in psychological theorizing. James (1890) argued that persons selectively attend to information that they find appealing. The Freudian (Freud, 1925) concept of repression is directly analogous to the selective learning hypothesis: psychologically painful events or memories will not be accessible for retrieval. As well, the hypothesis is congenial with findings demonstrating selective *perception* as a function of attitude (e.g., Postman, Bruner & McGinnies, 1948).

The selective learning hypothesis has been based, historically, on the assumption that attitude-relevant materials have affective implications that influence their processing and recall. Specifically, it has been assumed that attitude-consistent information arouses positive affect and attitude-inconsistent material arouses negative feelings. Such arousal has, in turn, been assumed to influence the processing of the information. Whether the hypothesized effects of the arousal on recall are mediated by input, consolidation, or retrieval differences is unclear—most theorists have not discussed the precise roles of these various stages. The general assumption seems to have been that all three may be involved (e.g., people may pay more attention to positively arousing material, may try to repress or forget negatively arousing information, and may retrieve positive material more easily).

At any rate, an attitude-memory relation has intuitive plausibility and is consistent with the more general hypothesis that affect plays a role in human information processing and memory (e.g., Higgins, Kuiper, & Olson, 1981; Schiffenbauer, 1974). The results from studies testing the selective learning hypothesis, however, can perhaps best be described as "unambiguously inconclusive" (Greaves, 1972). Experimental attempts to demonstrate an effect of attitudes on memory have resulted in inconsistent and contradictory findings. This inconsistency has recently led Greenwald (1975) to suggest that published results supporting the hypothesis were Type I errors.

Review of the Literature

Early Findings.   Perhaps the "classic" study demonstrating selective learning and retention was conducted by Levine and Murphy (1943). Pro- and anti-communist subjects were presented with pro- and anti-communist readings for a period of 5 weeks. For the following 5 weeks, subjects were asked to reproduce passages from the readings. As expected, subjects remembered significantly more material that supported their position than nonsupportive material, and this difference increased over time.

Jones and Kohler (1958) proposed a more fine-grained definition of attitudinal consistency than had been employed by Levine and Murphy (1943). They argued that selective learning should occur only if the subject can endorse comfortably both the *position* implied by the statement and the supporting *reasons* provided. Thus, they distinguished between plausible and implausible statements and proposed that this characteristic interacts with the same side/other side dimension to define phenomenologically "consistent" and "inconsistent" material (previous research had presented subjects only with plausible material for each side of the issue). Using segregation as the critical attitude topic, Jones and Kohler (1958) found that subjects scoring high in prejudice on an independent premeasure remembered more plausible prosegregation and implausible antisegregation statements, whereas subjects scoring low in prejudice remembered more plausible antisegregation and implausible prosegregation statements.

These two studies constitute the best-known of the early research testing the selective learning hypothesis. A number of other studies also provided at least partial support for the hypothesis (e.g., Alper & Korchin, 1952; Edwards, 1941; Garber, 1955; Jones & Aneshansel, 1956; Kanungo & Das, 1960; Taft, 1954; Watson & Hartmann, 1939). Thus, the early evidence concerning the attitude-memory relation consistently supported the notion that attitudes influence the learning and retention of related material.

Some Contradictory Results.   Unfortunately, a number of more recent attempts to replicate and extend these early findings failed to support the selective learning hypothesis. Using materials and procedures similar to those of Jones and Kohler (1958), Waly and Cook (1966) planned to capitalize on the attitude-memory relation for the purpose of indirect attitude measurement. Three experiments failed to reproduce the previous findings, however, and the authors concluded that the selective learning hypothesis "is limited by conditions as yet unspecified" (p. 288).

In another series of three experiments, Greenwald and Sakumura (1967) also failed to find a reliable relation between attitudes and recall. Using attitudes toward United States involvement in Vietnam as the critical variable, the authors attempted to demonstrate a selective learning effect in both intentional and incidental learning situations, and using subjects either aware or unaware that they had been selected on the basis of their pre-existing attitude. None of these variations produced the expected effect.

The inconsistent findings of studies testing the selective learning hypothesis (see also Brigham & Cook, 1969; Fitzgerald & Ausubel, 1963; and Smith & Jamieson, 1972, for additional failures to replicate) led one pair of authors to conclude after their negative results that:

Perusal of past research fails to unearth any clear-cut methodological differences which might account for the conflicting results of this and earlier studies.... It appears that we now must accept the conclusion that the attitude-memory relationship, if it exists at all, applies only under certain conditions. It is evident that the specific nature of these conditions is not as yet understood. (Brigham & Cook, 1969, p. 243)

Additional Supportive Findings.   Not surprisingly, research activity on the attitude-memory relation decreased substantially following these negative findings. Nevertheless, some researchers continued to look for factors that could account for the contradictory results. These efforts produced a number of supportive studies that hold promise for resolving past inconsistencies. Two of these studies are described below.

Malpass (1969) proposed that the selective learning hypothesis can be expected to hold only under conditions of incidental (as opposed to intentional) learning, because selective attention might underlie the effect. Using attitudes toward the draft as the critical variable, he found that the attitude-memory relation was supported only when the task instructions did not force the subject to pay close attention to the content of the material per se. When an intentional learning task was employed, no relation between attitudes and learning was obtained.

Feather (1969, 1970) departed from traditional methods for testing the selective learning hypothesis and obtained strong support for what he called "selective recall." He argued that attitudinal "consistency" involves both the side of the issue that the information supports (relative to the learner's attitude) and the extent to which the learner agrees with the material. Thus, for example, consistent material for procommunist subjects would be procommunist statements with which they agree and anticommunist statements with which they disagree. Inconsistent material for the same persons would be procommunist statements with which they disagree and anticommunist statements with which they agree. Consistent and inconsistent material for anticommunist persons would be exactly the converse of that for procommunist individuals.[1]

Employing attitudes toward American intervention in South Vietnam (Feather, 1969; 1970, Experiment 1) and attitudes toward student council financial support of student demonstrators (Feather, 1970, Experiments 2 and 3) as the critical variables, Feather showed that, when asked to report arguments about the issue, subjects will produce many more "consistent" than "inconsistent" argu-

---

[1]There are clear similarities between Feather's agree-disagree dimension and Jones and Kohler's (1958) plausibility dimension. Nonetheless, an individual could consider a statement plausible without necessarily agreeing with it. Plausibility is certainly related to agreeability (e.g., it is unlikely that one would agree with an implausible statement), but the latter dimension may require more psychological commitment.

ments. Although Feather has not tested the usefulness of his analysis for predicting the learning and recall of attitude-related information, his findings are compatible with the selective learning hypothesis. More importantly, his analysis raises interesting questions about the appropriate definition of attitudinal "consistency."

Resolving the Inconsistent Results.   The experiments by Malpass (1969) and Feather (1969, 1970) provide clues for resolving the inconsistent and contradictory findings of past research. Two factors seem particularly important: the learning paradigm that is employed and the way that attitudinal "consistency" is defined.

All of the nonsupportive studies, with the exception of two of the Greenwald and Sakumura (1967) experiments, employed intentional learning paradigms. Given Malpass's (1969) analysis and results, these negative findings are not surprising. What *is* surprising is that all of the early supportive studies, with the exception of Watson and Hartmann (1939), *also* employed intentional learning tasks and yet obtained positive results. The resolution to this anomaly might lie in the effects of familiarity on learning in an intentional learning situations. Familiar material is probably easier to memorize. Further, it seems likely that subjects in the early studies were more familiar with arguments that supported their side of the issue than with opposing arguments, since open and wide debate was not common on such issues as segregation (Jones & Aneshansel, 1956; Jones & Kohler, 1958), communism (Levine & Murphy, 1943), and the virtues of Russia (Garber, 1955). Thus, familiarity might have produced the differences in recall of "same side" versus "other side" material, which were then mistakenly attributed to the affective operations of attitudes. At the time of the later nonsupportive studies, however, familiarity could not reproduce the earlier effects because subjects had been exposed to more debate of the issues involved (this argument is consistent with the one proposed by Waly & Cook, 1966).

This perspective suggests that the early studies do not provide clearly supportive evidence for the selective learning hypothesis, nor do the later studies provide clearly invalidating evidence. None of the studies that employed an intentional learning task constitute unequivocal tests of the attitude-memory relation. Even if the familiarity argument is rejected and the early results are attributed to Type I errors (as was done by Greenwald, 1975), the selective learning hypothesis is not disproved: the evidence is not directly relevant.[2]

---

[2]We do not mean to imply that attitudes will never influence intentional learning, but rather that results may be inconsistent in such paradigms. There are, in fact, numerous reasons to expect that attitudinally consistent material should be easier to memorize (e.g., such material may be more compatible with existing cognitive structures). Nevertheless, incidental learning tasks seem more *likely* than intentional learning tasks to evidence the effects of attitudes (if the attitude-memory relation exists). For one thing, task demands influence learning. In the same way that subjects will

We are left, then, with the findings from studies that employed an incidental learning task. Considering only these studies, a second factor that may account for the inconsistency of the findings becomes apparent. In the supportive studies (Malpass, 1969; Watson & Hartmann, 1939), attitudinally consistent material was defined as that which supported the same side of the issue as the subject (i.e., pro material for pro subjects, and con material for con subjects). Greenwald and Sakumura (1967), on the other hand, defined consistent material as that with which the subject agreed (on the basis of ratings obtained from subjects). Although sidedness and agreeability are probably related characteristics of attitude-relevant material (e.g., people will tend to agree with "same side" information), they are not equivalent psychological concepts.

Thus, the inconsistency of the evidence relating to the attitude-memory relation may be attributable to differences in the nature of the learning tasks employed and the definitions of attitudinal "consistency." The fairest test of the selective learning hypothesis would seem to require that an incidental learning paradigm be employed and that both the sidedness and agreeability of the material be taken into account.[3]

An Individual Differences Perspective

One aspect of the attitude-memory relation that has not been widely discussed is possible individual differences in the selective learning of material consistent with one's attitudes. To the authors' knowledge, only two studies have directly examined personality differences in selective learning.

Kleck and Wheaton (1967) used an incidental learning paradigm to test selective learning by both high and low dogmatic subjects (Rokeach, 1960). The attitude topic was the age at which drivers' licenses should be issued. As predicted, high dogmatic subjects recalled more material that supported their own side of the issue than opposing information, whereas low dogmatic subjects showed no bias in recall. The authors interpreted these findings as showing that

---

remember inconsistent material if they expect to participate in a debate (e.g., Jones & Aneshansel, 1956), the demand to memorize *all* of the material, which is inherent in an intentional learning task, might preclude any effect of attitudes on learning. In addition, selective attention, which seems likely to contribute to any effect of attitudes on learning in real life situations, can be allowed to operate more freely in incidental than intentional learning paradigms, as long as the task does not demand close attention to all of the material (cf. Malpass, 1969). Thus, incidental learning tasks seem preferable to intentional learning tasks for testing the attitude-memory relations. Finally, note that the relative advantages of incidental learning tasks may be particularly strong when the delay between the learning trials and the recall test is short. Over long time intervals (e.g., weeks or months), there will be greater opportunity for attitudes to influence memory, and the nature of the learning task may be less important.

[3]Sidedness may be more important than agreeability (given past results), but the two dimensions together, as proposed by Feather (1969, 1970), may provide the best definition of consistency.

high dogmatic persons are less able to integrate new beliefs into their cognitive system than are low dogmatic persons.[4]

Thus, dogmatism would appear to influence the attitude-memory relation. There are a number of additional personality characteristics, however, that have not been examined in the selective learning literature but that seem theoretically relevant to attitudinal effects on recall.

As noted earlier, the selective learning hypothesis has been based, historically, on the assumption that attitude-consistent information arouses positive affect and attitude-inconsistent material is threatening or negatively arousing. The latter half of this assumption, in particular, has been supported by several studies (e.g., Kiesler & Pallak, 1976, Zanna & Cooper, 1976; Zanna, Higgins, & Taves, 1976). These findings suggest the hypothesis that the manner in which individuals deal, in general, with negatively arousing or threatening stimuli might influence the way that they deal with attitudinally inconsistent material.

The personality dimension "repression-sensitization" (Bell & Byrne, 1977; Byrne, 1964) is postulated to reflect chronic differences in exactly these sorts of tendencies. Repressors generally employ "avoidance" strategies (e.g., repression, denial) to deal with anxiety-provoking stimuli, and they accentuate positive or reassuring information about themselves and their environment. Sensitizers, on the other hand, generally employ "approach" strategies (e.g., intellectualization, rumination) to deal with threatening stimuli, and they do not focus on the positive as do repressors (Olson & Zanna, 1979a; Zanna & Aziza, 1976). Thus, repressors and sensitizers might differ in the extent to which they selectively recall attitudinally consistent and inconsistent information. Specifically, repressors should be more likely than sensitizers to manifest selective learning of material that is consistent with their own attitudes. Such an effect could result either from greater avoidance by repressors of inconsistent information (via selective attention) or from their active repression and forgetting of such mate-

---

[4]The second study on personality moderators of the attitude-memory relation is less pertinent to our analysis. Greaves (1972) investigated the implications for the attitude-memory relation of Harvey, Hunt, and Schroder's (1961) schema of conceptual development. His study dealt mainly with persons at two levels of conceptual development, whose chief behavioral characteristics included either a strong authority orientation (System 1 subjects) or a strong peer-group orientation (System 3 subjects). Subjects were presented with factual information about the United States and Sweden by a high status/high expertise source, who biased the presentation in favor of one of the countries. Some of the information favored the United States and some favored Sweden. An unexpected recall test followed the presentation of the material. System 1 subjects selectively recalled information that supported the side of the issue toward which the source was biased, whereas System 3 subjects selectively recalled information that supported their own side of the issue (favoring the United States). Thus, both groups manifested selective recall, but the direction of their bias depended on their level of conceptual development. This variable has clear implications for the effects of attitudes on the learning and recall of information presented by a high status source. Under other conditions, however, its relevance is less clear.

rial. A recent study by Olson and Zanna (1979a) supports these predicted effects for repression-sensitization: After making a decision, repressors visually attended to stimuli that were consistent with their decision more than to inconsistent stimuli, whereas sensitizers did not manifest such postdecisional "selective exposure" (Festinger, 1957).

A personality variable that has some conceptual similarities to repression-sensitization is self-esteem (indeed, these variables correlate significantly; repressors tend to have high self-esteem, e.g., Feder, 1968). There are a number of reasons to expect that high self-esteem persons will find inconsistent information more affectively disturbing than will low self-esteem individuals. First, the latter group may be less surprised than the former by such material (i.e., low self-esteem persons might expect that invalidating evidence for their opinions exists). Second, high self-esteem might *result from* (and therefore predict) the avoidance and/or repression of inconsistent material. Thus, high self-esteem persons should manifest a greater bias toward recall of attitudinally consistent information than low self-esteem persons.

Finally, Rotter's (1966) construct of internal-external locus of control might be expected to influence the attitude-memory relation. To the extent that internals believe that they control their environment, they may have a greater need than externals to believe that they are *correct* in their attitudes and opinions. Such confidence would allow them to act so as to further their desired ends (presumably, externals perceive less ability and/or opportunity to exert influence and may therefore be less concerned about the correctness of their attitudes). Thus, internals, relative to externals, may find attitudinally inconsistent information more disturbing, may be more likely to avoid such material, and may therefore manifest a greater bias toward recall of attitude-consistent information.

Experiment 1:   Individual Differences in Selective Learning

Olson and Zanna (1979b) conducted a study to determine the extent to which these various personality dimensions, singly or in combination, moderate the attitude-memory relation. Attitudes toward abortion constituted the critical variable.

Method.   Eighty-six female undergraduates participated in a preliminary personality and attitudes assessment session. Subjects completed Epstein and Fenz's (1967) repression-sensitization scale, Janis and Field's (1959) self-esteem scale, Rotter's (1966) internal-external locus of control scale, and Troldahl and Powell's (1965) short dogmatism scale. They also completed a questionnaire that assessed their opinions on a number of issues, including abortion. Two statements assessed opinions toward abortion: "The decision to terminate a pregnancy through abortion should be left up to the woman and her doctor," and

"Abortion should be available on demand." Responses were made on 6-point scales ranging from "Strongly agree" to "Strongly disagree." Subjects also indicated how important the issue was to them on 4-point scales ranging from "Not at all important" to "Extremely important."

To be included in the final sample, subjects had to respond consistently to both opinion statements (i.e., either pro- or con-abortion), and their responses had to be relatively extreme—an average across the two statements that was within one unit of either end of the 6-point scale. In addition, at least one of their importance ratings had to be either "3" or "4" on the 4-point scale, and the other rating could not be below "2" (in fact, all but six subjects included in the final sample responded "3" or "4" on both importance ratings). Fifty-four subjects satisfied these requirements; 39 were pro-abortion and 15 were con-abortion.[5]

Twelve statements on the issue of abortion were selected to vary independently sidedness and agreeability. The statements were chosen from a larger pool on the basis of pretests with subjects from the same population as the experimental group. Three statements were selected that almost all pilot subjects, irrespective of their own opinions about abortion, classified as *pro*-abortion and *agreed* with (e.g., "An unwanted pregnancy can be an unhappy, perhaps even traumatic experience"), three were chosen that were seen as *pro*-abortion and *disagreed* with (e.g., "Abortion is an acceptable means of birth control"), three were chosen that were seen as *con*-abortion and *agreed* with (e.g., "There are many families that want to adopt a baby"), and a final three were selected that were seen as *con*-abortion and *disagreed* with (e.g., "Every woman should have children").

Subjects participated individually in the second session. They were told that the study was an initial step in the development of a test of verbal comprehension and that feedback was needed on certain materials. They were told that the experimenter was designing statements on topical issues and that she was going to develop a test to measure certain ways of thinking. Subjects were told that it was important, therefore, that the statements be clear and not vague.

The experimenter (who was blind with respect to the experimental hypotheses and subjects' opinions and personality types) then played for the subject a taped reading of the 12 statements. The order of the 12 statements on the tape was determined randomly, with the constraint that each statement category from the sidedness × agreeability classification scheme had to be represented in each

---

[5]Actually, only 52 of the 86 subjects satisfied these requirements completely. Two additional subjects were subsequently added to create proportional cell sizes: each subject gave importance ratings of "2" to each statement. Note that our procedure ensured that the issue of abortion was relatively important to all subjects—a prerequisite for attitudes to have any affective influence on memory. Yet, many past studies have not limited their sample to highly involved subjects.

consecutive set of four statements. There was a 10-second pause between each statement, during which subjects rated it for clarity on a 5-point scale ranging from "Not at all clear" (1) to "Extremely clear" (5). The tape was then played again, and subjects rated each statment for complexity on a 5-point scale ranging from "Extremely simple" (1) to "Extremely complex" (5). Note that subjects were not instructed to learn or remember the statements; thus, Malpass's (1969) point about the kind of exposure subjects should have to the material was satisfied.

Subjects were then given a five-sentence paragraph on the possible separation of Quebec from Canada and asked to rate the paragraph as a whole for clarity and complexity. This task took 2 or 3 minutes and served as a filler between hearing the statements and the recall test.

Following this filler task, subjects were given a blank sheet of paper and asked to reproduce as many of the 12 statements on abortion as they could remember. They were told that reproducing the basic meaning of the statements was the important part. They were given up to 5 minutes to complete this unexpected recall test.

Results. Subjects' reproductions of the 12 statements were scored for accuracy of recall on a 5-point scale, ranging from "Not recalled" (0) to "Completely accurate in meaning" (4), by a judge who was blind with respect to the experimental hypotheses and subjects' opinions and personality types. (A second, "blind" judge scored the memory protocols of 27 randomly selected subjects. The recall scores for the 324 statements scored by both judges correlated highly, r (332) = .97, $p <$ .001, indicating that the scoring was highly reliable.)

Initially, the recall scores were submitted to a series of 2 (pro-con abortion subjects) × 3 (tertile split on the personality dimension, e.g., repressors-moderates-sensitizers) × 2 (pro-con abortion statements) × 2 (agree-disagree statements) factorial analyses of variance, with subjects' attitude and personality between-subjects factors, and statement sidedness and agreeability within-subjects factors. Four ANOVAs were performed, one for each personality dimension. In every analysis except the one involving dogmatism, the interaction between subjects' attitude, subjects' personality, and statement sidedness was significant. In each case, the interaction reflected better recall of "same side" than "other side" statements by subjects in the predicted tertile of the dimension (i.e., repressors, high self-esteem subjects, and internals), but not by moderates or subjects in the remaining tertile of the dimension (i.e., sensitizers, low self-esteem subjects, and externals). Thus, there was clear support for the selective learning hypothesis for subjects who could be described as repressing in defensive style, high in self-esteem, and internal in locus of control. Predictions for the dogmatism variable were not confirmed, however. Table 4.1 presents, for illustrative purposes, the means for the repression-sensitization analysis. It can

TABLE 4.1
Means for the Attitude × Defensive Style × Sidedness Interaction on
Statement Recall Scores[a]

Subject Attitude	Statement Sidedness	Subject Defensive Style		
		Repressors	Moderates	Sensitizers
Pro-abortion	Pro-abortion	2.36	1.83	1.61
	Con-abortion	1.42	1.44	1.71
Con-abortion	Pro-abortion	1.53	2.27	2.37
	Con-abortion	2.10	1.20	1.73

[a]Adapted from Olson & Zanna (1979b). Possible scores range from 0 to 4, with higher scores reflecting better recall. Cell n's for the pro-abortion subject attitude rows are 13 and for the con-abortion subject attitude rows are 5.

be seen from the table that pro-abortion repressors manifested better recall of pro- than con-abortion statements, whereas con-abortion repressors manifested better recall of con- than pro-abortion statements.

Across all subjects (i.e., ignoring the personality variables), there was no evidence of better memory for "same side" than "other side" statements, nor of better memory for "same side/agree" and "other side/disagree" than "same side/disagree" and "other side/agree" statements (contrary to our expectations based on Feather's, 1969, 1970, work). Although "agree" statements were better recalled, across all subjects, than were "disagree" statements, this effect cannot be attributed unequivocally to the agreeability of the statements per se. Specifically, subjects rates the "agree" statements as more clear than the "disagree" statements (there were no effects for sidedness of the statements on the clarity or complexity ratings). Finally, none of the personality measures interacted with statement agreeability in affecting recall.

Thus, a "sidedness" definition of attitudinal consistency, in conjunction with the personality measures, yielded support for the selective learning hypothesis. Because repression-sensitization, self-esteem, and locus of control were intercorrelated,[6] it is possible to characterize two personality "profiles." One profile involves a repressing defensive style, high self-esteem, and an internal locus of control; the second profile involves a sensitizing defensive style, low self-esteem, and an external locus of control. Within each profile, the defensive style, self-esteem, and locus of control characteristics make the same predictions for selective learning. To examine the predictive utility of the personality measures

---

[6]The correlations ranged from .21, in the case of repression-sensitization and locus of control, to −.49, in the case of repression-sensitization and self-esteem.

alone and in combination, a single score was calculated for each subject to reflect the extent to which she recalled more "same side" than "other side" material; these scores were regressed on the four personality measures (including dogmatism).

The multiple correlation between the four measures and the selective learning scores was significant, $R = .45$, $F (4, 49) = 3.04$, $p < .05$. When a step-wise regression was performed, repression-sensitization entered first and significantly predicted selective learning, $r^2 = .125$, $F (1, 52) = 7.41$, $p < .01$, with a repressing defensive style associated with greater recall of "same side" than "other side" material. Although the other variables did not significantly increase R^2 (the proportion of the variance in the dependent variable accounted for by variance in the predictors) when they were added to the regression equation, the effect for locus of control, which entered second, approached significance, $F (1, 52) = 3.86$, $p < .06$ (R^2 change $= .062$). Thus, repression-sensitization was the best single predictor of selective learning. It should be noted, however, that when either self-esteem or locus of control were intentionally entered first into the regression equation (and the remaining variables then entered freely), they, too, accounted for significant proportions of the variance (self-esteem, $r^2 = .100$, $F (1, 52) = 5.76$, $p < .02$; locus of control, $r^2 = .100$, $F (1, 52) = 5.75$, $p < .02$), with high self-esteem and an internal locus of control associated with greater selective learning. When self-esteem was entered first, the effects of the other variables were of marginal significance: repression-sensitization entered second, $F (1, 52) = 3.14$, $p < .09$ (R^2 change $= .052$), and locus of control entered third, $F (1, 52) = 2.66$, $p < .11$ (R^2 change $= .043$). When locus of control was entered first, repression-sensitization entered second and significantly increased R^2, $F (1, 52) = 5.44$, $p < .03$ (R^2 change $= .087$), while remaining variables added little to the prediction.

Discussion.   The present experiment tested the selective learning hypothesis under the conditions that, on the basis of past research and theory, seemed to allow the fairest test to be conducted. Incidental recall of the material was studied, so that subjects would not have an explicit "set" to retain the statements in memory. In addition, only highly involved subjects who were either clearly pro-abortion or clearly con-abortion were selected, thus ensuring that the sidedness of the materials for each subject could be specified with confidence and that the statements would have affective significance for the subjects. Further, statement sidedness and statement agreeability were varied independently, allowing a test of the selective learning hypothesis using different definitions of attitudinal "consistency." Finally, a number of personality variables that seemed theoretically relevant were also measured. Repression-sensitization, self-esteem, locus of control, and dogmatism were all expected to predict selective learning.

Analysis of the recall measure provided no clear evidence of selective learning across all subjects. When the personality variables were taken into account, however, clear support for the attitude-memory relation within particular sub-groups was obtained. Results showed that repressors manifested better recall of "same side" than "other side" material, whereas moderates and sensitizers did not. The relevance of defensive style for the closely related phenomenon of selective exposure has been demonstrated in past research (Olson & Zanna, 1979a); the present study extends the predictive utility of repression-sensitization to the selective learning hypothesis.

Self-esteem and internal-external locus of control also predicted selective learning (better recall of "same side" than "other side" statements). Indeed, these three personality measures were all significantly intercorrelated (except repression-sensitization and locus of control), and all reliably predicted selective learning. Consequently, although repression-sensitization was the best single predictor, one could focus on any of these dimensions to understand and/or explain the results. The most useful approach, however, might be to consider the three dimensions part of a general personality "profile" that is characterized by a positive self-image, an avoidance of threatening or negatively arousing stimuli, and a belief that one controls one's environment. Each of these characteristics might contribute to the memory bias evidenced in this study. Moreover, it seems impossible to determine the logical "ordering" of these variables in terms of their effects on tbe attitude-memory relation. For example, it may be that high self-esteem results, in part, from a repressing defensive style and that therefore defensive style is the critical operative variable in the profile. On the other hand, a repressing defensive style might spring from confidence in oneself and one's opinions; if such were the case, then self-esteem might be considered the primary operative variable (concerning the attitude-memory relation) in the profile.

There are some interesting similarities between the personality "profile" proposed here and Greenwald's (1980) concept of the "totalitarian ego." Greenwald characterizes the ego as a "personal historian," responsible for organizing knowledge about the self. He calls the ego "totalitarian" because it employs devices usually attributed only to dictators: "ego fabricates and revises history [memory], thereby engaging in practices not ordinarily admired in historians" (p. 604). These devices presumably enhance one's apparent power, goodness, and stability. Greenwald proposes that such an ego structure has evolved because cognitive systems characterized by beliefs in personal efficacy and self-esteem are associated with effective functioning and adaptation. Although his analysis is not directed at possible individual differences in ego, the personality measures employed in this study might have tapped into such differences. That is, a repressing defensive style, high self-esteem, and an internal locus of control might each be associated with a more "totalitarian ego." These speculations seem compatible with Greenwald's conceptual analysis of the totalitarian ego, and the predictive utility of the dimensions for selective recall of "same side" versus "other side" material (a memory bias that is similar to the kinds discussed by Greenwald) further supports the hypothesized similarity. Consequently, the most useful approach to understanding the present results again seems to be to consider the three predictive variables all part of a general personality (or ego) profile.[7]

A potentially important question is whether the selective learning manifested by repressors, high self-esteem subjects, and internals consisted of better recall of "same side" statements or impaired recall of "other side" statements, relative to the other personality groups. Taken as a whole, the results indicate that *both* improved recall of "same side" statements and impaired recall of "other side" statements contributed to the selective learning effect (see Table 4.1, for example, where pro-abortion repressors manifested better recall of pro-abortion statements and poorer recall of con-abortion statements than did pro-abortion moderates or sensitizers, and con-abortion repressors manifested better recall of con-abortion statements and poorer recall of pro-abortion statements than did con-abortion moderates or sensitizers). This conclusion suggests that repressors, high self-esteem subjects, and internals did not simply avoid "other side" statements; they also focused more than other personality types on "same side" statements. Thus, there seem to have been both "avoidance" and "approach" components in the learning manifested by these subjects. This analysis has implications for our conceptual understanding of both the personality dimensions and the attitude-memory relation. On the one hand, it suggests that the personality measures may reflect differences in the processing of both "pleasing" and "disturbing" information. Past theorizing on repression-sensitization, for example, has focused largely on the implications of this dimension for the processing of negatively arousing stimuli; the present study suggests that repressors and sensitizers may also process "pleasing" stimuli differently. On the other hand, it suggests that attitudes may both facilitate learning of consistent material and inhibit learning of inconsistent material, at least for some subjects.

---

[7]As noted earlier, dogmatism did not predict selective learning. Although Kleck and Wheaton (1967) found that high dogmatic subjects, relative to lows, recalled more "same side" than "other side" material, no such evidence was obtained in the present experiment. Indeed, the direction of the relation between dogmatism and selective learning was toward *low* dogmatic subjects manifesting more selective recall. It is not readily apparent why dogmatism failed to predict selective learning in this study. Kleck and Wheaton (1967) used a multiple choice test to assess recall, whereas the present study employed a free recall measure. Perhaps this methodological difference accounts for the conflicting results (e.g., perhaps dogmatism does not predict selective *accessibility*, as measured by free recall tests, but does predict selective *availability*, as measured by recognition type tests, Tulving & Pearlstone, 1966). Another possible explanation for the conflicting results involves the delay between exposure to the information and the recall test. There was a 2 week delay between exposure and recall in the Kleck and Wheaton (1967) study, whereas the present experiment assessed recall only minutes after exposure to the information. Perhaps dogmatism is associated with selective *forgetting* of attitude-related information and therefore predicts selective learning only after some passage of time.

The results improve our understanding of the attitude-memory relation in other ways. For example, they suggest that the sidedness of attitude-related material is particularly important in determining the probability that the material will be retained in memory. This hypothesis seems to conflict with a recent proposal by Judd and Kulik (1980), who argue that attitudes operate as "schemata," organized along an agreeability dimension. These authors present evidence that both extremely agreeable and extremely disagreeable materials are more memorable than less extreme material. In addition, they find no support for an effect of "pro" versus "con" material on recall. Unfortunately, Judd and Kulik did not assess the attitudes of their *subjects* on the relevant issues—information that is requisite for identifying the attitudinal consistency of pro and con material. Thus, their results are equivocal with respect to the importance of the sidedness dimension in memory.

Finally, it is interesting to speculate about why statement sidedness seemed more important, phenomenologically, than statement agreeability to the repressors, high self-esteem subjects, and internals in our study. One possibility is that the sidedness dimension reflected the relation of the statements to subjects' *overall* attitudes toward abortion, whereas the agreeability dimension reflected subjects' *"microattitudes"* toward the individual statements themselves. For example, the extent of someone's agreement with the statement "An unwanted pregnancy can be an unhappy, perhaps even traumatic, experience" might reflect his or her "attitude" (favorability) toward this specific idea, but the perception of the statement's sidedness (pro versus con) might reflect its relevance to the person's underlying attitude toward the more general issue of abortion. To the extent that it is more important to "defend" one's overall attitudes than one's "microattitudes," the sidedness dimension would be expected to predict selective learning by repressors, high self-esteem subjects, and internals, whereas the agreeability dimension would be expected to have less impact on these subjects' recall. This analysis might also help to explain Judd and Kulik's (1980) findings concerning the effects of agreeability. Perhaps "microattitudes" have different structural characteristics and different motivational implications than do more global, important attitudes. For example, perhaps "microattitudes" operate as schemata (consistent with Judd & Kulik's findings), whereas the sidedness dimension becomes affectively important for more global attitudes.

In conclusion, then, this experiment provided strong support for the selective learning hypothesis within particular personality subgroups. When conditions were set up that provided a fair test of the hypothesis, repressors, high self-esteem subjects, and internals manifested better recall of "same side" than "other side" material. A "sidedness" definition of attitudinal consistency was the only one that revealed selective learning by these subjects—a finding that is consistent with past research. Thus, the attitude-memory relation was supported when appropriate subgroups of subjects were identified and an appropriate definition of attitudinal consistency was employed.

ATTITUDES AND BEHAVIOR: THE DIRECT
EXPERIENCE HYPOTHESIS

The relation between attitudes and overt behaviors has been of even more interest to social psychologists than the attitude-memory relation. It has been widely assumed that attitudes predict overt behaviors (e.g., Allport, 1935; Campbell, 1950; Doob, 1947); indeed, the functional utility of the concept of attitude largely depends on this assumption. Unfortunately, research has often found the attitude-behavior relation to be weak. Wicker (1969), in an extensive review of the relevant literature, uncovered "little evidence to support the postulated existence of stable, underlying attitudes within the individual which influence both his verbal expressions and his actions" (p. 75). Although attitude-behavior consistency is increased when certain factors are taken into account (see Ajzen, this volume; Calder & Ross, 1973; Olson & Zanna, in press; Schuman & Johnson, 1976), the assumption that all attitudes strongly predict relevant, overt behaviors across situations has not been supported.

In response to this problem, some researchers have attempted to identify attitudinal characteristics that moderate the attitude-behavior relation. For example, Norman (1975) found evidence that attitudes predict actions more strongly if the cognitive and affective components of the attitude are consistent than if these components are inconsistent. In this section, we present data from a program of research that takes a similar approach. Rather than asking whether attitudes relate to behavior (clearly, they do under some circumstances), we consider the following questions: "What kinds of attitudes predict behavior?" and "What kinds of individuals are likely to possess these kinds of attitudes?" As mentioned at the outset, instead of assessing whether a given correlation coefficient between an attitude and a behavior measure is statistically significant and/or meaningful, we propose treating the strength of the attitude-behavior relation as we would treat any other dependent variable. Our goal is to achieve a better understanding of the mechanisms that produce attitude-behavior consistency. Some potentially specifiable attitudes, as we shall see, are more predictive of later behavior than are other attitudes. The research focuses on the effects of direct behavioral experience with the attitude object on attitude-behavior consistency.

Review of the Literature

It is interesting to note that although research has often found the attitude-behavior connection to be weak, the behavior-attitude link has been shown to be quite strong. Derived from both Festinger's (1957) cognitive dissonance theory and Bem's (1967) self-perception theory, the notion that attitudes will conform to freely performed behavior has been reliably demonstrated many times (e.g., Festinger & Carlsmith, 1959; Kiesler, Nisbett, & Zanna, 1969). An asymmetry seems to exist between the two possible directions of the attitude-behavior relation. As Abelson (1972) has put it, "we are very well trained and very good at finding reasons for what we do, but not very good at doing what we find reasons for" (p. 25).

An interesting question that arises from this possible asymmetry is whether an attitude that has formed as a result of direct, personal experience with the attitude object may better predict future behaviors than an attitude that is based on nonbehavioral information about the attitude object. The question can be phrased as follows: in a behavior-attitude-behavior sequence, will the attitude-behavior relation be stronger than is typically observed?

A number of studies have investigated this question and have found that attitudes based on direct behavioral experience with the attitude object are, indeed, more predictive of subsequent actions than are attitudes formed via indirect means (see Fazio & Zanna, 1981, for a review of this research). For example, Fazio and Zanna (1978) showed that prior experience in psychological experiments increased the strength of the attitude-behavior relation in this domain: Individuals who had participated in numerous psychological experiments expressed attitudes that better predicted their subsequent willingness to volunteer for studies, relative to individuals with little or no previous experience as subjects. It is important to note that the attitudes of experienced and inexperienced subjects did not differ in either variability or statistical reliability. Moreover, neither attitude extremity nor past behaviors per se (as predictors of future behaviors) accounted for the effects of past experience on the attitude-behavior relation.

Zanna, Olson, and Fazio (1981) more recently demonstrated that simply providing subjects with the opportunity to review, and therefore infer an attitude from, past religious behaviors resulted in greater attitude-behavior consistency. Subjects in this study indicated their attitudes toward being religious either before or after completing a "prior behavior inventory." Thus, in the Self-Perception condition, subjects reviewed their past religious behaviors before indicating their attitudes; in the Control condition, this review did not occur until after the attitude assessment. Approximately one month later, all subjects returned for a second session, during which self-report measures of their actual behaviors pertaining to religion since the first session were assessed (subjects had not been forewarned that such measures would be taken). Included among the measures were, "Since the last time you participated in this study, how many times did you: (1) attend a religious service? and (2) pray in private?"

Actually, two replications of the study were conducted. For each replication, the correlations between the religious attitudes measure and each of the measures of religious behavior were computed within each condition. As expected, these correlations were larger in the Self-Perception than in the Control condition. In the Control condition, the correlations ranged from .21 to .38, hovering around the traditional .30 mark. In the Self-Perception condition, the correlations were 20 points higher, hovering around .50 (the range was from .39 to .59).

Again, it should be noted that past behaviors per se (as predictors of future behaviors) could not account for the experimental effect. When we compared the partial correlations between attitudes and behaviors, holding constant the effects of prior behaviors, significant differences between conditions remained. In the Control condition, the partial correlations averaged .09; in the Self-Perception condition, the average partial correlation was .33.

Thus, past research suggests that attitudes which represent a summary of relevant past behaviors are more predictive of later behaviors than are attitudes formed outside the behavioral arena. Presumably, behavioral experience with an attitude object leads to a clearer attitudinal inference (cf. Bem, 1972), which is based on information that is directly pertinent to future behaviors toward the object.

An Individual Differences Perspective

One aspect of this "prior behavior" analysis that has not been examined in past research relates to possible individual differences in the extent to which attitudes represent inferences from past behaviors. That is, ignoring the absolute level of prior behavioral experience, might individuals differ in the extent to which their attitudes summarize their prior actions? Two requirements would seem necessary for an attitude to constitute an inference from past behaviors. First, past behaviors must have been sufficiently invariant that an attitudinal inference is possible; if past behaviors were highly variable, then no single attitudinal statement could accurately summarize all of the relevant actions. Second, the individuals must consider their past behaviors to be reflective of their attitudes and must infer their attitudes from those behaviors.

Thus, those persons who are most likely to express attitudes that summarize past behaviors (and that therefore predict future behaviors) are those whose past behaviors toward the attitude object have been relatively invariant *and* who base their attitudinal statements on their past behaviors. Individual differences on two dimensions appear relevant to this analysis. A parallel of the past behavioral variability notion has been discussed in the personality trait literature. Bem and Allen (1974) have shown that individuals who identify themselves as invariant on a particular trait dimension will, in fact, be less variable across situations on that trait. Thus, it should be possible to ask subjects how much they vary from one situation to another in their behavioral manifestations of a particular attitude, and their self-reports should reflect actual behavioral variability.

Low behavioral variability can be expected to increase attitude-behavior consistency, however, only if individuals employ their past behaviors as critical inputs from which to infer their attitudes. This tendency may be reflected in the construct of self-monitoring (Synder, 1974, 1979). Low self-monitors guide their behavioral choices mainly on the basis of salient information from relevant inner states, whereas high self-monitors guide their choices on the basis of situational information. That is, low self-monitors behave in accordance with their personal views and internal states, whereas high self-monitors change their behavior to match situational demands. Snyder and Tanke (1976) have shown that this construct is related to attitude change in an induced-compliance situation. After choosing to perform a counter-attitudinal behavior, low self-monitors manifested attitude change in the direction of their advocated position, whereas high self-monitors were unaffected by their attitude-discrepant behavior. One interpretation of this finding is that low self-monitors are more likely to consider their behavior to be reflective of their attitudes, and therefore more likely to infer attitudes from prior behavior.

Thus, an individual difference perspective on the prior experience hypothesis suggests that low self-monitors whose past behaviors toward the attitude object have been relatively invariant will manifest greater attitude-behavior consistency than either high self-monitors (irrespective of their prior behavioral variability) or low self-monitors whose past behaviors have been relatively variable. Note that we are not simply arguing, therefore, that persons whose past behaviors have been invariant will manifest greater attitude-behavior consistency; such a proposition would be open to the alternative interpretation that the future behaviors of previously invariant persons are more predictable per se. Rather, our analysis suggests that the self-perception of attitudes from prior behaviors, as mediated by the self-monitoring construct, is critical.

Experiment 2:   Individual Differences in Attitude-Behavior Consistency

In a test of this reasoning, Zanna, Olson, and Fazio (1980) examined the consistency between religious attitudes and religious behaviors. The study consisted of two sessions.

Method.   One hundred and three subjects (50 males and 53 females) participated in the study. In the first session, subjects (a) indicated their attitudes toward being religious, (b) indicated the degree to which they varied from one situation to another in how religious they were, and (c) completed Snyder's (1974) self-monitoring scale. In the second session, approximately one month later, subjects were asked to indicate the frequency with which they had performed several actions related to religion since the first session. Included among the acts were: became intoxicated on alcohol, used illegal drugs, attended a religious service, and prayed in private.

Each subject was classified as either a low or high self-monitor and as either a low or high variability subject, producing a 2 × 2 classification matrix. The former classification was performed by a median split of the distribution of self-monitoring scores. Following Bem and Allen (1974), the variability classification was performed by a median split of the distribution of variability scores at each point on the 11-point religious attitudes scale. This technique removed any possible confounding of attitude extremity and variability. Self-monitoring and variability were uncorrelated ($r = -.01$); as a result, the number of subjects classified into each cell of the matrix was approximately equal.

Because the frequencies with which subjects attended religious services and prayed in private were related (both conceptually and empirically), the two measures were standardized and summed to form one behavior measure. The alcohol and drug usage measures (which also correlated significantly) were similarly standardized and summed to form a second behavior measure.

Results.   Correlations between attitudes and each of the two measures of behavior were computed within each of the four cells produced by the classification scheme. Table 4.2 presents these within-cell correlations. On each measure, the correlations were larger in the low self-monitoring/low variability cell than in any of the other cells. Indeed, "low-low" subjects were the only group to manifest attitude-behavior correlations that were reliably different from zero on both measures, and their attitude-behavior correlations were typically 20 to 40 points higher than the correlations in the other groups.

Evidence that the pattern of findings should be interpreted as the "low-low" cell being different from the other three cells comes from contrasts of onecell versus the other three. When the correlations in the "low-low" cell were contrasted with the correlations across the other three cells, the alcohol/drugs measure yielded a significant difference, $r (26) = -.59$ versus $r (73) = .02$, $z = 3.01$, $p = .003$. Although the difference on the attended services/prayed measure was in the expected direction, $r (26) = .52$ versus $r (72) = .32$, this difference was not reliable, $z = 1.05$, $p = .294$. None of the contrasts involving any of the other cells versus the remaining three cells were significant (five of the six contrasts produced z's < 1).

TABLE 4.2
Attitude-Behavior Correlations as a Function of Self-Monitoring and Behavioral Variability[a]

	Self-Monitoring			
	Low		High	
	Variability			
Behavioral	Low	High	Low	High
Measure	(28)	(28)	(24)	(23)
Attended Services/Prayed	.52**	.38*	.34	.29
Alcohol/Drugs	-.59	-.06	-.21	.18

*p < .05.
**p < .01.
[a]Adapted from Zanna, Olson and Fazio (1980). Positive correlations would indicate that favorable religious attitudes were associated with more attending services and praying, or more alcohol and drug use, respectively. Cell *n*'s are in parentheses.

Discussion.   Results indicated that, as predicted, "low-low" subjects manifested greater attitude-behavior consistency than other subjects. The "low-low" cell represents those persons who report relatively invariant prior behavior and who are assumed to infer their attitudinal dispositions from their behavior. For these people, more so than for any others, attitudes presumably represent meaningful summaries of past actions. Consequently, these individuals' attitudes accurately predict their future behaviors.

Experiment 3:   A Replication and Extension

Although the Zanna, Olson, and Fazio (1980) study provides strong support for an individual difference perspective on the "direct experience" hypothesis, the study is limited in at least two ways. First, behaviors were assessed via retrospective self-reports, which may not constitute completely unbiased estimates of attitude-related behaviors (see Ross, McFarland, & Fletcher, 1981). Second, the findings were confined to only one attitudinal domain. A recent study by Olson and Zanna (1980) was designed, in part, to address these potential limitations.

Method.   Ninety-seven subjects (46 males and 51 females) participated in "a survey of university students' lifestyles." In the first session, subjects' attitudes toward a large number of topics were assessed, including attitudes toward the following 12 behaviors: watching television, listening to music, exercising, doing nonschool reading, reading newsmagazines, being religious, attending religious services, praying, drinking alcohol, using illegal drugs, wearing jeans, and opposing an increase in residence fees that was announced immediately prior to the study at the University of Western Ontario. Subjects also indicated how much they varied across situations and time in each of these behaviors (e.g., how much they varied in the amount of television they watched). Finally, subjects completed several personality measures, including Snyder's (1974) self-monitoring scale.

For the next 3 weeks, subjects maintained a daily diary of several behaviors. Specifically, they recorded the number of hours each day they spent watching television, listening to music, exercising, and doing nonschool reading; they also recorded the number of times they prayed, the number of alcoholic drinks they consumed, and whether or not they attended a religious service, used illegal drugs, and wore jeans.[8]

-----

[8]A major concern was that subjects might forget to maintain their diaries daily. To minimize this possibility, subjects were given a "reminder card" to put on their bathroom mirror and were reminded by phone twice during the 3 week period. They were also given seven preaddressed envelopes and asked to mail one envelope every 3 days, enclosing three diary pages. The vast majority of subjects adhered very well to this schedule; postexperimental interviews indicated that even those participants who were not strictly regular in returning their diary pages completed their diaries daily. Thus, although it is impossible to be totally certain, it seems that most subjects were conscientious in their maintenance of the dairies.

When each subject arrived for the second session, approximately 4 weeks after the first session, he or she was left alone for 5 minutes in a waiting area while the experimenter purportedly "prepared the necessary materials." On a table near the subject, several recent issues of newsmagazines were arranged haphazardly. The experimenter unobtrusively observed the subject from a room that adjoined the waiting area and recorded the number of minutes (out of 5) that the subjects read the newsmagazines. The experimenter also recorded whether or not the subject was wearing jeans. After the 5-minute delay, the experimenter emerged from this room with a stack of materials and apologized for keeping the subject waiting. He then said that he had promised a friend (supposedly a member of the students' council) to inform all participants about a petition that was being circulated to protest a proposed increase in residence fees for the coming year. The subject was told that he or she could sign the petition, or sign a list to receive more information from the students' council about the proposed increase, or do nothing. After subjects indicated their preference, they were debriefed, paid $7.00 for their participation, and dismissed.

As in Experiment 2, subjects were classified as either low or high self-monitors via a median split of the distribution of self-monitoring scores. Subjects were also classified *for each attitudinal domain* as either low or high in variability, by performing a median split of the distribution of that domain's variability scores at each point on that domain's 9-point attitude scale. Thus, subjects could be classified as "low variability" in one domain (e.g., watching television) and as "high variability" in some other domain (e.g., listening to music).[9]

Twelve measures of behavior were computed for each subject. From subjects' final 14 diary pages (the first week was excluded on the assumption that keeping a diary might have temporarily influenced subjects' behaviors), nine measures were obtained: the total number of hours subjects watched television, listened to music, exercised, and did nonschool reading, the total number of times subjects prayed, attended a religious service, used illegal drugs, and wore jeans, and the total number of alcoholic drinks subjects consumed. Three measures of actual, observed behavior (as opposed to self-report) were obtained from subjects' recorded behavior at the second session: the number of minutes they spent reading the newsmagazines, whether or not they wore jeans, and their actions concerning the petition (signing the petition was scored "2," requesting further information was scored "1," and doing nothing was scored "0").

Results. Sixteen correlations between attitudes and behaviors were computed within each of the four cells in the self-monitoring × variability matrix.

---

[9]In fact, the variability classifications were relatively uncorrelated. The mean of the 66 intercorrelations among the 12 variability dichotomies was only .07, indicating that subjects were not consistently classified as either "low variability" or "high variability" across all domains.

TABLE 4.3
Mean Attitude-Behavior Correlations as a Function of Self-Monitoring
and Behavior Variability[a]

	Self-Monitoring			
	Low		High	
		Variability		
	Low	High	Low	High
Mean of all 16 attitude-behavior correlations	.44	.24	.38	.30
Mean of 3 attitude-behavior correlations involving measures of observed behavior	.37	.15	.17	.23

[a]Adapted from Olson and Zanna (1980). Positive correlations indicate that attitudes and behaviors correlated in the predicted direction (e.g., more favorable attitudes toward watching television were associated with more reported television viewing). Cell n's varied for the different correlations.

For each behavioral domain (e.g., watching television), the correlation between the relevant attitude and the relevant behavior was calculated; the number of correlations totalled 16 because attitudes toward being religious were examined for their correlation with four different behavioral measures (the total number of times subjects prayed, attended religious services, used illegal drugs, and consumed an alcoholic drink), and attitudes toward wearing jeans were used to predict two behavioral measures (the total number of times subjects wore jeans, obtained from the diaries, and whether or not they wore jeans to the second session, as recorded by the experimenter).

Table 4.3 presents, for each cell, the mean of all 16 correlations and the mean of the three correlations involving measures of actual, observed behavior. It can be seen from the table that the low self-monitoring/low variability cell produced the largest means, particularly for the measures of observed behavior.

Twelve of the 16 attitude-behavior correlations were statistically significant ($p < .05$, one-tailed) in the "low-low" cell, whereas in the other three cells, statistically significant correlations numbered only six, nine, and six. This pattern makes the "low-low" cell reliably different from the combined, other three cells in the frequency of significant versus nonsignificant attitude-behavior correlations (i.e., "low-low" cell, 12 significant, 4 nonsignificant; other three cells, 21 significant, 27 nonsignificant, Chi-squared (1) = 4.69, $p < .05$). Parallel Chi-squared contrasts of one cell versus the other three were not reliable for any of the other cells.

Discussion.   Experiment 3 replicated the findings of Experiment 2 and extended them to multiple attitude-behavior domains and to measures of spontaneous, observed behavior.[10] In addition, the self-report measures were not long-term, retrospective estimates, but rather were recorded daily. Although the absolute magnitude of the differences in attitude-behavior consistency between the "low-low" cell and the other three cells was not as impressive in Experiment 3 as in Experiment 2, the methodological improvements and extensions increase our confidence in the reliability and importance of the effect. It seems clear that low self-monitors who have been relatively invariant in their prior behaviors toward some attitude object will manifest greater attitude-behavior consistency in that domain than will other personality subgroups. Note also that the particular subjects who were classified as "low-low" in Experiment 3 changed from one domain to another—separate variability classifications were made for each domain. Thus, the findings cannot be attributed to idiosyncrasies of some particular group of subjects.

What are the implications of these individual differences in attitude-behavior consistency for our understanding of the attitude-behavior relation? Perhaps most important, they validate the hypothesis that the attitude-behavior connection can be expected to be strong only when it has been preceded by a self-perception of attitude (i.e., a behavior-attitude link). Earlier research showed that behavioral experience with the attitude object is necessary for this requirement to be met. Experiments 2 and 3 extend this analysis by identifying two individual difference variables that moderate the behavior-attitude link. Low self-monitors are more likely than high self-monitors to consider their attitudes to be important determinants of their behavior. As a result, the former group is more likely to engage in a self-perception of attitude, i.e., to consider their past behaviors to be reflective of their attitudes. In addition, however, relatively invariant prior behaviors toward the attitude object are necessary to enable a clear inference of one's attitude. Thus, low self-monitoring/low variability subjects will manifest heightened attitude-behavior consistency.

Taken as a whole, this perspective suggests that attitudes are not mere justifications for past actions, despite the fact that individuals will often modify their attitudes to conform to freely performed behavior. Past behaviors certainly influ-

---

[10]This pattern of results was replicated in yet another study by Coreless and Zanna (1980). These authors investigated the relation between attitudes toward religion and the time subjects were willing to volunteer for a telephone survey designed to assess attitudes towards religious issues and the relation between attitudes toward energy conservation and subjects' willingness to sign an energy conservation petition which was to be published in a local newspaper. As would be expected with these single-act criteria, the correlations across the entire sample of 64 students were moderate (the religious attitude-behavior correlation was .29, $p < .05$; the energy conservation attitude-behavior correlation was .19, n.s.) When subjects were classified by self-monitoring and behavioral variability, however, subjects in the low self-monitoring/low variability cell produced the only reliable correlations. In the religious domain this correlation was .43 ($p < .05$), compared with an average correlation of .11 in the other three groups; in the energy conservation domain the correlation was .35 ($p < .10$), compared with an average correlation of .12 in the other three groups.

ence attitudes, but attitudes, in turn, influence future behaviors. Thus, attitudes consistitute an important mediating construct between past and future actions, exerting a directive influence on behaviors within the behavior-attitude-behavior sequence.

SUMMARY AND CONCLUSIONS

In this chapter, we have presented data from a program of research that explored personality trait moderators of two attitudinal relations—the attitude-memory relation and the attitude-behavior relation. Experiment 1 showed that repression-sensitization, self-esteem, and internal-external locus of control all predicted selective learning. Thus, attitudes were shown to influence memory within these personality subgroups. Experiments 2 and 3 revealed that low self-monitors who reported relatively invariant prior behaviors toward an attitude object manifested heightened attitude-behavior consistency in that domain. Thus, the effects of attitudes on behavior were shown to be moderated by individual differences that presumably reflect the extent to which attitudes represent inferences from past behaviors.

As we have pointed out, each of these individual difference findings has implications for our understanding of the relevant attitudinal relation. Consequently, we believe that an individual difference approach to the effects of attitudes can yield conceptual advances, in addition to increasing predictive power. Personality theorists have done much to improve our understanding of human behavior; we hope that social psychologists will recognize the value of an approach that integrates the individual difference constructs of traits and attitudes.

ACKNOWLEDGMENTS

The present research was supported by Canada Council Grant S76-0344 to the first-named author. We wish to thank Ronald Schlegel, Shelagh Towson, and Robert Wicklund for comments on an earlier draft.

REFERENCES

Abelson, R. P. Are attitudes necessary? In B. T. King and E. McGinnies (Eds.), *Attitudes, conflict, and social change*. New York: Academic Press, 1972.

Ajzen, I. On behaving in accordance with one's attitudes. In M. P. Zanna, E. T. Higgins, & C. P. Herman (Eds.), *Consistency of social behavior: The Ontario symposium* (Vol. 2). Hillsdale, New Jersey: Lawrence Erlbaum Associates, 1982.

Allport, G. W. Attitudes. In C. Murchison (Ed), *A handbook of social psychology*. Worcester, Mass.: Clark University Press, 1935.

Alper, T. G., & Korchin, S. J. Memory for socially relevant material. *Journal of Abnormal and Social Psychology*, 1952, *47*, 25–37.

Bell, P. A., & Byrne, D. Repression-sensitization. In H. London & J. E. Exner, Jr. (Eds.), *Dimensions of personality*. New York: Wiley, 1977.

Bem, D. J. Self-perception: An alternative interpretation of cognitive dissonance phenomena. *Psychological Review*, 1967, *74*, 183–200.

Bem, D. J. Self-perception theory. In L. Berkowitz, (Ed.), *Advances in experimental social psychology* (Vol. 6). New York: Academic Press, 1972.

Bem, D. J., & Allen, A. On predicting some of the people some of the time: The search for cross-situational consistencies in behavior. *Psychological Review*, 1974, *81*, 506–520.

Brigham, J. C., & Cook, S. W. The influence of attitude on the recall of controversial material: A failure to confirm. *Journal of Experimental Social Psychology*, 1969, *5*, 240–243.

Byrne, D. Repression-sensitization as a dimension of personality. In B. A. Maher (Ed.), *Progress in experimental personality research* (Vol. 1). New York: Academic Press, 1964.

Calder, B. J., & Ross, M. *Attitudes and behavior*. Morristown, N.J.: General Learning Press, 1973.

Campbell, D. T. The indirect assessment of social attitudes. *Psychological Bulletin*, 1950, *47*, 15–38.

Coreless, P., & Zanna, M. P. *Attitude-behavior consistency: Self-monitoring and behavioral variability aid in predicting real behavior*. Unpublished manuscript, University of Waterloo, 1980.

Doob, L. W. The behavior of attitudes. *Psychological Review*, 1947, *54*, 135–156.

Edwards, A. L. Political frames of reference as a factor influencing recognition. *Journal of Abnormal and Social Psychology*, 1941, *36*, 34–50.

Epstein, S., & Fenz, W. The detection of emotional stress through variations in perceptual threshold and physiological arousal. *Journal of Experimental Research in Personality*, 1967, *2*, 191–199.

Fazio, R. H., & Zanna, M. P. Attitudinal qualities relating to the strength of the attitude-behavior relationship. *Journal of Experimental Social Psychology*, 1978, *14*, 398–408.

Fazio, R. H., & Zanna, M. P. Direct experience and attitude-behavior consistency. In L. Berkowitz (Ed.), *Advances in experimental social psychology* (Vol. 14). New York: Academic Press, 1981.

Feather, N. T. Attitude and selective recall. *Journal of Personality and Social Psychology*, 1969, *12*, 310–319.

Feather, N. T. Balancing and positivity effects in social recall. *Journal of Personality*, 1970, *38*, 602–628.

Feder, C. Z. Relationship between self-acceptance and adjustment, repression-sensitization and social competence. *Journal of Abnormal Psychology*, 1968, *73*, 317–322.

Festinger, L. *A theory of cognitive dissonance*. Stanford: Stanford University Press, 1957.

Festinger, L., & Carlsmith, J. M. Cognitive consequences of forced compliance. *Journal of Abnormal and Social Psychology*, 1959, *58*, 203–211.

Fitzgerald, D., & Ausubel, D. P. Cognitive versus affective factors in the learning and retention of controversial material. *Journal of Educational Psychology*, 1963, *54*, 73–84.

Freud, S. Repression. In *Collected papers*, (Vol. 4). London: Hogarth Press, 1925.

Garber, R. B. Influence of cognitive and affective factors in learning and retaining attitudinal materials. *Journal of Abnormal and Social Psychology*, 1955, *51*, 384–389.

Greaves, G. Conceptual system functioning and selective recall of information. *Journal of Personality and Social Psychology*, 1972, *21*, 327–332.

Greenwald, A. G. Consequences of prejudice against the null hypothesis. *Psychological Bulletin*, 1975, *82*, 1–20.

Greenwald, A. G. The totalitarian ego: Fabrication and revision of personal history. *American Psychologist*, 1980, *35*, 603–618.

Greenwald, A. G., & Sakumura, J. S. Attitude and selective learning: Where are the phenomena of yesteryear? *Journal of Personality and Social Psychology*, 1967, *7*, 387–397.

Harvey, O. J., Hunt, D., & Schroder, H. *Conceptual systems and personality organization*. New York: Wiley, 1961.

Higgins, E. T., Kuiper, N. A., & Olson, J. M. Social cognition: A need to get personal. In E. T. Higgins, C. P. Herman, & M. P. Zanna (Eds.), *Social cognition: The Ontario symposium* (Vol. 1). Hillsdale, N.J.: Lawrence Erlbaum Associates, 1981.

James, W. *Principles of psychology*. New York: Holt, 1890.

Janis, I. L., & Field, P. B. Sex differences and personality factors related to persuasibility. In C. I. Hovland & I. L. Janis (Eds.), *Personality and persuasibility*. New Haven, Conn.: Yale University Press, 1959.

Jones, E. E., & Aneshansel, J. The learning and utilization of contravalent material. *Journal of Abnormal and Social Psychology*, 1956, *53*, 27–33.

Jones, E. E., & Kohler, R. The effects of plausibility on the learning of controversial statements. *Journal of Abnormal and Social Psychology*, 1958, *57*, 315–320.

Judd, C. M., & Kulik, J. A. Schematic effects of social attitudes on information processing and recall. *Journal of Personality and Social Psychology*, 1980, *38*, 569–578.

Kanungo, R. N., & Das, J. P. Differential learning and forgetting as a function of the social frame of reference. *Journal of Abnormal and Social Psychology*, 1960, *61*, 82–86.

Kiesler, C. A., Nisbett, R. E., & Zanna, M. P. On inferring one's belief from one's behavior. *Journal of Personality and Social Psychology*, 1969, *11*, 321–327.

Kiesler, C. A., & Pallak, M. S. Arousal properties of dissonance reduction. *Psychological Bulletin*, 1976, *83*, 1014–1025.

Kleck, R. E., & Wheaton, J. Dogmatism and responses to opinion-consistent and opinion-inconsistent information. *Journal of Personality and Social Psychology*, 1967, *5*, 249–252.

LaPiere, R. T. Attitudes vs. actions. *Social Forces*, 1934, *13*, 230–237.

Levine, J. M., & Murphy, G. The learning and retention of controversial statements. *Journal of Abnormal and Social Psychology*, 1943, *38*, 507–517.

Malpass, R. S. Effects of attitude on learning and memory: The influence of instruction-induced sets. *Journal of Experimental Social Psychology*, 1969, *5*, 441–453.

Norman, R. Affective-cognitive consistency, attitudes, conformity, and behavior. *Journal of Personality and Social Psychology*, 1975, *32*, 83–91.

Olson, J. M., & Zanna, M. P. A new look at selective exposure. *Journal of Experimental Social Psychology*, 1979, *15*, 1–15. (a)

Olson, J. M., & Zanna, M. P. *Opinions and memory: Individual differences in selective learning*. Paper presented at the American Psychological Association Meeting, New York, September, 1979. (b)

Olson, J. M., & Zanna, M. P. *Individual differences in attitude-behavior consistency: Replication and extension*. Unpublished manuscript, University of Western Ontario, 1980.

Olson, J. M., & Zanna, M. P. Changing attitudes and behavior. In D. Perlman & C. Cozby (Eds.), *Social psychology: SPSSI's perspective*. New York: Holt, Rinehart, & Winston, in press.

Postman, L., Bruner, J. S., & McGinnies, E. Personal values as selective factors in perception. *Journal of Abnormal and Social Psychology*, 1948, *43*, 142–154.

Rokeach, M. *The open and closed mind*. New York: Basic Books, 1960.

Ross, M., McFarland, C., & Fletcher, G. J. O. The effect of attitude on the recall of personal histories. *Journal of Personality and Social Psychology*, 1981, *40*, 627–634.

Rotter, J. B. Generalized expectancies for internal versus external control of reinforcement. *Psychological Monographs*, 1966, *80* (Whole No. 609).

Schiffenbauer, A. Effect of observer's emotional state on judgments of the emotional state of others. *Journal of Personality and Social Psychology*, 1974, *30*, 31–35.

Schuman, H., & Johnson, M. P. Attitudes and behavior. *Annual Review of Sociology,* 1976, *2,* 161–207.

Smith, S. S., & Jamieson, B. D. Effects of attitude and egoinvolvement on the learning and retention of controversial material. *Journal of Personality and Social Psychology,* 1972, *22,* 303–310.

Snyder, M. The self-monitoring of expressive behavior. *Journal of Personality and Social Psychology,* 1974, *30,* 526–537.

Snyder, M. Self-monitoring processes. In L. Berkowitz (Ed.), *Advances in experimental social psychology* (Vol. 12). New York: Academic Press, 1979.

Snyder, M., & Tanke, E. D. Behavior and attitude: Some people are more consistent than others. *Journal of Personality,* 1976, *44,* 501–517.

Taft, R. Selective recall and memory distortion of favorable and unfavorable material. *Journal of Abnormal and Social Psychology,* 1954, *49,* 23–28.

Troldahl, V., & Powell, F. A short-form dogmatism scale for use in field studies. *Social Forces,* 1965, *44,* 211–214.

Tulving, E., & Pearlstone, Z. Availability versus accessibility of information in memory for words. *Journal of Verbal Learning and Verbal Behavior,* 1966, *5,* 381–391.

Waly, P., & Cook, S. W. Attitude as a determinant of learning and memory: A failure to confirm. *Journal of Personality and Social Psychology,* 1966, *4,* 280–288.

Watson, W. S., & Hartmann, G. W. The frigidity of a basic attitudinal frame. *Journal of Abnormal and Social Psychology,* 1939, *34,* 314–335.

Wicker, A. W. Attitudes versus actions: The relationship of verbal and overt behavioral responses to attitude objects. *Journal of Social Issues,* 1969, *25,* 41–78.

Zanna, M. P., & Aziza, C. On the interaction of repression-sensitization and attention in resolving cognitive dissonance. *Journal of Personality,* 1976, *44,* 577–593.

Zanna, M. P., & Cooper, J. Dissonance and the attribution process. In J. H. Harvey, W. J. Ickes, & R. B. Kidd (Eds.), *New directions in attribution research,* (Vol. 1). Hillsdale, N.J.: Lawrence Erlbaum Associates, 1976.

Zanna, M. P., Higgins, E. T., & Taves, P. A. Is dissonance phenomenologically aversive? *Journal of Experimental Social Psychology,* 1976, *12,* 530–538.

Zanna, M. P., Olson, J. M., & Fazio, R. H. Attitude-behavior consistency: An individual difference perspective. *Journal of Personality and Social Psychology,* 1980, *38,* 432–440.

Zanna, M. P., Olson, J. M., & Fazio, R. H. Self-perception and attitude-behavior consistency. *Personality and Social Psychology Bulletin,* 1981, *7,* 252–256.

5 When Believing Means Doing: Creating Links Between Attitudes and Behavior

Mark Snyder
University of Minnesota

There is an old saying—in fact, a very old saying—that "A superior man is ashamed if his words are better than his deeds." This bit of wisdom has been attributed to Confucius (circa 500 B.C.). Now, I don't know whether or not superior people really are ashamed when their words are better than their deeds. And, I don't know whether or not superior people (or, for that matter, not-so-superior people) ought to be ashamed when their words are better than their deeds. But I do know this: oftentimes people's words are better than their deeds. The fact of the matter is that the attitudes expressed by individuals when surveyed about their positions on social and personal issues are all too often not reflected in their actions in relevant life situations. Consider these rather telling examples.

When queried about their viewpoints, most people express rather positive attitudes toward good health and a long life; nevertheless, substantially fewer individuals translate these positive attitudes into actions (e.g., diet, exercise, checkups) that will produce good health and a long life. Similarly, support for protecting the environment and conserving energy is substantially more widespread at the level of attitudes than it is at the level of actions that fulfill these goals. And, as lobbyists who have worked the halls of state legislatures in search of votes for the ratification of the Equal Rights Amendment know, there exist substantial numbers of legislators who, in principle, claim to value and favor equal rights but who, in practice, will not support the Equal Rights Amendment.

Moreoever, not only do individuals' actions not always live up to the promises of their attitudes, but also there seem to be reasons to question the existence of any meaningful relations whatsoever between attitudes and behaviors. Despite the fact that theoretical statements (e.g., McGuire, 1969) on the nature of attitudes have stressed the links, both predictive and causal, between attitudes and behavior, empirical researchers all too frequently have found weak and inconsistent relations between the attitudes expressed by individuals and their actions in relevant life situations (for reviews, see Calder & Ross, 1973; Deutscher, 1973; Fishbein & Ajzen, 1975; Kiesler, Collins, & Miller, 1969; Wicker, 1969). Similarly, and again all too often, empirical investigators have been disappointed to find that hardwon changes in attitudes may not necessarily be translated into corresponding changes in behavior (e.g., Festinger, 1964). And, to complete the picture, the impact of behavioral experience on relevant underlying attitudes is often small and occasionally hard to detect (e.g., Collins, 1973).

Perhaps the lesson to be learned from the empirical search for pervasive consistencies between social behavior and underlying attitudes is a negative one. Long-standing assumptions to the contrary, there may be no necessary relations between private attitudes and public actions. It simply may be the case that knowing what people think and believe about social issues may have little or no utility for understanding what people actually say and do in relevant life situations. However, such a conclusion would be an overly pessimistic one. For, it appears that correspondence between attitudes and behavior is, in large measure, a question of "some individuals more than others" and "some situations more than others." Thus, searches for consistency between attitudes and behavior have been successful to the extent that they have identified accurately those individuals who characteristically display substantial correspondence between their attitudes and their behavior, and those situations within which marked congruence between attitude and actions typically is observed. This chapter is concerned with one program of research devoted to the identification of "those individuals" and "those situations," the exploration of the psychological processes by which attitudes are translated into corresponding actions by "those individuals" and in "those situations," and the articulation of guidelines for developing strategies for linking attitudes and behavior.

ATTITUDES AND BEHAVIOR: SOME INDIVIDUALS MORE THAN OTHERS

Who are those individuals who characteristically manifest substantial consistencies between their attitudes and their actions? One answer to this question is provided by theory and research on self-monitoring processes (e.g., Snyder, 1979b). According to the self-monitoring formulation, an individual in a social setting actively attempts to construct a pattern of social behavior appropriate to that particular context. Diverse sources of information are available to guide this choice, including (a) cues to situational or interpersonal specifications of appropriateness and (b) information about inner states, personal dispositions, and social attitudes.

Furthermore, according to the self-monitoring formulation, individuals differ in the extent to which they rely on either source of information. For those individuals who monitor or guide their behavioral choices on the basis of situational information (high self-monitoring individuals), the impact of situational and interpersonal cues to social appropriateness ought to be considerable. These individuals ought to demonstrate considerable situation-to-situation specificity in their social behavior. Moreover, for these high self-monitoring individuals, correspondence between behavior and attitude ought to be minimal. By contrast, persons who monitor or guide their behavioral choices on the basis of information from relevant inner states (low self-monitoring individuals) ought to be less responsive to situational and interpersonal specifications of behavioral appropriateness. Their social behavior ought to manifest substantial cross-situational consistency and temporal stability. Furthermore, for these low self-monitoring individuals, the covariation between behavior and attitude typically ought to be quite substantial.

Empirical evidence has provided documentation for these theoretical propositions (for reviews, see Snyder, 1979a, 1979b). Consider, specifically, the relation between self-monitoring and the links between attitudes and behavior. Individual differences in self-monitoring are measured by the Self-Monitoring Scale. Details of the psychometric construction of this instrument, as well as demonstrations of its convergent and discriminant validity, have all been presented elsewhere (Snyder, 1972, 1974).[1] In terms of the links between attitudes and behavior, the self-monitoring formulation suggests that high self-monitoring individuals are aware that what they say and do may not necessarily reflect what they think and feel. Specifically, they endorse such self-report Self-Monitoring Scale items as:

I sometimes appear to others to be experiencing deeper emotions than I actually am.

I am not always the person I appear to be.

I may deceive people by being friendly when I really dislike them, etc.

In contrast, low self-monitoring individuals report that their behavior is under the guidance of relevant dispositions, attitudes, and other internal states. They report that they value correspondence between who they think they are and what they try to do. They endorse such Self-Monitoring Scale items as:

My behavior is usually an expression of my true inner feelings, attitudes, and beliefs.

---

[1]For information on the internal structure of the Self-Monitoring Scale, see Briggs, Cheek and Buss (1980) and Gabrenya and Arkin (1980). For information on the independence of self-monitoring and other potentially related concepts, see Snyder (1974, 1979b).

I can only argue for ideas which I already believe, etc.

It follows that consistency between attitudes and behavior should be moderated by self-monitoring: low self-monitoring individuals should manifest substantially greater consistency than high self-monitoring individuals. A series of empirical investigations have documented the role of self-monitoring in determining the relation between measured attitudes and observed behavior.

In one typical investigation, Snyder and Swann (1976) examined the relation between measured attitudes toward affirmative action and verdicts 2 weeks later in a mock court case involving alleged sex discrimination. Attitudes were measured with a psychometrically reliable set of items designed to tap the cognitive, affective, and intentional components of general attitudes toward affirmative action. Two weeks later participants offered judicial judgments in the case of "Ms. C. A. Harrison vs. the University of Maine." As mock jurors, they read summary curriculae vitae for two biologists, Ms. C. A. Harrison and Mr. G. C. Sullivan, both of whom had applied to the University of Maine for a position as assistant professor of biology. The vitae described each applicant's training, honors, professional experience, and publications. The vitae presented different, but equally impressive, patterns of qualifications. One candidate held a Ph.D. from Harvard University; the other candidate, a Ph.D. from Yale University. One candidate had slightly more research experience than the other candidate, but the other candidate had more teaching experience. One candidate had more published reports of research, but the other candidate's fewer publications had been published in more prestigious journals.

The University of Maine appointed Mr. Sullivan to the position. Ms. Harrison filed suit. She insisted that this decision reflected a bias against females. All jurors then considered the arguments advanced in court on behalf of the plaintiff (Ms. Harrison) and on behalf of the defendant (The University of Maine). The case for the female plaintiff emphasized not only Ms. Harrison's outstanding pattern of qualifications for a professorial appointment, but also the fact that the faculty of the University of Maine was 65% male and that the University of Maine was far behind the schedule that it had set to equalize the faculty sex ratio. The case for the defense emphasized that decisions concerning the appointments and promotion of faculty were too subjective to be realistically evaluated in court. Moreover, the defense stressed the fact that the University had made significant strides toward attaining equal representation of males and females within the faculty, and that the University was progressing toward the goal of equal employment opportunity at an above-average rate.

Jurors were charged with studying both sides of the case, weighing all of the evidence, and reaching a verdict in the court case. After reaching their verdicts, the jurors communicated them in written essays explaining their behavioral decisions. From these "essay verdicts", raters assessed the favorability toward Ms. Harrison, the female plaintiff, of each juror's judicial decision-making behavior.

What was the relation between general attitudes toward affirmative action and verdicts in the specific sex discrimination court case? Overall, for all participants, the correspondence between initial attitudes and judgment behavior was, at best, modest ($r = .22$). However, when the relation between attitudes and behavior was considered separately for high self-monitoring (that is, individuals with scores above the median on the Self-Monitoring Scale), and low self-monitoring individuals (that is, individuals with scores below the median on the Self-Monitoring Scale), the following pattern emerged. Covariation between attitude and behavior was considerably larger for low self-monitoring individuals ($r = .42$) than for high self-monitoring individuals ($r = .03$). Evidently, it is possible to identify those individuals (i.e., low self-monitoring individuals) for whom correspondence between attitudes and behavior is substantial and those individuals (e.g., high self-monitoring individuals) for whom correspondence between attitudes and behavior is minimal.

Not only is it possible to predict accurately the future behavior of low self-monitoring individuals from measures of their present attitudes, but also it is possible to forecast the attitudes that they will express in the future from knowledge of their current actions (e.g., Snyder & Tanke, 1976). However, there may be costs associated with the low self-monitoring individuals' concern that their behavior accurately reflect their personal attitudes. When low self-monitoring individuals are induced to engage freely in behaviors that are discrepant from their attitudes (in the classic forced compliance situation familiar to dissonance researchers), they are particularly likely to accept their counterattitudinal behavior as representative of their true attitudes (Snyder & Tanke, 1976). By contrast, high self-monitoring individuals, who regard what they do and what they believe as not necessarily equivalent, are relatively unaffected by their attitude-discrepant behavior. Their private attitudes tend to remain stable despite changes in their public behavior.

Evidently, when it comes to correspondence between the private realities of beliefs and attitudes and the public realities of words and deeds, low self-monitoring individuals do seem to display substantial consistency between their private attitudes and their public actions (for other demonstrations of the contributions of self-monitoring to covariation between measured attitudes and intentions and observed behaviors and actions, see Ajzen, Timko, & White, in press; Becherer & Richard, 1978; Lutsky, Woodworth, & Clayton, 1980; Zanna, Olson, & Fazio, 1980; Zuckerman & Reis, 1978). Moreover, self-monitoring is not the only moderator variable that has proven its utility for determining the predictive relationship between attitudes and action. Within the domain of altruism, Schwartz (1973) has found that measures of personal norms could only be used to successfully predict volunteering behavior for those individuals who claimed personal responsibility for their actions. Similarly, Norman (1975) could only predict volunteering behavior from previous measures of attitudes for individuals with consistent affective and cognitive components of the relevant attitudes. Finally, there are indications that individuals who are highly self-con-scious are more likely to manifest consistency between attitudes and behavior than are individuals low in self-consciousness (e.g., Scheier, Buss, & Buss, 1978). In each case, the message seems to be the same one: Attempts to docu-ment consistency between attitudes and actions have been successful to the extent that they have identified those classes of individuals who characteristically manifest such consistencies.

ATTITUDES AND BEHAVIOR:
SOME SITUATIONS MORE THAN OTHERS

Just as it is the case that individuals differ meaningfully in the propensity to engage in attitude-guided behaviors, so too do social settings and interaction contexts differ in the extent to which they include individuals to use relevant attitudes as guides to action. That is, some situations more than others promote a "believing means doing" orientation. And, it is in such situations that substan-tial correspondence between attitudes and actions is to be found.

In one attempt to create an environment that would promote such a "believing means doing" orientation and in which actions would meaningfully reflect atti-tudes, Snyder and Swann (1976) constructed a social situation in which indi-viduals, faced with an opportunity to engage in activities that might or might not reflect underlying attitudes, were encouraged to reflect upon attitudes of poten-tial applicability to their current situations before embarking on any course of action. The theory behind this procedure was a simple one: If individuals would only think before they acted, they might take their attitudes into account when choosing their actions.

To create this "thinking person's environment," Snyder and Swann (1976) had students participate, as mock jurors, in a judicial decision-making task in which they prepared written communications about their judgments of liability in a sex discrimination court case in anticipation of discussing their verdicts with another individual. The court case was, once again, that of "Ms. C. A. Harrison vs. the University of Maine," the details of which have already been described. Some mock jurors were encouraged to think over, reflect upon, and privately articulate their general attitudes toward affirmative action before considering the specific court case. To help them organize their thoughts and views on the issue of affirmative action, these mock jurors were encourged to mull over their personal answers to the questions: "Is it important to you that everyone be given equal opportunity in obtaining employment?" "Should women and minorities be actively recruited to help equalize employment ratios?" "Is it a good idea to have men and women equally represented in employment?" "If you were an employer, how would you feel about regulations specifying how many women and minorities to hire?" These "thought catalysts" were designed to encourage participants to consider privately and to articulate their general attitudes toward the policies and procedures of affirmative action and the behavioral implications of their attitudes.

In this "thinking person's environment," mock jurors offered judicial verdicts that reflected, communicated, and embodied their general attitudes toward affirmative action: Covariation between the favorability of their judicial judgments toward Ms. Harrison, the female plaintiff, and their attitudes toward affirmative action that had been measured 2 weeks before participation in the judicial decision-making task was substantial ($r = .58$). By contrast, the judicial verdicts of mock jurors who were given no opportunity to reflect upon their attitudes before considering the court case were virtually independent of their previously stated attitudes ($r = .07$).

Clearly, then, the "thinking person's environment," in which individuals were encouraged to adopt a contemplative orientation to choosing a course of action, generated substantial correspondence between attitudes and actions. Moreover, the "thinking person's environment" is not the only environment that is known to promote correspondence between attitudes and behavior. In particular, there are numerous demonstrations of the power of environments that induce the state of objective self-awareness to generate marked covariation between measured attitudes and actual behavior (e.g., Carver, 1975; Gibbons, 1978; Pryor, Gibbons, Wicklund, Fazio, & Hood, 1977; Wicklund, 1975, this volume). And, in environments that encourage individuals to form their attitudes on the basis of direct behavioral experience, consistency between these attitudes and subsequent behaviors typically is quite substantial (e.g., Fazio & Zanna, 1978, 1981; Regan & Fazio, 1977; Zanna & Fazio, 1977). In each case, the message seems to be the same one: Searches for manifestations of meaningful correspondence between attitudes and subsequent behaviors have been successful to the extent that they have identified those situations and environments within which marked congruence between attitudes and actions typically is generated.

THE ORIGINS OF CORRESPONDENCE: THE AVAILABILITY PRINCIPLE AND THE RELEVANCE PRINCIPLE

This, then, appears to be the lesson to be learned from the long and arduous empirical search for evidence of a meaningful relation between attitudes and behavior. There may not exist pervasive consistencies between actions in life situations and underlying attitudes, but there do exist some individuals who characteristically manifest such consistencies and some situations within which such consistencies typically are to be found.

In light of the evident success of attempts to define the "who" and the "where" of the relation between attitudes and behavior, the time has come to pose questions about the "how" and the "why" of correspondence between attitudes and behavior. What are the psychological processes that join attitudes to behavior? When individuals have opportunities to engage in activities that might or might not reflect underlying attitudes, what are the psychological requirements that must be fulfilled before general attitudes will be faithfully translated into specific actions? How, for example, are these psychological requirements fulfilled by low self-monitoring individuals, who typically display substantial congruence between their attitudes and their actions? How, for example, are these psychological requirements fulfilled by the thinking person's environment, which generated substantial correspondence between attitudes and behavior?

From theoretical attempts to answer these questions, there have emerged two principles, the availability principle and the relevance principle, each of which has the potential to account for the origins of correspondence between attitudes and behavior (Snyder, 1977). Consider, first, these two theoretical principles and, then, the empirical evidence of their contributions to the creation of links between attitudes and behavior.

The Availability Principle

It has been said, by the poet R. W. Emerson, that "Thought is the seed of action" (1885, p. 42). If so, it may be the case that, before an individual can use attitudes as guides to action, he or she must know his or her attitudes and the behavioral implications of those viewpoints. That is, knowledge of one's general attitudinal orientation must be available to the individual before that individual can use attitudes as guides to action.

This apparent necessity notwithstanding, all too often attitudes simply may not be available to serve as guides to action. To the extent that individuals are confronted with the demands of coping with their immediate situations, with all of the situations' attendant social and interpersonal pressures impinging on them, individuals may have little psychological time and/or energy to devote to any attempts to determine whether they possess any general attitudes of potential application to the specific behavioral choices that confront them. Even individuals who do make an effort to define general attitudinal domains applicable to their particular situations may yet encounter difficulty in deriving clear behavioral implications from those viewpoints. For, as individuals think through their beliefs, feelings, and intentions within an attitudinal domain, they may be dismayed to discover structural inconsistencies among the cognitive, affective, and intentional components of that attitude. And, these structural inconsistencies may pull them in different behavioral directions.

Any and all of these outcomes may contribute to deficits in the availability of knowledge of general attitudes and the specific behavioral implications of those viewpoints. And, in the absence of such knowledge, attitudes simply are not available to serve as potentially useful guides to action. After all, only individuals who know what they believe and who know the implications of "what they believe" for "what they do" are in a position to put their beliefs into practice.

From these theoretical considerations of the availability principle emerges this strategy for bridging the gap between attitude and behavior: To the extent that deficits in availability prevent attitudes from serving as guides to action, then it follows that any circumstances that increase the availability of knowledge of one's general attitudes and the specific behavioral implications of one's viewpoints ought to promote correspondence between attitude and behavior.[2] Thus, from the perspective of the availability principle, low self-monitoring individuals may be more likely than high self-monitoring individuals to act upon their attitudes because attitudes of low self-monitoring individuals typically may be more available as potential guides to action than those of high self-monitoring individuals. Furthermore, with reference to the "thinking person's environment", these considerations of the availability principle suggest that the activities of contemplating one's general attitudes before choosing one's specific actions may have succeeded in promoting substantial correspondence between attitudes and behavior because these activities increased the availability of attitudes to serve as guides to action.

The Relevance Principle

Just as it is the case that deficits in availability of attitudes may contribute to lack of correspondence between attitudes and behavior, so too may deficits in the relevance of attitudes as guides to action create gaps between attitude and behavior. It has been said, by the British poet and essayist W. S. Landor, that "We talk on principle, but we act on interest" (1883, p. 511). If this observation of human nature is a valid one, individuals can be expected to act upon their attitudes only when it is in their interests to act upon their attitudes. That is, before one can act upon one's attitudes, one must define one's attitudes as relevant and appropriate guides to the behavioral choices at hand.

Yet, individuals need not, and often do not, define their attitudes as necessarily relevant to their actions. For a variety of pragmatic reasons, individuals may choose to define situational and interpersonal specifications of behavioral

---

[2]It should be clear to the reader that, in the use of the terms "available" and "availability," no reference is made to the use of the term "availability" to describe a heuristic for estimating frequency: Events that are easy to bring to mind are thought to occur with greater frequency than are events that are difficult to bring to mind. Rather, in the use of the terms "available" and "availability," reference is made only to their dictionary definitions: something that is available is of potential use. Accordingly, when knowledge of an attitude is in a form that is of potential use for guiding one's actions, that knowledge of that attitude may be said to be available.

appropriateness as the relevant guidelines for their actions. If there is one message that comes through loud and clear from generations of research in social psychology, that message is the power of situational forces to influence social behavior. Peer group pressures, reference group norms, role requirements, incentives and sanctions may singly and together appear to be impossible to ignore. Accordingly, it may be these situational guidelines to action that individuals define as relevant to their behavioral choices. And, as often as not, these situational influences may dispose actions that contradict the dictates of one's attitudes. Accordingly, as a consequence of molding their actions to the prescriptions of such situational forces, individuals' actions often may be clearer reflections of their current situations than of their enduring attitudes.

From this perspective, it may be only when individuals explicitly define their attitudes as relevant and appropriate guides to action that they can be expected to turn to their general attitudinal orientations for guidance in making their behavioral choices. Only when individuals have adopted such a "believing means doing" orientation can they be expected to strive for congruence between their attitudes and their actions in life situations.

From these considerations of the relevance principle emerges this strategy for linking attitudes and behavior: To the extent that deficits in the relevance of attitudes account for lack of correspondence between attitude and behavior, then it follows that any circumstances that increase the relevance of attitudes as guides to action ought to enhance correspondence between an individual's general attitudes and his or her specific actions. Thus, from the perspective of the relevance principle, low self-monitoring individuals may be more likely than high self-monitoring individuals to act upon their attitudes because low self-monitoring individuals typically may regard their attitudes as more relevant guides to action than do high self-monitoring individuals. Furthermore, with reference to the "thinking person's environment," these considerations of the relevance principle suggest that the activities of contemplating one's general attitudes before choosing one's specific actions may have succeeded in promoting substantial correspondence between attitudes and behavior because these activities increased the relevance of attitudes as potential guides to action.

The Contributions of Availability and Relevance

What are the contributions of availability and relevance to the translation of attitudes into behavior? In answering this question, one must resist the temptation to pit availability against relevance in any competitive attempt to determine which principle provides the better account of the origins of correspondence between attitude and behavior. Rather, one ought first to document empirically the involvement of availability and relevance in the generation of correspondence between attitude and behavior, and only then consider, from a theoretical standpoint, the utility of conceptualizing the links between attitudes and behavior in terms of either the availability principle or the relevance principle.

To observe availability and relevance in action, Snyder and Kendzierski (1982) created three experimental situations: (1) a situation that made attitudes neither available nor relevant as potential guides to action, (2) a situation that increased the availability of general attitudes as potential guides to action, and (3) a situation that increased the relevance of general attitudes as potential guides to action. In these experimental situations, Snyder and Kendzierski (1982) examined the extent to which low self-monitoring individuals and high self-monitoring individuals manifested correspondence between their attitudes and their actions.[3]

For their purposes, Snyder and Kendzierski (1982) examined the relationship between general attitudes toward the issue of affirmative action and the behavioral verdicts that individuals subsequently offered (2 weeks later) in the now familiar court case of "Ms. C. A. Harrison vs. the University of Maine," an affirmative action lawsuit in which the female plaintiff, Ms. C. A. Harrison, alleged that she had been a victim of sex discrimination in hiring after the defendant, the University of Maine, had denied her an appointment to their faculty. Accordingly, the Basic Courtroom situation provided an opportunity for individuals to engage in specific activities (here, their judicial decision-making behaviors) that might reflect, to greater or lesser degree, potentially applicable underlying general attitudes (here, their attitudes toward affirmative action).

What was the relation between attitudes toward affirmative action and verdicts in the court case? In this Basic Courtroom situation, the correspondence between initial attitudes and judicial decision-making behavior was minimal ($r = .08$), both for low self-monitoring individuals and for high self-monitoring individuals. Knowing what jurors thought and felt about the issue of affirmative action had virtually no utility for predicting their actions in the courtroom.

Why was correspondence between attitudes and behavioral minimal in the Basic Courtroom? The structural features of court cases typically focus jurors' activities on the weighing of evidence presented by attorneys for the plaintiff and by attorneys for the defendant in an effort to decide the relative merits of the arguments advanced by each side. Thus, courtroom situations inherently provide little opportunity for individuals to reflect on their general attitudes in the context of their judicial activities. Moreover, courtroom situations inherently provide little opportunity for jurors to define their personal attitudes as relevant guides to reaching their verdicts. From this perspective, the Basic Courtroom neither made attitudes toward affirmative action available to serve as potential guides to action; nor did the Basic Courtroom encourage jurors to define their attitudes as relevant guides for reaching their verdicts. And, in the absence of availability and in the absence of relevance, correspondence between attitudes and behavior

---

[3]Essentially, this investigation employs a 3 (experimental situations) $\times$ 2 (self-monitoring classifications) factorial design in which the dependent variable is the correlation between attitudes and behavior in each of the six cells of the factorial design. For details of the appropriate statistical analysis, see Snyder and Kendzierski (1982).

ought to have been minimal—and, as we have seen, was decidedly minimal—in the Basic Courtroom.

Into this Basic Courtroom situation, Snyder and Kendzierski (1982) injected structural features designed to create two new courtroom situations: one that increased the availability of attitudes, and another that increased the relevance of attitudes. They then examined the ability of these features to overcome the inherent attributes of courtroom situations that generate minimal correspondence between attitudes and behavior. And, indeed, despite the inherent impediments to correspondence between attitudes and behavior that characterize courtroom situations, it was possible to witness substantially and reliably increased covariation between general attitudes toward affirmative action and specific verdicts in the court case. And these substantial increments in predictability occurred in circumstances that proved themselves to be most revealing about the psychological processes by which attitudes are translated into action.

The Attitude Available Courtroom.   According to the strategy derived from the availability principle, to the extent that one increases the availability of knowledge of applicable general attitudes, one ought to promote correspondence between attitudes and behavior. Therefore, to increase the availability of potentially applicable attitudes, Snyder and Kendzierski (1982) created the Attitude Available Courtroom. In the Attitude Available Courtroom, they provided jurors with an opportunity to think over, reflect upon, and privately articulate their general attitudes toward the policies and procedures of affirmative action before considering the specific court case. These jurors thus had an opportunity to bring to mind the general attitudinal domain of potential applicability to the court case, to think through their beliefs, feelings, and intentions within that attitudinal domain, discover and resolve any structural inconsistencies among the components of that attitude, and to define the behavioral implications of their general attitudes.

For some individuals, the reflective and contemplative activities of the availability strategy were sufficient to generate substantial correspondence between the favorability toward the female plaintiff of their verdicts and their general attitudes toward affirmative action. For low self-monitoring individuals, the correlation between attitudes and behavior in this situation was substantial ($r = .47$). By contrast, for high self-monitoring individuals, the correlation between attitudes and behavior remained minimal ($r = .18$).

Why was the availability strategy sufficient to generate marked correspondence between attitudes and behavior for low self-monitoring individuals? One set of answers is to be found in the conceptions of self that characterize low self-monitoring individuals (e.g., Snyder, 1979b; Snyder & Campbell, 1982). Low self-monitoring individuals regard themselves as rather principled beings who value congruence between the private realities of their self-conceptions and the public realities of their words and deeds. These individuals are the ones among us who claim to believe that their actions should be true and accurate reflections of their attitudes. These individuals are the ones among us who profess to value consistency between what they believe and what they do. These individuals are the ones among us who proclaim (with their responses to items on the Self-Monitoring Scale) that "My behavior is usually an expression of my true inner feelings, attitudes, and beliefs" and "I can only argue for ideas which I already believe." Accordingly, for low self-monitoring individuals, the presence of available knowledge of their attitudes ought to be sufficient to induce them to adopt, on their own, a "believing means doing" orientation that ought then, in turn, to produce correspondence between their attitudes and their actions. And, indeed, in the Attitude Available Courtroom, believing meant doing: Their verdicts in the court case did embody their attitudes toward affirmative action.

By contrast, high self-monitoring individuals regard themselves as somewhat more pragmatic creatures (e.g., Snyder, 1979b). These individuals are both willing and able to mold and tailor their self-presentations to fit situational and interpersonal specifications of behavioral appropriateness (e.g., Lippa, 1976; Snyder & Monson, 1975). They claim that these impression management activities may create gaps and contradictions between their attitudes and their behaviors. They report (in their responses to items on the Self-Monitoring Scale) that "I sometimes appear to others to be experiencing deeper emotions than I actually am," "I'm not always the person I appear to be," "I may deceive people by being friendly when I really dislike them." For these high self-monitoring individuals, who claim what they do and what they believe may not be the same thing, available knowledge of attitudes may not be sufficient—and, in the Attitude Available Courtroom, certainly was not sufficient—to guarantee correspondence between attitudes and behavior.

The Attitude Relevant Courtroom. According to the strategy derived from the relevance principle, to the extent that one increases the relevance of attitudes as guides to action, one ought to promote correspondence between attitudes and behavior. One type of situation that ought to promote such a "believing means doing" orientation is the one that induces individuals to adopt an "advocacy" role. When individuals regard their actions as instrumental in promoting the wider acceptance of their attitudes and in creating worlds compatible with their attitudes, they ought to be studiously attentive to the links between their attitudes and their actions. Thus, for example, when individuals with positive attitudes toward affirmative action adopt advocacy roles, they may seek every opportunity to say or do things that reflect and communicate their positive attitudes, to attempt to influence others, to share their positive attitudes, and to try to promote the development of affirmative action programs.

Accordingly, to induce individuals to define attitudes as behaviorally relevant and situationally appropriate guides to action, Snyder and Kendzierski (1982) created the Attitude Relevant Courtroom. In the Attitude Relevant Courtroom, they provided jurors with an opportunity to adopt an advocacy role in the courtroom. Specifically, the judge's charge to the jury reminded jurors of the precedent-setting nature of courtroom decisions: What jurors decided in this specific court case might help determine how other court cases may be decided. Implicit in the judge's charge was the inference that, with their verdicts in the court case, jurors in the Attitude Relevant Courtroom potentially could influence the fate of affirmative action policies and programs.

In these circumstances, in the presence of an advocacy orientation to reaching one's judicial decisions, believing meant doing. For all individuals—both high self-monitoring individuals and low self-monitoring individuals—in the Attitude Relevant Courtroom, covariation between verdicts in the specific court case and general attitudes toward affirmative action measured 2 weeks before entering the courtroom was substantial ($r = .51$).

What accounts for the effects of the relevance strategy? For low self-monitoring individuals, the relevance strategy may have affirmed, supported, and encouraged their characteristic inclinations to strive for congruence between their attitudes and their actions. And, in accord with these characteristic inclinations, they translated their attitudes toward affirmative action into corresponding verdicts in the sex discrimination court case. But why was the Relevance Strategy so effective for high self-monitoring individuals, who do not share their low self-monitoring counterparts' faith in the intrinsic value of consistency between attitudes and behavior? Perhaps, for high self-monitoring individuals, the relevance strategy effectively placed them in a situation that called for public self-presentations that reflected private attitudes. Accordingly, high self-monitoring individuals, who pride themselves on being creatures of their situations, proceeded to tailor their self-presentations to their situations. And, in the Attitude Relevant Courtroom, being creatures of their situations required them to adopt a "believing means doing" orientation. Indeed, high self-monitoring individuals in the Attitude Relevant Courtroom effectively carried out the mandate of this "believing means doing" orientation by offering judicial verdicts that embodied their own general attitudes toward affirmative action.

It appears, then, that relevance functions as a sufficient requirement to generate correspondence between attitudes and behavior both for low self-monitoring individuals and for high self-monitoring individuals. By contrast, availability was sufficient only for low self-monitoring individuals. Moreover, there are reasons to believe that relevance actually may subsume availability. When one regards attitudes as relevant guides to choosing one's behavioral choices, one must be knowledgeable about one's attitudes before one can use those attitudes to guide one's actions. Accordingly, increasing the relevance of attitudes as guides to action may induce individuals on their own to increase the availability of their attitudes to serve as guides to action.

If indeed, relevance itself may generate availability, then any procedures that increase both the relevance and the availability of attitudes should produce amounts of observed correspondence between attitude and behavior that are not detectably different from the amounts of correspondence produced by the strategy of increasing only the relevance of attitudes. As a test of this derivation, Snyder and Kendzierski (1982) had jurors in an Attitude Available and Attitude Relevant Courtroom not only contemplate their attitudes toward affirmative action (the same procedure that they used in the Attitude Available Courtroom) before encountering the court case, but also think through the implications of their verdicts (the same procedure that they used in the Attitude Relevant Courtroom) before reaching their judicial decisions. Not only was the observed correspondence between attitude and behavior substantial both for low self-monitoring individuals ($r = .42$) and for high self-monitoring individuals ($r = .44$), but also the correspondence between attitude and behavior observed in this Attitude Available and Attitude Relevant Courtroom was not detectably different from that observed in the Attitude Relevant Courtroom.

Evidently, the procedures that increase both relevance and availability produce outcomes no different from those produced by a procedure that increases only the relevance of attitudes. Presumably, then, the strategy of increasing the relevance of attitudes is sufficient to generate correspondence between attitudes and behavior because it induces individuals on their own to make potentially applicable attitudes available to serve as relevant guides to action, and the resultant presence of both relevance and availability then may set the stage for the translation of attitudes into corresponding behaviors.

From this perspective, although both availability and relevance may be necessary requirements for generating correspondence between attitudes and behavior, relevance itself—because it subsumes availability—may function as a sufficient requirement. Furthermore, from this perspective, those types of individuals (e.g., low self-monitoring individuals) who characteristically manifest substantial correspondence between their attitudes and their behavior may do so because they characteristically define their attitudes as necessarily relevant guides for choosing their actions. Similarly, those types of situations (e.g., the "thinking person's environment") that generate substantial correspondence between attitudes and behaviors may do so because they induce individuals in those situations to define their attitudes as situationally relevant guides to action.

TO THE PRACTITIONER: STRATEGIES FOR LINKING OTHER INDIVIDUALS' ATTITUDES AND BEHAVIOR

Frequently, practitioners of the techniques of social influence seek to design successful strategic programs to encourage other individuals to translate their existing attitudes into actions. Indeed, the same gaps that can and do exist between believing and doing that have prompted researchers to seek greater understanding of the links between attitudes and behavior often prompt practitioners to seek means of bridging those gaps. For it is those cases when individuals who obviously possess favorable attitudes but who equally obviously don't live up to the favorable promise of their attitudes that motivate efforts to encourage those individuals to behave in accord with their attitudes. Consider again the examples—those of health care, the environment, and equal rights—with which this chapter began.

Advocates of preventive health care programs often define their goal not so much in terms of encouraging individuals to have positive attitudes toward good health and a long life, but rather in terms of inducing individuals to translate those positive attitudes into a regimen of specific activities (e.g., diet, exercise, checkups) that will produce good health and a long life. Proponents of the protection of the environment and the conservation of energy frequently target their efforts on those large numbers of individuals with favorable attitudes who have yet to act upon those favorable attitudes. And, lobbyists who have worked the halls of state legislatures in search of votes for the ratification of the Equal Rights Amendment often find that their toughest customers are the ones who claim to value equal rights but still will not vote for the Equal Rights Amendment ("I'm for equal rights; I'm just not for the ERA").

How are practitioners of social influence to induce individuals to live up to the behavioral implications of their existing attitudes? What words of advice might be offered to those practitioners concerned with bridging the gap from attitudes to behavior? What, specifically, would be the assets and liabilities of designing programs that incorporate the defining characteristics of the availability strategy and the relevance strategy? Consider the case of the lobbyist for the Equal Rights Amendment.

The Potential of the Availability Strategy

As a strategy for enforcing correspondence between attitudes and behavior, the availability strategy was a successful strategy only for some people; specifically, only for low self-monitoring individuals. Perhaps the source of the limited effectiveness of the availability strategy lies in its rather indirect approach. The availability strategy, limiting itself as it does to essentially cognitive tactics, provides the individual with the necessary knowledge of attitudes, but relies on the individual himself or herself to supply the necessary motivational linkage between that knowledge and his or her actions. However, it is only the low self-monitoring individuals of this world who feel any necessary obligation to supply this linkage: Only low self-monitoring individuals characteristically regard available knowledge of attitudes as behaviorally relevant knowledge. For these reasons, I would hesitate to recommend the widespread application of the availability strategy. Thus, for example, I would not advise the lobbyist who seeks to induce legislators who value equal rights to vote for ratification of the Equal

Rights Amendment to pursue a strategy of encouraging these legislators to contemplate their attitudes toward equal rights before voting. Such a strategy would, at best, be effective only for low self-monitoring legislators.

The Potential of the Relevance Strategy

By contrast, the relevance strategy was an effective strategy for enforcing correspondence between attitude and behavior for all individuals, both for low self-monitoring individuals and for high self-monitoring individuals. The source of the particular effectiveness of the relevance strategy may be found, perhaps, in the fact that this strategy concentrates its effects directly on the forging of a link between general attitudes and specific behaviors—a link that endows attitudes with necessary implications for action. That is, the Relevance Strategy is a fundamentally motivational strategy that provides individuals with a "believing means doing" *action structure* (cf. Snyder, 1977) for linking their attitudes to their behaviors. An action structure essentially is a set of instructional rules (or, if you will, a "plan" or a "script") that directs individuals to use general attitudes of relevance to their current situation as guidelines for enacting specific behaviors that accurately reflect those relevant general attitudes. An action structure essentially mandates individuals to ask themselves the question "What course of action do my attitudes suggest that I pursue in this situation?" and then to instruct themselves "If that is what my attitudes say that I should do, then that is what I must do" (for a highly related analysis, see Abelson, 1972).

For these reasons, I would enthusiastically recommend the relevance strategy to those practitioners of the techniques of social influence who seek to design successful programs to encourage individuals to translate their existing attitudes into actions that meaningfully reflect those attitudes. Thus, to the lobbyist who solicits votes for the ratification of the Equal Rights Amendment, the following advice is offered: Attitudes will be translated into behavior only when attitudes and behavior are linked by a "believing means doing" action structure that endows attitudes with necessary implications for behavior. The lobbyist must focus his or her efforts on creating and solidifying links between attitudes and behavior. The lobbyist must persuade legislators that they possess their favorable attitudes toward equal rights only to the extent that they translate these attitudes into relevant action. The lobbyist must persuade legislators that it is not enough to talk as if they value equal rights; rather, they also must act as if they value equal rights.

The Relevance Strategy in Action

How effectively may the relevance strategy be used to induce other individuals to translate their existing attitudes into corresponding behaviors? To document the effectiveness of the relevance strategy to induce individuals to perform the "good" deeds implied by their "good" attitudes, Snyder and Kendzierski (1982) chose a particularly demanding situation, one that would provide little or no incentive to individuals for acting on their potentially applicable attitudes. Individuals were asked to volunteer for a time-consuming and inconvenient activity in return for next to no tangible reward, possibly save the knowledge that they were acting in accord with their attitudes. The sacrifice of time and the involvement of effort mirrored the sacrifice and the involvement that are required in many everyday situations in which acting in a manner congruent with one's attitudes is both time-consuming and effortful. Consider, for example, the acts of volunteering to give blood or to collect donations for a charity. In each case, the individual with attitudes favorable to the "cause" must forego other, definitely more habitual and perhaps more rewarding, activities in order to help other people who essentially are strangers. Furthermore, the pressures against volunteering may be compounded by the realizations not only that few people ever will know or even will care about whether or not one volunteered but also that the job probably will get done by someone else if one chooses not to volunteer. These and other considerations of time and effort may singly and together prompt the potential volunteer to ignore whatever favorable attitudes might dispose him or her to volunteer. Accordingly, the "volunteering" situation contains many features and pressures that work against the translation of favorable attitudes into corresponding actions. It is thus an excellent situation within which to examine the effectiveness of the relevance strategy for creating links between attitudes and behavior.

In their investigation, Snyder and Kendzierski (1982) provided individuals with favorable attitudes toward psychological research an opportunity to act upon these attitudes and to volunteer to participate in extra sessions of a psychology experiment. This request was a particularly demanding one. Participants were asked to return for two additional one-hour sessions on two different days for the meager compensation of a total of only $1.50 when the "going rate" was at least $3 per hour. Furthermore, to avoid pressuring participants into volunteering, the actual request for volunteers was not delivered personally by the experimenter; rather, it appeared in a notice posted on a wall in a waiting room. So demanding was this request that, on its own, it attracted very few volunteers. To be precise, only 25% of individuals who were exposed to this request (all of whom were known to have favorable attitudes toward psychological research) were willing to volunteer for extra sessions of the psychology experiment.

Could a relevance strategy induce individuals to translate their favorable attitudes toward psychological research into participation in extra sessions? To document the effectiveness of the relevance strategy in action, Snyder and Kendzierski (1982) arranged for some individuals, who were to be the targets of the relevance strategy, to encounter the same request for volunteers, only for them the request was accompanied by procedures designed to increase the relevance of their favorable attitudes toward psychological research as potential guidelines for deciding whether or not to accept the request to volunteer for extra sessions of the psychology experiment.

Specifically, the targets of the relevance strategy were individuals who had agreed to participate in an experiment on interviewing processes. When they arrived, one at a time, at a waiting room, they encountered two other individuals who were, in actuality, confederates of the investigators. Shortly after the target individual had arrived, one of these confederates stood up and read the notice, posted on the wall, that solicited volunteers to return for extra sessions of the psychology experiment. After reading the notice, one confederate turned to the other confederate and said "I don't know if I should volunteer or if I shouldn't volunteer. What do you think?" The second confederate then replied offhand-edly "Well, I guess that whether you do or whether you don't is really a question of how worthwhile you think experiments are."

This conversation was designed to encourage, by example, the target individual to define attitudes toward psychological research as being relevant guides to action in this situation. At the same time, this conversation was designed to provide no direct pressure on the target individual to volunteer or not to volunteer. Toward this end, the confederates offered their comments in as neutral a tone as possible. Thus, nothing in the confederates' expressive behavior could have been interpreted as an indication of the confederates' own desires to see other people volunteer or not volunteer. Moreover, both confederates fully expected that some target individuals would choose to volunteer and that other target individuals would choose not to volunteer, supposedly as a function of an undisclosed personality variable under investigation. Accordingly, confederates did not view the decisions of target individuals to volunteer or not to volunteer as indicators of their own effectiveness in the roles of confederates. Finally, neither confederate ever expressed to the target individual any interest in this or her intentions about volunteering or not volunteering. Therefore, confederates had no opportunity to directly encourage the target individuals to volunteer or not to volunteer. After the confederates had together implemented the relevance strategy by means of their conversation, the target individual and both confederates filled out forms on which they indicated whether or not they would volunteer for the extra experimental sessions.

Was the strategy of increasing the relevance of potentially applicable attitudes an effective strategy for generating correspondence between attitudes and behavior? Did the relevance strategy provide target individuals with an action structure for effectively bridging the gap between attitudes and behavior? Indeed, in this investigation, the relevance strategy demonstrated its effectiveness in a particularly demanding set of circumstances. Despite the fact that volunteering to participate in extra sessions of the psychology experiment would be very time consuming, highly inconvenient, and minimally lucrative, the relevance strategy nevertheless succeeded in inducing a clear majority (fully 60%) of individuals to translate their favorable attitudes toward psychological research into actions that meaningfully reflected these favorable attitudes. When one recalls that the request for volunteers for extra sessions of the psychology experiment, when it was not accompanied by any strategic procedures designed to increase the relevance of attitudes toward psychological research, on its own managed to induce very few individuals (only 25%) to commit the time and effort necessary to act upon their favorable attitudes toward psychological research, the effectiveness of the relevance strategy becomes all the more impressive.[4] Moreover, the relevance strategy was an effective strategy both for low self-monitoring individuals and for high self-monitoring individuals.

Evidently, at least when it comes to favorable attitudes toward psychological research, the relevance strategy effectively persuaded individuals that "believing means doing." That is, the relevance strategy effectively provided individuals with an action structure for linking their attitudes and their behavior. For other demonstrations that reinforce these assertions about the effectiveness of relevance-based strategies, see McArthur, Kiesler and Cook (1969) and Kiesler, Nisbett and Zanna (1969). Clearly, then, the outcomes of this investigation of the relevance strategy in action reinforce and bolster the advice to those practitioners of the techniques of social influence who seek strategies to encourage other individuals to bridge the gaps between their attitudes and their actions: concentrate your efforts on creating and/or solidifying links between attitudes and behavior by persuading individuals to define their attitudes as the relevant guides for action; only when attitudes and behavior are linked by an action structure that endows attitudes with necessary implications for behavior will individuals translate their existing attitudes into actions that meaningfully embody those attitudes.

TO THE INDIVIDUAL:
STRATEGIES FOR LINKING ONE'S OWN
ATTITUDES AND ONE'S OWN BEHAVIOR

Of course, the foregoing words of advice are directed at those practitioners who seek to encourage *other people* to bridge the gap between attitudes and behavior. What about some words of advice for those individuals who seek to translate *their own* attitudes into actions that meaningfully reflect their attitudes? The time has come to consider strategies by which individuals may create, promote, and enforce correspondence between their own attitudes and their own behavior.

Consider the case of an individual who possesses a variety of liberal attitudes on social and political issues. Suppose, further, that this individual desires to live

---

[4]In this comparison condition, the second confederate's response was a simple "Beats me—it's up to you." This comment was designed to end the conversation between the two confederates as naturally as possible without making any mention of anything that possibly could be interpreted as a guide to action. Thus, the comparison paralleled the experimental condition in all respects save the comment that increases the relevance of attitudes toward psychological research.

a life filled with actions that reflect those liberal attitudes. This individual might want to choose friends who possess similarly liberal attitudes. This individual might want to join and become active in various liberal organizations. This individual might want to vote for liberal candidates for public office. By what strategic vehicles might this individual promote the translation of his or her liberal attitudes into liberal actions? Clearly, that individual's liberal attitudes are available to him or her, and that individual has defined these attitudes as relevant to action. So, neither the availability strategy nor the relevance strategy have anything more to offer in the quest for correspondence between attitudes and behavior.

Nevertheless, there are strategies that are well-suited for use by that individual. These strategies involve the situations, surroundings, and circumstances within which one chooses to live one's life.

Choosing The Situations of One's Life

In the course of their lives, individuals typically have considerable freedom to chose where to be, when, and with whom. Accordingly, the interpersonal situations in which individuals find themselves may be partially of their own choosing. It has been suggested that these choices of the interpersonal settings in which to live one's life may reflect relevant features of one's conceptions of self, including one's attitudes (for details of the argument, see Snyder, 1981). How might one's attitudes be reflected in one's choices of the settings of one's life? In particular, how might one's choices of the settings of one's life be utilized strategically to promote correspondence between one's attitudes and one's actions? Consider the case of the liberal who seeks to enforce correspondence between his or her liberal attitudes and those actions that might reflect those attitudes.

Now, as you know, some communities may provide an individual with greater opportunity to perform "liberal" actions than may other communities. It's easy to make friends with liberals in communities where liberals live. It's easy to join liberal organizations in communities where liberal organizations exist. It's easy to vote for liberal candidates in communities where liberals run for public office. The strategy, then, for the individual with liberal attitudes who seeks to translate those liberal attitudes into liberal actions is to choose to live his or her life in liberal surroundings. For, these liberal surroundings actually will dispose or constrain the individual to perform liberal actions. After all, the combined influence of the good examples set by one's liberal friends and acquaintances, the frequent appeals for membership in liberally oriented organizations, and the persuasive campaigns of liberal candidates for elected office will together increase the likelihood that any individual living in those surroundings would think and act in a liberal fashion. Of course, this correspondence between liberal attitudes and liberal actions may be purchased at the cost of having the impact of one's liberal actions diminished in the context of all the other liberal actions by all the other liberal thinkers in liberal environments.

Accordingly, by means of the strategic choice of the surroundings within which to live their lives, individuals may enforce correspondence between their attitudes and their behavior. To the extent that individuals know their attitudes, and to the extent that individuals believe that their actions ought to be meaningful reflections of relevant attitudes, they may enforce correspondence between their attitudes and their behaviors by choosing preferentially to enter, and to spend time in, those social situations that will dispose them to perform the actions implied by their attitudes.

Clearly, the strategic choice of the situations of one's life constitutes one vehicle by which individuals potentially may enforce correspondence between their attitudes and their behavior. But, do individuals employ this strategic vehicle to provide themselves with opportunities to act upon their attitudes? Empirical investigations have documented, at least for some individuals, the relationship between attitudes and the strategic choice to enter and to spend time in social situations.

In one investigation of the strategic choice of situations, Snyder and Kendzierski (1982) allowed individuals to choose to enter and spend time in, or not to enter and not to spend time in, a social situation that would provide relatively strong normative supports for the behavioral expression of favorable attitudes toward affirmative action. For some individuals, willingness to enter and spend time in this social situation was a direct reflection of their personal attitudes toward affirmative action. Specifically, for low self-monitoring individuals, those with favorable attitudes toward affirmative action were particularly eager to enter and to spend time in this social situation that would encourage, promote, and facilitate the behavioral expression of their favorable sentiments toward affirmative action. By contrast, low self-monitoring individuals with unfavorable attitudes toward affirmative action were distinctly unwilling to enter and to spend time in this social situation that not only would provide little support for them to express and act upon their own attitudes but that also might actually tempt them to behave in ways that would betray their own attitudes. And, in clear contrast to the choices of low self-monitoring individuals, the willingness of high self-monitoring individuals to choose to enter and to choose to spend time in this social situation was in no way whatsoever a reflection of their personal attitudes toward affirmative action: High self-monitoring individuals whose attitudes were favorable to affirmative action were neither more nor less willing to enter and to spend time in this situation than were high self-monitoring individuals whose attitudes were unfavorable to affirmative action.

Transforming The Situations of One's Life

To the extent that one may generalize from the demonstration of Snyder and Kendzierski (1982), it would appear that low self-monitoring individuals actively gravitate toward social situations and interpersonal settings that provide supports for acting in ways that would reflect their attitudes. For these individuals, the strategic choice of the situations of their lives may represent a major vehicle by which they may enforce and enhance correspondence between their attitudes and their behavior. Of course, the ability of low self-monitoring individuals to strategically choose situations to enforce consistency between attitudes and behavior may be constrained to the extent that these individuals have little or no choice in the situations of their lives.

Nevertheless, even when these individuals are thrust into situations that do not inherently dispose actions supportive of their attitudes, these individuals still may have the opportunity to exert influence on their situations, to change the character of their situations to make them more supportive of actions congruent with their attitudes. Consider once again the individual with liberal attitudes toward social and political issues. Imagine that that individual has been forced (perhaps by economic circumstances) to work and live in a community populated largely by people of rather conservative persuasion. Perhaps the individual might adopt an activist or missionary orientation to altering the attitudes and behaviors of others in the community to move the community in the direction of a more liberal orientation. To the extent that these activities are successful, it will become all the more easy for that individual to live out his or her liberal attitudes and values.

Accordingly, the strategic transformation of the situations of one's life may consistute another vehicle by which individuals potentially may enforce correspondence between their attitudes and their behavior. To the extent that individuals know their attitudes and the behavioral implications of those attitudes, and to the extent that they believe that their actions should reflect those attitudes, they may enforce a consistency between attitudes and behaviors by actions that transform their situations into ones that dispose the behaviors that are implied by their attitudes. And, to the extent that one may generalize from empirical investigations of the strategic choice of situations (e.g., Snyder & Kendzierski, 1982), it very well may be that it is the low self-monitoring individuals among us who are particularly likely to actively transform the situations of their lives into ones that promote correspondence between their attitudes and their actions. Together, the vehicles of strategic choice and strategic transformation may enable these individuals to live lives filled with actions that accurately reflect, meaningfully communicate, and faithfully embody their own personal attitudes—lives in which believing means doing.

CONCLUSIONS

Central to the activities of social scientists are attempts to define the relations between attitudes and behavior. If indeed there did exist reliable covariation between an individual's attitudes and behavior, it would be possible to predict future behavior from measures of relevant present attitudes. Similarly, it would be possible to infer private attitudes from observations of ongoing behavior. Furthermore, if attitudes and behavior were causally linked, one could change behavior by influencing relevant attitudes and modify attitudes by altering behavioral experience.

Such links between attitudes and behavior seem to be characteristic of some classes of individuals more so than other classes of individuals. Specifically, this chapter has focused on the role of self-monitoring processes in the creation of links between attitudes and behavior. For low self-monitoring individuals, covariation between attitudes and behavior typically is quite substantial; by contrast, for high self-monitoring individuals, covariation between attitudes and behavior often is minimal. Moreover, links between attitudes and behavior are to be found in some classes of situations more often than in other classes of situations. Specifically, this chapter has focused on those situations that increase the availability of attitudes as potential guides to action and those situations that increase the relevance of attitudes as potential guides to action. Situations that increase the availability of attitudes as potential guides to action succeed in generating substantial correspondence between attitudes and behavior only for low self-monitoring individuals. By contrast, situations that increase the relevance of attitudes as potential guides to action effectively generate substantial correspondence between attitudes and behavior not only for low self-monitoring individuals but also for high self-monitoring individuals.

From these considerations of the contributions of self-monitoring, availability, and relevance to the creation of links between attitudes and behavior emerge some guidelines for the design of strategies for generating correspondence between attitudes and behavior. Specifically, this chapter has focused on the potential of relevance strategies for use by practitioners who seek to design programs to encourage other individuals to translate their existing attitudes into actions that embody those attitudes. Furthermore, this chapter has focused on the manner in which individuals may strategically choose and may strategically transform the settings of their lives to create, promote, and enforce correspondence between their attitudes and their behavior. Indeed, it is these considerations of strategies for linking attitudes and behavior that provide some of the most compelling justifications for inquiries into the relations between attitudes and behaviors.

ACKNOWLEDGMENTS

This research and the preparation of this manuscript were supported in part by National Science Foundation Grant BNS 77-11346, ''From Belief to Reality: Cognitive, Behavioral, and Interpersonal Consequences of Social Perception,'' to Mark Snyder. Portions of this manuscript were prepared while Mark Snyder was a Fellow at the Center for Advanced Study in the Behavioral Sciences.

The empirical investigations reported in this manuscript were conducted in collaboration with Deborah Kendzierski, William B. Swann, Jr., and Elizabeth Decker Tanke. For their comments on the manuscript, thanks go to Robert P. Abelson, Norman Endler, and Mark P. Zanna.

REFERENCES

Abelson, R. P. Are attitudes necessary. In B. T. King & E. McGinnies (Eds.), *Attitudes, conflict, and social change*. New York: Academic Press, 1972.

Ajzen, I., Timko, C., & White, J. Self-monitoring and the attitude-behavior relation. *Journal of Personality and Social Psychology*, in press.

Becherer, R. C., & Richard, L. M. Self-monitoring as a moderating variable in consumer behavior. *Journal of Consumer Research*, 1978, *5*, 159–162.

Briggs, S. R., Cheek, J. M., & Buss, A. H. An analysis of the self-monitoring scale. *Journal of Personality and Social Psychology*, 1980, *38*, 679–686.

Calder, B. J., & Ross, M. *Attitudes and behavior*. Morristown, N.J.: General Learning Press, 1973.

Carver, C. S. Physical aggression as a function of objective self-awareness and attitudes toward punishment. *Journal of Experimental Social Psychology*, 1975, *11*, 510–519.

Collins, B. E. *Public and private conformity: Competing explanations by improvisation, cognitive dissonance, and attribution theories*. New York: Warner Modular Publications, 1973.

Confucius. *Analects*. Book XIV, Chapter 29, circa 500 B.C.

Deutscher, I. *Why do they say one thing, do another?* Morristown, N.J.: General Learning Press, 1973.

Emerson, R. W. *Society and solitude, twelve chapters*. Boston: Houghton, Mifflin & Company, 1885.

Fazio, R. H., & Zanna, M. P. Direct experience and attitude-behavior consistency. In L. Berkowitz (Ed.), *Advances in experimental social psychology*. (Volume 14). New York: Academic Press, 1981.

Fazio, R. H., & Zanna, M. P. Attitudinal qualities relating to the strength of the attitude-behavior relationship. *Journal of Experimental Social Psychology*, 1978, *14*, 398–408.

Festinger, L. Behavioral support for opinion change. *Public Opinion Quarterly*, 1964, *28*, 404–417.

Fishbein, M., & Ajzen, I. *Belief, attitude, intention, and behavior*. Reading, Mass.: Addison-Wesley, 1975.

Gabrenya, W. K. Jr., & Arkin, R. M. Factor structure and factor correlates of the Self-Monitoring Scale. *Personality and Social Psychology Bulletin*, 1980, *6*, 13–22.

Gibbons, F. X. Sexual standards and reactions to pornography: Enhancing behavioral consistency through self-focused attention. *Journal of Personality and Social Psychology*, 1978, *36*, 976–987.

Kiesler, C. A., Collins, B. E., & Miller, N. *Attitude change: A critical analysis of theoretical approaches*. New York: Wiley, 1969.

Kiesler, C. A., Nisbett, R. E., & Zanna, M. P. On inferring one's beliefs from one's behavior. *Journal of Personality and Social Psychology*, 1969, *11*, 321–327.

Landor, W. S. *Imaginary conversations* (Fourth Series: Dialogues of literary men—cont., Dialogues of famous women, and miscellaneous dialogues). Strand, London: J. C. Nimmo & Bain, Publishers, 1883.

Lippa, R. Expressive control and the leakage of dispositional introversion-extraversion during role-played teaching. *Journal of Personality*, 1976, *44*, 541–559.

Lutsky, N., Woodworth, W., & Clayton, S. *Actions-attitudes-actions: A multivariate, longitudinal study of attitude-behavior consistency*. Paper presented at Midwestern Psychological Association, St. Louis, Mo., 1980.

McArthur, L. A., Kiesler, C. A., & Cook, B. P. Acting on an attitude as a function of self-percept and inequity. *Journal of Personality and Social Psychology,* 1969, *12,* 295–302.

McGuire, W. J. The nature of attitudes and attitude change. In G. Lindzey & E. Aronson (Eds.), *The handbook of social psychology* (2nd Edition), (Vol. 3). Reading, Mass.: Addison-Wesley, 1969.

Norman, R. Affective-cognitive consistency, attitudes, conformity, and behavior. *Journal of Personality and Social Psychology,* 1975, *32,* 83–91.

Pryor, J. B., Gibbons, F. X., Wicklund, R. A., Fazio, R., & Hood, R. Self-focused attention and self-report validity. *Journal of Personality,* 1977, *45,* 513–527.

Regan, D. T., & Fazio, R. H. On the consistency between attitudes and behavior: Look to the method of attitude formation. *Journal of Experimental Social Psychology,* 1977, *13,* 28–45.

Scheier, M. F., Buss, A. H., & Buss, D. M. Self-consciousness, self-report of agressiveness, and aggression. *Journal of Research in Personality,* 1978, *12,* 133–140.

Schwartz, S. H. Normative explanations of helping behavior: A critique, proposal, and empirical test. *Journal of Experimental Social Psychology,* 1973, *9,* 349–364.

Snyder, M. Individual differences and the self-control of expressive behavior (Doctoral dissertation, Stanford University, 1972). *Dissertation Abstracts International,* 1972, *33,* 4533A–4534A.

Snyder, M. The self-monitoring of expressive behavior. *Journal of Personality and Social Psychology,* 1974, *30,* 526–537.

Snyder, M. *When believing means doing: A cognitive social psychology of action.* Paper presented at American Psychological Association, San Francisco, Calif., 1977.

Snyder, M. Cognitive, behavioral, and interpersonal consequences of self-monitoring. In P. Pliner, K. R. Blankstein, & I. M. Spigel (Eds.), *Advances in the study of communication and affect* (Volume 5). *Perception of emotion in self and others.* New York: Plenum Press, 1979. (a)

Snyder, M. Self-monitoring processes. In L. Berkowitz (Ed.), *Advances in experimental social psychology* (Vol. 12). New York: Academic Press, 1979. (b)

Snyder, M. On the influence of individuals on situations. In N. Cantor & J. F. Kihlstrom (Eds.), *Personality, cognition, and social interaction.* Hillsdale, N.J.: Lawrence Erlbaum Associates, 1981.

Snyder, M., & Campbell, B. H. Self-monitoring: The self in action. In J. Suls (Ed.), *Psychological perspectives on the self* (Vol 1). Hillsdale, N.J.: Lawrence Erlbaum Associates, 1982.

Snyder, M., & Kendzierski, D. Acting on one's attitudes: Procedures for linking attitude and behavior. *Journal of Experimental Social Psychology,* 1982.

Snyder, M., & Kendzierski, D. Choosing social situations: Investigating the origins of correspondence between attitudes and behavior. *Journal of Personality,* 1982.

Snyder, M., & Monson, T. C. Persons, situations, and the control of social behavior. *Journal of Personality and Social Psychology,* 1975, *32,* 637–644.

Snyder, M., & Swann, W. B., Jr. When actions reflect attitudes: The politics of impression management. *Journal of Personality and Social Psychology,* 1976, *34,* 1034–1042.

Snyder, M., & Tanke, E. D. Behavior and attitude: Some people are more consistent than others. *Journal of Personality,* 1976, *44,* 510–517.

Wicker, A. W. Attitudes versus actions: The relationship of verbal and overt behavioral responses to attitude objects. *Journal of Social Issues,* 1969, *25,* 41–78.

Wicklund, R. A. Objective self-awareness. In L. Berkowitz (Ed.), *Advances in experimental social psychology* (Vol. 8). New York: Academic Press, 1975.

Zanna, M. P., & Fazio, R. H. *Direct experience and attitude-behavior consistency.* Paper presented at American Psychological Association, San Francisco, Calif., 1977.

Zanna, M. P., Olson, J. M., & Fazio, R. H. Attitude-behavior consistency: An individual difference perspective. *Journal of Personality and Social Psychology,* 1980, *38,* 432–440.

Zuckerman, M., & Reis, H. T. A comparison of three models for predicting altruistic behavior. *Journal of Personality and Social Psychology,* 1978, *36,* 498–510.

6 Three Modes of Attitude-Behavior Consistency

Robert P. Abelson
Yale University

Many discussions of attitude and behavior focus on the observation that attitude toward a social object often does not predict behavior toward that object (Abelson, 1972; Ehrlich, 1969; Schuman & Johnson, 1976; Wicker, 1969). There are almost as many explanations for attitude-behavior inconsistencies as there are commentators, but two lines of argument are usually invoked in sophisticated discussions:

Definitional Specificity. Attitudes and behaviors can be characterized on many different levels of generality. Many specifications can be placed upon attitude objects, and attitudes are not invariant over the set of such specifications. Attitudes toward blacks as hypothetical neighbors need not coincide with attitudes toward black co-workers or with attitudes toward specific blacks. Similarly behavior can be specified in many ways: having a casual conversation with someone is not of a piece with inviting them home for dinner. In this view it is naive to talk of *the* attitude and *the* behavior toward some object class.

Situational Context Factors. Even when the attitude/behavior object is specifically defined, however, circumstances surrounding the expression of attitudes or the elicitation of behavior can vary from one occasion to the next, either through slow evolution or by the sudden introduction of transient influences. Stress, social pressure, anonymity, motivation to reflect, and other conditions can alter either attitude or behavior or both. Many apparent inconsistencies can thus be understood as a change in context between the attitude measurement and behavioral elicitation situations.

In this chapter, I give emphasis to the situational context explanation rather than to definitional specificity. The latter is an important consideration for the attitude-behavior question, but there is danger in too single-minded a pursuit of this factor. Ajzen & Fishbein (1977), as the leading expositors of the definitional view, make the matter almost exclusively methodological, pushing into the background some important psychological considerations.

They maintain that attitude object and behavior object must correspond in both their "target components" and "action components" (among others) in order for attitudes to predict behaviors successfully. Thus if one wanted to predict the behavior of attending church services, it would not be too helpful to measure attitudes toward religion or even toward churches or church services. One would need to assess attitudes toward *attending* church services. Ajzen & Fishbein marshall a good deal of evidence which makes a strong overall case that the closer the correspondence in objects measured, the higher the attitude-behavior correlation.

While this is certainly an important practical admonition for those who would wish to predict a particular behavior from some attitude, it leaves a great many questions unanswered. It tells us that to predict a specific act, you must measure attitude toward that specific act, but it doesn't shed light on whether general dispositions might not sometimes relate reasonably well to specific actions, or indeed, on what basis different specific attitudes or actions might sometimes cluster well with each other to produce coherent relationships even without an obvious correspondence in objects of measurement. A case in point is the study by Sears, Hensler, and Speer (1979), showing that the general attitude of "symbolic racism" is a rather good predictor of opposition to school busing, on the face of it quite a different target object. Thus Ajzen & Fishbein's advice leaves us traveling a road paved with psychometric intentions, which does not necessarily take us near to understanding the dynamics of attitudes and behaviors.

By contrast, an emphasis on situational context factors gives insight into the psychological relation between attitudes and behaviors. Often such factors can be experimentally manipulated. It is especially interesting when such manipulations alter attitude-behavior correlations, holding constant the definitional specificity of what is measured. Much of the research reviewed in the present volume falls in this category. I would like to pull together here several of the relevant ideas, in an attempt to extract general principles.

Recent Research on Mediating Context Factors

Several studies have shown that attitudes learned via direct experience with an object or issue correlate better with behavior than attitudes learned without direct involvement. Fazio and Zanna (1978) assessed subjects' attitudes toward being in psychological experiments, along with their frequency of volunteering. For subjects who previously had been in at least four experiments, the correlation between attitude and behavior toward experiments was .42. For subjects who had been in no more than one experiment, the corresponding correlation was −.03.

Regan and Fazio (1977) have obtained similar results on two other issues, one a real campus housing crisis, the other a set of puzzle materials with prior experience manipulated in the laboratory. A related result was obtained by Songer-Nocks (1976), who showed that prior experience with a Prisoner's Dilemma game considerably strengthened the relationship between attitudes toward cooperative choices and actual performance of those choices.

Meanwhile, Snyder and Swann (1976) have shown that thinking about a general issue (Affirmative action) before filling out an attitude scale results in a correlation of .58 with a behavior in a later specific case, whereas without prior thought, this correlation is a mere .07. A similar type of result has been obtained by Fendrich (1967) for racial attitudes. Pryor, Gibbons, Wicklund, Fazio, and Hood (1977) and several other studies reviewed by Wicklund & Frey (1980) and Wicklund (this volume) have shown that self-awareness, usually manipulated by placing a mirror opposite the subject during attitude measurement (or even during behavior), increases attitude-behavior correlation.

These several results are not all attributable to shifts in the reliability of attitude measurements. Rather, they seem to involve the distinction between an academic attitude and a practical attitude. In Snyder's (this volume) theoretical analysis, he says that attitudes must be well-organized in both their "cognitive component"—what they are about—and in their "action component"—how and when to apply them—before they can be expected to correlate well with behavior. It is not automatic to know how to act on one's attitudes. Fazio and Zanna (1978) attribute the effects of direct experience to the confidence with which the attitude is held: "During a direct experience, because of more information and better focus, the individual forms a relatively clear, strong, and confident attitude . . . which better predicts behavior."

Meanwhile, Kahle, Klingel, and Kulka (1981), in reviewing the attitude-behavior literature, propose that during "adaptive ambiguity", attitudes and behaviors are tentative, but when the adaptive significance of attitudes is known, they then tend to guide behavior.

These three strands of research—on direct experience with the attitude object, on thinking about the attitude object, and on self-awareness in general—seem tantalizingly related to each other. What is their common conceptual core?

In all three phenomena, what seems to be involved is a sharpening of the individual's preparation to respond in terms of private values and beliefs. The manipulations of giving relevant experience or thought or self-awareness all serve in one way or another to *individuate* the subject, that is, to increase awareness of essential self-orientations. It is interesting that there is also a personality construct, *private self-consciousness,* containing items such as "I am often aware of my thoughts and feelings". People scoring high on this scale have shown higher attitude-behavior correlations than people scoring low on the scale (Buss, 1980, p. 59). One way, then, that attitudes and behavior might be mediated so as to be consistent would be if in both attitude measurement and behavior situations the individual was disposed or prodded to apply convictions well-integrated in his or her personality (or even to work towards such integration on the spot). If such individuating conditions are manipulated for attitude measurement only, then the degree of consistency presumably would depend on whether an individuated style would be likely to carry over into the behavioral performance, as opposed to other factors impinging on that performance.

In the absence of the special phenomena we have called individuating conditions, the correlation between attitude and behavior can sometimes be quite low. This implies that normally, responses may not be individuated (Abelson, 1972). The inner personal considerations brought to bear by coaxed rehearsal otherwise lie dormant, and attitude elicitation and behavioral expression are governed in other modes, often independently. It will be theoretically useful to puzzle out what some such other modes of attitudinal and behavioral governance might be. I will do this indirectly, by discussion on two other modes which especially interest me.

Scripted Behavior

In recent years, I have been exploring the concept of ''scripts,'' both for story understanding and for behavioral performance (Abelson, 1976, 1981; Schank & Abelson, 1977). A script is one kind of cognitive ''schema'' (Bobrow & Norman, 1975; Rumelhart & Ortony, 1976; Taylor & Crocker, 1981), i.e., knowledge structure governing perceptual and cognitive processes. In particular, a script is an organized bundle of expectations about an event sequence; for example, the typical series of actions at a restaurant, a laundromat, a supermarket, a wedding, etc. When a script is activated, it aids the individual in disambiguating ongoing social and physical reality.

Scripts can govern one's own behavior as well as the passive understanding of the behavior of others. To behave a script, that is, to play a role such as a customer in a restaurant, you must not only understand that such a possibility exists, but you must commit yourself to the performance of it. (The concept of ''commitment'' is used deliberately here. Starting a script performance usually entails a commitment to finish it. One doesn't readily leave a restaurant once seated or walk out of a dentist's office before he is through.) I have hypothesized (Abelson, 1981) that commitment to a particular scripted behavior is contingent upon an ''action rule'' which the individual has developed and attached to the particular script representation. An action rule consists of a set of criteria which if affirmed will lead the person to enter the script, but if negated will lead the person not to enter the script. For example, the action rule for the little script of giving someone a light might be, ''Did they ask politely?'' and ''Do I have a light?'' Action rules are not necessarily consciously articulated by the individual. However, it does seem a reasonable hypothesis that they are based upon very few relevant criteria—especially if a lengthy decision process is not feasible on each occurrence of the script's evoking context.

What is the implication of scripted behavior, if and when it occurs, for attitude-behavior consistency? The classic LaPiere (1934) study provides a good starting point, even though there are alternative interpretations of his findings (e.g., Ajzen & Fishbein, 1980, p. 23, invoking Campbell, 1963). LaPiere and two Chinese traveling companions were received at virtually all of the two hundred motels and restaurants they visited during a tour of the U.S. Six months after a visit, a letter from LaPiere asked each establishment whether it would "welcome members of the Chinese race as guests." Ninety% of the returns said "No," a huge discrepancy between attitude (or behavioral intention) and actual behavior.

In script terms, we would say that when the Chinese arrived, the management representatives played standard script scenes from their role perspectives. In the restaurant, the crucial scene is "seating the customer"; in the hotel, "registering the guest." Given very well-practiced scripts, the action rules—the policies for whether to enter the scripts—are presumably very well learned. What a hotel manager is likely to check before registering a guest is whether a room is available and the guest looks able to pay. Hotel managers (and clerks) are very well practiced at going ahead if the answers are yes, but refusing the guest politely if either answer is no. On the other hand, it seems quite unlikely that managers would ask themselves, "Do I feel favorable towards these potential guests?" Liking the guest is not a good action criterion if the commercial establishment is to turn a profit. Thus "attitude" is manifestly not relevant for hotel (and restaurant) welcoming behavior. Even if a negative attitude exists toward a particular rare minority, this attitude (with some exceptions) has not been practiced as a non-action reason. Emergent doubts have little chance of deflecting scripted behavior when standard action criteria are satisfied.

Here we have a potentially general basis for attitude-behavior inconsistency: behavior is controlled by a particular script for which the attitude in question is not relevant to its action rule. This plausible suggestion, however, raises further issues. Are these cases in which attitudes *are* relevant to action rules? And what about the possible scriptedness of the attitude measurement situation? (One might, for example, want to understand better the context for the respondents to LaPiere's letter.)

Certainly it seems possible for an attitude to be a relevant condition for scripted action. If you are invited to dinner at someone's house, (thus to be a participant in the "dinner guest script"), or are asked out on a date, your liking for the one who invites you is clearly relevant. It is thus important to analyze the behavior in question to see whether and where it permits attitudes to enter.

Sometimes there are places within scripts where attitudes are explicitly recognized as relevant. These are at choice or decision points marked in the script. For example, deciding what to order is an essential event in the restaurant script. Deciding for whom to vote is an explicit step (albeit vague as to when it should occur) in the script of voting in an election.

To the extent that such marked choice points are available in a given script, we should expect that attitudes toward the available choice objects will correlate with behavior toward them. We tend to eat what we prefer, to dance more with those we like more, and to vote for those we favor. When a person does not behave consistently with his or her attitudes, it may be that there was no place in the flow of action set aside for the explicit purpose of considering the options toward the target objects of attitude.

In this analysis, we note the importance not only of explicit choice points, but also of the particular choice targets. In the department store script, for example, one explicitly decides which items of clothing to buy; one does not as a standard matter choose whether to snub given salespersons in advance of any information about their demeanor. Thus attitudes toward types of clothes should correlate well with the behavior of buying those clothes, whereas attitudes toward categories of salespersons need not correlate at all with the behavior of buying from those salespersons. This point seems obvious enough, but the finding some years back that the racial integration of the sales force at Macy's department store (Saenger & Gilbert, 1950) had no effect on the purchasing behavior of prejudiced buyers occasioned a good deal of surprise at the time.

An enterprising individual perhaps can create choice points where none exist in a script, but this is not easy! Individuating manipulations can be viewed in part as providing help to the subject in stopping the flow of events to ask, "Can I apply some personal feeling or belief to this situation?" and also, "What is it that I really feel and believe?"

We have been discussing the case where attitudes and behavior are inconsistent because the subject exercises a free choice during attitude measurement, but has no chance to make a (presumably corresponding) behavioral choice because behavior is co-opted by a script which does not explicitly provide an opportunity for such a choice. In principle, there is another interesting case. Suppose that attitude measurement were scripted (or at any rate, heavily governed by normative constraints), such that no real opportunity for individuated choice occurred?

Let us reexamine the LaPiere situation, imagining that his traveling companions were black instead of Chinese, and that their excursion covered the pre-Civil Rights Law South. Presumably they would have been almost universally denied accommodations. "Are the potential guests colored?" was in that time and place an explicit action criterion for refusing service. In like fashion, a letter asking, "Do you welcome members of the Negro race as guests?" would have been accorded a comparably negative response, also because of normative constraints (as probably was the Chinese question for LaPiere's respondents). Thus attitude and behavior might come out the same because both are governed by comparable norms.[1] This would be a case of culturally enforced consistency, a phenomenon quite different from the individuated consistency produced by pushing people toward close examination of what they really think and feel.

---

[1] I am indebted to Robert Wicklund for suggesting this possibility.

To complicate matters still further, one can imagine attitude-behavior *incon*-sistency because attitudes and behavior are each normatively controlled such as to produce institutionalized hypocrisy. Public attitude expression and private behavior toward liquor during Prohibition would be one example. LaPiere (1934) suggests another, with brothels as response object. He asked his readers to imagine what attitude would be expressed toward brothels on a questionnaire given to a Midwestern businessman, and how the same businessman would behave toward brothels on a binge in Paris. Inconsistently, one supposes.

In sum, ''scriptedness'' is a mediating context factor which can produce attitude-behavior consistency when both attitude measurement and behavioral elicitation situations happen to be proscribed similarly to one another. Scripted-ness can also (unlike individuation) produce attitude-behavior *in*consistency when one of the two situations is scripted and the other isn't, or in the extreme, when they are scripted to opposite effect, as in institutionalized hypocrisy.

Both scriptedness and individuation serve a defining or constraining function: They focus the individual on the most well-structured aspects of the relevant attitudes and potential behaviors. Scriptedness refers to socially defined, and individuation to individually defined structure. Although well-structuredness is an important condition in the production of consistency in both cases, there is an important difference in the kind of consistency that may be produced.

In a heterogeneous sample of individuals, individuation tends to accentuate the underlying differences between people, and the *correlation over individuals* between attitudes and behavior tends to increase. By contrast, scriptedness sup-presses and obscures individual differences, and the consistency (or inconsisten-cy) it governs between attitudes and behaviors consists in the *co-occurrence of extreme marginal distributions*. The LaPiere study illustrates this latter effect: Almost all his respondents expressed an intolerant attitude, but behaved with tolerance toward the Chinese. In the other three cells of the 2×2 table fell either zero cases or one case, and thus no meaningful correlation over respondents could even be calculated. This distinction between individual consistency and group consistency has often been noted in the attitude-behavior literature, and it is important again to be mindful of it here.

Deindividuation

The claim that individuation is a common theme in many experiments producing attitude-behavior consistency suggests an examination of the conceptual op-posite: What happens to attitudes and behavior under conditions of *deindividua-tion?* That is, suppose that instead of reminding the individual of who he or she is and encouraging thoughtful processing of underlying beliefs, suppose we remove such reminders, provide anonymity, and promote thoughtlessness and impulsivity?

Zimbardo (1970) lists a number of conditions promoting deindividuation: arousal, sensory overload, novelty, altered states of consciousness, diffusion of responsibility within an active group, an orientation toward the immediate present rather than past or future, etc. A mob on a rampage of cruelty and destruction is a vivid illustration of deindividuation, but there are a number of more modest or partial illustrations as well, including Zimbardo's (1970) own experimental demonstration of the increase in aggressive behavior of undergraduates in hooded groups given an opportunity to administer electric shocks to a peer.

In our present context, the theoretical problem is how to place the particulars of deindividuated behavior into some coherent framework. How can we predict (if at all) *which* behaviors will be forthcoming under deindividuating circumstances? A concrete image may make the problem clearer: Picture the TV coverage of the crowds outside the U.S. Embassy in the early days of the Iranian hostage crisis. Many in the crowd shouted slogans such as "Death to Carter, the great Satan," and burned Carter effigies and American flags. As attitude theorists, how well could we have predicted such behavior under the circumstances, either on a group or individual basis?

Some in the crowd were much more active than others. Suppose we had had prior attitude measures toward the burning of effigies, toward Carter, America, the Iranian revolution, the Shah, etc. What kinds of measures in what contexts would best have predicted which individuals would be the most active in slogan-chanting and effigy-burning? It seems implausible to suppose that *individuating* the attitude measure and/or the behavioral situation would help prediction. The very notion of putting mirrors in front of Iranians, or asking them to take time to think about the issues, does not seem appropriate to tap the wellsprings of excitement and rage let loose in mass demonstrations. The behavior being deindividuated would suggest that one should attempt to predict it from attitudes measured in deindividuated circumstances.

But is deindividuated attitude measurement plausible? It seems both difficult to arrange and intrinsically self-contradictory. One can't have people aroused and dedifferentiated, with impulses at the dispensation of mob stimulation, and then ask them soberly whether they strongly agree, moderately agree, slightly agree, etc., with each of a list of rather tedious and wordy propositions. We shall return to the question below, but for the moment let us set aside the concept of deindividuated attitude measurement. As we do so, however, we note that attitude measurement is an American invention (Thurstone 1928; Likert, 1932). It presupposes a respondent who is a reflective, autonomous being who can be seated quietly in a room with pencil and paper so as to tell us social truths. It is nevertheless still necessary to individuate attitudinal and behavioral situations to make salient the American idealization of the individualist and give coherence to the attitude-behavior link. In cultures where attitudes and behaviors are more group-centered than individual-centered, individuation might produce confusion rather than coherence.

We are still left with the problem of whether one can predict deindividuated behaviors from standard attitude measures. Relevant evidence is scarce. One major study using riot participation as a dependent variable is by Sears and McConahay (1973), who tried to find variables which would relate to the degree of activity of individual blacks in the Watts rebellion of 1965.

Their extensive pattern of results on many measures can essentially be summarized in terms of the symbolic self-identification of some respondents. So-called "new urban blacks" were much more likely than others to have participated in the riot. This identification is "symbolic" because it represents a cluster of value orientations which are not usually well-articulated in terms of the instrumentalities of real-world policies, but rather in terms of the shared feelings of a social group. These feelings are often tacit, but can be acknowledged and evoked by gestures and "code words" or other symbols. The raised fist salute and terms such as "brothers (sisters)" are examples of such symbols for the "new urban blacks" of the 1960s. In the Sears and McConahay (1973) study, the existence of such a symbolic identity was inferred from the profile among rioters of demographic characteristics (young, born in the North) and aggrieved attitudes (hostility toward police, distrust of white authorities, cyncism about the "system") which suggested a solidarity of general group interest without any necessary cohesion on concrete policy questions.

That the attitudes predictive of riot behavior were indirect and "symbolic" is a very important point. Ajzen and Fishbein's (1980) dictum is that to predict behavior one needs to measure behavioral intention which in turn is a function of attitude toward the specific behavioral act. In the Watts case, it is not necessary to suppose that the typical rioter had favorable prior attitudes toward, say, the burning of particular buildings, or had any focused bebavioral intentions of this sort. It is in the nature of deindividuated behavior that products of the group's energies can be quite spontaneous. Though an observer might well be able to predict in broad terms the sort of destructiveness an angry crowd would wreak, many of the participants caught up in the process find themselves suprised the morning after at their own particular actions.[2]

The moral of our story is that straightforward attitude measurement in the Ajzen and Fishbein tradition is really oriented toward the prediction of individuated behavior (though for good prediction, individuating *contexts* may even then

---

[2]There are important qualifications to these assertions. It is of course possible for a group committed to a social cause to plan unusual actions. Members of an urban squatters movement in West Berlin, for example, recently staged a premeditated demonstration during which glue was poured into the door locks to the office buildings of local authorities! It is also possible for riot behavior to be repeated according to a familiar pattern, moving toward becoming scripted. Accompanying such subcultural institutionalization of rebellious behavior may be a growing commitment to an ideology of violence, so that there comes to be a scripted correlation between participation in violent actions and favorable general attitude toward violence in the service of one's cause (Campbell & Schuman, 1968, p. 55). The point we wish to make is not that deindividuated behavior is always unpredictable but only that it *can* be very fluid.

be required). For the prediction of degree of susceptibility to deindividuated behavior, on the other hand, the relevant attitudes are "symbolic."

What do we mean by a symbolic attitude? Intuitively, it has to do with a "gut issue" such as abortion, gun control, or the Equal Rights Amendment where there is great emotional involvement and a sense that one's self-identity is at stake when the issue is debated. There is a sometimes surprising insensitivity to rational-instrumental considerations, as for example with strong adherents of capital punishment who say they favor it primarily because it deters crime—but would favor it just as strongly even if it didn't deter crime (Ellsworth & Ross, in press). The symbolic character arises because the manifest issue stands in for a deeper, more "real" issue (e.g., punitiveness toward those who violate social order). Symbolic attitudes involve a heavy moral concern with what is right and what is wrong, and a strong orientation against an outgroup whose actions are "wrong," and emphasis on the feeling state of the respondent's ingroup (e.g., righteous indignation). A symbolic attitude is a general attitude which has (possibly remote) ramifications for specific attitudes and behaviors. For example, Sears et al. (1979) found that strong political conservatism and "symbolic racism" predicted opposition to school busing. Sears, Tyler, Citrin, & Kinder (1978) identified hostility to local government authorities as the chief determinant of nonconformance to emergency gasoline-saving policies. In both these examples, the symbolic attitudes predicted the resultant behaviors better than indices of rational self-interest, e.g., whether the respondent had a child who was being bused to school; whether the respondent had high gasoline needs. (See also Sears, Lau, Tyler, & Allen, 1980.)

Symbolic attitudes presumably spring from general emotional orientations (toward authority, toward death or violence, toward nonconformity, etc.), but these orientations need not be so general as to characterize the whole personality, as with the authoritarian personality scoring extremely high on the F-scale. Rather, one might think of streaks or strains in the personality, such as distrust of the dangers of unbridled power, which resonate with particular attitude positions such as opposition to nuclear energy.

Although our analysis here is speculative, the fit between the nature of symbolic attitudes and of deindividuated behaviors seems a good one. Deindividuation under provocation from the ingroup can mobilize and release the feelings central to the symbolic attitude, and play them out against the outgroup target. Thus black rioters focus their rage on the police and other symbols of the white establishment; conversely, white busing protests unleash violence against blacks; committed Iranian revolutionaries symbolically enact moral indignation against the "Great Satan U.S."; anti-nuclear mass arrest protests express scorn for the establishment; in Jonestown, paranoia about the outside world and glorification of their own leader enabled a mass suicide to occur. In many such examples, the specific form that behavior may take may not be known in advance, although of course in repeated mass demonstrations certain activities may become scripted, and thus predictable.

Not enough is known about symbolic attitudes at this time to go further in our analysis. Despite decades of research in psychology on attitudes, symbolic attitudes have received only desultory attention. Among the many possible reasons for such inattention is the tendency toward "cognitive imperialism" as noted by Tomkins (1981), the reduction of mental life to rational information processing at the expense of a full theory of the nature of affects. In studying attitude-behavior linkage, we should be aware of such a possible bias, and not restrict our attention only to those attitudes and behaviors which represent self-conscious policy decisions. ("What do I believe is best for me? What do others expect of me? Therefore, what shall I do?"). Symbolic attitudes and deindividuated behaviors are interesting partly because of their distance from rational-instrumental cases in which values and emotions enter only derivatively.

Returning for a second look at the question of whether the measurement of attitudes can be deindividuated, we can now view the question more productively than we did before. The appropriate measures are symbolic attitudes, which involve moral sentiments anchored in an ingroup. Various manipulations could be considered to hype up the symbolic aspect of symbolic attitude questions, downplaying whatever rational-instrumental aspect they might happen to have.

For one thing, some symbol of the ingroup identity (logo, photograph, bumper sticker) could be "accidentally" present in the measurement situation, much in the fashion that a mirror is accidentally present in Wicklund's (this volume) self-awareness manipulation. Or a confederate could fortuitously drop some reminder making the group salient, or group composition in the testing situation could serve as an implicit cue (Shomer & Centers, 1970), or some pre-questionnaire task could contain material relevant to the group, as was done in a study many years ago by Kelley (1955). In addition, instructions to the subjects could emphasize feeling rather than thinking. ("Give your gut reaction to these statements. . . ." "How do you feel about this issue?" etc., as opposed to "Carefully consider the statements below. . . ." "In your opinion, which do you think is more advisable. . . ?" etc.) Whether such variations would be effective in producing more "symbolification" of appropriate issues is open to empirical exploration.

Restatement

We have invoked three types of mediating situational contexts—individuated, scripted, and deindividuated—and discussed the different types of relations between attitudes and behavior that each would imply. Certain clarifications are now in order.

The three types are not mutually exclusive. It is perfectly possible for individuated attitudes/behaviors to be scripted. The highly committed role participant in (say) a religious ceremony may both believe in what he or she is doing and do it automatically. It is also perfectly possible, as we have noted, for deindividuated performances to become scripted. Can a behavior be both individuated and deindividuated? No, not in terms of the contradictory contexts required to produce them. Yes, in the sense that the resulting behaviors might turn out to be the same. Many Iranian revolutionaries, for example, might not require the mobilizing influence of an angry mob to express militant anti-U.S. sentiments.

Thus any of the three modes of attitudes and behaviors could happen to agree, depending on circumstances. When all three agree simultaneously, the result may be a satisfying concordance for the individual, since conflict and hypocrisy would be avoided (Abelson, 1972). However, we should in general allow for any possible discrepancy among the three modes.

Another question pertains to the mediation of attitude and behavior in the absence of general individuating, deindividuating, or scripting contexts. We shall refer to such absence as the "underdetermined" context, although it is clearly possible for any given individual to respond in an individuated or scripted fashion even in a generally underdetermined context. Some individuals may typically reflect deeply in filling out attitude measures and/or in engaging in social or political behavior. Individuation in particular content areas is a habit of mind for some people, as Schwartz (1977) has made clear in the domain of helping behavior, where certain individuals are typically more aware of the moral consequences of their behavior and are more willing to accept responsibility for their actions. Such individuals show higher attitude-behavior correlations than others. Similar correlation differentials are produced by Snyder's (1974) self-monitoring and Buss' (1980) private self-consciousness variables. Individual difference variables relevant to individuation, in other words, can produce the same amplification in attitude-behavior correlations as do individuating context manipulations.

A related point could be made about individual variations in scriptedness. Some people may behave in socially determined, stereotyped fashion toward particular attitude objects even where the majority of people do not. Scripted behavior is probably more common than scripted attitude expression. In any case, the net effect could easily be to lower attitude-behavior correlations.

The "underdetermined" context thus contains a mix of all sorts of influences for different individuals. Among the influences not even mentioned yet are transient or idiosyncratic variations in how attitude questions are construed, and accidents of what situations present themselves as contexts for behaviors for different individuals. Even when the behavior is the "same," say, attending church on Sunday, there are all kinds of personal influences such as health, other activities, etc., which are not the same over sets of individuals, however similar their attitudes. It is thus not surprising that attitude-behavior correlations are often quite low.[3]

We can restate our analysis in terms of the kinds of influences present in the various contexts. In the underdetermined contexts for attitude measurement and behavioral performance, transient influences on individuals can be strong, and obscure potential attitude-behavior relationship. What individuation does at best is to introduce stable common influences into both attitude and behavior contexts for each individual. This promotes the revealed relationship between the two. The effect of scriptedness, on the other hand, is massively to introduce stable and probably irrelevant social influences into behavior (and possibly also attitude) contexts. The result is to produce group consistency of behavior (and/or attitude), obscuring attitude-behavior correlation over individuals. It is possible to obtain a kind of forced consistency, where the whole group is pushed correspondingly in their attitude statements and their behavioral expressions. However, it is also possible to produce forced group inconsistency, or "institutionalized hypocrisy" if the scripts or norms for attitude and behavioral expression point in opposite directions.

The effects of deindividuation on behavior are of a different order. While further analysis is clearly needed, our premise is that deindividuation brings to the fore for a group of individuals their symbolic attitudes which revolve around the ingroup's sense of common identity and their (usually negative) feelings toward a target out-group. Behavioral deindividuation of the ingroup's members thus can produce consistency with attitude measures, provided those measures are of a symbolic nature. Such consistency would tend to be collective rather than individual, although one might imagine a high attitude-behavior correlation over individuals being produced from a mixture of people differentially committed to the ingroup, and correspondingly differentially susceptible to deindividuation.

The effects of deindividuation could thus be of comparable nature to those of individuation—in both cases context changes can sharpen an attitude-behavior correlation otherwise hidden by ordinary underdetermined contexts. The difference is in the nature of the attitudes expressed: individuated attitudes spring from values which have been personally developed, symbolic attitudes usually from values which embed themselves in group causes; individuated attitudes are often instrumental and reasoned, whereas symbolic attitudes are typically expressive and passionate. These differences are probably more pronounced in general American (or Western) culture than in countries or groups where individuated attitudes are not acknowledged and respected (the Soviet Union, for

---

[3]Of course the size of attitude-behavior correlations is also heavily influenced by the number of attitude and behavior items sampled, as Epstein (1980) has yet again reminded us. Random transient influences will tend therefore to wash out in multi-item measures. But systematic irrelevant influences differentiating individuals will remain even then.

example, or in revolutionary Iran). In these latter cultures, we might not need two contextual categories, indviduated and deindividuated, but simply one— "aroused"—and our general proposition would be that attitude-behavior correlations are increased when individuals are aroused.

The astute reader may have noticed that our three modes of potential attitude-behavior consistency—individuation, scripting, and deindividuation—bear strong family resemblances to Kelman's (1958) formulation of three attitude change processes—internalization, compliance, and identification, albeit the questions we are addressing are different from his. There are also family resemblances to the distinctions made long ago by Katz (1960) and Smith, Bruner, & White (1956). It is reassuring to find such a continuity of psychological theorizing. However, it is unsettling to realize how little systematic attempt until recently has been made in all the years of the attitude-behavior dilemma to consider the mediating or moderating effects of situational and personality factors. Perhaps that is now changing.

REFERENCES

Abelson, R. P. Are attitudes necessary? In B. T. King & E. McGinnies (Eds.), *Attitudes, conflict and social change*. New York: Academic Press, 1972.

Abelson, R. P. Script processing in attitude formation and decision making. In J. S. Carroll & J. W. Payne (Eds.), *Cognition and social behavior*. Hillsdale, N.J.: Laurence Erlbaum Associates, 1976.

Abelson, R. P. The psychological status of the script concept. *American Psychologist*, 1981, *36*, 715–729.

Ajzen, I., & Fishbein, M. Attitude-behavior relations: A theoretical analysis and review of empirical research. *Psychological Bulletin*, 1977, *84*, 888–918.

Ajzen, I., & Fishbein, M. *Understanding attitudes and predicting behavior*. Englewood Cliffs, N.J.: Prentice-Hall, 1980.

Bobrow, D. G., & Norman, D. A. Some principles of memory schemata. In D. G. Bobrow & A. Collins (Eds.), *Representation and understanding*. New York: Academic Press, 1975.

Buss, A. H. *Self-consciousness and social anxiety*. SanFrancisco: W. H. Freeman, 1980.

Campbell, A., & Schuman, H. *Racial attitudes in 15 American cities*. Ann Arbor: Institute for Social Research, 1968.

Campbell, D. T. Social attitudes and other acquired behavioral dispositions. In S. Koch (Ed.), *Psychology: A study of a science* (Vol. 6). New York: McGraw-Hill, 1963.

Ehrlich, H. J. Attitudes, behavior, and the intervening variables. *American Sociologist*, 1969, *4*, 29–34.

Ellsworth, P. C. & Ross, L. Public opinion and capital punishment: A close examination of the views of abolitionists and retentionists. *Crime and Delinquency* (in press).

Epstein, S. The stability of behavior: II. Implications for psychological research, *American Psychologist*, 1980, 790–806.

Fazio, R. H., & Zanna, M. P. Attitudinal qualities relating to the strength of the attitude-behavior relationship. *Journal of Experimental Social Psychology*, 1978, *14*, 398–407.

Fendrich, J. M. A study of the association among verbal attitudes, commitment, and overt behavior in different experimental situations. *Social Forces*, 1967, *45*, 347–335.

Kahle, L. R., Klingle, D. M. & Kulka, R. A. A longitudinal study of adolescents' attitude-behavior consistency. *Public Opinion Quarterly*, 1981, *45*, 402–414.

Katz, D. The functional approach to the study of attitudes. *Public Opinion Quarterly*, 1960, *24*, 163–204.

Kelley, H. H. Salience of membership and resistance to change of group-anchored attitudes. *Human Relations*, 1955, *8*, 275–289.

Kelman, H. C. Compliance, identification and internalization: Three processes of opinion change. *Journal of Conflict Resolution*, 1958, *2*, 51–60.

LaPiere, R. T. Attitude vs. actions. *Social Forces*, 1934, *13*, 230–237.

Likert, R. A technique for the measurement of attitudes. *Archives of Psychology*, 1932, No. 140.

Pryor, J. B., Gibbons, F. S., Wicklund, R. A., Fazio, R. & Hood, R. Self-focused attention and self-report validity. *Journal of Personality*, 1977, *45*, 513–527.

Regan, D. T., & Fazio, R. H. On the consistency between attitudes and behavior: Look to the method of attitude formation. *Journal of Experimental Social Psychology*, 1977, *13*, 28–45.

Rumelhart, D. E., & Ortony, A. The representation of knowledge in memory. In R. C. Anderson, R. J. Spiro, & W. E. Montague (Eds.), *Schooling and the acquisition of knowledge*. Hillsdale, N.J.: Lawrence Erlbaum Associates, 1976.

Saenger, G., & Gilbert, E. Customer reactions to the integration of Negro sales personnel. *International Journal of Opinion and Attitude Research*, 1950, *1*, 57–76.

Schank, R. C., & Abelson, R. P. *Scripts, plans, goals and understanding*. Hillsdale, N.J.: Lawrence Erlbaum Associates, 1977.

Schuman, H., & Johnson, M. P. Attitudes and behavior. *Annual Review of Sociology*, 1976, *2*, 161–207.

Schwartz, S. Normative influences on altruism. In L. Berkowitz (Ed.), *Advances in experimental social psychology*, (Vol. 10). New York: Academic Press, 1977.

Sears, D. O., Hensler, C. P., & Speer, L. K. Opposition to busing: self-interest or symbolic politics? *American Political Science Review*, 1979, *73*, 369–384.

Sears, D. O., Lau, R. R., Tyler, T. R., & Allen, H. M. Self-interest vs. symbolic politics in policy attitudes and presidential voting. *American Political Science Review*, 1980, *74*, 670–684.

Sears, D. O., & McConahay, J. *The new urban Blacks and the Watts riot*. Boston: Houghton Mifflin, 1973.

Sears, D. O., Tyler, T. R., Citrin, J. & Kinder, D. R. Political system support and public response to the 1974 energy crisis. *American Journal of Political Science*, 1978, *22*, 56–82.

Shomer, R. W., & Centers, R. Differences in attitudinal responses under conditions of implicitly manipulated group salience. *Journal of Personality and Social Psychology*, 1970, *15*, 125–132.

Smith, M. B., Bruner, J. S., & White, R. W. *Opinions and personality*. New York: Wiley, 1956.

Snyder, M. The self-monitoring of expressive behavior. *Journal of Personality and Social Psychology*, 1974, *30*, 526–537.

Snyder, M., & Swann, W., Jr. When actions reflect attitudes: The politics of impression management. *Journal of Personality and Social Psychology*. 1976, *34*, 1034–1042.

Songer-Nocks, E. Situational factors affecting the weighting of predictor components in the Fishbein model. *Journal of Experimental Social Psychology*, 1976, *12*, 56–69.

Taylor, S. E., & Crocker, J. Schematic bases of social information processing. In E. T. Higgins, C. P. Herman, & M. P. Zanna (Eds.), *Social cognition: The Ontario symposium on personality and social psychology* (Vol. 1). Hillsdale, N.J.: Lawrence Erlbaum Associates, 1981.

Thurstone, L. L. Attitudes can be measured. *American Journal of Sociology* 1928, *33*, 529–554.

Tomkins, S. The quest for primary motives: Biography and autobiography of an idea. *Journal of Personality and Social Psychology*, 1981, *41*, 306–329.

Wicker, A. W. Attitudes vs. actions: The relationship of verbal and overt behavioral responses to attitude objects. *Journal of Social Issues*, 1969, *25*, 41–78.

Wicklund, R. A., & Frey, D. Self-awareness theory: When the self makes a difference. In D. M. Wegener & R. R. Vallacher (Eds.), *The self in social psychology*. New York: Oxford University Press, 1980.

Zimbardo, P. The human choice: Individuation, reason and order versus deindividuation, impulse and chaos. In W. J. Arnold & D. Levine (Eds.), *Nebraska Symposium on Motivation, 1969.* Lincoln: University of Nebraska Press, 1970.

THE PERSONALITY-
BEHAVIOR RELATION

7 Self-Focused Attention and the Validity of Self-Reports

Robert A. Wicklund
University of Texas at Austin

THE PROBLEM

The lack of consistency between two different facets of the human is the central problem dealt with in this chapter. These two facets are (1) behaviors—the sort we prefer to call "overt"—and (2) attitudes, personality traits, or even simpler self-descriptions that have some ostensible bearing on overt behaviors. In many cases these two facets appear to be almost identical—differing only in mode of expression. For instance, someone is observed to eat three pieces of apple pie and is then asked to rate, on a Likert scale, how much he enjoys eating apple pie. It is hard to imagine that there would be much inconsistency here. In other cases, the connection between these two facets may be less clear. An individual can be observed to be a very good organizer and manager, letting each employee know exactly what is expected and attending to every rule and detail. Should the same person then score high on the California F scale? Maybe so, but this issue is better dealt with empirically. In fact, even the apple pie case needs to be dealt with empirically. Just because the behavior and self-report seem obviously tied together is no cause to conclude that they are tied together in the individual's mind. That is, the two may not correlate.

One of the better summaries of evidence relating to inconsistency between these two facets of the human is by Wicker (1969), whose focus is slightly more specific than the one here. He concentrates on research that has correlated overt behavior with behavior-relevant attitudes, and finds such phenomena as the following:

Three Examples

The subject of a study by Carr and Roberts (1965) was the participation of black college students in civil rights activities. The authors obtained attitudes toward civil rights participation from their black respondents with a straightforward, Likert-type instrument. Then the same students' behavioral participation in civil rights activities was assessed, using behavioral indices such as the depth of involvement in civil rights activities and frequency of participation. The behavioral index was then correlated with the previously measured attitude. For the male respondents these correlations ranged between .25 and .29, and for the females the range was between .10 and .25. These levels of correlation are exemplary, in that they are pointed to as characteristic of attempts to validate attitude measures, personality measures, or more generally, self-reports of any kind.

A conceptually similar effort was undertaken by Freeman and Ataov (1960). College students' attitudes toward cheating were measured on four projective measures, as well as on a more direct measure. When the relationship between each measure and actual cheating behavior was examined, the resulting correlations were found to vary between .10 and −.19.

Finally, a somewhat more recent study by Gibbons (1978) looked at the relationship between self-rated sex guilt and subsequent appreciation for pornographic literature. The sex guilt scale was a rather lengthy scale developed by Mosher (1968), and included items referring to obscene literature. For the behavioral measure, all subjects had an opportunity to examine a pornographic passage and then rate it on several dimensions, including how arousing, enjoyable, and well-written it was. The subsequent correlations between scale score and each of the three behavioral indices of enjoyment were .10, .20, and −.23, respectively. Again, a seemingly face valid measure of an attitude seems to have practically no bearing on a behavior that would ordinarily be considered as closely germane to the attitude.

A LIST OF FIRST SOLUTIONS

After reviewing numerous articles akin to those just described, Wicker delves into some of the factors that might be responsible for these low correlations.

Other Influences.   One such problem was cited by Allport in 1937, and is the observation that any given behavior is probably affected by more than one attitude. Thus if a number of mutually orthogonal, or mutually contradictory attitudes are simultaneously relevant (or salient), it is no longer clear which direction will be taken in behavior. The *other influences* factor is much broader than simply a question of conflicting attitudes: Wicker also cites competing motives, normative prescriptions for behavior that interfere with people acting

upon their attitudes, unforeseen events that might affect behavior, and interviewer bias.

Possibility of the Behavior's Being Manifested.   Another reason for not finding correlations has to do with a ceiling effect on behaving. If there are severe
constraints on what subjects can do in the measurement situation, the behavioral
variability might be insufficient for a correlation to emerge. For instance, much
of the research cited by Wicker (1969) correlates work-related attitudes with job
performance. If a sample happened to consist just of apprentices, it might be that
their abilities were at a low and homogeneous level, thereby not giving work
attitudes an opportunity to affect performance.

Relation Between Attitude and Behavior.   This factor comes close to the
central theme of the present chapter. Wicker invokes what may be called the
specificity hypothesis, by which is meant that the attitude object may be defined
so vaguely, in measurement, that responses have little to do with concrete,
behavioral settings. For instance, suppose a sample of people is given the item,
"Do you like children"? Subsequently, their contraceptive-usage is monitored,
and correlated with the "like children" item. The correlation is found to be
exactly .00. Why? Because the object of attitude was simply children; there was
no differentiation between having one's own children, having one's own children
now versus later, enjoying others' children, teaching children, appreciating them
from afar, etc. By the reasoning of the specificity hypothesis it should come as
no surprise when vague items, or perhaps projective tests, show no relationship
with specific behaviors.

Measurement Problems.   Although this source of problem was not discussed
in detail by Wicker, it receives a great deal of attention in research involving
validation of personality measures. Commonly the discussion centers around the
reliability of the measuring instrument. Suffice it to say that an unreliable instrument will reduce the correlation between self-report and behavior. At the same
time, many of the measures to be discussed here (as that used by Gibbons, 1978)
have been shown to be highly reliable; thus unreliable measurement is by no
means the sole problem.

THE PSYCHOLOGICAL CONNECTION BETWEEN SELF-
REPORT AND BEHAVIOR

Wicker's list of stumbling points is an important one, and no doubt many of the
low correlations he cites are attributable to one or another of the factors cited.
However, there is one serious omission. In discussing the validity of self-reports
there is never any reference to the psychological state of the person whose self-
reports and behaviors are being assessed. What is the person trying to do at the

time of making the report or while performing the overt behavior? Is the individual trying to be consistent? Can we conceivably speak of a psychological state—perhaps a motivated state—that could be engaged in the interest of greater consistency?

All of the factors emerging from Wicker's article may be seen as prerequisites for the emergence of a correlation. Clearly the person must have the ability to perform the behavior, and to be sure, no correlation will emerge if interview bias governs the responses. It is also evident that the attitude object must be sufficiently specific. But given that all of these prerequisites are met, should we not then turn our attention to the psychological state of the person, in order to try to understand whether the person is trying to be, or oriented toward being, consistent? If this latter state of the person varies, we should then have a handle on why people are only variously consistent.

Automated Behaviors as Responsible for Low Correlations.   Assume for a moment that all of the Wicker criteria are satisfied. The attitude items are highly specific, the reliability of the attitude measure is high, there are no competing attitudes or motives and so forth. Even against the backdrop of these seemingly ideal circumstances we might still find a correlation of 0. And the reason would be this: Either the behaviors entailed in answering the attitude items, or else the overt behaviors correlated with the attitude, or both, might be automated. By *automated* is meant a certain over-rehearsed quality of behavior, such that the behavior simply "goes off" in a particular situation without the person's having to think about its connection to any specific goal state, rules, attitudes, or anything else (Kimble & Perlmuter, 1970). One may also apply the term *automated* to the highly trained behavior of animals, as it is also likely that they do not cogitate a great deal about responses that are so conditioned that they emerge 100% of the time. Now, in terms of the kinds of situations dealt with by Wicker, why would automation lead to low correlations?

Consider for a moment the remarkable report by La Piere (1934). La Piere took a Chinese couple for a drive through parts of the United States, and found that they were accepted at virtually every restaurant-hotel establishment they chose to patronize. But in contrast to the seemingly non-prejudiced attitudes of this sample of proprietors, those same people evidenced heavily anti-Oriental attitudes when surveyed via a mail questionnaire. Nearly all of them said they would refuse Chinese customers. Was the questionnaire unreliable? Was its specificity inadequate? Conceivably so, but it is also very possible that either or both sides of the hypocrisy—the accepting overt behavior and the rejecting private questionnaire response—were automated. For instance, if an automobile with three adults drives up to a restaurant, the manger may well go automatically into a set of highly rehearsed responses that simply belongs to the situation (cf. Abelson, 1976). The exact characteristics of the adults may play no role in determining the manner in which this over-rehearsed set of responses is run off. Thus it is not as though the manager was necessarily responding to the Orientals as marginal customers, about whom he had to make a decision. Instead, it is likely that no thought was devoted to the issue of whether his behavior coincided with his previous verbal statements, or internal values, regarding Orientals.

Similarly, the questionnaire may well have been filled out in an automated fashion. It would not be surprising to learn that people have an over-rehearsed repertoire of verbal response about ethnic groups that bear little relation to their overt behavior. This would be especially likely if they seldom have contact with such groups.

In summary, the typically low correlations between self-reports and overt behavior may have to do simply with the individual's not thinking about the inconsistency, and/or not being motivated to remove or minimize that inconsistency. Instead, many overt behaviors—and self-reports as well—might be so over-rehearsed that they take place in isolation, with no psychological connection to other facets of the person.

Automated Behaviors as Responsible for High Correlations. But the intrusion of automated behaviors into the attitude-behavior link does not stop with the low end of the correlation continuum. It is also very likely that many of the high correlations, of which psychologists would be so proud, have no *psychological* basis. That is to say, such correlations may not be the result of individuals trying to be consistent, but instead, only a by-product of automated behaviors and automated answers. For instance, if we re-arrange the La Piere study so that the couple with whom he traveled was black, alter the time in history to the 1950s, and focus on the South and West as areas for sampling hotels and restaurants, we would expect much different results. Southern restaurant-hotel owners would have turned the black couple away, and they also would have indicated discriminatory attitudes on the questionnaire. In the West, the couple would likely have been accepted, and owners would have been considerably less negative toward black clientele. The result: a definite positive correlation between overt behavior and attitude. But exactly as in the analysis of La Piere's original study (above), there is no reason to think that the restaurant-hotel owners would be making a conscious endeavor to bring their verbal reports and behavior into alignment. Rather, the behavior would be an over-rehearsed rejection (southern) or over-rehearsed acceptance (western). And the attitude statements would probably be equally over-rehearsed.

We might look at an even simpler example to illustrate the point once again. Consider two extreme samples of subjects, such that one believes firmly in obeying the law, while the other is generally ambivalent toward the law. The members of both groups are then observed, and their incidence of jay-walking in a downtown area is tabulated. A high positive correlation between attitude toward the law and jay-walking is noted.

Now obviously this does not have to mean that the person who waits for the green light before crossing is trying to bring his overt behavior into coordination with his attitudes, nor does it mean that the person who violates the light, or crosses at a non-pedestrian location, is trying to act in an illegal manner. No doubt the street-crossing repertoire is over-rehearsed, based on thousands of repetitions. Thus the question is this: Should the psychologist who finds a positive correlation in this instance be so pleased? The correlation exists simply because two overlearned responses (one verbal; one more overt) happen to coincide. But there is no evidence that the individual was thinking about the two facets in relation to one another.

Has there been a direct answer to this kind of problem? Or has the question even been raised? We will now look briefly at some of the recent attempts in psychology to raise correlations between overt behavior and self-reports.

A HANDFUL OF SOLUTIONS

The Idiographic Approach.   One of the best-known, direct confrontations with the low correlation issue began with Bem and Allen (1974). The idea was to assume that consistency cannot be expected of all people on all dimensions; thus the issue becomes one of ferreting out those individuals who tend toward being inconsistent. This was accomplished, interestingly, by self-report. Subjects were asked if they were generally consistent on some given dimension, and it was indeed then established that the consistency among their behaviors on a given dimension was higher when they described themselves as being consistent on that dimension. A similar strategy was followed by Kenrick and Stringfield (1980), although they asked subjects to discriminate between *most* and *least* consistent traits. Again, subjects seemed to have a veridical sense of which behavioral dimensions were consistent and which were inconsistent. Unfortunately, this approach tells us nothing about the psychology of the individual at the time he is acting consistently or inconsistently. Thus it does not advance our knowledge of the factors that steer a person toward coordinating verbal reports with behavior.

An idiographic approach to the test-validity issue does not need to be limited to the individual difference of self-reported consistency. For instance, Mabe and West (in press), in a review of validity of self-reports of ability, have pointed to such variables as intelligence and internal locus of control as mediators of validity. Still, a further analysis remains to be done, in the sense of uncovering the psychological bases for the workings of such individual differences.

"Maximal" Personality Measures.   Willerman, Turner, and Peterson (1976) tried two alternative methods of asking subjects about their expression of anger. One approach asked for typical levels, and another approach asked the subject for the *maximum* level of anger he might display. Subjects then had the opportunity to express overt hostility, and interestingly, it turned out that the maximal measure was a better predictor. The reasons for the operation of the maximal measure are at

least three: (1) the maximal measure would seem to have a greater specificity, thereby coinciding with one of Wicker's (1969) more salient suggestions; (2) maximal reports may bear more similarity to aggression-eliciting conditions, in that aggressive behavior might usually be enacted under freer conditions than self-reports; and (3) normative proscriptions against describing oneself in an antisocial way can be overridden by asking people for maximal level. Still, none of these factors has much to do with the psychology of the person who is more (or less) consistent. The improvement in specificity of the measure, or the reduction in constraints against admitting to hostility, do not tell us what factors motivate a person to bring self-reports into line with behavior.

Cognitive Dissonance. Cognitive dissonance theory (Festinger, 1957) comes to this area in a rather oblique manner, in that the theory has practically never been associated with the test-validity issue. And it must be said at the outset that the theory applies only to self-reports that are made quite soon *following* behavior (cf. Brehm & Cohen, 1962; Wicklund & Brehm, 1976). Prediction of behavior from attitudes is out of the realm of the theory. However, the theory is potentially fruitful here in that it says something theoretical about the conditions conducive to consistency between freely chosen behaviors and subsequent self-reports about those behaviors. The variables of free choice, responsibility, justifications for behavior, and a variety of other variables all have a definite theoretical meaning in the context of behavior-attitude consistency. Thus with dissonance theory we have a start: At least the theory addresses the issue of the psychological state of the person who is trying (or not trying) to be consistent, and it is very precise in specifying variables antecedent to consistency. This leads us to the next section, where the consistency idea is elaborated within a much different theoretical context.

SELF-FOCUSED ATTENTION: A THEORETICAL BACKGROUND

Breaking up Automation

From the previous line of reasoning we might think that if the automatic character of responding—whether verbal self-descriptions or overt behavior—were broken, the person would then direct thought onto the nature of the verbal utterances and behaviors. This much comes directly from Kimble and Perlmuter's (1970) analysis of automated action, which notes that the automation of an act and conscious attention to that act are virtually mutually exclusive. To turn one's attention suddenly to what one is typing, or to the individual words of a memorized poem, is to destroy the automation that seems to be associated with not thinking about the components of the act. Thus a first step should be to vary the individual's attention toward the content of what is going on. And what is the content? In this case, it is relatively simple to describe: We are talking about content in the sense of attitudes, values, traits, or behaviors. In short, we are talking about various facets of the self. Thus if the person's attention can be turned inward, toward those self-elements, the automatic character of the act should be affected, and the result should be a clearer picture of the components of one's own attitudes and behaviors. But self-directed attention has more than just automation-breaking consequences, and at this point we will describe a theoretical notion that spells out some of these comsequences.

Self-Awareness Theory

The theory of self-awareness (Duval & Wicklund, 1972; Frey, Wicklund, & Scheier, 1978; Wicklund, 1975, 1979a, 1979b, 1980) begins with a simple distinction between attending to the self and attending elsewhere. It has been documented that a certain class of stimuli can bring the individual's attention increasingly onto the self—as assessed by the frequency with which the person makes self-references in response to ambiguous verbal material. For instance, studies by Carver and Scheier (1978), Davis and Brock (1975), and Giuliano and Wegner (1981) have confronted people with verbal material in which there was an opportunity to impute oneself into the situation, via first-person pronouns or first-person references of other kinds. As independent variables, the kinds of stimuli that have been used most commonly are the person's mirror image, tape-recorded voice, a camera trained on the subject, and making the person feel unique (for a review see Wicklund, 1979a, 1980).

Another class of stimuli has been conceived as having distracting power—i.e., as taking attention away from the self. Such events as a television program (Ferris & Wicklund, in Wicklund, 1975), engaging in a simple motor activity (Duval & Wicklund, 1973), or deindividuation in a small group (Pennebaker, 1979; Wegner & Giuliano, in press) have been shown to have self awareness-decreasing properties.

Not only can we speak of environmental stimuli that will draw the person's attention alternately toward or away from the self, but it also makes sense to characterize individuals as relatively high, or low, in chronic self-focused attention. A measure of "private self-consciousness" (Fenigstein, Scheier & Buss, 1975) has been shown to correlate with the same kinds of effects that are produced by manipulations involving such stimuli as mirrors or tape-recorded voices.

The Motivational Consequences.   The condition of self-awareness has a number of consequences, not all of which are completely germane here. The important one for our purposes concerns the premise that self-focused individuals come to realize their personal inconsistencies, or inadequacies, on whatever dimensions that are salient in the condition of self-focused attention. Most people commit countless hypocrisies, or other kinds of inconsistent behaviors, without attending regularly to the fact of the inconsistency. The stereotypical Christian goes to church regularly, assents to the Ten Commandments, then proceeds to cheat his neighbor on Monday morning. The moralizing mother instructs her children in attending to the rules and laws, then does her best to speed without getting picked up by the police.

The person committing these inconsistencies does not necessarily suffer guilt feelings because of the actions. It is as though the act is carried out without any thought directed toward the moral principle, the value, or the attitude, and it is also as though one is able to espouse the principle without thinking of past behaviors to the contrary. In other words, each component of the attitude-behavior relationship might be automated.

The impact of self-awareness is to make it more difficult for attitudes and attitude-relevant actions to remain psychologically dissociated. Consider the jay-walker once more. If a person who normally insists upon his strict obedience of the law were made self-focused in a potential jay-walking situation, the automaticity of the act should break down. Rather than the law-breaking (or law-abiding) response simply "going off" in its habitual way, the person will come to think of himself and his behaviors along the dimension of obedience to the law. The relation among the relevant parts of the self, i.e., the moral principle and the relevant behaviors, will be considered when in the self-aware state.

The result of this self-evaluative process is a motivational consequence: If it is difficult to remove oneself from the self-aware condition, then the person can be expected to show an increase in consistency. Consistency in this case is possible in primarily two ways: to behave in accord with one's principles or attitudes, or to alter the attitude to fit the behavior. If the act has not yet been performed, but the person is at the choice point, then the act will be carried out such that it conforms more to the moral principle (self-report). On the other hand, if one has just performed an act, and becomes self-aware only after the action is unequivocal, then the self-report can be altered to fit the behavior. In each of these cases an increase in self-consistency is the result—and this leads us directly to the topic of self-description validity.

SELF-AWARENESS WHILE REPORTING ABOUT THE SELF

Personality Tests

Pryor, Gibbons, Wicklund, Fazio and Hood (1977) assembled a simple, highly face valid test of sociability with a very high degree of face validity. The items were the following:

1. I feel that I can usually communicate well with members of the opposite sex.
2. I feel that I can find something in common with most people.
3. Sometimes I ''freeze up'' when around very attractive women.
4. Some people consider me quite talkative.
5. I consider myself a sociable person.
6. I usually have difficulty in starting conversations with strangers.
7. I prefer my own company.
8. When with others I do not speak until spoken to.
9. I have difficulty in making new friends.
10. I sometimes avoid social contacts for fear of doing or saying the wrong thing.
11. I usually take the initiative in making new friends.
12. I often feel ill at ease with other people.
13. Sometimes I am so shy it bothers me.
14. I enjoy getting acquainted with most people.
15. It is important to me that people like me.
16. I am shy with all but good friends.

A sample of male subjects was asked to take this test individually, then they returned approximately two days later—again individually—for an experiment that ostensibly had no relationship to the initial testing session. Upon arriving for the second session they found that they would have to wait in a small room with an attractive female undergraduate, and during the ensuing 3-minute waiting period two behavioral indices of sociability were taken. One consisted of the number of words the subject spoke to the woman (tape-recorded), and the other was the woman's subjective rating of his sociability. In fact, she was a confederate of the experimenter.

The two behavioral indices correlated together very highly (over .80), thus were combined via z-scores into a single behavioral index, and the index was then correlated with the sociability scale score. The experiment was conducted twice (i.e., two replications), each time with a different experimenter and confederate, and the results for the two highly similar replications are shown in Table 7.1. Note first that in the control conditions there is practically no relationship between scale score and the behavioral sociability index—.03 in the first replication and .28 in the second.

Now the theory becomes relevant. Approximately half of the subjects were administered the scale while they were looking into a mirror. The mirror was said to belong to another researcher, a justification that has proven generally plausible in numerous studies with a mirror manipulation. According to the previous reasoning the impact of the mirror should be one of heightening self-awareness, and since sociability was the central feature of the situation, the subject should

TABLE 7.1
Correlation of Sociability Score with Behavioral
Index of Sociability

	Mirror	Control
Replication I	.55	.03
Replication II	.73	.28

have come to concentrate increasingly upon his sociability. The outcome, according to the theory, would be an increased effort to bring the self-report into line with the usual level of sociability, and this is evidently what happened. Table 7.1 shows that the correlations for the mirror conditions are .55 for the first replication and .73 for the second, and the combination of these is significantly higher than the combined control condition correlations. Thus it begins to appear that self-focused attention can steer self-reports into the direction of one's habitual behavior, meaning that test validity can be the outcome of self-focus-engendering situations.

There is a question that may already have occurred to the reader. If someone is engaged in filling out a questionnaire that asks very direct questions about one's sociability level, wouldn't that already maximize self-awareness on the sociability dimension? Of what additional value, then, is the mirror manipulation? The answer is that it is possible to fill out a questionnaire without focusing directly on the self. In fact, a person can deviate from answering directly about the self in two different ways. On the one hand, the answer can be totally automated, such as the answer to "Do you like Christmas?" or "Do you enjoy music?" Thus if it is automated, the answer is not predicated on any special contents of self, but rather, is nothing more than a habitual response set off by a certain questioning format. The second possibility is that the person bases the answers on some particular content, but not necessarily on what is characteristic of the self. For instance, when asked "How many friends do you have?" a person might answer in terms of how many friends the usual person has, or perhaps just give a random estimate, without focusing on what is true of one's own self.

There is also another answer to the question of "Why isn't the questionnaire sufficient to create self-awareness?" It is possible that direct questions of a person do generate the self-focused state. This issue had never been considered experimentally. At the same time, it is also important to keep in mind that the self-focused attention concept is not an either-or distinction. The human is not totally self-aware or totally un-self-aware. Rather, it is sensible to speak in terms of the proportion of time spent in self-focused attention, and it might be that an initial instance of self-awareness generated by an unusual, self-directed question is quickly replaced by a less-self-focused condition. In other words, a stronger, more dominant stimulus (such as a mirror) would be necessary to create the prolonged self-focused state necessary for the increased correlations.

Another exploration of a personality test was by Scheier, Buss and Buss (1978)—this time with a test that had been documented and used some years earlier. This was the Buss and Durkee hostility inventory (1957), an inventory with 66 items that has both an attitudinal factor, with resentment and suspicion scales, and aggressiveness factor that includes several scales related to overt aggressive behaviors. In one sitting subjects were administered both the hostility inventory and the self-consciousness measure. It would be expected, based on earlier research, that the subjects high in "private self-consciousness" would be the more self-focused, thus more likely to be consistent between self-reports and behavior.

Later in the semester subjects had the opportunity to administer shock to a victim, using the Buss (1961) shock machine apparatus. The shock level administered was taken as the behavioral index of aggressiveness. When correlations between the Buss and Durkee (1957) inventory and overt aggressiveness were computed, the difference between high and low private self-conscious subjects was striking. The low self-conscious group showed a correlation of only .09, while the group high in self-consciousness was remarkably consistent ($r = .66$).

There is one ambiguity associated with the individual difference definition of self-focus. One cannot be certain whether the results are due to highly self-focused subjects' steering their questionnaire responses in the direction of their usual behaviors, or their behaviors in the direction of their attitudes. This is because they are self-focused both at the time of making verbal reports and at the time of overt behavior. Independent of this issue, it is useful to know that chronic self-focus operates similarly to the manipulated condition. In one sense, the Scheier et al. research may be seen as a theoretical improvement on the Bem and Allen approach. While the Ben and Allen technique and the Scheier et al. technique may both be characterized as idiographic strategies, the Scheier et al. paradigm at least has a definite theoretical rationale for thinking that a certain class of people will be more consistent.

Reporting One's Test Score

A second experiment by Pryor et al. (1977) also manipulated self-awareness by using a mirror, but this time it is more accurate to call subjects' self-descriptions *post*-dictive rather than predictive. Our hypothesis was a simple one: People should be more accurate in reporting their test scores if they are self-focused while making the self-report. This time undergraduate males were asked simply to record their combined verbal and quantitative SAT scores on a piece of paper, and at the time were either seated before a mirror or not. Following that pro-

cedure the discrepancies between that report and actual SAT score were calculated. Overall, subjects tended quite strongly toward self-aggrandizement: inaccuracies were almost invariably in a positive direction, and the average
discrepancy was approximately 50 points. The presence of the mirror caused this
discrepancy to drop to a relatively accurate 16 points. Further, the effect was
especially strong for subjects whose actual scores were below the median. Without the mirror their average discrepancy was 78 points, but the effect of self-
awareness was to bring this to 25 points.

It is interesting that the inaccuracies in self-reporting were highly directional
in this study, for there was no hint of a bias, or direction distortion, in sociability
self-reports in the first experiment by Pryor et al. (1977). That is, in that experiment there were no differences between the control and mirror groups in either
mean or variance on the sociability scale. The contrast between these two studies
underlines a point that is seldom noted in research on test validity. A report can
be invalid either because of mere sloppiness (i.e. randomness, neglect, effect of
various sources of error), or because subjects are systematically interested in
fudging the self-report in a given direction. The self-awareness reasoning is
applicable in either case, as the idea is that the person will attempt to become
more consistent vis-á-vis the relation between self-report and behavior.

Recently-Acquired Attitudes: Behavior as an
Antecedent of Attitude Formation

It was already noted previously that cognitive dissonance theory gives us a
theoretical orientation toward the human's striving to be consistent between self-
reports and behaviors. Specifically, given a paradigm in which the individual
first chooses, and then attitudes toward the choice alternatives are measured, the
theory predicts that the person becomes increasingly attracted to the chosen
course of action. Within such a simple paradigm one can arrive at the same
prediction with Bem's self-perception theory (1965), although with a much
different theoretical language. Rather than the creation of a motivational state of
cognitive dissonance, Bem refers only to a simple judgmental process, whereby
the choosing person comes to infer a positive attitude toward what is chosen
simply because of having chosen it.

Thus no matter which of these formulations we begin with, the implication of
making a decision is a clear one. The person should come to make a self-
description, i.e., adopt an attitude about one's relation to the choice objects, that
is consistent with the direction taken in the choice.

In a third experiment reported by Pryor et al. (1977) subjects were given a
simple, five-way choice. They were given a number of intellectual puzzles to
play with for 10 minutes—consisting of the games "letter series, cube comparison, Gestalt completion, hidden figures, and nearer point." The subjects had two

mimeographed pages of each type of problem, and were instructed to work only as many of each problem as they desired. There were no requirements and no implication for evaluation.

Following the 10-minute work period the subject was taken to a different location, then filled out a simple rating scale on each of the five puzzles, rating them on a continuum of "extremely boring" to "extremely interesting." In order to examine consistency between choice of a puzzle and later self-report of interest in that same puzzle, a correlation was computed for each subject, consisting of the relationship between the quantity of work on a given puzzle and the rating of that same puzzle. Thus a positive correlation would mean that the more a subject worked on a given puzzle, the higher rating it received.

The results in the control condition were hardly suggestive of a consistency process: The average correlation of those subjects was only .13. Other subjects filled out the rating questionnaire with a mirror before them, and the average correlation for this group was a surprisingly high .74. Thus it would appear again as if the provocation to self-focused attention brings subjects to base their interest ratings very much on their freely chosen behaviors. The results would suggest that Bem's self-perception theory has perhaps not been interpreted literally enough, for "self" in "self-perception" has not heretofore been treated as a variable. If one can maximize the self-examination experimentally, the attitudes that are then inferred are based to a much greater extent on the free behavior.

A related, and more elaborate experiment by McCormick (1979) underlines this conclusion even further. One might ask in the context of the Pryor et al. study whether subjects were forming their attitudes simply from the mere quantity of each puzzle performed, or from their knowledge of having freely chosen to work on those particular tasks. Both dissonance theory and self-perception theory would view the volitional element as important. And in the context of speaking of the *self*, it is important that the attitude is based on something initiated by the self—not just on behaviors that are totally constrained by the environment. McCormick conducted a study within the Pryor et al. paradigm,

TABLE 7.2
Correlations Between Quantity of Work on
Task and Interest in Task

	Mirror	*Control*
Choice	.56	.15
No Choice	−.01	.17

Note—A separate rank order correlation was computed for each subject. The two variables were (a) relative work done on the five tasks, and (b) relative interest ratings of the five tasks. The values in the table are the means of these rank-order correlations.

but added another pair of conditions in which the quantity of each task performed was dictated by the previous *choice condition* subject's performance. In other words, each *no choice* subject was yoked to an earlier choice subject. The results, in terms of average correlation between quantity of task accomplished and interest rating, are shown in Table 7.2. It is immediately apparent that the self-awareness manipulation, again introduced only during the interest-rating phase, enhances consistency only as long as the consistency involves behaviors chosen by the self. If the behaviors are exterior to the self, i.e., totally constrained, the self-awareness manipulation makes little difference.

SELF-AWARENESS WHILE BEHAVING

This chapter opened with an orientation toward two facets of the human—the self-report (i.e., reflection of attitude, value, personality trait) and the relatively overt behavior. The central issue here is one of consistency between these two facets, and from the theory, it is easy to imagine two alternatives uses of the induction of self-awareness. The person can be brought into a self-reflexive state while reporting on the relevant attitude or trait, as in the preceding research, or else self-awareness can be bolstered during the overt behavior. The behavior should then be steered more in the direction of the attitude or trait. Theoretically, these two lines of research are practically identical. We will now turn to three illustrations of the impact of self-awareness while the person is behaving.

The study of Gibbons (1978) was discussed above briefly, although not in entirety. Subjects first filled out the Mosher sex guilt inventory, then read an erotic passage from a paperback book, and finally rated the passage on the criteria of "arousing, enjoyable, and well-written." The results mentioned earlier referred only to the control conditions, in which there was no introduction of self-awareness. About half of the subjects sat before a mirror while they made this tri-partite rating of the pornographic passage, and the resulting correlations between the scale socre and the three dependent measures are shown in Table 7.3. Note that the correlations become higher with the mirror, no matter which

TABLE 7.3
Correlations Between Sex Guilt Score and
Three Indices of Enjoyment of Pornographic
Passage

	Mirror	*Control*
Arousing	.45	.10
Enjoyable	.74	.20
Well-written	.58	−.23

TABLE 7.4
Mean Values for Originality of Associations

	Mirror	*Control*
High Creative Group	737	336
Low Creative Group	341	524

Note—Maximum possible value is 1742. A higher score represents a more creative response.

index is used. In short, the results say that the sex guilt inventory becomes a much better predictor if the criterion behaviors (enjoyment ratings of pornography) are observed while subjects' attention is directed inward.

An earlier experiment within this kind of paradigm was by Carver (1975), and used a self-report measure of punitiveness as the predictor. Subjects had the opportunity to act punitively via giving electirc shocks to a target person, and the results were very clear: With no self awareness induction there was almost a perfect 0 relationship between self-rated punitiveness and shock administered, but people who delivered punishment while sitting before a mirror behaved much more in line with their earlier-recorded punitiveness scores.

Finally, even the dimension of creativity can be dealt with in this same manner. Hormuth (in press) measured a sample of subjects on several of the creativity-tapping items of a Personal Value Scale by Scott (1965). Then, during an experimental session, subjects' actual creativity was operationalized in terms of the uncommonness of words chosen for responding to stimulus words. It was assumed, quite reasonably, that a non-common word associate may be taken as an operational definition of creativity. When there was no inducement to self-awareness during the association task, the Scott measure tended to predict *backward,* although that trend was not significant. And when subjects were made self-focused during that task, the creativity scale then showed a definite predictive validity. These data are shown in Table 7.4. A second, highly germane finding takes us back to the research results of Pryor et al. (Experiment III) and McCormick (1979). Hormouth asked subjects how much effort they expended in trying to be original while making their associations. Such a self-description would be expected to relate more closely to actual creativeness under self-awareness-prompting conditions, and indeed, control subjects showed a correlation between self-rated effort and actual creative output of just .34, while the self-awareness condition resulted in a correlation of .80.

In summary, the validity of self-reports in a variety of settings can be improved by bringing the individual's attention to bear on the self. The self-reports involved can consist of simple attitudes toward choice objects as well as what are normally called personality traits. Further, it doesn't matter whether attention is brought to the self at the time of self-report, or at the time of overt behavior. In either case the result is an improvement in the predictive or postdictive power of the measures.

It might be noted that the extremely meager correlations found in the control conditions of these studies may actually be under-representative of what would be found in normal testing conditions. In almost all of the research reported, subjects were alone while responding, and the only element that varied was the presence of a mirror. The characteristic testing situation, with others including experimenters or proctors present, is no doubt more conducive to self-focus than are the bare walls of a laboratory cubicle. Thus "characteristic" correlations might be expected to fall somewhere between those of the control and self-awareness conditions discussed here. But this is a small practical point: The more important issue is that it now seems to be possible to describe, in a theoretical language, a controllable psychological mediator of the self-report-behavior relationship.

TWO PRACTICAL QUESTIONS

Controlling Self-Awareness

With the exception of the Scheier, Buss and Buss (1978) study, which used an individual difference operationalization of self-focus, the rest of this research has employed mirror manipulations exclusively. The reason for the frequent use of this manipulation is its minimal, unconfounded nature—it is largely free of artifacts that might clutter the meaning of the results. But at the same time, given that the basic effect seems to be replicable, it is fruitful to think in terms of stimuli to self-focus that might either have a more direct applied value and that tend more to occur in natural settings.

The first of these to come to mind is simply an evaluative audience (cf. Duval & Wicklund, 1972), a stimulus that has been employed with some success in at least two studies (Carver & Scheier, 1978; Scheier, Fenigstein & Buss, 1974). Very recently there has been some evidence (Kenrick & Stringfield, 1980) that people who feel that certain classes of their behaviors are observed are likely to be more consistent on those same behavioral dimensions. While this correlational finding is probably open to more than one interpretation, there is a definite suggestion that feeling observed creates the same kind of self-focus, hence consistency, that has been considered in the last several pages.

Another stimulus to self-focus that is a common part of the social milieu is the condition of being unique, or standing out. Research by Duval (1976) and Wegner and Schaefer (1978) has manipulated the person's feeling a certain minority status, and Wicklund and Frey (1979) have found that uniqueness-generating traveling circumstances can also have such effects. In the latter study it was found that European travelers, interviewed in a certain country (e.g., Germany, Sweden, Switzerland) showed higher self-consciousness scores if they had never been in that country before. It would appear that traveling to a foreign country more than once can lower the initial impact of standing out or estrangement.

Finally, at the suggestion of C. H. Cooley (1902), Stephenson and Wicklund (1980) have looked at the effect within a dyad of one member's ostensible self-consciousness. Prior to interacting with one another, members of a dyad were given false feedback about the other's level of self-consciousness. Some subjects saw a self-consciousness questionnaire, representing the other, that indicated a great deal of self-focus. Other subjects expected to interact with someone who had only a minimal level of self-directed attention. The result, no matter whether measured in terms of attribution toward the self or tendency to use first-person pronouns, was an increased self-awareness as a result of anticipation of interaction with a self-conscious other.

Consistent With What?

The characterization of the human being as having two facets—self-report and behavior—that can either be consistent with one other or not, is perhaps a bit naive. As it happens, the research based on this premise has been profitable, in that the subjects of the above studies do seem to behave as though these two facets are highly salient components of the self-aware process. However, there are some important questions that can be asked about this simple conception of the human, and it is hoped that asking these questions will enable researchers to form a clearer picture of the potential complexities associated with trying to bring self-reports into closer conjunction with behavior.

When Self-Reports are Based on Recent Decisions.   For one, it would seem reasonable that self-awareness might heighten the *reliability* of an attitude or personality measure. There is no direct evidence for this point, but the thesis is plausible. The *two facets* being made consistent in such a case would simply be the attitude report at Time 1 and the corresponding report at Time 2. But suppose that behavior intervenes, within the context of a dissonance-arousing setting. When the Time 2 attitude measure is then taken, what are the relevant two facets that the self-aware person will try to bring into coordination—Attitude 1 and Attitude 2, or the chosen behavior and Attitude 2? All of the relevant evidence would indicate that Attitude 1 is at that point neglected, and that the person's primary concern is with consistency between the behavior and the second report of attitude. Interestingly then, self-awareness could in fact operate in the direction of reducing the reliability of the attitude report, simply because the person is oriented toward increasing the consistency between the freely chosen behavior and the final attitude. In short, the question "Consistent with what?" is answered in this context in terms of an orientation around a recent, freely chosen behavior. To be consistent with previously stated attitudes is not necessarily a vital concern of the self. James (1910) anticipated this development precisely when he said that of the many components of self, "volitional decisions" have a particularly profound impact on the individual's functioning, relative to more static aspects of self such as attitudes. And as we have seen above, in the third study by Pryor et al. (1977) and the one by McCormick (1979), subjects are very likely to make a self-report congruent with a recent decision, particularly under conditions of self-focus.

When Self Reports are Based on Self-Defining Goals.   Suppose that a number of individuals are highly committed to their self-images as budding psychotherapists. It is a personal goal, part of the self-definition, that they can administer therapy successfully to others. Then they receive failure (or success) feedback regarding their effectiveness as therapists. We might think that self-descriptions would fall into line with the feedback received, and more so under self-aware circumstances. All of the preceding research would imply that the self-focused individual's self-descriptions are more in tune with actual performance than are the self-descriptions of non-self-aware people. Thus the two facets of the human here are simply performance and self-report. However, what about the commitment to a conception of oneself as successful therapist? Such a personal goal could conceivably constitute another import facet of self—one that could become involved in a consistency-increasing effort. As it happens, the results of an experiment by Federoff and Harvey (1976), using students as "therapists," found that the self-aware subjects were disinclined to take blame for failing in a therapy session. Rather, they attributed blame to the patient. It would appear from these results that subjects were clinging to their self-conceptions of being decent therapists, and aligning their self-descriptions with that self-conception rather than with their knowledge of their own failure performance. The point here is a more general one: Self-reports of self-aware people do not necessarily have to be brought into conjunction with prior behavior or performance. In the event that performance conflicts with a central self-conception, the resulting self-description can take on a defensive character, such that the positive self-conception comes to guide the self-description.

A series of studies by Wicklund and Gollwitzer (1981) goes still further in elaborating the conditions under which the person's orientation toward a self-defining goal (e.g. therapist, violinist) is likely to become a center point for the consistency process. For example, in the fourth study by Wicklund and Gollwitzer, subjects who were strongly committed to particular self-defining goals, such as "tennis player, journalist, mathematician," were asked to write an essay about a former teacher. Half of the subjects were requested to write about the best teacher in their history, while the others wrote about the *worst* teacher. It was proposed that those in the "worst-teacher" condition would react defensively to the fact of a negative teacher being made salient, and would then try to bolster the security of the striven-for self-definition. Consistent with this thinking, subjects who wrote about their worst teacher were more positive about themselves later than were those who wrote about their best teacher.

What do these results say about the validity of self-reports? The crucial point is that the self-report in this case was clearly oriented toward consistency with the sought-after self-definition (i.e., tennis player, journalist, and so forth). If subjects had been the least bit oriented toward trying to be consistent with their educational histories, then we might have expected those with a salient negative teacher to be more negative in their self-descriptions.

If one can assume, with Federoff and Harvey (1976), that self-focused attention will exacerbate the tendency for self-reports to be congruent with a striven-for self-definition, or aspired status, we now have a major issue to contend with in understanding the dynamics of self-report consistency. Sometimes self-reports will be congruent with "what the researcher wants them to be congruent with," i.e. with past behaviors, degree of training, or other observable features of the subject's history, and at other times the congruency will be oriented around self-defining goals. From the research reported by Wicklund and Gollwitzer (1981), it seems likely that this second kind of consistency process is put into gear by recent and/or salient experiences that undermine a person's self-definition. Further, and highly important in this context, this process is instigated only to the degree that the person is indeed committed to a self-definition that is relevant to the dimension tapped by the self-report.

Accordingly, the kind of self-consistency effects we have reported above (Gibbons, 1978; Pryor et al., 1977, etc.) are to be expected as long as the person does not have a strong commitment to a self-definition in the area being tapped. If there is a strong commitment, the consistency effects might still be expected as long as there is no recent, salient undermining of the self-definition. Otherwise an ostensible lack of self-report validity will result. But only ostensibly: In fact, the self-reports of subjects who are defending a self-definition are being made congruent with the aspired-to self, and this is an important kind of consistency that is invariably overlooked by that part of psychology which studies self-reports.

When Self-Reports are Based on Emotional States.   Scheier (1976) has shown that personal values about being aggressive are disregarded when subjects are aroused to anger, and that self-awareness actually serves to heighten the anger state, rather than to coordinate level of aggression to earlier-stated values. The finding is intriguing, for Carver (1975, above) had found that personal values about punitiveness were very useful predictors of the self-aware individual's aggression. It appears from Scheier's study, and from subsequent work by Scheier and Carver (1977) that an emotional state can come to dominant the person's thinking, such that self-reports are guided by the character of the emotion rather than the more static attitudes or personal values. James (1910) anticipated this result exactly, in viewing the emotions as a more gripping component of self than the more static components such as attitudes.

SUMMARY

The foregoing discussion of "consistent with what?" underscores the central purpose of this chapter. The view taken here is that the question of the validity of self-reports is only in part a methodological one—in the sense of issues of item specificity, scale reliability, and other factors cited by Wicker (1969). The other part of the question, this being the dynamics of the consistency process underlying valid self-reports, has been the central theme here. Consistency between self-report and behavior, where the behavior is variously aggressive behavior, sociability, enjoyment of pornography, among others, can be shown to increase when individuals are made to focus increasingly on themselves. The reasoning, based on a theory of self-awareness, is that the human is not necessarily *internally* consistent without first focusing attention inward, upon relevent parts of the self. Only then is the person moved to steer the self-report in the direction of characteristic behavior, or analogously, to steer behavior in the direction of self-reported attitudes and values. Thus self-consistency is not to be viewed as a static process, to be tapped into directly as long as the measuring instrument is sufficiently precise. We must think of the human as potentially very *in*consistent, more than willing to show blatant disregard for the researcher's desired goal of attaining validity coefficients of .30 and above.

There is more to the dynamic picture of the human. The consistency that researchers choose to examine when doing studies of self-report validity is not always the kind of consistency that will be of foremost concern for the subject being measured. The researcher should, according to the dynamic view outlined here, keep an eye toward the possibility that the individual might be basing a self-report on a recent decision rather than on some observed characteristic or attitude. And second, the researcher should be sensitive to the possibility that self-reports can easily be put into the service of the person's striving after particular self-definitions. Thus in such cases one would use as a criterion for validity the person's aspired-to self-definition, and not some pre-conceived criterion for validity that is drawn from the subject's behavioral history, such as performance or education. Finally, the emotionally aroused person might simply disregard any cognitive point of orientation for self-reports, tending instead to report more emotion to the extent that he is asked to look inward and reflect on the self.

ACKNOWLEDGMENTS

The author is indebted to Jeffrey S. Berman, Frederick X. Gibbons, Daniel M. Wegner, and Mark P. Zanna for their critical remarks on an earlier version of this chapter.

REFERENCES

Abelson, R. P. Script processing in attitude formation and decision making. In J. S. Carroll & J. W. Payne (Eds.), *Cognition and social behavior*. Hillsdale, N.J.: Lawrence Erlbaum Associates, 1976.

Allport, G. W. *Personality: A psychological interpretation*. New York: Holt, 1937.

Bem, D. J. An experimental analysis of self-persuasion. *Journal of Experimental Social Psychology*, 1965, *1*, 199–218.

Bem, D. J., & Allen, A. On predicting some of the people some of the time: The search for cross-situational consistencies in behavior. *Psychological Review*, 1974, *81*, 506–520.

Brehm, J. W., & Cohen, A. R. *Explorations in cognitive dissonance*. New York: Wiley, 1962.

Buss, A. H. *The psychology of aggression*. New York: Wiley, 1961.

Buss, A. H., & Durkee, A. An inventory for assessing different kinds of hostility. *Journal of Consulting Psychology*, 1957, *21*, 343–349.

Carr, L., & Roberts, S. O. Correlates of civil-rights participation. *Journal of Social Psychology*, 1965, *67*, 259–267.

Carver, C. S. Physical aggression as a function of objective self-awareness and attitudes toward punishment. *Journal of Experimental Social Psychology*, 1975, *11*, 510–519.

Carver, C. S., & Scheier, M. F. Self-focusing effects of dispositional self-consciousness, mirror presence, and audience presence. *Journal of Personality and Social Psychology*, 1978, *36*, 324–332.

Cooley, C. H. *Human nature and the social order*. New York: Charles Scribner's Sons, 1902.

Davis, D., & Brock, T. C. Use of first person pronouns as a function of increased objective self-awareness and prior feedback. *Journal of Experimental Social Psychology*, 1975, *11*, 381–388.

Duval, S. Conformity on a visual task as a function of personal novelty on attitudinal dimensions and being reminded of the object status of self. *Journal of Experimental Social Psychology*, 1976, *12*, 87–98.

Duval, S., & Wicklund, R. A. *A theory of objective self-awareness*. New York: Academic Press, 1972.

Duval, S., & Wicklund, R. A. Effects of objective self-awareness on attributions of causality. *Journal of Experimental Social Psychology*, 1973, *9*, 17–31.

Federoff, N. A., & Harvey, J. H. Focus of attention, self-esteem, and the attribution of causality. *Journal of Research in Personality*, 1976, *10*, 336–345.

Fenigstein, A., Scheier, M. F., & Buss, A. H. Public and private self-consciousness: Assessment and theory. *Journal of Consulting and Clinical Psychology*, 1975, *43*, 522–527.

Festinger, L. *A theory of cognitive dissonance*. Stanford, Calif.: Stanford University Press, 1957.

Freeman, L. C., & Aatov, T. Invalidity of indirect and direct measures of attitude toward cheating. *Journal of Personality*, 1960, *38*, 443–447.

Frey, D., Wicklund, R. A., & Scheier, M. F. Die Theorie der objektiven Selbstaufmerksamkeit. In D. Frey (Ed.), *Theorien der Sozialpsychologie*. Bern, Switzerland: Huber, 1978.

Gibbons, F. X. Sexual standards and reactions to pornography: Enhancing behavioral consistency through self-focused attention. *Journal of Personality and Social Psychology*, 1978, *36*, 976–987.

Giuliano, T., & Wegner, D. M. *Social awareness and justice*. Presented in symposium: Justice as a pervasive theme in everyday behavior. Annual Meeting of the American Psychological Association, Los Angeles, Calif., 1981.

Heinemann, W. The assessment of private and public self-consciousness: A German replication. *European Journal of Social Psychology*, 1980, in press.

Hormuth, S. E. Self-awareness, internal standards, and response dominance. *European Journal of Social Psychology*, in press.

James, W. *Psychology: The briefer course*. New York: Holt, 1910.

Kenrick, D. T., & Stringfield, D. O. Personality traits and the eye of the beholder: Crossing some traditional philosophical boundaries in the search for consistency in all of the people. *Psychological Review*, 1980, *87*, 88–104.

Kimble, G. A., & Perlmuter, L. C. The problem of volition. *Psychological Review*, 1970, *77*, 361–384.

La Piere, R. T. Attitudes vs. actions. *Social Forces*, 1934, *13*, 230–237.

Mabe, P. A., & West, S. G. Validity of self-evaluations of ability: A review and meta-analysis. *Journal of Applied Psychology*, in press.

McCormick, T. F. *An investigation of standards of correctness by inducing conformity and consistency pressures within the framework of objective self-awareness*. Unpublished doctoral dissertation, University of Texas, 1979.

Mosher, D. L. Measurement of guilt in females by self-report inventories. *Journal of Consulting and Clinical Psychology*, 1968, *32*, 690–695.

Pennebaker, J. W., McElrea, C. E., & Skelton, J. A. *Levels of selfhood: From me to us*. Paper presented at the annual meeting of the American Psychological Association, New York, 1979.

Pryor, J. B., Gibbons, F. X., Wicklund, R. A., Fazio, R. H., & Hood, R. Self-focused attention and self-report validity. *Journal of Personality*, 1977, *45*, 513–527.

Scheier, M. F. Self-awareness, self-consciousness, and angry aggression. *Journal of Personality*, 1976, *44*, 627–644.

Scheier, M. F., Buss, A. H., & Buss, D. M. Self-consciousness, self-report of aggressiveness, and aggression. *Journal of Research in Personality*, 1978, *12*, 133–140.

Scheier, M. F., & Carver, C. S. Self-focused attention and the experience of emotion: Attraction, repulsion, elation, and depression. *Journal of Personality and Social Psychology*, 1977, *35*, 625–636.

Scheier, M. F., Fenigstein, A., & Buss, A. H. Self-awareness and physical aggression. *Journal of Experimental Social Psychology*, 1974, *10*, 264–273.

Scott, W. *Values and organizations: A study of fraternities and sororities*. Chicago: Rand McNally, 1965.

Stephenson, B. O., & Wicklund, R. A. *The contagion of self focus*. Unpublished manuscript, University of Texas, 1980.

Wegner, D. M., & Giuliano, T. The forms of social awareness. In W. J. Ickes & E. S. Knowles (Eds.), *Personality, roles and social behavior*. New York: Springer Verlag, in press.

Wegner, D. M., & Schaefer, D. The concentration of responsibility: An objective self awareness analysis of group size effects in helping situations. *Journal of Personality and Social Psychology*, 1978, *36*, 147–155.

Wicker, A. W. Attitudes versus actions: The relationship of verbal and overt behavioral responses to attitude objects. *Journal of Social Issues*, 1969, *25*, 41–78.

Wicklund, R. A. Objective self awareness. In Berkowitz (Ed.), *Advances in experimental social psychology*, (Vol. 8). New York: Academic Press, 1975.

Wicklund, R. A. The influence of self-awareness on human behavior. *American Scientist*, 1979, *67*, 187–193. (a)

Wicklund, R. A. Die Aktualisierung von Selbstkonzepten in Handlungs-vollzügen. In Filipp, S-H. (Ed.), *Selbstkonzept Forschung: Probleme, Befunde, Perspektiven*. Stuttgart: Klett-Cotta, 1979. (b)

Wicklund, R. A. Group contact and self-focused attention. In P. B. Paulus (Ed.), *Psychology of group influence*. Hillsdale, N. J.: Lawrence Erlbaum Associates, 1980.

Wicklund, R. A., & Brehm, J. W. *Perspectives on cognitive dissonance*. Hillsdale, N.J.: Lawrence Erlbaum Associates, 1976.

Wicklund, R. A., & Frey, D. *The alienated traveller and self-awareness*. Unpublished manuscript, University of Texas, 1979.

Wicklund, R. A., & Gollwitzer, P. M. Symbolic self-completion, attempted influence, and self-deprecation. *Basic and Applied Social Psychology*, 1981, *2*, 89–114.

Willerman, L., Turner, R. G., & Peterson, M. A comparison of the predictive validity of typical and maximal personality measures. *Journal of Research in Personality*, 1976, *10*, 482–492.

8 Persons, Situations, and Template Matching: Theme and Variations

Daryl J. Bem
Cornell University

The twin themes of this volume are the variability and the consistency of behavior. Happily, many of us believe in both. We believe in the variability of behavior as a matter of established fact and in the consistency of behavior as a matter of epistemological necessity, the article of faith that prompts some of us to be personologists rather than plumbers. As most observers of contemporary personality research are now aware, the apparent contradiction between the personological view that behavior is person-determined and transsituationally consistent and the situationist view that behavior is situation-determined and context-specific has now been resolved: We are all now "interactionists," dedicated to raising the status of the old adage that behavior is a function of both the person and the situation above the cliché level of, say, "it will never heal if you pick at it." (See, for example, Endler & Magnusson, 1976, and Magnusson & Endler, 1977.)

And because personological theories and methods for assessing persons have been around a long time, much of the current concern in interactional psychology centers upon the challenge of incorporating the situation into the enterprise (e.g., Magnusson, 1981). My own initial response to this challenge was to attempt to fashion a method for characterizing both persons and situations in a commensurate language (a goal pursued earlier, of course, by Murray, 1938). This exercise produced the template-matching technique, a general tool for predicting the behavior of particular persons in particular situations (Bem & Funder, 1978; Bem & Lord, 1979), and this article describes and evaluates some of the variations of the basic method that have been explored so far.

TEMPLATE MATCHING

The template-matching technique is actually a formalization of a procedure that we often use in everyday life when asked to describe a situation (Bem & Funder, 1978; Cantor, 1981). Consider, for example, a student who wants to know how he or she would fare at a particular college. Note that this is, in fact, a question about person-situation interaction: The student is not interested in how he or she might do at colleges in general or in how students in general do at this particular college. What the student seeks is information about how his or her unique characteristics mesh or interact with the unique characteristics of that particular college. One particularly common way to give this student information about the college is to describe how several types of students fare there: "Students with varied interests tend to get caught up in extracurricular activities, have a marvelous college experience, but get rather poor grades; students who work hard, but who are somewhat shy obtain good grades but are unlikely to have much interaction with the faculty; students who . . ."; and so forth. With this kind of description in hand, the student has only to match his or her own characteristics to the various "templates" we have provided in order to predict his or her probable outcomes at the college. Rather than describing the college in terms of the physical plant, faculty-student ratios, graduation requirements, and so forth, we have instead characterized it in terms of a set of template-outcome, or template-behavior pairs. The language system used to characterize the situation is the same system the student uses to characterize himself or herself.

Our formal proposal, then, was that each outcome or behavior of interest be characterized by a template, a personality description of a hypothetical ideal individual most likely to display that behavior in the situation under scrutiny. The behavior of any particular individual is predicted by comparing a description of his or her own personality with each template in turn and predicting that he or she will display the behavior associated with the template of closest match or greatest similarity.

In order to operationalize the template construct, I deliberately sought an assessment technique that would be person centered rather than variable centered, that is, a technique that would assess the relative salience and configuration of variables within an individual rather than the relative standing of individuals across each variable. Accordingly, I chose the Q-sort technique, utilizing the items of the California Q set devised by Block (1961/1978). This Q set consists of 100 descriptive personality statements (e.g., "is critical, skeptical, not easily impressed") which are sorted by the assessor into nine categories, ranging from the least to the most characteristic of the person being described. Although not derived from any particular theoretical orientation, many of the items have a psychodynamic flavor, and both phenotypic and genotypic levels of description are included. (An extensive description of the Q-sort methodology in general and a detailed history of the California Q set in particular will be found in Block (1961/1978).) Because this item set was originally designed for use by professionally trained clinicians, we modified it so that it could be used for peer and self-descriptions by our subjects (Bem & Funder, 1978).

Operationally, then, a template is a Q-sort description of an idealized person to which one compares or matches Q-sort descriptions of particular individuals, using either a correlational index of similarity or an additive "template" score (see Green, 1980, and Hoffman & Bem, 1981).

One virtue of the template-matching technique is that it can be employed both as a tool of verification and as a tool of exploration. For example, Bem and Lord (1979) used it as a verification procedure in a study designed to test the ecological validity of mixed-motive games (e.g., the Prisoner's Dilemma Game). First we constructed templates or personality descriptions of hypothetical individuals who would be expected to follow distinctively different strategies of play in such games. This was accomplished by having five judges who were familiar with these games independently rate items from the California Q set for their relevance to each strategy. For example, the most cooperative strategy was characterized by such items as "behaves in a giving way toward others," whereas the most competitive strategy was characterized by such items as "is power oriented; values power in self and others." College undergraduates were then recruited to participate in a series of mixed-motive games, and Q sorts were obtained on each subject from two of his or her acquaintances. By matching each subject's Q sort against the several templates, Bem and Lord were able to verify that the templates could significantly predict which strategy a subject would adopt.

As a tool of exploration, the technique enables an investigator to identify empirically those personality attributes that are functionally important for the observed behaviors. For example, by examining the individual Q-item correlates of the subjects' game-playing strategies, Bem and Lord found that the women who pursued the most competitive strategy were described by their peers as people who tend to undermine, obstruct, or sabotage; keep people at a distance; avoid close interpersonal relationships; and so forth. In contrast, these women rated themselves as likable, personally charming, feminine, and socially poised. Not surprisingly, their peers rated these women significantly lower than they rated themselves on the item "has insight into her own motives and behavior." Note that the Q-item descriptions thus provided three distinct kinds of information: peer perceptions, self-perceptions, and discrepancies between the two (see also Bem & Funder, 1978).

THEORY TESTING WITH THE TEMPLATE-MATCHING TECHNIQUE

The purpose of the template matching in the Bem-Lord study was to predict which of several alternative behaviors each subject would display. A variation of the procedure enables the technique to test competing psychological theories against one another. Rather than associating each template with a different behavior, one instead associates each template with a different theory of a single behavior, and the purpose of the matching is to determine which template best predicts the criterion behavior. This variation was illustrated in a study by Bem and Funder (1978), who sought to test three competing theories of the forced-compliance situation. In this setting, individuals are induced to advocate attitudes contrary to their own positions. The classical finding is that, subsequent to their compliance and under theoretically specified conditions, individuals report attitudes that are closer to the advocated positions than were their initial attitudes.

Several theories offer explanations of this attitude-change effect. Cognitive dissonance theory, the original source of the paradigm, asserts that an aversive state of "dissonance" aroused by the discrepancy between their behavior and their contrary attitudes motivates subjects to change their attitudes (e.g., Festinger & Carlsmith, 1959). Self-perception theory (Bem, 1967, 1972) proposes that the subjects observe their own behavior of advocating the designated position and then infer their final attitudes from that behavior in much the same way that an external observer of their behavior would do. A third group of theories emphasizes the self-presentational demands of the setting and suggests that the final attitude reports given by subjects are motivated primarily by an attempt to make a particular impression on the experimenter (Tedeschi, Schlenker & Bonoma, 1971), evaluation apprehension (Rosenberg, 1965, 1969), or a desire to project a particular "situated identity" to themselves as well as to others (Alexander & Knight, 1971).

To test these theories, Bem and Funder first derived a separate template for each theory by having three researcher/theoreticians in the forced-compliance paradigm independently select Q items that would describe the hypothetical person who, according to each theory, should show the most attitude change in that situation. For example, the dissonance theory template contained items such as "is uncomfortable with uncertainties and complexities," and "prides self on being 'objective,' rational."

Bem and Funder then recruited college undergraduates to participate in a classical forced-compliance experiment, and Q sorts were obtained on each subject from two of his or her acquaintances. Each subject's Q sort was matched with the template constructed for each theory, and the resulting template-similarity scores for each theory were then correlated across subjects with their attitude change scores; the higher this correlation, the better the theory is predicting attitude change. In this way, the theories were pitted against one another in predicting the individual-difference variance in attitude change.

The results showed that cognitive dissonance theory was not successful at predicting attitude change, the template-similarity scores actually correlating negatively with attitude change scores, $r = -.25$; self-perception theory was moderately successful, $r = .32$, $p < .10$, two-tailed. And self-presentation theory was the most successful of all, $r = .53$, $p < .005$, two-tailed.

As Bem and Funder noted, the study did demonstrate that the self-presentation template accounted for more of the individual-difference variance in attitude change than the other templates, but it might be that some theories are simply more capable of generating individual-difference predictions than others, and a greater ability to predict person effects does not strictly imply a greater ability to predict situation effects. Thus we ran only the "choice" condition of the typical forced-compliance experiment, and our contest required the theories to account for within-cell variance (person effects); conceivably our winners and losers could have fared differently in a battle over the between-cell variance (situation effects). Indeed, most social-psychological theories are designed to predict treatment differences, including the theories tested in our study. It was only we who coerced them into playing the unaccustomed role of personality theories.

But this points up the real value of the template-matching technique: If personological theories have not lived up to expectations because they have limited themselves to person effects in a world populated by person-situation interactions, then we should not be more hopeful about theories that limit themselves to situation effects. The template-matching technique thus provides a potential tool for expanding such social psychological theories into genuine theories of person-situation interaction. And in pursuit of this promise, Funder (1982) used the technique in a forced-compliance experiment that required the theories to address both within-cell and between-cell variance simultaneously, finding that a template based on the concept of "scripted" behavior (Abelson, 1976; Langer, 1978) did better than the original theories tested by Bem and Funder (1978).

The Funder study illustrates that template matching can be a useful supplement to the traditional experimental approach of designing treatments that will discriminate among theories of hypotheses. In some cases, template matching can undertake tasks that would be extraordinarily unwieldy or complex if one relied solely on the between-cell approach. For example, Ransen (1980) sought to test five different explanations of the finding that children who are rewarded for engaging in an intrinsically interesting activity show a subsequent loss of motivation for it. Moreover, Ransen wanted to test for possible interactions between the underlying mechanisms and the sex and age of the children. He found that three of the five theories had explanatory power, but only for males. Moreover, one of the theories accounted for the motivation decrement in younger boys, but not in older boys, a finding that was consistent with Ransen's theoretical speculations. The template-matching technique thus has the potential for going beyond the simple detection of interaction effects to their explanation; at the least it can provide promising leads to be followed up with more traditional experimental procedures.

ASSESSING THE INDIVIDUAL'S OWN PERCEPTIONS OF SITUATIONS

In introducing the template-matching procedure at the beginning of this article, I noted that it is simply a formalization of a procedure that we already use in everyday life, thereby implying—with no hard evidence whatsoever—that the layperson may spontaneously categorize situations according to how particular types of people behave within them. The utility of template matching did not hinge upon the validity of this casual observation since the technique does not entail asking the subjects themselves to construct the templates. Interestingly, however, Cantor (1981) has now obtained evidence that individuals often do, in fact, appear to categorize situations spontaneously in this way. Quite independently, it occurred to Lord (1982) that template matching might provide a new way of tapping an individual's perception of situations. In particular, he proposed that the technique might enable one to predict when a person will behave consistently across two situations by assessing the person's perception of similarity between the two settings. To test this possibility, Lord measured the "conscientiousness" of 40 subjects in six real-life situations during an academic quarter, repeatedly recording the neatness of their closet and desk, their personal appearance, their promptness in returning forms, the degree to which they were caught up on. their course readings, the neatness of their lecture notes, and the regularity of their scheduling of non-class time. By standardizing these observations across subjects, Lord was able to assess the degree to which an individual behaved consistently—that is, equally conscientiously—across each of the 15 pairs of situations constituted from the six different situations assessed. Each subject also provided six templates, Q sorts of the hypothetical ideal person who would be most conscientious in each situation. The intercorrelations between each of the 15 pairs of the individual's templates provided the indices of perceived situation similarity. In addition, each subject provided a self-sort.

Lord found that the template-template similarity measure did, in fact, predict the cross-situational consistency of behavior: If the individual's Q-sort conceptions of the "most conscientious individual" were highly similar for two situations, then the individual himself or herself displayed comparable conscientiousness (or non-conscientiousness) across them. In addition, Lord found that the matches between the templates and the individual's own self-Q-sort also predicted cross-situational consistency: If an individual's self-sort correlated similarly with two of the templates, he or she behaved comparably across the two situations. (These two findings are not necessarily constrained to be jointly true or false; for example, two situation templates can be quite dissimilar from one another, and yet the person's self-sort might be equally correlated with the two of them. In other words, a person might be equally conscientious—but for different reasons—across two dissimilar situations.)

In contrast, consistency could not simply be predicted form direct similarity ratings between the pairs of situations ("In relation to conscientiousness, how similar are organizing one's closet and desk and taking lecture notes?"). Nor did simple consensual templates work: Only the individual's own templates and self-sort could predict his or her behavior. And finally, the Q-sort information itself again proved heuristically useful. Lord was able to find systematic personality differences (as measured by the self-sorts) between individuals who saw maintaining a neat personal appearance as similar to other types of conscientiousness and those who did not so include personal neatness in their "equivalence class" for conscientiousness (Cf. Bem & Allen, 1974).

CONTEXTUAL TEMPLATE MATCHING

Although the technique of template matching has been versatile and empirically successful both as a tool of verification and of exploration, it is incomplete in two closely related ways. First, it lacks a systematic way of characterizing situations independently of personality attributes. As Bem and Funder point out, it fails to address the problem of specifying "how the templates themselves relate to independently assessed properties of the situation (e.g., What are the functional properties of the forced-compliance situation that cause it to evoke attitude change in such individuals?)" (1978, p. 487).

Second, the technique embraces only the weakest form of the interactionist thesis, namely the simple assertion that both person factors and situation factors need to be considered in accounting for human behavior. This version of interactionism has long been a part of traditional personality theorizing. For example, Cattell's "specification equation" is an explicit statement of such a person-situation combination (1965), and Eysenck incorporates this kind of interaction in the observation that extraverts perform better when in groups, introverts when alone (1970). And like these approaches, the template-matching procedure also characterizes persons in context-free dispositional terms first, and then attempts to combine this information with situational information after the fact. A stronger version of the interactionist thesis maintains that persons and situations are inseparable from the outset and that the enterprise ought to begin with persons-in-situations as the fundamental unit of analysis: "The organism and its milieu must be considered together, a single creature-environment interaction being a convenient short unit for psychology" (Murray, 1938, p. 40).

It was to remedy these twin deficiencies that Curt Hoffman and I developed the method of contextual template matching (Hoffman & Bem, 1981). The major feature of contextual template matching is the substitution of a contextual or situation-specific description of the individual's personality for the global Q sort in the template-matching procedure, a modification that dramatically augments both the amount and the kind of information that one obtains.

The first step in developing a method for assessing persons-in-context was the construction of a feature set for characterizing situations; and, after examining a number of existing taxonomies, we evolved our own set of 150 items that appeared both applicable to a wide variety of situations and compatible with the California Q set. Some of the items are physicalistic (e.g., "is noisy"); others refer to the interpersonal situations (e.g., "is characterized by the presence of authority figure[s]''); and still others refer to the environmental "press" (Murray, 1938) (e.g., "encourages or demands psychological closeness, intimacy"). Since the list of personality descriptors is referred to as a Q set, we designated our list of situation descriptors an S set.

To characterize a particular situation, observers or judges go through the S set and check those features that are present in the setting. To obtain a contextual or situation-specific description of an individual, we list each of these characteristic features of the situation at the top of a separate page, followed by 100 blanks corresponding to the 100 items of the California Q set. For each Q item, the individual indicates whether it is more or less characteristic of him or her in situations having the indicated feature. (For example, an individual may judge that he or she is more "critical and skeptical" than usual in situations "characterized by interaction with strangers.") The individual's score on a particular Q item is the sum of the ratings he or she assigns to that item across the set of situational features, and the full set of 100 summary Q-item scores is the contextual personality description that replaces the usual global Q sort in the template-matching procedure. Note that the absolute placement of a Q item in the person's global Q sort does not enter explicitly into the contextual personality description.

In order to assess whether or not contextual personality descriptions have any incremental predictive utility over global Q-sort descriptions, we returned to the forced-compliance experiment by Funder (1982), cited above. Although he had obtained some results of interest, none of the three original templates had displayed significant predictive utility within the treatment condition corresponding most closely to the classical forced-compliance situation, and hence, to the original Bem-Funder study. The two experiments were different from one another in several respects, and thus it was not clear why the same pattern of findings did not emerge. Accordingly, Hoffman and I decided to adopt this study as a particularly stringent test for contextual template matching: Could it succeed in replicating the pattern of findings from the original Bem-Funder experiment on a set of data on which global template matching had failed?

First we had two judges assess the salient features of Funder's forced-compliance situation by participating as "subjects" in independent sessions of the actual experiment and then independently selecting items from the S set that they felt characterized the situation. Twelve of the 150 items from the S set were selected in this way (e.g., "encourages or requires one to 'play a role' other than the true self"; "involves being an object of study—as in a psychological experiment"; "encourages or demands active imaginative involvement"). These were entered into a 12-page contextual personality description form according to the format described above. We then recruited most of the subjects who had participated in the relevant condition of Funder's original study to come in and fill out this form. (This took place several weeks after their original participation, and they were not informed of the connection between the two studies.) This provided us with the information we needed for contextual template matching.

The results showed that contextual template matching was quite successful. Not only were the validity coefficients very high and significant in absolute terms, but their pattern replicated the findings for global template matching reported by Bem and Funder, and they were significantly higher than the nonsignificant coefficients obtained from applying global template matching to the original Funder data. And once again, by correlating the scores for each Q item with the dependent variable (attitude change), the technique functioned as a tool of exploration by identifying personality attributes that appear to be functionally important for the observed behavior.

The novel contribution of contextual template matching, however, derives from the S items. Just as it is possible to consider each of the Q items separately, so it is possible to consider each of the S items separately as well in order to discern which of the specific features of the setting are "doing the work" for each template. This can be interpreted as discerning which features of the situation are salient and effective in producing attitude change (or whatever) for particular kinds of persons. For example, our data implied that being required to play a role other than the true self was the situational factor that most evoked attitude change among persons concerned with self-presentation, whereas expressing counterattitudinal views and being involved in imaginative activity most evoked attitude change in individuals who function according to the processes postulated by self-perception theory.

And finally, it is even possible to correlate each of the person-by-situation ratings made by the subjects with the criterion behavior—although this provides only the roughest exploratory information unless one has enormous subject samples. Thus, without putting too fine a point on it, Hoffman and I noted that less attitude change was shown by individuals who tend to undermine, obstruct, or sabotage when in situations that involve being an object of study or who express hostile feelings directly when required to play a role other than the true self—findings consistent with self-presentation theory. Similarly, less attitude change is shown by individuals who are self-defensive or guileful and deceitful when expressing a point of view not their own—findings consistent with self-perception theory.

In sum, contextual template matching not only functions as a tool of verification better than does global template matching, but it also permits one to perform three kinds of exploratory analysis: Q-item analysis uncovers the personality attributes that are associated with the criterion behavior *within* particular situations; S-item analysis uncovers the situational features that are associated with the criterion behavior for particular prototypic persons (templates); and Q × S item analysis provides leads about how particular person attributes interact with particular situational features to determine behavior.

The moral, of course, is interactionism. Moreover, it is interactionism in its stronger sense. One cannot simply add together person information and situation information obtained independently; the unit of analysis must itself be the person-in-context. And that is why contextual template matching succeeded on the same set of data on which global template matching had failed. Furthermore, by outfitting the general technique with a more dynamic, less trait-like language, template matching might be capable of addressing an even stronger version of interactionism, one that incorporates the reciprocal or dynamic interactions between the person and the situation, the transactions between them. The logic of template matching transcends the particular descriptive language we have employed in implementing the technique, and there is nothing in its logic that precludes it from embracing such interactions.

ADDITIONAL VARIATIONS OF TEMPLATE MATCHING

The existence of a broad set of situation descriptors should provide a useful complement to the personality Q set in ways other than contextual template matching. For example, just as we have used the personality Q set to characterize both hypothetical ideal individuals (the templates) as well as actual individuals, so too, we can use the S set to characterize both the individual's situation prototypes as well as his or her own definition of particular concrete situations. To put this a bit more formally, we, the investigators, can define a situation by selecting the set of situation descriptors that apply to a situation, but our subjects can then rate or weight these items to define the "interpreted" situation, the salience of these features as they see them. This can be done for hypothetical situations (e.g., "a situation that makes you most anxious") or for actual situations (e.g., "the session you just went through").

And finally, the Q set and the S set in combination can be used to explore a number of hypotheses about self-schemata, the ways in which individuals process and organize information about the self (Markus, 1977). Bem and Allen (1974) suggested that each individual has a small number of personality traits that are highly salient or central and around which his or her personality is organized; accordingly, any given trait is likely to be irrelevant for many people (cf. Allport, 1937). If this idiographic view of personality is correct, then it seems plausible that the individual might have a rich associative network, an available and well-articulated cognitive schema of behaviors and situations that are relevant to each of these central traits. For example, Markus (1977) has shown that individuals who are "schematic" for independence, that is, who rate themselves as extremely independent *and* who regard this trait as important to their personalities are better able than "aschematics" to generate behaviors relevant to the trait, can respond more quickly to independence-relevant traits as self-descriptive, and so forth. The general hypothesis, then, is that individuals should be better able to delineate equivalence classes of behaviors and situations for those personality characteristics they deem central to their personalities than for characteristics they consider irrelevant (an intraindividual comparison) and that, given a particular characteristic, individuals who deem it central will have better delineated equivalence classes of behaviors and situations for it than individuals who deem it irrelevant (an interindividual comparison).

Because a personality Q sort specifies which traits are characteristic, uncharacteristic, and irrelevant for the person, it can be used to identify each individual's central traits. The richness of the self-schemata surrounding each trait could be indexed by the number and diversity of situations the individual could generate in which he or she would and would not display that trait. The S set of situation features could be used to characterize the sets of situations that compose the "equivalence class" for each trait, providing another way of assessing the schemata surrounding the trait. In general, all of the experimental procedures used by Markus (1977) to demonstrate the existence of the independence schema and by S. L. Bem (1981) to investigate the gender schema can also be employed to explore intraindividual and interindividual differences in self-schemata.

This, then, is a proposal for taking one operational step towards the Bem-Funder tongue-in-cheek suggestion that one should be able to shuffle both the Q and S decks and then predict how *that* hypothetical person would behave in *that* hypothetical situation; in other words, to predict all of the people all of the time (Bem & Funder, 1978).

TOWARD A THEORY OF PERSONS-IN-SITUATIONS

As noted at the outset, the template-matching technique was my first pass at a general method for characterizing persons and situations in a commensurate language. It has been a useful exercise. The technique and its variations are, I think, clever, and the research reviewed here has shown them to have some utility for predicting and understanding the behavior of persons-in-situations. There is, however, one aspect of the entire enterprise that severely limits its future: the absence of a substantive personality theory behind it. It is true that the broad eclectic vocabulary of both the personality Q set and the situation S set makes template matching and its variations compatible with almost any social-psychological or personality theory. Thus we have seen that the original variation of the technique can, in principle, adopt of several existing theories of situations—social psychological theories concerning the conditions that produce attitude change, for example—and push them to expand into theories of person-situation interaction. In analogous fashion, the variations that use the set of situational descriptors can adopt any of several personality theories and push them to incorporate situational factors.

But being theory compatible is not the same as being theory generated or even theory guided. The template-matching technique remains just that, a technique; and, in this regard, it is similar to most of current interactional psychology, which seems long on method and short on theory. I find this unsatisfactory and now believe that one cannot fashion a genuinely useful and compatible language for characterizing situations until one has a substantive theory of persons (cf. Murray, 1938).

My own biases and interests incline me to a personality theory that is, first of all, person-centered rather than variable-centered, a theory that focuses upon the configurations of variables within a person rather than upon the relative standing of persons across variables. (Such an approach tends to lead to typologies of persons—about as fashionable in personality research these days as miniskirts are with feminists.) Second, I think that the personality variables of such a theory should not be the kinds of phenotypic traits whose varying relevance across persons make them useful only for idiographic characterization; rather, the variables should be the more genotypic variables that Cattell, for example, would place at the level of temperament or general personality traits (1965). And among these, I would favor those traits that refer specifically to the individual's stylistic ways of processing information and interacting with the internal and external environment. These would permit situational variables to be incorporated into the theory from the outset, possibly producing a typology of situations or situational task demands that parallels the typology of persons. Witkin's field dependence variable (Witkin, Dyk, Faterson, Goodenough, & Karp, 1962) and, especially, the Blocks' work with ego control and ego resilience (Block & Block, 1979, 1981) are illustrative, although my own view is that several such stylistic variables will have to be incorporated into the theory simultaneously in order to encompass their interactions (Cf. the Jungian typology [Myers, 1962]). And finally, I should like the theory to contain some ideas about the ontogenetic development of the variables and their interactions.

This, then, is the direction of my current work and is the enterprise that will constitute my second pass at fashioning a theory of persons-in-situations.

REFERENCES

Abelson, R. P. A script theory of understanding, attitude, and behavior. In J. Carroll & T. Payne (Eds.), *Cognition and social behavior*. Hillsdale, N.J.: Lawrence Erlbaum Associates, 1976.

Alexander, C. N., & Knight, G. W. Situated identities and social psychological experimentation. *Sociometry*, 1971, *34*, 65–82.

Allport, G. W. *Personality: A psychological interpretation*. New York: Holt, 1937.

Bem, D. J. Self-perception: An alternative interpretation of cognitive dissonance phenomena. *Psychological Review*, 1967, *74*, 183–200.

Bem, D. J. Self-perception theory. In L. Berkowitz (Ed.), *Advances in Experimental Social Psychology* (Vol. 6). New York: Academic Press, 1972.

Bem, D. J., & Allen, A. On predicting some of the people some of the time: The search for cross-situational consistencies in behavior. *Psychological Review*, 1974, *81*, 506–520.

Bem, D. J., & Funder, D. C. Predicting more of the people more of the time: Assessing the personality of situation. *Psychological Review*, 1978, *85*, 485–501.

Bem, D. J., & Lord, C. G. The template-matching technique. A proposal for probing the ecological validity of experimental settings in social psychology. *Journal of Personality and Social Psychology*, 1979, *37*, 833–846.

Bem, S. L. Gender schema theory: A cognitive account of sex typing. *Psychological Review*, 1981, *88*, 354–364.

Block, J. *The Q-sort method in personality assessment and psychiatric research*. Palo Alto: Consulting Psychologists Press, 1978. (Originally published in 1961.)

Block, J., & Block, J. H. Studying situational dimensions: A grand perspective and some limited empiricism. In D. Magnusson (Ed.), *Toward a psychology of situations*. Hillsdale, N.J.: Lawrence Erlbaum Associates, 1981.

Block, J. H., & Block, J. The role of ego-control and ego-resiliency in the organization of behavior. In W. A. Collins (Ed.), *Minnesota Symposia on child psychology* (Volume 13). Hillsdale, N.J.: Lawrence Erlbaum Associates, 1979.

Cantor, N. Perceptions of situations: Situation prototypes and person-situation prototypes. In D. Magnusson (Ed.), *Toward a psychology of situations*. Hillsdale, N.J.: Lawrence Erlbaum Associates, 1981.

Cattell, R. B. *The scientific analysis of personality*. Chicago: Aldine, 1965.

Endler, N. S., & Magnusson, D. (Eds.). *Interactional psychology and personality*. Washington, D.C.: Hemisphere Publishing, 1976.

Eysenck, H. J. Explanation and the concept of personality. In R. Borger & F. Cioffi (Eds.), *Explanation in the behavioural sciences*. Cambride: Cambridge University Press, 1970.

Festinger, L., & Carlsmith, J. M. Cognitive consequences of forced compliance. *Journal of Abnormal and Social Psychology*, 1959, *58*, 203–210.

Funder, D. C. On assessing social psychological theories through the study of individual differences: Template matching and forced compliance. *Journal of Personality and Social Psychology*, 1982, in press.

Green, B. F. A note on Bem and Funder's scheme for scoring Q sorts. *Psychological Review*, 1980, *87*, 212–214.

Hoffman, C., & Bem, D. J. *Contextual template matching: A progress report on predicting all of the people all of the time*. Unpublished manuscript, Stanford University and Cornell University, 1981.

Langer, E. J. Rethinking the role of thought in social interaction. In J. H. Harvey, W. Ickes, & R. F. Kidd (Eds.), *New directions in attribution research*, (Vol. 2). Hillsdale, N.J.: Lawrence Erlbaum Associates, 1978.

Lord, C. G. Predicting behavioral consistency from an individual's perception of situational similarities. *Journal of Personality and Social Psychology*, 1982, in press.

Magnusson, D. (Ed.). *Toward a psychology of situations*. Hillsdale, N.J.: Lawrence Erlbaum Associates, 1981.

Magnusson, D., & Endler, N. S. (Eds.). *Personality at the crossroads: Current issues in international psychology*. Hillsdale, N.J.: Lawrence Erlbaum Associates, 1977.

Markus, H. Self-schemata and processing information about the self. *Journal of Personality and Social Psychology*, 1977, *35*, 63–78.

Murray, H. A. *Explorations in personality*. New York: Oxford, 1938.

Myers, I. B. *Manual for the Myers-Briggs type indicator*. Palo Alto: Consulting Psychologists Press, 1962.

Ransen, D. L. The mediation of reward-induced motivation decrements in early and middle childhood: a template matching approach. *Journal of Personality and Social Psychology*, 1980, *39*, 1088–1100.

Rosenberg, M. J. When dissonance fails: On eliminating evaluation apprehension from attitude measurement. *Journal of Personality and Social Psychology,* 1965, *1,* 18–42.

Rosenberg, M. J. The conditions and consequences of evaluation apprehension. In R. Rosenthal & R. W. Rosnow (Eds.), *Artifacts in behavioral research.* New York: Academic Press, 1969.

Tedeschi, J. T., Schlenker, B. R., & Bonoma, T. V. Cognitive dissonance: Private ratiocination or public spectacle? *American Psychologist,* 1971, *26,* 685–695.

Witkin, H. A., Dyk, R. B., Faterson, H. F., Goodenough, D. R. & Karp, S. A. *Psychological differentiation.* Hillsdale, N.J.: Lawrence Erlbaum Associates, 1974. (Originally published, 1962).

9 In Search of Consistency: Measure for Measure

Walter Mischel and Philip Peake
Stanford University

The controversy concerning the relative specificity versus consistency of social behavior and of the breadth of the dispositions underlying such behavior continues; the themes highlighted in the past by Thorndike (1906), Hartshorne and May (1928), Allport (1937, 1966), Fiske (1961), and many others are still very much with us. The doubts about the breadth of personality traits and the utility of inferring them, raised in *Personality and Assessment* (Mischel, 1968) and so ardently debated in the past decade (see Endler & Magnusson, 1976; and Magnusson & Endler, 1977, for reviews), are still central to the fields of both personality and social psychology, as the present volume attests.

One response to the issues raised in such critiques as Mischel's *Personality and Assessment* has been to search for alternative ways of conceptualizing person variables (e.g., Bandura, 1978; Cantor & Mischel, 1979; Mischel, 1973, 1979) and for studying person-situation interactions through more fine-grained analyses (e.g., Magnusson & Endler, 1977; Moos & Fuhr, in press; Patterson, 1976; Patterson & Moore, 1979; Raush, 1977). A second response, however, is that the issues raised reflect not the inadequacy of traditional conceptualizations of broad traits that yield cross-situationally consistent behaviors but rather the inadequacy of earlier searches for such traits (e.g., Block, 1977; Bowers, 1973; Olweus, 1977). Of the many efforts to pursue this "better methods" approach to the consistency problem, the two that appear to be most dramatic, and that currently have been greeted as most promising, are the reliability solution (Epstein, 1979) and the template-matching solution (Bem & Funder, 1978). They are the focus of the present chapter not only because they deserve serious attention in their own right but because they are excellent exemplars of the "better methods" approach to the consistency issue and their analysis may teach some highly instructive lessons.

Our analysis of these approaches will reveal that, in spite of the attention they are attracting currently, the ''solutions'' they propose do not resolve the basic issues raised by the consistency debate. Recent studies by the present authors also are discussed and document the empirical limitations of both the Epstein and Bem-Funder approaches in the search for behavioral consistency.

THE RELIABILITY SOLUTION

Epstein's Study

Epstein (1979) asserts that the consistency debate in psychology, rather than meriting deep and enduring discussion, should never have happened. In his view, the consistency issue in personality is ready (indeed, overdue) for ''A solution . . . so obvious that once pointed out, it reminds one of the fairy tale of *The Emperor's New Clothes.*'' The solution is to realize that ''The issue can be resolved by recognizing that most single items of behavior have a high component of error of measurement and a narrow range of generality'' (Epstein, 1979, p. 1097). In other words, the problems of demonstrating broad behavioral consistency to support global traits are simply the result of unreliable measurement in past research.

Challenging ''the charge that personality traits do not exist,'' Epstein (1979, p. 1098) recently demonstrated that coefficients of temporal stability (e.g., of self-reported emotions and experiences recorded daily, and of observer judgments) become much larger when based on averages over many days. In essence, Epstein computed split-half reliabilities for samples of behavior varying from 2 days up to about 28 days. He found that as the number of observations included in the composite increased, the split-half reliability also increased. Of course, this phenomenon is a fundamental premise of classical reliability theory (Gulliksen, 1950; Lord & Novick, 1968; Thurstone, 1932). The increase in reliability through use of aggregated composites is exactly what the Spearman-Brown formula has been used to estimate for years; Epstein's demonstration thus provides a nice empirical verification of the Spearman-Brown prophecy. (See Horowitz, Inouye, & Siegelman, 1979, for a more statistically sophisticated empirical demonstration.)

However, the recognition that reliability is important and increases with the number of items aggregated is hardly new to the consistency debate. Even introductory statistics texts routinely intone that we cannot have either validity or utility without reliability and it is remarkable to suggest that the consistency debate has suffered from mass amnesia for the reliability construct. Far from overlooking reliability, it was noted in 1968 that:

> There is nothing magical about a correlation coefficient, and its interpretation depends on many considerations. The accuracy or reliability of measurement in-

creases with the length of the test. Since no single item is a perfect measure, adding items increases the chance that the test will elicit a more accurate sample and yield a better estimate of the person's behavior. . . . (Mischel, 1968, p. 37)

Epstein believes that the "classic debate" can be resolved simply by aggregating our measures to enhance reliability. But the OSS project in World War II, the Michigan V. A. project, the Harvard Personologists, and The Peace Corps projects—all the large-scale applied assessment projects of the 1940s, 1950s, 1960s—used aggregated measures, pooled judgments, assessment boards, multiple-item criteria, and nevertheless yielded overall results that raised basic questions about the usefulness and limitations of the traditional personality assessment enterprise (e.g., Peterson, 1968; Vernon, 1964; Wiggins, 1973). Although those who critically evaluated the state of the field in the 1960s did not overlook the issue of reliability, they nevertheless concluded, as Vernon did in 1964, that:

The real trouble (with the trait approach) is that it has not worked well enough, and despite the huge volume of research it has stimulated, it seems to lead to a dead end. (p. 239)

Tempting as simple solutions might be, the problems raised by the consistency debate cannot be dismissed as the result of forgetfulness for the basic concepts of measurement error and neglect of the Spearman-Brown formula. How, then, can Epstein conclude that the consistency debate should never have occurred because it is resolved when reliability is taken into account? Put another way, how can the use of aggregated measures resolve a debate in 1980 that it was unable to resolve throughout the 40s, 50s, and 60s? The answer to this seemingly puzzling shift becomes quite simple once one recognizes that the discrepancy is one of interpretation, not effect. Reliability is doing nothing more (or less) for Epstein than it did for any of the earlier large scale assessment projects.

Adequate reliability coefficients can surely be found, as Epstein has demonstrated and as earlier work amply attests, especially for similar measurements with similar instruments taken repeatedly over time (Mischel, 1968). But we have to discriminate clearly between demonstrations of impressive temporal stability on the one hand, and cross-situational generality or consistency in behavior on the other. By collecting specific observations over a series of days, and then computing split-half "stability" coefficients, most of Epstein's data (Tables 1, 2, 3 of Epstein, 1979) are relevant only to the temporal stability of behavior. But temporal stability has never been a central issue in this debate. As noted in 1968: "Considerable stability over time has been demonstrated . . ." (Mischel, 1968, p. 36). And: "Although behavior patterns may often be stable, they are usually not highly generalized across situations . . ." (Mischel, 1968, p. 282).

More than a decade ago the available research provided evidence for significant temporal stability. To quote from *Personality and Assessment* again:

The trait-descriptive categories and personality labels with which individuals describe themselves and others on questionnaires and trait-rating scales seem to be especially long-lasting. E. L. Kelly (1955) compared questionnaire trait self-descriptions obtained almost twenty years apart. . . . the stability coefficients for self-descriptions of interests, of economic and political values, of self-confidence and sociability were high. The coefficients . . . ranged from about .45 to slightly over .60, indicating impressive stability, considering the long temporal delay between assessments.

As another example, the test-retest correlations on the California Psychological Inventory scales for high school students retested after one year, and for a sample of prisoners retested after a lapse of seven to twenty-one days, were also high (Gough, 1957). In general, trait self-descriptions on many personality questionnaires show considerable stability. . . .

and it was noted in summary that:

. . . behaviors sampled in closely similar situations generally yield the best correlations. Considerable stability over time has been demonstrated for some domains. . . . Self-descriptions on trait dimensions also seem to be especially consistent even over very long periods of time. (Mischel, 1968, pp. 35–36)

To reiterate, temporal stability is not the basic issue and often has been demonstrated: The crux of the "classic debate" is the breadth of noncognitive social traits, the cross-situational discriminativeness of behavior, and the utility of inferring traits for the prediction of an individual's actions. While Epstein purports to resolve the debate by using aggregated measures, most of his data are relevant only to an issue that has never been seriously questioned.

Epstein presents some data (in Tables 4 and 5 of his 1979 paper) that do go beyond the demonstration that aggregation increases reliability coefficients and enhances temporal stability. Let us consider those data in some detail. He presents (in his Table 4) "intercorrelations of objective events with each other and with self-rated emotions for a 12-day sample." Since the consistency of self-ratings is also not controversial, only the data intercorrelating aggregated objective events are directly relevant to the issue of behavioral consistency. Table 9.1, adapted from Epstein's Table 4, shows these coefficients. First note that each of the measures listed in Table 9.1 is the aggregate of a 12-day sample. As such, the corresponding reliability coefficients (first column) are as substantial as they are noncontroversial.

Now, consider the more interesting question: What is the evidence for cross-situational consistency when highly reliable measures of objectively observed behavior are intercorrelated? Among the 105 relevant correlations computed, the 7 that reached significance (at the $p < .01$ level) were: letters written with letters received; calls made with calls received; stomachaches with headaches; heart rate mean with heart rate range; errors with heart rate range; erasures with letters

TABLE 9.1
Summary of Epstein's (1979) Significant Behavior Inter-correlations

Behaviors	Aggregated Reliability	1	2	3	4	5	6	7	8	9	10	11	12	13	14	15
1. Heart Rate Mean	1.0	XX														
2. Heart Rate Range	.88	.74	XX													
3. Calls Made	.91			XX												
4. Calls Received	.94			.77	XX											
5. Letters Written	.79				.42	XX										
6. Letters Received	.90				.46	.79	XX									
7. Headaches	.90							XX								
8. Stomachaches	.91							.77	XX							
9. Entertainment	.70									XX						
10. Errors	.88										XX					
11. Erasures	.60		.57			.52	.42					XX				
12. Papers Missing	NA					.43	.45						XX			
13. Absences	NA										.64			XX		
14. Lateness	.94														XX	
15. Pencils Forgotten	.93															XX

N=26 except for pencils forgotten and lateness for which N=15. (Adapted from Epstein, 1979, Table 4, p. 1114.)

written; absences with erasures. Significant intercorrelations among such items hardly suggest that the solution to the consistency issue has arrived. Most of the obtained interrelations seem virtually automatic; the more doors I open, the more I tend to close. And we also predict a significant correlation between how often you say "hello" to people and how often they say "hello" to you. Demonstrating some links between bits of behavior (letters written, letters received) that may cohere (often almost by definition and because they are functionally related, virtually demanding each other) does not provide impressive evidence for cross-situational consistencies.

Epstein also provides coefficients between aggregated objective events and trait inventory scores (his Table 5). Most of the significant associations he found were between self-reported headaches, self-reported stomachaches, and other self-reported physical complaints and troubles (e.g., muscle tension, autonomic arousal on the Epstein-Fenz Anxiety Scale). It is no news to personality assessors that some people do sensitize and complain more than others about their well-being (e.g., Byrne, 1964; Mischel, Ebbesen, & Zeiss, 1973). The remaining coefficients were extremely unimpressive. Such objective events as calls made, calls received, letters written, and letters received—the items of behavior that do interrelate—even when aggregated and highly reliable, turn out to correlate significantly with none of the inventories. Epstein's consistency data, far from offering a solution to the problems raised by the consistency debate, demonstrate and illustrate those problems vividly.

The Stanford-Carleton Study

An adequate empirical search for behavioral consistency requires data aggregated to achieve reliability. But it also needs to go beyond reliability, beyond temporal stability, and beyond scattered self-report and behavior correlations. It needs to explore cross-situational consistency in behavior with appropriate and reliable behavior measures sampled across a range of presumably similar situations. Furthermore, such a search needs to be informed by some conceptualization—even if rudimentary—of how behavior is organized or should be categorized for particular goals (e.g., Cantor & Mischel, 1979; Mischel, 1979). That is exactly what we have been trying to do over the last 3 years, studying behavioral consistency among college students at Carleton College in Northfield, Minnesota. In collaboration with Neil Lutsky, we began by replicating the work of Bem and Allen (1974), extending greatly the behavioral referents and battery of measures employed.

Specifically, 63 Carleton College volunteers have participated in extensive self-assessments relevant to their friendliness and conscientiousness. They were assessed by their parents and a close friend, and were observed systematically in a large number of situations relevant to the traits of interest. We are currently replicating and extending the first wave of this study. The overall results so far are presented elsewhere (Mischel & Peake, 1982), and we can only summarize selected features that allow us to explore empirically the cross-situational consistency obtained when reliability and appropriate aggregation are taken into account.

To illustrate the gist of our results as they bear on the issues of this volume and particularly on Epstein's thesis, we consider only selected examples from the domain of conscientiousness/studiousness (henceforth called simply "conscientiousness"). The behavioral referents of conscientiousness in this work consist of 19 different measures. For example, our behavioral assessment of conscientiousness included such measures as: psychology class attendance, study session attendance, assignment neatness, assignment punctuality, reserve reading punctuality, room neatness, and personal appearance neatness. It is important to note that the specific behaviors selected as relevant to each trait were supplied by the subjects themselves as part of the pretesting at Carleton College to obtain referents for the trait constructs as perceived by the subjects, in contrast to many studies in which these referents are selected exclusively by the assessors. For each different measure, repeated observations (ranging in number from 2 to 12) were obtained. Thus, for example, we obtained 3 observations of assignment punctuality and 9 observations of appointment punctuality.

First we computed the percentage of significant coefficients among all the possible coefficients of temporal stability. To qualify as a coefficient of temporal stability, the correlation had to consist of two observations of the same type of measure. For example, lecture attendance on Day 1 correlated with lecture attendance on Day 6 is a correlation of temporal stability. This analysis revealed that nearly half of the single-item temporal stability coefficients (specifically 46%) were statistically significant. Note that this is prior to any aggregation to enhance reliability. Here, then, is another clear indication that even at the single item level, temporal stability can be demonstrated readily: It is at issue neither theoretically nor empirically and therefore we need not debate it further. Given the high level of temporal stability among the single items, it is not surprising either conceptually or empirically that when these single items are aggregated into composite measures, all of the resulting reliability coefficients are significant (with the mean correlation being .66).

We performed a similar analysis for all the correlations relevant to cross-situational consistency. At the single item level, cross-situational consistency coefficients consist of such correlations as a single observation of appointment punctuality with a single observation of lecture punctuality, or with a single observation of class note neatness (i.e., with any other single observation except another observation of appointment punctuality). As is now typical for research findings of this type, while the percentage of significant correlations (11%) exceeded chance, the obtained correlations were highly erratic. The critical question then becomes what gains in cross-situational consistency are evidenced when our more reliable aggregates are intercorrelated?

To address this question we must examine such correlations as aggregated lecture attendance with aggregated appointment punctuality, or aggregated lecture attendance with aggregated appointment attendance. For this purpose 171 cross-situational consistency coefficients were computed by intercorrelating the 19 different aggregated measures of conscientiousness. Of the 171 coefficients, 20% (35 coefficients) reached significance—a number considerably above chance. Some of these coefficients reached substantial levels. For instance, aggregated class attendance correlates highly with aggregated appointment attendance ($r = .67$, $p < .001$). Furthermore, there are patterns of meaningful coherences among the correlations. For instance, aggregated class attendance correlates significantly with aggregated assignment punctuality ($r = .53$, $p < .001$), with completion of class readings ($r = .58$, $p < .001$), and with amount of time studying ($r = .31$, $p < .05$). These coherences once again testify that individual differences are patterned and organized rather than random. But it is just as clear from the results that behavior is also highly discriminative and that broad cross-situational consistencies remain elusive even with reliable measures. Thus, while aggregated class attendance correlates impressively with the above measures, it does not correlate significantly with aggregated class note thoroughness ($r = .14$, n.s.), aggregated punctuality to lectures ($r = -.03$, n.s.) or aggregated assignment neatness ($r = -.04$, n.s.). This discriminativeness is further reflected in the fact that for the 19 aggregated measures, the mean cross-situational consistency coefficient was only .13.[1]

It is possible that our data do not adequately reflect the gains in cross-situational consistency attainable through aggregation because several of our measures evidenced low reliability coefficients even after aggregation. To apply a more stringent test of the effects of increased reliability for demonstrating cross-situational consistencies, we focused our analysis on those measures whose estimated reliability exceeded an arbitrary selected level of .65. In all, 14 of the 19 original measures met this breakoff point, and the mean reliability (temporal stability) estimate of these measures is .74. Intercorrelating these 14 measures results in 91 consistency coefficients with a mean level of .14. Thus restricting our attention to our most reliable measures results in a minimal gain (.13 to .14) in the mean cross-situational consistency coefficient.

While restricting our attention to our most reliable measures does not seem to have a substantial effect on the cross-situational consistency evidenced in the

---

[1]Unless the single items within one aggregate show a stable (albeit low) pattern of association with the items in the comparison aggregate, substantial increases in validity should not be expected to result from aggregation (Lord & Novick, 1968). That is, gains in cross-situational consistency should not be expected from aggregation when the measures being compared show erratic validity coefficients prior to aggregation. Interestingly, the persistent finding of such erratic relations is precisely what led to the controversy over the breadth and generality of behavioral consistency in the first place.

data, one might argue that a mean reliability coefficient of .74 is still too low to evaluate the "reliability solution." What would happen if all our mean reliability coefficients were .95? More impressively, what kinds of cross-situationally consistency would be evidenced if we were to use perfectly reliable measures? Of course, to answer this type of question is precisely why one applies the correction for attenuation in classical test theory.

By correcting each of the obtained correlations in our matrix for attenuation due to low reliability, we can estimate the maximal ("true") level of association between each of our measures. In this sense, correcting for attenuation is the logical extreme, or ultimate test, of the "reliability solution" as proposed by Epstein. When we apply the correction as described above, the mean consistency coefficient increases to .20. Thus, if we were to collect a large number of observations for each measure such that the reliability of each of the composites (aggregations) of these observations is 1.0, the mean level of cross-situational consistency evidenced between these measures still would not exceed .20.

Given the various results summarized to this point, what can one conclude about the promise of "the reliability solution" for the consistency debate? First of all, it is clear that aggregation of repeated observations in order to obtain adequately reliable measures yields, as expected (and hardly to anyone's surprise), gains in the percentage of significant correlations and the mean levels of correlations both for measures of temporal stability and for cross-situational consistency in behavior. These gains are most impressive for measures of temporal stability (mean $r = .66$) and document that aggregation over occasions is a useful method for increasing the reliability of a measure. The results also indicate, however, that aggregating observations over occasions does not necessarily lead to high cross-situational consistency (mean $r = .13$ or at best up to .20 if perfect reliability is assumed). While aggregation over occasions has the desirable effect of enhancing reliability, it does not provide a simple solution to the consistency debate.

Our results do not imply, however, that there is little coherence among the behaviors studied. While the overall patterning of correlations is erratic and on the average low level (even when we restrict our analysis to our most reliable measures or employ the correction for attenuation), the results do not suggest that the individual's behaviors are random and unorganized. As was noted above, some impressive coefficients emerge, and coherent patterns of correlations are apparent among some of the variables. In addition, 78% (133 of 171) of the obtained correlations are positive, and of the 38 negative correlations, only 2 reach statistical significance. Thus, we obtained considerably more positive significant correlations and also obtained considerably fewer negative significant correlations than would be expected by chance. So while the data reflect behavioral discriminativeness, there is also a positive trend, a coherence or gist among the behaviors sampled, suggesting a relatively stable mean level of individual differences.

In this regard, it is also worth remembering that a mean cross-situational coefficient of the sort we are finding can be construed either as evidence for the relative discriminativeness of behavior or for its coherence, either as evidence for a stable thread of individual differences or for the need to take account of situations not just as sources of "error." How to interpret the results depends on many considerations, not just on the coefficients achieved, as often noted before. For example:

> . . . The relative importance of individual differences will depend on the situation selected, the type of behavior assessed, the particular individual differences sampled, and the purpose of the assessment. . . . (Mischel, 1973, p. 255)

In our view, the challenging problems in the consistency debate require more than searching for significant correlations, and recognizing coherence in obtained results. We need to understand why the obtained coherences emerge and when and why expected coherences do not. The technologies of psychometrics supply us with ample methods for distilling the coherence among our measures, for accentuating the mean levels of individual differences we have identified, and for focusing on and distilling their gist. As our analysis continues, we intend to employ these various technologies in hopes of fully illuminating the psychological significance of these coherences. However, we simultaneously intend to pursue the oft-neglected alternative path of attempting to understand the discriminativeness that also clearly exists in our data and which we believe demands an interactional perspective that treats situations as sources of meaningful variance. For instance, in our research at Carleton College we plan to search for consistency at different levels of abstraction-generality in the data, from the most "subordinate" or molecular to increasingly broad, "super-ordinate," molar levels, guided by a cognitive prototype and hierarchical levels analysis of the sort proposed by Cantor and Mischel (1979). We also plan to explore the comparative usefulness of measures specifically designed to tap such cognitive social learning person variables as the individual's relevant competencies, encodings, expectancies, values, and plans (Mischel, 1973, 1979).

Such analyses should help illuminate processes that underlie both the significant and the nonsignificant coefficients yielded by personality research, the "uneven and erratic patterns" of behavior that characterize person-situation interactions. Aggregation of repeated observations over occasions will aid in these analyses by providing a more accurate (reliable) picture of the significant *and* nonsignificant links that characterize our research. The reliability solution, rather than providing a simple answer to the issues raised regarding the cross-situational consistency of behavior, highlights the complexity of those enduring issues. Rather than resolving the consistency debate, the reliability solution points rather directly to the need to employ alternative conceptualizations of personality that might lead us to a better understanding and appreciation of both the coherence and the discriminativeness of human behavior.

THE TEMPLATE-MATCHING SOLUTION

A second "solution" for the consistency problem is offered by Bem and Funder (1978). Their aim was to utilize Block's California Child Q-sort to find a common language for the description of both persons and situations, and to develop a "template-matching technique" that allows one to examine the interface of person and situation characteristics. Because of the great promise it offers, and the substantial attention it already has attracted, the Bem and Funder contribution merits careful analysis and a thorough examination of its findings and implications. In this analysis the focus will be on the content area of "delay of gratification," the domain Bem and Funder chose to illustrate their approach as it speaks to the consistency problem.

The Bem-Funder Study

Bem and Funder note the failure to obtain more impressive cross-situational consistency coefficients in personality research generally and for delay of gratification in particular. They suggest that the "inconsistencies" obtained are due to the erroneous equation of situations that are superficially similar but "functionally" different. To identify situations that are functionally dissimilar though apparently similar, they propose examining the rated personality characteristics associated with the behavior in these situations. Their ultimate hope is to increase the predictive power of trait information by matching the individual's personality characteristics with the "personality of the situation," defined by Q-sort ratings that supply "portraits" of both the individual and the setting. They see their work as relevant to the consistency issue by showing that situations that seem alike may actually be dissimilar, as evidenced by discrepant patterns of Q-sort correlates. We therefore should not expect behavior in such situations to be highly intercorrelated. Moreover, they argue that only when situations are characterized by similar Q-sort portraits should we expect—and find—high intercorrelations among the behaviors displayed in them.

Their procedure and results require close consideration. They exposed 29 preschool children to a version of the traditional delay of gratification situation. While Bem and Funder retained the basic features of the delay paradigm (e.g., Mischel & Ebbesen, 1970) there was an important difference: The experimenter remained in the room with the child during the delay period rather than leaving the room as in the traditional paradigm. Correlations were computed between a child's delay time and each of the 100 items in the Q-set (i.e., the parents' trait ratings of this child).

Some of the correlations they obtained were highly consistent with previous findings on the rated characteristics of children who are high versus low in their ability to wait in the standard delay situations (see Table 9.2, reproduced from Table 1 of Bem & Funder, 1978, p. 490). Bem and Funder note the existence of these expected correlations (e.g., "Has high standards of performance" is relat-

TABLE 9.2
Table 1 (from Bem & Funder, 1978, p. 490) Q-Item Correlates with
Delay Scores

Item	r
Positively Correlated	
Has high standards of performance for self.	.48[c]
Tends to imitate and take over the characteristic manners and behavior of those he or she admires.	.39[b]
Is protective of others.	.39[b]
Is helpful and cooperative.	.36[a]
Shows a recognition of the feelings of others (empathic).	.35[a]
Is considerate and thoughtful of other children.	.34[a]
Develops genuine and close relationships.	.31[a]
Negatively Correlated	
Appears to have high intellectual capacity.	−.62[c]
Is emotionally expressive.	−.56[c]
Is verbally fluent, can express ideas well in language.	−.50[c]
Is curious and exploring, eager to learn, open to new experiences.	−.49[c]
Is self-assertive.	−.47[b]
Is cheerful.	−.43[b]
Is an interesting, arresting child.	−.43[b]
Is creative in perception, thought, work, or play.	−.40[b]
Attempts to transfer blame to others.	−.37[b]
Behaves in a dominating way with others.	−.34[a]
Is restless and fidgety.	−.31[a]
Seeks physical contact with others.	−.31[a]
Is unable to delay gratification.	−.31[a]

[a]$p < .10$ (two-tailed).
[b]$p < .05$ (two-tailed).
[c]$p < .01$ (two-tailed).

ed to duration of delay, as earlier research suggests it should be). However, they emphasize that the rest of the portrait: ". . . introduces a more *dissonant note,* a picture of the long-delaying child as *not very intelligent, not verbally fluent, not eager to learn, or not open to new experiences*—a child, moreover, who is *not self-assertive, cheerful, interesting, or creative.* The very strong negative relationship between delay and rated intelligence is particularly inconsistent with theories of ego control . . ." (p. 490).

Bem and Funder then confront the consistency issue by comparing the Q-sort portrait from their version of the delay situation with the portrait that emerged from a study of "gift delay" by Block (1977) in an effort to show why behavioral consistency in these two situations has not been found. In Block's procedure, the child sits in front of a gaily-wrapped gift that is not to be opened until he or she has completed a puzzle. The measure of delay is the length of time the child waits before reaching out and taking the gift. Bem and Funder compare their own results with the Q-sort items that were associated with long delay time on Block's measure and note that the two Q-sort portraits: ". . . show very little overlap, and the dull-passive-obedient cluster of items that emerged in our experiment is completely absent from the Block data. *What we have here, then, are two situations that appear conceptually equivalent* but that are functionally quite different, and it would appear that different subsets of children are delaying in the two settings. Typically, one learns only that behavior across two theoretically similar situations is disappointingly inconsistent. By collecting Q-sort data, however, one can see in exquisite detail the nature of that inconsistency and draw plausible inferences about its source in the nonoverlapping features of the setting . . ." (p. 491).

The Bem-Funder approach promises to help resolve the consistency issue by identifying those situations that are psychologically equivalent rather than merely superficially similar, but in fact their data provide no evidence whatsoever for cross-situational consistency. The design of their study does not allow them even to make any estimates about potential consistency since evidence for cross-situational consistency can only be obtained if the same subjects are observed in at least two or more situations. Rather, their conclusions are based on a comparison of the Q-correlates of delay in two different delay situations, for two different sets of children, samples not even matched in age. Their paper thus raises the prospect of improving evidence for cross-situational consistency in behavior but it does not take the essential step of doing so. That is exactly why the present authors proceeded to try to fill this void and tested the Bem-Funder promise empirically with an appropriate design for assessing cross-situational consistency.

The Mischel-Peake Study

Mischel and Peake (1982) attempted to replicate the Bem-Funder study, with some important additions. We exposed children to the Bem-Funder paradigm using identical procedures, the same immediate and delayed rewards, subjects of the same age drawn from the same population (Stanford University's Bing Nursery School), whom we tested at about the same time of year as those in the Bem-Funder study. These children also participated in the standard delay paradigm (described in Mischel & Ebbesen, 1970), which differs from the Bem-Funder procedure only in that the experimenter is absent during the delay period. This design made it possible for us to assess the consistency of the children's delay behavior across the two situations (experimenter present versus absent) and to compare the Q-correlates for the two situations systematically. The children participated in the two situations in random order and within a period of 3 weeks. To enhance reliability, the sample size was nearly twice that in the Bem-Funder study.

Delay behavior in the two situations was correlated at a modest level ($r = .22$, n.s.). According to Bem and Funder's reasoning, this low level of association provides an ideal test of their proposition on two counts. First, the two situations appear to be similar (indeed, the two vary only in the experimenter's presence versus absence—an aspect apparently so trivial that Bem and Funder employed it as a substitute for the standard Mischel delay paradigm). Second, behavior in the two situations proves to be not strongly intercorrelated empirically. Applying the Bem-Funder Q-sort approach to the two situations should reveal the "distinctive features" that make these seemingly similar situations psychologically different: showing their "unique personalities," and revealing why behavior in the two situations is not more closely intercorrelated.

The results of our investigation surprised us greatly. In spite of our considerable efforts to conduct an exact replication of the Bem-Funder delay study, the data we obtained not only did not support their basic findings, it reversed them. The major distinctive Q-correlates obtained by Bem-Funder are shown in the first column of Table 9.3; the Q-correlates yielded by the replication are given in the second column. The resulting portrait, far from replicating the Bem-Funder distinctive features, is the very opposite of the one they drew.

For example, on the identical measure (i.e., with experimenter present), the high-delay child rather than being intellectually dull and uneager to learn appears to have high intellectual capacity ($r = .23$, $p < .10$) and is curious and exploring, eager to learn, open to new experiences ($r = .27$, $p < .05$). Bem-Funder's strong negative correlations between high delay and verbal fluency; self-assertiveness, and creativity in perception, thought, work or play are all lost ($r = .06$, .09, and .00, respectively). The other remaining "distinctive features" either fail to approach significance or reach significance in the opposite direction ("needs physical contact" changes from $-.31$ to a positive .24, $p < .10$).

Interestingly, it is only the distinctive features that are lost or reversed in the replication. The Q-sort correlates that are theoretically consistent with the previously established view of the "ego strength" correlates of high delay remain intact, indicating that the delay measure employed had validity even though the Q-correlates reported as distinctive by the Bem-Funder methodology turned out to be unstable. Thus "traditional" ego strength correlates for the delay measure (Mischel, 1974) such as "has high standards of performance for self," and "develops genuine and close relationships" were in the expected direction and statistically significant. In the same vein, the replication yielded the expected correlations between high delay time and such ratings as "is competent and skillful" ($r = .38$, $p < .005$); "is planful, thinks ahead" ($r = .36$, $p < .01$); uses and "responds to reason" ($r = .27$, $p < .05$); and "is reflective, thinks and deliberates before he or she speaks or acts" ($r = .26$, $p < .10$).

Moreover, the correlates obtained for the "standard delay" (experimenter absent) procedure were generally similar to those for the Bem-Funder (experi-

TABLE 9.3
Comparative Correlates for Significant "Distinctive" Items of Bem-
Funder (1978) Delay (Mother–Father Q-sorts)

Item	Bem and Funder (1978) r (N = 29)	Bem and Funder Replication r (N = 52)
Appears to have high intellectual capacity	− .62[c]	.23[a]
Is verbally fluent, can express ideas well in language	− .50[c]	.06
Is curious and exploring, eager to learn, open to new experiences	− .49[c]	.27[a]
Is self-assertive	− .47[b]	.09
Is cheerful	− .43[b]	− .19
Is an interesting, arresting child	− .43[b]	− .17
Is creative in perception, thought, work, or play	− .40[b]	.00

[a]$p < .10$ (two-tailed).
[b]$p < .05$ (two-tailed).
[c]$p < .01$ (two-tailed).

menter present) version and were entirely coherent with the expected "ego strength" portrait (Mischel, 1966, 1974). Namely, we found low-level but statistically significant associations between the standard delay measure and such ratings as: appears to have high intellectual capacity; has high standards of performance for self; uses and responds to reason; is curious and exploring, eager to learn, open to new experiences; is reflective, thinks and deliberates before he or she speaks or acts.

Although the obtained Q-sort portraits proved neither stable nor distinctive, we must still consider the utility of the "template-matching technique" for making predictions about the delay behavior of children within our study. So far we have considered only the Q-sort correlates of the measures, without applying the template-matching procedures proposed by Bem-Funder to the data. Their "weighting" procedure was intended to allow them to transport "the relevant information . . . from one subject sample to another . . ." and thus to "generate templates which retain their situation-characterizing properties while simultaneously characterizing most closely the particular sample of individuals whose behavior is to be predicted" (Bem & Funder, 1978, p. 492). Given that the distinctive features of the Q-sort portrait for the Bem-Funder measure proved to be so unstable, it is not surprising that application of the original Bem-Funder template "weights" to our replication turned out to have no predictive value, producing a negligible correlation ($r = .05$, n.s.). More distressing is the fact that within the replication sample itself, efforts to internally cross-validate the template-matching technique did not succeed in spite of our attempts to closely adhere to the original procedures.[2]

In sum, the Bem-Funder technique held out the exciting promise of yielding distinctive personality portraits that would "explain" why two situations that seem alike may not be very closely associated empirically in the behaviors that they evoke. Unfortunately, this promise appears to remain unrealized at least as it applies to the delay paradigm, both when we search for the distinctive Q-sort portrait suggested by the Bem-Funder approach and when we seek to apply their template-matching technique to new data. In situations that yield similar rather than distinctive Q-sort portraits, their argument predicts that one should be able to show high cross-situational consistency in behavior. We did not find that to be true in our data. How can this failure be understood?

In our view, we failed to replicate the distinctive Q-sort correlates because when the sample size is small and when the associations are purely empirical (with no theoretical hypotheses a priori), correlations with Q-sort items may be extremely unstable. In that case, "distinctive" actuarially-achieved portraits can vanish rapidly, as often happens with other "cookbooks" (see Mischel, 1968, p. 134). Moreover, the weighting procedures of the Bem-Funder template-matching technique may inadvertently serve to compound error (by weighting chance findings) and thus hurt rather than help. Certainly, the reliability of the assigned weights should have been assessed empirically, for example, by using a "jack-knife technique" (Mosteller & Tukey, 1977) or a "bootstrap" technique (Efron, 1979). In the absence of such assessment the confidence intervals for the true weights are unknown. And since their method of cross-validation also used only a single (albeit random) split of the sample, it does not preclude that any reliability obtained may be spurious; at the minimum, one needs a series of split-halves within the original sample to allow a more stable estimate of generalizability.

It seems worth remembering that often simple linear combinations of single scale scores have been found to be more accurate than complex, sophisticated configural models, including the Meehl-Dahlstrom Rules (e.g., Goldberg, 1965). Simple cooking with simple recipes may work better than more esoteric methods. At a minimum it seems wise to compare the increments that fancier (thus costlier) methods (like template matching) provide when tested against old-fashioned, basic-fare methods (like linear regression to predict a particular

---

[2]Although our focus here is only on the application of the Bem-Funder template-matching approach to the delay situation, there also have been attempts to replicate their effort to predict attitude change in the forced-compliance paradigm. These attempts at extended replication so far also seem to have failed (Funder, 1979; Hoffman & Bem, 1980). A more situation-specific or "contextual" procedure now has been substituted for the global Q-sort descriptions (Hoffman & Bem, 1980) and seems promising, yielding high coefficients but it might be wise to await replication of these new efforts before judging them.

behavior in a given situation from any cross-validated items shown to have predicted it before). It may be less exciting, but often it is more efficacious (Mischel, 1968). If personality assessment has taught us any lesson, it is that it is generally not worth offering "conclusions" about actuarially-obtained performance correlates unless they are based on careful cross-validation.

The present results have considerably more significance than a failure to replicate the Bem-Funder distinctive portraits. They more importantly speak to the value of their approach for resolving the consistency issue in the directions they proposed. Recall that we not only found that the Bem-Funder delay situation and the classical delay situation were not reliably differentiated by distinctive Q-sort portraits; on the contrary, we also found the two situations share highly similar and familiar patterns of correlations. According to Bem and Funder, here then are two situations revealed by their method to have similar correlates and therefore expected by their analysis to yield cross-situational consistency in behavior. Yet in fact, the inter-correlation for behavior in these two situations is only .22 in our data. Disappointingly, the Bem-Funder approach, at least in the delay context, provides no perceptible increment in the usual level of cross-situational consistency obtained.

Of course one might concede that the Bem-Funder approach did not improve consistency where it was expected to do so and yet go on to argue that .22 is "really" not a poor correlation if one corrects for the unreliability of measurement (considering each delay situation as if it were a single item on a test). In that case, we have come full-circle back to Epstein's solution, and we invite any hardy readers not yet exhausted to review the promise and the results of the reliability solution to the consistency issue discussed previously.

SOME IMPLICATIONS

In sum, Epstein's solution for the consistency issue asks us to remember the issues of reliability and the Spearman-Brown formula—which comprehensive reviews of the consistency debate (including Hartshorne & May's 1928 classic) never forgot in the first place. Analysis of Epstein's data, and of our own, reveals that aggregation of course enhances reliability just as expected. The evidence for temporal consistency—never in dispute in this debate—is impressive, but the evidence for cross-situational consistency in behavior remains as complex and as debatable as ever.

The Bem-Funder efforts towards a solution of the consistency issue in the delay domain is most disappointing. When the sample is adequate (as in our replication), one finds the typical, replicable low-level theory-consistent Q-sort correlates of delay behavior. But no advance is made by use of their methods to show replicable distinctive portraits, to demonstrate improved cross-situational breadth in the domain, or to powerfully explain its phenotypic absence. The promise that the Bem-Funder technique would allow demonstrations of impressive cross-situational consistency by identifying measures that have similar rather than distinctive Q-sort correlates still awaits realization.

Recognition of the limitations in these proposed solutions does not leave us pessimistic. Indeed, it is exciting to see that in recent years the consistency debate has stimulated a great deal of interesting research and even more discussion. As the present volume attests, much of this activity has been refreshing, offering some new perspectives, insights, and methods for pursuing dispositions and inferring their links to behavior fruitfully. In our view, the bulk of the evidence still provides at least as much documentation for the discriminativeness and flexibility of behavior as for its cross-situational consistency. But an insistence that human conduct is more flexible, adaptive, and individually patterned than traditional nomothetic trait theories implied in no way suggests that behavior is either chaotic or unpredictable.

The consistency of behavior and its potential predictability are hardly equivalent. Yet the issue of consistency is often transformed into one of predictability with the implication that if something (sometimes almost anything) can be predicted, then traditional trait constructs are alive and well. But in fact all sorts of predictability can be obtained without evidence for cross-situational consistency. As a case in point, take the demonstration of significant links between self-reports and relevant behavior. Consider, for example, the phenomenon of selective attention to self-relevant information. The correlations between scores on self-report trait measures (the R-S Scale based on the Minnesota Multiphasic Personality Inventory; see Byrne, 1964) and attention to one's personal assets and liabilities as objectively measured were explored by Mischel, Ebbesen, and Zeiss (1973). Theoretically interesting and substantial associations were found. Thus, for example, people who presented themselves in a positive ("repressing") rather than in a self-critical ("sensitizing") fashion on this 127-item scale also tended actually to spend more time attending to positive (.51) and less time to negative ($-.61$) information about themselves on the behavioral measure of selective attention. This finding clearly illustrates a respectable link between a self-report and a relevant specific behavior (even without any aggregation). Links of this sort have been reported before and self-reports not infrequently are the best predictors of behavior (as discussed, for example, in Mischel, 1968 and 1972). However, such links between what a person says and what he does are not necessarily evidence for consistency in behavior across situations. It would be a mistake to confuse the predictability of behavior (which can be highly specific, yet orderly) with its cross-situational consistency.

In our view, an adequate resolution of the many issues raised in the long debate about consistency requires a theoretical reconceptualization of the issues, and of personality and situation constructs themselves (e.g., Cantor & Mischel, 1979; Mischel, 1973), not merely more clever methods for applying everyday trait terms to people's behavior in particular contexts. It is tempting to tire of the consistency debate, to trivialize it by focusing on its obvious qualities: surely each person's behavior shows some consistency, some discriminativeness, some continuity, some change. But this tempting stance has nontrivial consequences, diverting attention from the serious questions that have been raised by evidence of unexpected discontinuities and discriminativeness in behavior (e.g., Baltes, 1980; Brim & Kagan, 1980; Mischel, 1968, 1979), which suggest the potentially disturbing (but equally exciting) plasticity of social life. In our view, such evidence calls for a reconceptualization of traditional personality theory in ways that unify the analysis of person characteristics with the analysis of cognitive-learning processes (e.g., Mischel, 1973). Such a reconceptualization requires that the person and the situation be analyzed in light of the same psychological principles, and not merely described with the same trait terms. It also requires a deeper analysis of the nature of natural person and situation categories, and the bases of psychological similarity (Cantor & Mischel, 1979; Cantor, Mischel, & Schwartz, 1981). In the absence of an appropriate theoretical framework, the search for consistencies can become an ultimately uninteresting hunt for statistically significant coefficients neglecting their psychological significance and their links to psychologically interesting processes.

ACKNOWLEDGMENTS

Portions of this chapter are based on Mischel and Peake, 1982.

Preparation of this paper and the research by the authors were supported in part by Grant HD MH-09814 from the National Institute of Child Health and Human Development and Grant MH 6830 from the National Institute of Mental Health. We have benefitted from the thoughtful help of more colleagues than we can list, and are grateful to them all. Among the most detailed comments on earlier drafts were those offered by Albert Bandura, Nancy Cantor, Lee Cronbach, Leonard Horowitz, Anne Locksley, and Neil Lutsky.

REFERENCES

Allport, G. W. *Personality: A psychological interpretation*. New York: Holt, Rinehart & Winston, 1937.

Allport, G. W. Traits revisited. *American Psychologist*, 1966, *21*, 1–10.

Baltes, P. B. Life-span developmental psychology: Observations on history and theory. In P. B. Baltes & O. G. Brim, Jr. (Eds.), *Life-span development and behavior*, (Vol. 2). New York: Academic Press, 1980.

Bandura, A. Reflections on self-efficacy. In S. Rachman (Ed.), *Advances in behaviour research and therapy*, (Vol. 1). Oxford: Pergamon Press, 1978.

Bem, D. J., & Allen, A. On predicting some of the people some of the time: The search for cross-situational consistencies in behavior. *Psychological Review*, 1974, *81*, 506–520.

Bem, D. J., & Funder, D. C. Predicting more of the people more of the time: Assessing the personality of situations. *Psychological Review*, 1978, *85*, 485–501.

Block, J. Advancing the psychology of personality: Paradigmatic shift or improving the quality of research. In D. Magnusson & N. S. Endler (Eds.), *Personality at the crossroads: Current issues in interactional psychology.* Hillsdale, N.J.: Lawrence Erlbaum Associates, 1977.

Bowers, K. Situationism in psychology: An analysis and a critique. *Psychological Review,* 1973, *80,* 307–336.

Brim, O. G., Jr., & Kagan, J. (Eds.). *Constancy and change in human development.* Cambridge, Mass.: Harvard University Press, 1980.

Bryne, D. Repression-sensitization as a dimension of personality. In B. A. Maher (Ed.), *Progress in experimental personality research,* (Vol. 1). New York: Academic Press, 1964.

Cantor, N., & Mischel, W. Prototypes in person perception. In L. Berkowitz (Ed.), *Advances in experimental social psychology,* (Vol. 12). New York: Academic Press, 1979.

Cantor, N., Mischel, W., & Schwartz, J. Social knowledge: Structure, content, use and abuse. In A. Hastorf and A. Isen (Eds.), *Cognitive social psychology.* New York: Elsevier North-Holland, 1982, in press.

Efron, B. Bootstrap methods: Another look at the jackknife. *Annals of Statistics,* 1979, *7,* 1–26.

Endler, N. S., & Magnusson D. (Eds.). *Interactional psychology and personality.* New York: Wiley (Halsted Press: Hemisphere Publishing), 1976.

Epstein, S. The stability of behavior: I. On predicting most of the people much of the time. *Journal of Personality and Social Psychology,* 1979, *37,* 1097–1126.

Fiske, D. W. The inherent variability of behavior. In D. W. Fiske & S. R. Maddi (Eds.), *Functions of varied experience.* Homewood, ILL.: Dorsey Press, 1961.

Funder, D. C. *The person-situation interaction in attitude change.* Unpublished doctoral dissertation, Stanford University, 1979.

Goldberg, L. R. Diagnosticians vs. diagnostic signs: The diagnosis of psychosis vs. neurosis from the MMPI. *Psychological Monographs,* 1965, 79 (Whole No. 602).

Gough, H. G. *Manual, California Psychological Inventory.* Palo Alto: Consulting Psychologists Press, 1957.

Gulliksen, H. *Theory of mental tests.* New York: Wiley, 1950.

Hartshorne, H., & May, M. A. *Studies in deceit.* New York: Macmillan, 1928.

Hoffman, C., & Bem, D. J. *Contextual template matching: A progress report on predicting all of the people all of the time.* Unpublished manuscript, 1980.

Horowitz, L. M., Inouye, D., & Siegelman, E. Y. On averaging judges' ratings to increase their correlation with an external criterion. *Journal of Consulting and Clinical Psychology,* 1979, *47,* 453–458.

Kelly, E. L. Consistency of the adult personality. *American Psychologist,* 1955, *10,* 659–681.

Lord, F. M., & Novick, M. R. *Statistical theories of mental test scores.* Reading: MASS.: Addison-Wesley, 1968.

Magnusson, D., & Endler, N. S. Interactional psychology: Present status and future prospects. In D. Magnusson & N. S. Endler (Eds.), *Personality at the crossroads: Current issues in interactional psychology.* Hillsdale, N.J.: Lawrence Erlbaum Associates, 1977.

Mischel, W. Theory and research on the antecedents of self-imposed delay of reward. In B. A. Maher (Ed.), *Progress in experimental personality research,* (Vol. 3). New York: Academic Press, 1966.

Mischel, W. *Personality and assessment.* New York: Wiley, 1968.

Mischel, W. Direct versus indirect personality assessment: Evidence and implications. *Journal of Consulting and Clinical Psychology,* 1972, *38,* 319–324.

Mischel, W. Toward a cognitive social learning reconceptualization of personality. *Psychological Review,* 1973, *80,* 252–283.

Mischel, W. Processes in delay of gratification. In L. Berkowitz (Ed.), *Advances in experimental social psychology,* (Vol. 7). New York: Academic Press, 1974.

Mischel, W. On the interface of cognition and personality: Beyond the person-situation debate. *American Psychologist,* 1979, *34,* 740–754.

Mischel, W., & Ebbesen, E. B. Attention in delay of gratification. *Journal of Personality and Social Psychology,* 1970, *16,* 329–337.

Mischel, W., Ebbesen, E. B., & Zeiss, A. R. Selective attention to the self: Situational and dispositional determinants. *Journal of Personality and Social Psychology,* 1973, *27,* 129–142.

Mischel, W., & Peake, P. K. Beyond déjà vu in the search for cross-situational consistency. *Psychological Review,* 1982, in press.

Moos, R. H., & Fuhr, R. The clinical use of social-ecological concepts: The case of an adolescent girl. *American Journal of Orthopsychiatry,* in press.

Mosteller, F., & Tukey, W. *Data analysis and regression: A second course in statistics.* Reading, MASS.: Addison-Wesley, 1977.

Olweus, D. A critical analysis of the "modern" interactionist position. In D. Magnusson & N. S. Endler (Eds.), *Personality at the crossroads: Current issues in interactional psychology.* Hillsdale, N.J.: Lawrence Erlbaum Associates, 1977.

Patterson, G. R. The aggressive child: Victim and architect of a coercive system. In L. A. Hamerlynck, L. C. Handy, & E. J. Mash (Eds.), *Behavior modification and families: 1. Theory and research.* New York: Brunner/Mazel, 1976.

Patterson, G. R., & Moore, D. R. Interactive patterns as units. In M. Lamb, S. Suomi, & G. Stephenson (Eds.), *Methodological problems in the study of social interaction.* Madison: University of Wisconsin Press, 1979.

Peterson, D. R. *The clinical study of social behavior.* New York: Appleton, 1968.

Raush, H. L. Paradox levels, and junctures in person-situation systems. In D. Magnusson & N. S. Endler (Eds.), *Personality at the crossroads: Current issues in interactional psychology.* Hillsdale, N.J.: Lawrence Erlbaum Associates, 1977.

Thorndike, E. L. *Principles of teaching.* New York: Seiler, 1906.

Thurstone, L. L. *The reliability and validity of tests.* Ann Arbor, MICH.: Edwards Brothers, 1932.

Vernon, P. E. *Personality assessment: A critical survey.* New York: Wiley, 1964.

Wiggins, J. S. *Personality and prediction: Principles of personality assessment.* Reading, MASS.: Addison-Wesley, 1973.

10 Interactionism Comes of Age

Norman S. Endler
York University

Interactionism is an idea whose time has come. This is reflected both in theorizing and research during the past few years. A perusal of the various psychological journals and recent personality texts readily attests to the impact of interactionism, as do the various conferences and symposia on this topic. Does interactionism deserve all the recent attention it has received? Is it a viable concept? Have the recent discussions on interactionism shed more light than heat?

The concept of interactionism is not a new one, but can be traced back at least to the time of Aristotle (see Shute, 1973), Descartes, and other philosophers. In the seventeenth century, the physicist Robert Hooke proposed Hooke's law, which stated that "within the elastic limit, strain is proportional to stress. For fluids and gases elasticity has a different meaning" (Bridgwater & Kurtz, 1963, p. 637). That is, the elasticity of a substance is an interactive function of the degree of situational stress, and the nature of the material. Empirical evidence (see Endler & Edwards, 1978) suggests that there may well be a Hooke's law for personality. That is, there is evidence that behavior (e.g., anxious behavior, conforming behavior), is an interactive function of personality traits (material) and situational impact (stress). Persons and situations interact jointly to influence the nature and the direction of behavior.

Kantor (1924, 1926) was probably one of the first to propose a psychological interpretation of interactionism. According to Kantor "no biological fact may be considered as anything but the mutual interaction of the organism and the environment" (1926, p. 369). He believed that "the individual as he interacts with all the various types of situations which constitute his behavior circumstances" (1924, p. 92), should be the unit of analysis. Kantor proposed that "a personality conception must be predominantly functional and must place great emphasis upon the stimuli conditions and the interaction of the person with them'' (1924, p. 91). He was one of the first to distinguish between the physical and psychological environments. Kantor (1969) emphasized the physical environment, as distinguished from Lewin's (1936) field theory and the theories and models of most interactionists. Nevertheless, Kantor's behavioristic field theory did emphasize the reciprocal interaction between the person and the environment.

In parallel to the early "interbehavioral psychology" of Kantor, the Gestalt psychologist Koffka, in his studies on perception, also distinguished between the physical environment and the psychological environment. Koffka (1935) proposed a very precise distinction between the "geographical" (physical) and "behavioral" (psychological) environment. For him the psychological environment was a function of the interaction between the physical environment and the person.

Lewin (1935, 1936) was another psychologist who emphasized the distinction between the psychological environment and the physical environment. For behavior, it was the psychological environment or psychological situation, or psychological ecology, that was important. Lewin also focused on the relationship between the individual and the environment, in his theorizing. The units of organization, for Lewin, were holistic entities. The various elements within the person-situation relationship were mutually interdependent and not independent. Both Kantor and Lewin emphasized the reciprocal interaction between the person and his or her environment.

Murray (1938) postulated a need-press theory of personality, whose essential characteristic was the interaction between personal and situational factors. "Since at every moment, an organism is within an environment which largely determines its behavior, and since the environment changes—sometimes with radical abruptness—the conduct of an individual cannot be formulated without a characterization of each confronting situation, physical and social" (Murray, 1938, p. 39). He used the parallel constructs of presses and needs for environments and persons, respectively, and therefore, it is possible to examine person by situation interactions within the theoretical context of his theory. Murray also distinguished between *Alpha* press (physical environment) and *Beta* press (psychological environment).

Angyal (1941), like Lewin, emphasized the person by environment system as an inseparable entity. He believed that the person and the situation interpenetrate one another so thoroughly that it is impossible to unravel them without destroying their unity or wholeness. Angyal coined the term *biosphere* to refer to his holistic entity, which included the sociological, psychological, and biological facets of the person by environment constellation. This seems to be analogous to what Dewey and Bentley (1949) called transactionalism.

Whereas Kantor and Lewin emphasized the interdependence of situation variables and person variables, Tolman (1935/1951) regarded the various components as independent. Tolman also focused on the physical environment in contrast to Lewin, Koffka, and Angyal, who emphasized the psychological environment. Nevertheless, Tolman did conceptualize behavior as being a function of the stimulus setup, heredity, training and physiological state of the organism.

Murphy (1947) formulated a *biosocial* theory of personality which is essentially an interactional theory. According to Murphy, personality was a function of two factors, one residing within the biological organism, and the other located in the social environment. He favored an interactional view of personality, but did not explicitly distinguish between the psychological environment and the physical environment. Furthermore, Murphy had nothing to say about the units of analysis necessary for an interactional psychology of personality.

Rotter (1954), however, in his social learning theory formulation of personality, proposes that the unit of analysis for the investigation of personality should be the interaction of the person and his or her meaningful environment. Meaningful environment as proposed by Rotter appears to be the same as the psychological environment as proposed by Lewin and Murray.

Jessor (1956, 1958) has also emphasized the psychological environment and has attempted to relate this to phenomenological theories of personality. He is in favor of phenomenological personality theories, that is, theories that use concepts that are relevant to the psychological environment. In most cases the psychological environment refers to the person's perception of the situation or the meaning that the situation has for him or her.

Despite the theoretical formulations about person by situation interactions in the 1920s, 1930s, 1940s, and 1950s, the mainstream of empirical research on interactionism did not start until the late 1950s and early 1960s. Surprisingly, the empirical research developed almost independently of the theoretical aspects of the person by situation interaction issue. The early empirical studies on interactionism by Raush, Dittmann, and Taylor (1959a, 1959b), and by Endler, Hunt, and Rosenstein (1962), and by Endler and Hunt (1966) show no readily discernible relationship with the theorizing of Kantor, Koffka, Lewin or Murray. The reason for the almost independent development of the theoretical and empirical streams is not readily apparent, but it does raise an interesting question for the sociology of science. It was only towards the mid- and late 1960s and the 1970s that the interest in the theoretical aspects of interactionism redeveloped (e.g., Endler 1976; Endler & Hunt, 1969; Endler & Magnusson, 1976b, 1976c; Hunt, 1965; Magnusson & Endler, 1977; Raush, 1965). There have also been extensive reviews of the empirical literature on interactionism (e.g., Argyle & Little, 1972; Bowers, 1973; Ekehammar, 1974; Endler, 1976; Endler & Magnusson, 1976b, 1976c; Magnusson, 1976; Magnusson & Endler, 1977; Mischel, 1973; and Pervin, 1968).

SOCIOPOLITICAL AND PERSONAL SOURCES OF INTERACTIONISM

What are the various sources that have influenced the research and theorizing on interactionism during the last twenty years? Basically I want to discuss two general types of sources of influences, namely, a situation factor and a person factor. The situation factor refers to sociopolitical influences and the person factor refers to some of my own personal background and influences.

Pervin (1978a) has noted that "The general public and many scientists have the view of science as a purely objective pursuit and the view of scientists as purely rational individuals. Yet, considerable evidence suggests that scientists are very much influenced by their personal histories and by the societal views of the time" (p. 269). It is most likely that personal variables and experiences have a more profound role in psychological theory and research than in the fields of chemistry and physics, because the latter two disciplines are exact sciences whereas psychology is not. This is most pronounced in personality research where the ambiguity of the subject matter may be propitious for projection on the part of the investigator. The scientist and his field of study *interact* and this affects the content areas of the research under investigation.

Stolorow and Atwood (1979) have suggested that one determinant of a personality theory is the life experiences of the scientist postulating the theory. Personal and subjective factors affect the nature of personality theories as does the sociopolitical climate. Ichheiser (1943) is one investigator who has noted the role of sociopolitical factors in personality research. He believes, for example, the overestimation of the role of personal factors and the underestimation of situational factors, in personality theorizing and research, had its roots in the social system and ideology of nineteenth-century liberalism. The notion was that "our fate in social space depended exclusively, or at least predominantly, on our individual qualities—that we, as individuals, and not the prevailing social conditions shape our lives" (Ichheiser, 1943, p. 152). The sociopsychological and sociopolitical forces since the 1930s (e.g., unemployment, the depression, World War II, the Cold War, the revolution of rising expectations, Viet Nam) seem to have shifted the emphasis towards explaining behavior on the basis of social conditions.

All scientific endeavors have historical, political, social, and scientific contexts. The scientific perspectives about the nature-nurture issue, for example, are intricately related to political factors. Behaviorism, for example, is intimately related to the American ideology of "doing and action" as opposed to "thinking and reflection" (See Buss, 1975; and Pervin, 1978a). Obviously research in personality is not value free, nor should we claim that it is. We should, however, attempt to *minimize* the influence of social, political, and personal factors on the scientific enterprise.

In addition to personality theory and content being influenced by extrascientific considerations, the methodology and tactics of research are also influenced by personal and social factors. Whom should we use as subjects for our research? Adults or children? Normals or abnormals? Blacks or whites? Males or females? This has obvious political implications. Should our research be conducted in real-life situations, where we can obtain "wide band-low fidelity" information or should it be conducted in the laboratory where we can obtain "narrow band-high fidelity" information? Will our research have more relevance if it is conducted in natural settings than if it is conducted in the laboratory? Are idiographic methods more appropriate for collecting personality data than nomothetic methods? Should our research be guided by theory or by practical concerns?

Lewin (1952) proclaimed "that there is nothing so practical as a good theory" (p. 169). Both theory and practice can mutually benefit one another. A theory of personality can be tested in an applied setting (e.g., a clinical setting) and this might lead to improved methods of assessment. Work in an applied setting can generate hypotheses which can frequently be tested under rigorous experimental methods. Freud's theories of personality were based primarily on clinical observations. My own interest in interactional psychology grew out of very practical concerns.

It is quite frequent that research is instigated by the need to solve a practical problem. This type of research can be designated *action-oriented* research. In the field of personality, *action-oriented* research was conducted by Henry Murray for the *Office of Strategic Service* (OSS) during World War II. Murray and his co-workers were faced with the task of assessing and selecting men for intelligence work, as undercover agents, spies, and resistance leaders. The assignment for the OSS (the precursor of the CIA) Assessment Staff, as presented in the *Assessment of Men* (1948), was to determine which persons would do well in a number of different military intelligence situations. The OSS action-oriented study, influenced by political considerations, was concerned with the intensive study of the individual, with the person as the unit of analysis.

We have seen how the sociopolitical or situational context has influenced the research on personality. What are some of the personal factors that led me to become interested in and to investigate an interactional psychology of personality? During my late teens and early twenties I was a counsellor and then a head counsellor at a summer camp. While working at camp I was puzzled and fascinated by the fact that various counsellors described each camper in a somewhat different manner. The nature-study counsellor, for example, might describe Bill, one of the campers, as very brave, because Bill is not afraid of handling snakes. However, the waterfront counsellor disagrees and describes Bill as a very anxious person, because Bill is afraid to jump into the water. The bunk counsellor describes Bill as being afraid of the dark, but being very relaxed while playing volleyball. I was somewhat puzzled by the fact that different counsellors perceived the same camper differently, and that the same counsellor perceived Bill differently at different times. I respected all the counsellors and trusted their judgment. At first I thought that they might not be describing the same camper. However, they were describing the same camper, but I realized later they were observing him in different situations. At that time, when I tried to make some sense of all this, the answers did not come very readily or easily.

A few years later when I started my doctoral training for my Ph.D. in Clinical Psychology at the University of Illinois (after completing a Master's Degree in Social Psychology at McGill University) I again had an experience during my practicum training and internship that puzzled me. During case conferences about patients, I discovered that the various mental health workers (psychiatrists, psychologists, and social workers) all described the same patient differently from one another, and differently from me, who had assessed the patient via various psychological tests. Since I respected the ability and judgment of the psychiatrists, psychologists, and social workers, I was concerned when they described the patient differently from one another.

At about this time I was taking a graduate course in Personality from J. McV. Hunt. In the context of this course, he presented a logical analysis of what is meant by saying that one person manifests more than another person of a given adjectively designated common trait (e.g., anxiety, dependence, hostility). During these class seminars we discussed the fact that observers do not always agree about the degree to which any given trait or characteristic is manifested in an individual or sample of individuals. One of the bases of disagreement among raters is that they may very well observe persons' responses in different contexts or situations. For example, Bill the camper, discussed above, may be anxious in the swimming situation but not in the snake-handling situation. The discrepancy between the two counsellors regarding Bill's anxiety, may well be due to the fact that the counsellors observed Bill in two different situations. A psychiatrist, in interviewing a patient, may focus on the patient's psychodynamics, whereas the social worker may focus on the family constellation of the patient.

Endler, Hunt, and Rosenstein (1962) developed the *S-R Inventory of Anxiousness* out of the concerns discussed above. The distinctiveness of this inventory is that it separates *stimulus situation* from *response* in its format. This self-report inventory, because of its format, makes it possible to calculate the percent of variance due to persons, situations, modes of response, and to various interactions among these main effects. The intensity of the person's responses is assessed as well as the factor structure of the 11 situations (e.g., you are going to meet a new date; you are alone in the woods at night) and the 14 modes of response (e.g., perspire, heart beats faster).

The field of interactional psychology which focuses on person-by-situation interactions is influenced by both situational or sociopolitical factors (situations) and by personal experiences of investigators (persons).

CONCERNS ABOUT PERSONALITY RESEARCH

A major problem with respect to personality research during the 1950s, 1960s, and 1970s, is that it has been basically piecemeal, and ad hoc, rather than programmatic. In addition, much of the personality research has serious methodological flaws (Block, 1977). Carlson (1971), in reviewing all of the articles published in 1968 in the *Journal of Personality* and in the *Journal of Personality and Social Psychology,* has pointed out that research in the area of personality emphasizes undergraduates, relies to a great extent on the experimental methods, collects data on a small sample of responses from each person, and that the relationship between the subject and the experimenter is artificial and impersonal. She notes that *"not a single published study attempted even minimal inquiry into the organization of personality variables within the individual"* (Carlson, 1971, p. 209). Carlson was concerned about the underemphasis with respect to intensive studies of the individual. She asks "Where is the person?" in current personality research. Earlier, Allport (1961) had the same concern, and two years after Carlson, Bowers (1973) questioned the overemphasis on the situation and the environment, and the underemphasis on the individual. However, a few years after Bowers, Sechrest (1976) in his *Annual Review of Psychology* paper on "Personality" noted that emphasis on individual differences could possibly be counterproductive to progress in the field of personality. The issue of studying *the* individual versus groups of individuals, where the emphasis is on variables (e.g., traits), is comparable to debate about the merits of the nomothetic (universal variables) versus the idiographic (individual) approach to personality. An integration of both approaches, where one first isolates the essential variables, and then examines their unique constellation within the person, is most desirable.

The emphasis on the individual or the lack of emphasis on the individual comes and goes in waves. Freud and Piaget, the two persons who have made the greatest impact in psychology, both made their reputations studying persons, in great detail. The monumental research by Henry Murray (1938) and his collaborators on *Explorations in Personality,* and their subsequent work on the *Assessment of Men* (1948), both focused on the person and person variables. In fact, Murray coined the term *personology* to refer to this approach rather than use the more general term personality. The investigations conducted at the Berkeley Institute of Personality Assessment and Research have also focused on studies of the individual. Recently Block (1971, 1977), at Berkeley, has reported on his longitudinal studies of personality, and White (1966, 1976) has reported on in-depth case studies. Mischel, who has been mistakenly accused of being a situationist, has recently noted that "The person is what personality psychology must be about; no one really disputes that" (Mischel, 1976, p. 497). Interactionists also believe in people, but they believe that situations are important (Endler & Magnusson, 1978).

A greater concern, to my mind, than whether or not the person has been overemphasized or underemphasized is the impression that a fair amount of research has been atheoretical and has focused on what is flashy and trendy, rather than on what is theoretical, meaningful and substantive. Contributing to this is the value system of Universities, where "publish or perish" is the norm. This makes it impractical and very difficult for faculty and students to become involved in intensive, longitudinal, relevant, and detailed studies of individual persons. It also makes it difficult to become involved in theorizing when the emphasis is on collecting bushels of data.

There is no really comprehensive theory of personality. There are a number of models and issues, and hopefully from this we can eventually conduct methodologically adequate research, and develop some meaningful theoretical integration.

At this point let us briefly summarize some of the models and issues in the field of personality.

MODELS OF PERSONALITY AND RESEARCH ISSUES

Endler and Magnusson (1976c) have discussed the fact that research and theory, in personality, have been influenced by four prime models: trait psychology, psychodynamics, situationism, and interactionism. (A fifth model, *pheomenology,* focuses on the person's self-concept, personal constructs, and introspective and internal subjective experiences. A sixth model, the *type* model [see Endler & Edwards, 1978] is a precursor of the trait model. A discussion of these last two models is not relevant for some of the key issues in personality research that we will be discussing.)

Personality Models

An extended discussion of personality models is presented in Endler and Magnusson (1976c). Here, we will merely summarize the most salient points.

The Trait Model.   The trait model assumes that internal factors or stable, latent dispositions are the major determinants of actual behavior. Traits serve as a predispositional basis for response-response consistencies of behavior in a wide variety of different situations (e.g., Cattell, 1957; Guilford, 1959). Although the trait model does *not* suggest that individuals behave the same way in various situations, it does, however, postulate that the rank order of individuals, for a specified personality variable (e.g., anxiety), is the same across a variety of situations. Allport (1937) did not believe that traits were linked to specific stimuli or responses, but instead conceptualized traits as enduring and general predispositions. Trait theorists agree that traits are the basic personality units, leading to behavior consistency, but disagree as to the specific structures, numbers, and types of traits. They now recognize that traits interact with situations influencing behavior.

Psychodynamics.   The psychodynamic models, especially psychoanalysis, also emphasize internal determinants of behavior. However, there are important differences between the psychodynamic and trait models. Psychodynamic models postulate an essential personality core which acts as an instigator for behavior in various situations. Psychoanalysis emphasizes the structure of personality (id, ego, and superego), the dynamics of personality, and personality development (Freud, 1959). Experiences, developmentally, modify the expression of instinctual impulses, according to Freud. The neo-Freudians (e.g., Erikson, 1963; Fromm, 1955; Horney, 1945; Sullivan, 1953), nevertheless, have minimized the role of the psychosexual stages and the role of instincts, and have emphasized social factors, the psychosocial stages of development and the ego. The trait model assumes a one-to-one positive and monotonic relationship between underlying hypothetical constructs and responses; the psychodynamic model does not.

Situationism.   The situationism model emphasizes external factors as the prime determinants of behavior (e.g., see classical social learning as represented by Dewey & Humber, 1951; Dollard & Miller, 1950). The social learning models as espoused by various theories represent a heterogeneous set of viewpoints (Endler & Edwards, 1978). For example, Dollard and Miller (1950), classical behavior theorists, investigate organismic variables, and modern behavior theorists such as Bandura (1971), Mischel (1973), and Rotter (1975) are primarily concerned with the person's behavior rather than with traits, attributes, and motives, although they do incorporate person factors into their theories.

Interactionism.   The interaction model of personality (Endler & Magnusson, 1976c; Magnusson & Endler, 1977) emphasizes the role of person by situation interactions with respect to the behavioral manifestations of personality. There is a continuous interaction between the person and the situations that he or she encounters or selects. There is an ongoing process since situations affect persons, who subsequently affect these situations.

Interactional psychology, according to Endler and Magnusson (1976c), postulates that behavior is a function of a continuous and bidirectional process of person-by-situation interactions; that the individual is an intentional active agent in this process; that motivational, emotional and cognitive variables play important determining roles on the person side; and that the psychological meaning that the situation has for the person is an essential determining factor of behavior.

Let us now, briefly, discuss some of the issues in personality research including personality theories and their measurement models, reaction variables versus mediating variables, persons versus situations, and situational specificity versus trans-situational consistency.

Issues in Personality Research

Personality Theories and their Measurement Models.   Theoriests and research investigators frequently fail to differentiate between personality theories that are *models of psychological processes* and the *measurement models* that are pertinent to these theories (Endler, 1977; Magnusson, 1976; Magnusson & Endler, 1977). Oftentimes investigators also fail to distinguish between the reactions (responses) they are investigating and the methods that they are using to collect their data (Magnusson & Endler, 1977). Measures of overt behavior can be obtained by ratings, by self-reports, or by objective measures.

The trait measurement model assumes that there is a *true* trait score for each individual, and that individual positions on the trait dimension are *stable* across situations. Consequently, the behavior (test score) that is an indicator of the trait is also *stable* across situations. However, empirical studies have failed to provide evidence for stable rank orders or transsituational consistency (Endler, 1973, 1975a, 1975b; Mischel, 1968, 1969).

The trait and psychodynamic models, although both accentuating the role of person factors in behavior, differ in their measurement models. Whereas the trait measurement model postulates a positive and monotonic relationship between hypothetical constructs (mediating variables) and overt behavior, the psychodynamic model does not.

Mediating Variables Versus Reaction Variables.   Consistency at the reaction (behavioral) level is not necessarily related to consistency at the mediating variable level. There are at least four classes of reaction variables. These are overt behavior, physiological reactions, covert reactions (feelings, etc.), and artificial behavior ("test" behavior, role playing). Mediating variables are inferred from behavioral observations, and from phenomenological self-reports. Mediating variables, such as traits and motives, assist us in explaining, understanding, and predicting the processes whereby both stored information and concurrent stimuli are selected. Magnusson and Endler (1977) have discussed three types of mediating variables: structural, content, and motivational.

Structural variables include abilities, competence, cognitive complexity, and intelligence. These variables are not affected by situational factors, within a normal range of situational conditions. Nonetheless, extreme situations such as threatening stimuli, can and do often modify the manifestation of these variables. Mischel (1968, 1969), and Rushton and Endler (1977) have provided empirical evidence for the consistency of structural variables.

Content variables include situationally determined or stored information, e.g., the content of anxiety-arousing situations. The content processed by the mediating system is determined by the precise stimulus cues that are selected by (or imposed on) the individual and by the stored information that is activated by sensory stimulation. Situational factors influence the content of the mediating process.

Motivational variables refer to attitudes, drives, motives, needs, and values, and are actively involved in the arousal, maintenance, and direction of behavior. Different situational and stored contents elicit different motivational factors and these are influenced by situational factors.

Persons Versus Situations.   What is the major source of behavioral variance? Is it persons or situations? Is it internal or external determinants? Sociologists, social psychologists, and social learning theorists (e.g., Cooley, 1902, Dewey & Humber, 1951; Mead, 1934; Mischel, 1968; Rotter, 1954) have postulated that situations and the meanings that the situations have for individuals are the major determinants of behavior. On the other hand, personality trait theorists (e.g., Allport, 1966; Cattell, 1946; Guilford, 1959), and clinicians (e.g., Freud, 1959; Rapaport, Gill, & Schafer, 1945) have believed that traits and their dynamic sources within persons are the major determinants of behavior. It is our contention that behavior is a function of the interaction of person by situation variables.

Trans-Situational Consistency Versus Situational Specificity.   Is behavior stable or consistent across situations or is it situation specific? This controversy is related to the person versus situation issue. As indicated earlier there is no one-to-one relationship between consistency at the reaction variable level and consistency at the mediating variable level. There are at least three different meanings of ''consistency'' at the reaction variable level (see Magnusson & Endler, 1977; and Endler, 1977): (1) *absolute consistency* suggests that an individual manifests a behavioral trait (e.g., honesty) to the same degree in various situations; (2) *relative consistency* states that the rank order of persons for a specified behavior (e.g., aggressiveness) is stable across situations; (3) *coherence* proclaims that behavior is predictable and inherent without necessarily being stable in either absolute or relative terms. The person's *pattern* of stable and changing behavior across a wide variety of situations is characteristic for the individual (see Block, 1977; Endler, 1977; Magnusson, 1976; Magnusson & Endler, 1977). Coherence denotes the fact that ''the *rank order* of a person's behavior in various situations with respect to a number of variables is stable and predictable, but his (or her) rank order may differ from another person's rank order of the situations'' (Endler, 1977, p. 348).

Although it is possible to classify behavioral consistency in terms of temporal (longitudinal) versus spatial (cross-sectional) variable, it is more useful (Magnusson & Endler, 1977) to distinguish consistency on the basis of reactions to similar and dissimilar situations. Spatial and temporal factors are not independent of one another. Basically, cross-sectional studies have been concerned with consistency across *dissimilar* situations (usually over a short period of time). Longitudinal studies have primarily focused on consistency of persons across *similar* situations, ontogenetically over time.

Most longitudinal researchers have investigated the correlation for a specific personality variable (e.g., dependency) over two time periods (e.g., adolescence and adulthood) and have often ignored specific situational variables. Block (1977), for example, has empirically demonstrated the existence of longitudinal consistency. Most researchers conducting cross-sectional studies have investigated the correlation for a specific personality variable (e.g., nurturance) in two different situations (e.g., at home and at school), usually occurring over a very short time span. For personality and social variables, the evidence for cross-sectional consistency is neither impressive nor encouraging. Cross-situational correlations have averaged about .30 (e.g., see Endler, 1973, 1975a; Mischel, 1968, 1969).

Consistency of structural, content, and motivational variables refers to consistency of mediating processes. Structural variables are consistent and coherent in the *manner* in which they select and process content and motivational variables. Nevertheless, the *expression* of the content and motivational variables may vary from one situation to another. Social learning processes are related to the coherent or consistent style of *processing* both motivational and content variables.

There have been at least three empirical methods that have been used to examine the issue of cross-situational consistency versus situational specificity: (a) the multidimensional variance components research strategy; (b) the correlational research strategy; and (c) the personality by treatment analysis-of-variance, experimental design. For a review of the empirical literature relevant to the consistency versus specificity issue the reader is directed to Argyle and Little, 1972; Bowers, 1973; Endler, 1973, 1977; Endler and Magnusson, 1976c; Magnusson, 1976. In general, there is some evidence for trans-situational consistency *over time* for structural variables such as cognitive and intellectual factors. There is very little evidence of cross-situational consistency regarding personality-social (content) variables and personality-motivational variables.

Multidimensional Variance Components.   This approach demonstrates interactions but doesn't explain them. The original investigations employing the variance-components methodology were those done by Raush, Dittmann, and Taylor (1959a, 1959b), and by Endler and Hunt (1966, 1969). Bowers (1973), summarizing the results of 11 studies, found that person by situation (P × S) interactions accounted for more variance than either P or S for 14 out of 18 comparisons.

Correlations.   For a more direct test of the assumption of cross-situational stability or relative consistency, one correlates the responses of persons across situations. However, as indicated earlier, there is no evidence, using this strategy, to indicate that there is any cross-situational consistency with respect to personality and social variables. There is some evidence for moderate consistency for: (1) the structural variables of cognition and intelligence (Mischel, 1968, 1969; Rushton & Endler, 1977); (2) types of situations that are similar (Magnusson, Gerzén & Nyman, 1968; Magnusson & Heffler, 1969; Magnusson, Heffler, & Nyman, 1968); and (3) stability over time (longitudinal studies) across similar situations (Block, 1971, 1977). There may be more consistency for some variables (e.g., hostility) than for others (e.g., anxiety).

Personality by Treatment Experimental Designs. The variance components strategy and the correlational strategy both demonstrate that interactions are important but do not explain the nature of the interactions. Experimental research that incorporates both situational and personality variables in its design enables us to predict the nature of interactions, particularly if the research is guided by theory. Endler and Magnusson (1977), Hodges (1968), Flood and Endler (1980), and Diveky and Endler (1977) have, in separate studies, demonstrated an interaction between trait anxiety (a person variable) and situational stress, regarding state-anxiety arousal. Berkowitz (1977) has demonstrated an interaction of persons and situations with respect to aggression, and Fiedler (1971, 1977) discovered that situational variables interact with leadership style (a person variable) in affecting group effectiveness.

All these studies, employing three different research strategies, obviously cast serious doubt on the trait model assumption that the rank order of persons is consistent and stable across various situations.

The recent emphasis on interactionism has been primarily empirical, whereas classical interactionism was primarily theoretical. However, there has been a recent reemergence of interest in theory. Ekehammar (1974) states that "Whereas the classical interactionist views were usually formulated within comprehensive personality theories, most often without empirical support, the more recent conceptualizations have usually been proposed in the absence of any elaborate theories, but often with some empirical support" (p. 1032). However, as a result "of the first empirical studies on person-situation interactions during the early 1960s, the interest in the theoretical aspects of the issue redeveloped" (Endler & Magnusson, 1976c, p. 968). Analyses of situations, and the examination of person by situation interactions are the two basic tasks of interactional psychology.

THE NATURE OF SITUATIONS IN PERSONALITY RESEARCH

What is a situation? What is a stimulus? What is an environment? Social learning theorists and sociologists have emphasized situations as the prime determinants of behavior. Ecological psychologists (e.g., Barker, 1965) have emphasized environmental factors. Endler (1975a) has pointed out that there have been very few attempts at integrating ecological psychology and personality research. Craik (1973) has suggested a personality research paradigm for environmental psychology. Mehrabian and Russell (1974) have conducted research that notes the relevance of personality psychology and environmental psychology for interactional psychology.

Frederiksen (1972) has stated that "We need a systematic way of conceptualizing the domain of situations and situation variables before we can make rapid progress in studying the role of situations in determining behavior" (p. 115). Pervin (1978b) has noted that there has been a failure in defining and adequately differentiating among the terms stimuli, situations, and environments.

Moos (1973) has described six major methods for characterizing environments as related to human functioning: (1) ecological dimensions (e.g., architectural-physical variables, geographical-meterological variables; (2) behavior settings involving both ecological and behavioral properties; (3) parameters of organizational structure; (4) personal and behavioral parameters of the environment; (5) climate, organizational, and psychosocial variables; and (6) variables related to reinforcement or functional analyses of environment. According to Moos (1973), "The six categories of dimensions are non-exclusive, overlapping and mutually interrelated" (p. 652).

Feshbach (1978) has discussed two levels of a dimension that he calls the environment of personality, namely the *situational* level and the *sociocultural* level. There is also a third class of variables that is part of the environment of personality, and a definite and distinct subset of our sociocultural environment. This third class, according to Feshbach, is concerned with the theories, perspectives, and points of view that influence and to a great extent determine a particular investigator's program of research. This third class of variables is similar to the sociopolitical factors or political ideologies that we discussed earlier.

Five major methods of studying the problem of situational description and classification have been discussed by Ekehammar (1974). These are: "(a) a priori defined variables of *physical* and *social* character; (b) *need* concepts; (c) *some single* reaction elicited by the situations; (d) individuals' *reaction patterns* elicited by the situations; and (e) individuals' *perception (cognitions)* of situations" (pp. 1041–42).

A number of investigators (Ekehammar, 1974; Endler & Magnusson, 1976b, 1976c; Magnusson, 1978; and Pervin, 1978b) have made the fundamental distinction between the subjective (psychological) aspects and the objective aspects of environments and situations. This distinction has also sometimes been called the physical versus psychological environment distinction. As indicated earlier, Kantor (1924, 1926) distinguished between biological and psychological environments; Koffka (1935) distinguished between the geographical and behavioral environments; and Murray (1938) distinguished between *alpha press* (objective) and *beta press* (subjective) environments or situations. These are all analogous, but not identical distinctions. The prime conceptual distinction in all cases is between the *objective* "external world" that affects the person, and the *subjective* "internal world," as the individual perceives it, and reacts to it (Magnusson, 1978).

According to Endler and Magnusson (1976b), the subset of the "external world" with which the person interacts (including both physical and social environmental factors) can be conceptualized as the ecology (see Brunswik, 1952, 1956). Actual behavior occurs in a *situation* or that part of the ecology that a person perceives and reacts to immediately (Murray, 1938, p. 40) or the momentary *situation* (Lewin, 1936, p. 217). The psychological meaning or perception or significance of the environment (the subjective world), for the individual, can be discussed and described at different levels of generality (Endler & Magnusson, 1976b; Magnusson, 1978). Similarly, the objective "external world" or the environment as it actually is, independent of the person's interpretations, can be discussed and described at different levels of generality. Both micro- and macro-environments can be described and discussed.

The "external world" or environment can be conceptualized in terms of physical factors, social factors, or some combination of the two. Examples of the *physical macro-environment* are buildings, cities, lakes, and parks. Examples of the *physical micro-environment* are single stimulus variables. Examples of the *social macro-environment* are norms, cultural values, and roles common to the whole society. Examples of the *social micro-environment* are norms, values, habits, and attitudes common to the specific individuals and groups with whom the individual interacts directly, and specifically at school, work, or home. In effect this refers to the social environment unique to the person. It is the individual's idiosyncratic environment and is based on his (her) unique life experiences interacting with experiences that are common to most members of the culture.

Stimuli, Situations and Environments

What is the basic distinction among stimuli, situations, and environments? At an approximate and general level it is possible to distinguish among the three of them. The environment is the persistent and general background or context within which behavior occurs. The situation is the momentary or transient background. Stimuli can be conceptualized as the elements within a situation. The environment-situation distinction is analogous to the trait-state distinction, with environments conceptualized as the enduring background ("traits") and situations conceptualized as the momentary or transient background ("states"). One can compare elements (stimuli) *within* a situation and judge how this influences behavior. One can also conduct a comparison *between* situations, assessing the influence of situations as wholes on behavior.

One can distinguish among stimuli, situations, and environments at a crude level, but the borderline between any two of them is frequently fuzzy. Stimuli spill over into situations, and situations into environments. One individual's situation might be another individual's environment, and one person's stimulus might be another person's situation. One very important determinant of behavior is the person's *perception* of the situation (or environment, or stimulus). The exact specific or same environment (or stimulus or situation) can, and does have a different impact on different individuals. Pervin (1978b), in discussing the relationships among stimulus, situation, and environment, points out that "The major distinction appears to have to do with the scale of analysis—ranging from the concern with molecular variables in the case of stimulus to molar variables and behaviors in the case of the environment" (p. 79). In practice, however, this is not always the case.

Perception psychologists, and most experimental psychologists, have focused on the stimulus. Ecologists or environmental psychologists have focused on the environment. Personality theorists, emphasizing person by situations interactions, have focused on situations. Whether we can define the situation (or the environment, or the stimulus) independent of the perceiver is a very important issue. Because the meaning or significance of a situation is an important determinant of behavior, it is necessary to focus on the perception of situations when examining the person by situation interaction issue.

Sells (1963) has defined situations on the basis of *objectively* measured external characteristics as have Rotter (1955) and Barker (1965). Frederiksen (1972), however, defines situations in terms of *reactions* or behaviors associated with the situation. Endler and Magnusson (1976c), Endler (1978), and Magnusson (1978) define situations in terms of a person's *perception* of the situation. Persons react to situations, but they also affect the situations with which they interact. "Situations are as much a function of the person as the person's behavior is a function of the situation" (Bowers, 1973, p. 327). There is a constant and continuous interplay between person and situations.

"Shopping" for Situations or Having them Imposed

We frequently select and choose the situations with which we interact, and the situations that we encounter in our day-to-day lives. Nevertheless, there are obviously instances and circumstances where situations are imposed on us. This is necessarily a lifelong and continuous ongoing process. However, instead of investigating situations longitudinally, we tend to observe and examine a cross-sectional slice of situations, at one specific point in time.

As Endler (1981) has noted, by selecting (or being born in) a city instead of a rural area, we are more apt to encounter subways, tall buildings, areas of high population density, and less likely to have contact with unpolluted air and farm animals. If an individual decides to go to University, he or she is, in effect, probably eliminating labor occupations such as assembly line operators, farmhands, taxi drivers, and is minimizing the opportunity of interacting with people in these occupations. If then the individual decides to go into graduate school, he or she is further limiting the situations (including other individuals) that he or she encounters. Almost all of us are creatures of habit, and except for vacations and other unusual events (e.g., marriage, illness, change of occupation), we routinely interact in the same types of situations from day to day, and from weekend to weekend. If there is any consistency in behavior, it is due, to a fair extent, to the fact that we experience similar situations (both at work and during our lesiure hours) from day to day. We shape our environment and our environment shapes us. One of the reasons that longitudinal studies on the consistency versus specificity issue have shown a fair amount of consistency, while cross-sectional studies have not, is that for the former type of studies the various situations are similar, whereas for the latter they are not. As we go through life we select those situations (as much as we can and to the degree that we can control this) that are rewarding and satisfying to us. If we enjoy playing tennis, then we will select those situations that enable us to play tennis. We "shop around" for situations that will benefit us. (I am thankful to Jerry Patterson for suggesting the delicious phrase "shopping for situations".) Therefore to a great extent we restrict and limit the situations we experience, and this usually leads to satisfaction and simultaneously increases the probability of consistency of behavior. If a situation is painful we avoid it; if pleasurable we try to experience it, and encounter it with gusto.

All of us encounter complex stimuli at various levels. Magnusson (1978) has noted that "The total environment—influencing individuals' lives—consists of a complex system of physical-geographical, social, and cultural factors which are continuously interacting and changing at different levels of proximity to the individual" (p. 1). Various forms of stimulation affect behavior not only on the basis of information processed at the moment, but also on the basis of interaction with previously stored information (Endler, 1981).

A Differential Psychology of Situations

Typically, when psychologists use the term differential psychology, they are referring to the study of individual differences. Magnusson (1978, 1980) has recently proposed a differential psychology of situations to complement the differential psychology of persons. What should be the nature of a differential psychology of situations? Along what dimensions should we scale situations? Should it be in terms of impact, complexity, objectiveness, relevance, subjectiveness? How do we obtain adequate and representative samplings of situations? Should we attempt to develop a taxonomy of situations? There may be problems connected with this, since different investigators may focus on different attributes and thus produce different taxonomies. This is one of the major problems concerning traits; different trait theorists have developed different taxonomies of traits. It is important that taxonomies of situations (or traits) be derived from a theoretical context rather than being arbitrary. Ideally a classification system should be based primarily on the situations that individuals encounter, and on the perception or meaning of these events.

Pervin (1977) has examined the natural habitats that persons encounter, and has sampled situations ecologically. He has examined the free responses of persons' perceptions, and their behavioral and affective responses to their daily situations. He then classified his variables via factor analysis and on the basis of his results concluded that it is desirable to focus on the person by situation interaction as the unit of analysis. Magnusson (1978) suggests that the *actual* situation is central for "understanding the development of process and actual behavior" (p. 8). The *total situation,* serving as a frame of reference, and actual situational settings should serve as our major focus. Runyan (1978) has proposed the investigation of the *life course* in terms of sequences of person by situation interactions.

Perhaps it may be appropriate and desirable to have individuals keep diaries or daily logs of their activities and the situations that they encounter and experience. Our data base should probably be in terms of how individuals construe their daily life encounters, and which situations they consider stressful and which ones they consider pleasurable. It is advisable to examine real-life situations. One approach might be to investigate the personal *projects* of individuals. All of us have certain goals in life and certain projects that we engage in (e.g., going on vacation, building furniture, buying a home, obtaining a degree, getting married). However, projects differ in size, scope, relevance, and intensity. This problem could be partially overcome by asking individuals to scale their projects along these dimensions. We need to examine situations in terms of the meaning they have for persons and in terms of how they affect peoples' lives.

Perceptions of and Reactions to Situations

Two of the five strategies suggested by Ekehammar (1974) for investigating situations are conducive to a psychological perspective: namely, *situation perception* and *situation reaction* studies. Endler and Magnusson (1976b) have noted that "They psychological significance of the environment can be investigated by studying the individual's *perception* of the situation (the meaning he assigns to a situation) and *reaction* to a situation (a specific situation or the general environment)" (p. 15).

Magnusson (1971, 1974) has proposed and used an empirical psychophysical method for investigating the *perception of situations*. Magnusson and Ekehammar (1973), using the psychophysical method, examined situations common to University students in their studies, and found two bipolar dimensions: positive versus negative; and active versus passive. These are similar to the semantic differential factors. Furthermore, they also found one unipolar dimension, a social factor. They then extended their research to stressful situations, and found essentially the same results (Ekehammar & Magnusson, 1973) as in their previous studies.

The *situation reaction* investigations have emphasized individuals' responses to situations. Rotter (1954) and Frederiksen (1972), who advocate the development of taxonomies of situations, have proposed that situations should be classified on the basis of the similarity of behavior that they evoke in persons. Many of the investigations of reactions to situations have employed data from inventories originally constructed for research purposes (e.g., the S-R Inventory of Anxiousness, Endler et al., 1962; the Interactional Reactions Questionnaire, Ekehammar, Magnusson, & Ricklander, 1974). Endler et al. (1962) factor analyzed persons' responses to various situations of the S-R Inventory of Anxiousness and found three situational factors: interpersonal threat, inanimate physical danger, and ambiguous.

Magnusson and Ekehammar (1975, 1978), and Ekehammar, Schalling, and Magnusson (1975) have investigated the relationship between persons' *perceptions* of situations and their *reactions* to situations. Situation *reaction* and situation *perception* data were collected on the same individuals. The coefficient of congruence between perceptions and reactions for three of four a priori groups of situations ranged from .89 to .92; for a fourth group of situations the coefficient of congruence was .69.

With respect to the psychological significance of situations, it is important to differentiate between situation *perception* dimensions and situation *reaction* dimensions. Two persons may *perceive* the same situation as threatening. However, one person may *react* by attacking the situation and another may *react* by withdrawing from the situation. Another aspect of the relationship between perception and reaction is the temporal one. At one time a person may react to (perceived) stress by attacking, at another time by withdrawing. Contextual and motivational factors are also important.

Another approach to the study of situations is to differentiate between *objective* and *subjective* (or psychological) characteristics of situations. Gibson (1960), Sells (1963), and Tolman (1951) have proposed an analysis of environments in objective terms. As indicated earlier, Kantor (1924, 1926) using the terms biological and psychological environment, Koffka (1935) using the terms geographical and behavioral environment, and Murray (1938) using the terms alpha press and beta press have all differentiated between objective and subjective (psychological) environments. There have been, unfortunately, very few systematic analyses of the relationships between objective and subjective (psychological) environments. It is important to emphasize the psychological characteristics of situations and environments; and also to evaluate the objective characteristics of situations as one of the important determinants (in addition to cognitions, past experience, and needs) of the perception of situations (psychological meaning), and of behavior.

Elements within a Situation and Whole Situations

Much of the research on situations and interactional psychology has emphasized the situation as a *whole,* and has compared the effects of different situations. These studies on situations as *wholes* have examined how each situation is interpreted or experienced in its total context (see Magnusson, 1971). In addition, one can study the situational cues or elements *within* a situation. How do the various cues *within* a situation interact with one another and how do they change in the process (Magnusson & Endler 1977)? During the intermission at a concert, for example, Betty's reaction to Bill is influenced by Bill's reaction to Betty, and both of their reactions to this situation might be influenced when Ruth (Bill's wife) appears. This is an ongoing and continuous process (Endler, 1978; Magnusson, 1976). "One can construe a situation as a dynamic process in which a person selects certain elements or events (primarily other persons) and is in turn affected by these other elements" (Endler, 1977, p. 356). It is necessary to empahsize the various elements within a situation, when one is investigating situations. These elements include both person by situation interactions, and person by person interactions.

Units of Analysis, Situations and Events

We frequently obtain representative samplings of persons in our research. However, we rarely obtain representative samplings of environments and situations. Brunswik (1952, 1956) was among the first to alert us to the need to obtain representative samplings of situations. He noted that if we did not do this we might very well bias our conclusions. There are also various definitional and conceptual problems. How long is a situation? When does it begin and end? What is the impact of a situation? When do we respond independent of situations?

What is the relevance of Skinner's (1938) distinction between operants (reactions independent of observable stimuli) and respondents for the situational-specificity versus cross-situational consistency issue? One would expect greater consistency for operant reactions than for respondent reactions. The individual may have situations imposed on him or her for respondents, and may therefore have to respond primarily to the demands of the situation, rather than on the basis of his or her own interests and tendencies. When it comes to operants, the person may *select* his or her situations, and search for or "shop" for situations similar to those that be or she has found reinforcing in the past.

Situational Units.   What *size* and *kind* of situational unit should be used in personality research? What *size* and *kind* of person unit should be used? With respect to persons, the kinds of units that have been used most frequently have been traits, but some researchers have used defenses and motives. However, there has not been any systematic parallel research with respect to situations, and environments, in personality research. Nevertheless, there has been a recent increase in personality research related to the role of situations and environments. A number of investigators (Endler, 1981; Pervin, 1977; and Raush, 1977) have suggested that the person by situation interaction unit is the most appropriate unit of analysis for personality research.

To date, no one has systematically investigated the person-situation interaction unit. Over 40 years ago, Murray (1938) proposed that need-press units or themas were desirable for personality research. Yet, no one has conducted intensive and/or systematic investigations of themas, even though there have been systematic longitudinal and/or intensive studies of persons (e g., Block, 1977; Levinson, 1978; White, 1966, 1976). It is now desirable and necessary to have longitudinal investigations of the situations that persons experience and encounter, and longitudinal studies of person by situation interactions. According to Murray (1938) "much of what is now *inside* the organism was once *outside*. For these reasons, the organism and its milieu must be considered together, a single creature-environment interaction being a convenient short unit for psychology. A *long* unit—an individual life—can be most clearly formulated as a succession of related *short units* or *episodes*" (p. 40). Empirically nothing much has happened with Murray's proposal of over 40 years ago!

With respect to size of units, it is often very difficult, in practice, to determine when an event or situation begins and when it ends. What do we focus on? Is it the elements within a situation, is it the total situation, or is it both? Do we examine only one event or do we investigate a family of events and the various permutations, combinations, and interrelationships of these events? Do certain situations elicit certain responses? Do other situations inhibit and constrain responses?

We can conceptualize person by person interactions as a subset of person by situation interactions, in that other persons serve as stimulus (situational) input for us. Patterson and Moore (1978) define interactionism in terms of person by person interactions. Other persons serve as important cues for our behavior. When we behave, the other person is part of our situation, and we anticipate how the other person will react to our behavior. The other person's response serves as a stimulus for us. There is a continuous ongoing process.

One should examine the *dynamic* ongoing process of events, as well as isolating the important personal and situational variables. Situations have an impact on individuals, but individuals actively seek out and select the situations and persons with whom they interact. It's a two-way street. Every individual is an active and intentional stimulus-seeking organism. People are not passive victims of situational encounters. Interaction is an important ongoing process. To fully understand interactionism and the role of situations, it is necessary to investigate real-life situations rather than depending only on laboratory procedures and studies. Admittedly, real-life behavior is more difficult and more complex to study than behavior in the laboratory. However, the potential extra benefits are worth the extra effort. We need a combination of real-life and laboratory studies (see Endler, 1981).

PERSON BY SITUATION INTERACTIONS

The two basic tasks for an interactional psychology of personality are: (1) the description, classification, and systematic analyses of situations, stimuli, and environments; and (2) the examination of how persons and situations interact in evoking behavior. In the previous sections we discussed the situational task. Now let us examine the interactional task.

Endler and Edwards (1978) have differentiated mechanistic from dynamic models of interaction and have discussed the research on person by situation interactions, for the personality variables of anxiety, locus of control, and conformity. Let us briefly summarize the concepts of mechanistic and dynamic interaction and then we will discuss some of the empirical research on person by situation interactions.

In general, the concept of interaction has been used in a number of different ways. Olweus (1977) has referred to four different meanings of the term interaction: (1) in a *general sense* to characterize how situations and individuals combine or connect (unidirectional interaction); (2) in terms of the *interdependency* of persons and situations; (3) in terms of *reciprocal action,* and (4) in terms of its use in the *analysis of variance*. The fourth meaning, like the first, refers to unidirectional interaction and is really a methodological subset of the first meaning.

Basically then, Olweus (1977) is discussing three types of interaction: unidirectional (mechanistic), reciprocal (dynamic), and a third kind where one cannot really separate persons from situations. Because of our current lack of methodological sophistication, it is not possible to study this last type of interaction, empirically, at the moment. Therefore, we are left with two meaningful conceptions of interaction: mechanistic (unidirectional) and dynamic (reciprocal action).

Mechanistic Interaction

The mechanistic model of interaction uses analysis of variance procedures in its measurement model and is concerned with interactions of main factors such as persons, situations, and modes of responses, within a data matrix. This interaction model makes a clear distinction between independent and dependent variables, and assumes a linear and additive relationship between person and situational factors (both independent variables) in determining behavior. For the mechanistic model, interaction describes the interdependency of determinants (independent variables) of behavior. It is not concerned with the interaction between independent and dependent variables. The "interaction is not between cause and effect, but between causes" (Overton & Reese, 1973, p. 78). Mechanistic interaction is concerned with the structure of the interaction and not with the process.

Person (P) by situation (S) interactions, person (P) by modes of response (M-R) interactions, situations (S) by modes of response (M-R) interactions, and P by S by M-R interactions have all been investigated by variance components techniques, and via person by (experimental) treatment analyses of variance techniques. Most of the focus has been on P by S interactions. The strength of the variance components technique is that it has *demonstrated* the existence of strong interactions. The weakness of this approach is that it cannot *explain* the interactions. This approach leads to insight concerning the direction for formulating a more effective measurement model, and a more effective behavioral model, than the usual trait personality and measurement models (see Magnusson & Endler, 1977). The person by treatment experimental design enables us to *explain* interactions. Nevertheless, both the person by treatment design and the variance components strategy represent a mechanistic model. Therefore, they are insufficient for studying the dynamic interaction process, within the context of the interaction model of personality.

Dynamic Interaction

The dynamic (organismic) model of interaction involves the reciprocal interaction between behavior and situational (or environmental) events. It is concerned with the relationship between independent and dependent variables; with reciprocal causation. "*Reciprocal Causation* means that not only do events affect the behavior of organisms but the organism is also an active agent influencing environmental events" (Endler & Magnusson, 1976c, p. 969). Dynamic interaction is multidirectional and refers "to the mutual interdependence of person-situations and behavior so that persons-situations influence behavior and vice versa" (Endler, 1975a, p. 18). Dynamic interaction is process oriented and attempts to integrate situations, mediating variables, and person reaction variables. As indicated earlier, persons not only react to situations, but to a certain degree they select (or shop for) the situations in which they interact, encounter, and experience.

Raush (1977) has noted that for the dynamic model of interaction, the usual and typical distinction between independent and dependent variables may not be a very useful one. An examination of the empirical research on interactionism reveals that most of it has been concerned with mechanistic interaction. This is basically due to the fact that we have not yet developed and perfected the techniques, strategies, and measurement models for studying dynamic interaction.

Person by Situation Interactions and Locus of Control

In the next few sections, we summarize the literature on person by situation interactions with respect to the personality variables of locus of control, conformity, and anxiety. It should be noted that these studies are primarily illustrative of the mechanistic model of interaction. These three content areas were chosen because each represents an important research and theoretical area in social-personality psychology, and also because the three variables represent quite diverse types of research activities and variables. Internal-external locus of control, although usually conceptualized primarily as a person variable, is theoretically applicable to both persons and situations. Conformity is dependent upon a social situation for its meaning. Anxiety has been defined in a number of different ways, but has been associated primarily with the person. For a more detailed summary of the interactional research on these three variables, the reader is referred to Endler and Edwards (1978).

Rotter (1966) has been the driving force behind the internal-external (I-E) locus of control of reinforcement construct. Locus of control is a cognitive expectancy (belief) with respect to the contingency between a person's actions and reinforcements. Internal locus of control means that one believes that one's reinforcements are contingent upon one's own behavior or characteristics. External locus of control means one has the expectancy that reinforcements are not contingent on one's own actions but are "the result of luck, chance, fate . . . under the control of powerful others, or . . . unpredictable because of the great complexity of forces . . ." (Rotter, 1966, p. 1).

Theoretically, Rotter (1966) has presented internal-external (I-E) locus of control as a continuum. Empirically, for much of the research subjects have been dichotomized into internals (I's) and externals (E's). Empirically, the I-E construct has usually been used as a global, person variable, without regard for the multidimensionality of the construct, and without regard for situational constraints. However, locus of control, as part of social learning theory, focuses on the interaction between the person and his meaningful environment in determining the outcomes of behavior (Rotter, 1954; Rotter, 1975). Definitionally, I-E suggests that I's attribute their outcomes to person variables and E's attribute their outcomes to situational variables. The empirical studies suggest that it is necessary to qualify these conclusions. Davis and Davis (1972), and Gilmor and Minton (1974), for example, have found that the I-E person variable interacts with the situational success-failure outcome variable and this determines whether attributions are made to external or internal factors. Facets of the situation, in addition to those of the I-E person variable, must be taken into account when one is predicting causal attributions.

Locus of control is both a person variable and a situational variable, according to Rotter (1966, 1975). A number of person by situation interaction studies have investigated the consequences of incongruence and congruence between the locus of control in the situation and the person's generalized locus of control expectancy. Under conditions when the situational locus of control is operationally defined as a skill versus chance task description or perception, person by situation interactions affected reward value (e.g., Lefcourt, Lewis, & Silverman, 1968), information seeking (e.g., Davis & Phares, 1967), and performance (e.g., Houston, 1972). Sherman (1973) found that I-E interacted with various attitude change procedures (e.g., reading a persuasive communication versus writing a counterattitudinal essay) to determine the degree of attitude change. Baron and Ganz (1972), and Baron, Cowan, Ganz, and MacDonald (1974) found that type of reinforcement (intrinsic versus extrinsic) interacted with I-E to affect performance.

Rotter (1966) originally presented I-E as unidimensional, and his scale was developed to measure a general locus of control expectancy. This was done by sampling beliefs regarding a wide variety of situations. Nevertheless, factor analyses of the Rotter Scale and some modified scales have yielded two or more factors (see Lefcourt, 1976 and Phares, 1976, for reviews). Reid and Ware (1973) have identified a Fatalism dimension (e.g., the belief that outcomes are determined by luck, chance, or fate, versus hard work), and a Social System Control factor (e.g., the extent to which people believe they can or cannot induce sociopolitical change in society). The dimensionality of I-E has relevance for interactional psychology, since it is predicted that interactions would occur when the facet of the locus of control person variable is congruent with the salient control dimension in the situation.

Person by Situation Interactions and Conformity

Wiesenthal, Edwards, Endler, Koza, Walton and Emmott (1978) have defined conformity as a "change in behavior caused by social influence such that a conflict exists between a person's judgments and publicly presented social pressure by others" (p. 43). This approach emphasizes movement conformity instead of the more inclusive and comprehensive area of all kinds of social influence processes. Blake and Mouton (1961), Endler (1966), Rhine (1968), in the 1960s, all pointed to the fact that conforming behavior is a function of person by situation interactions. For example, Rhine (1968) noted that conformity is "a complex behavior resulting from the interaction of an individual's motives and his perception of the relative instrumental value of conformity or non-conformity in the influence situation" (p. 989). Nevertheless, there has been very little actual research on person by situation interactions with respect to conforming behavior. Most of the research on conformity has focused either on the effects of personality variables (e.g., authoritarianism, need achievement, dependence) or on the effects of situational variables (e.g., stimulus characteristics, reinforcement). Wiesenthal et al. (1978), in an extensive review of the conformity litera-ture, found that only 15 percent of the 326 articles that they reviewed included both situational and personality variables. Even the majority of these 15 percent of the studies did *not* examine the interaction of the personality and situational variables.

McDavid (1959) and Sistrunk (1973) both developed personality tests that measured differential responsiveness to normative (motivational) versus infor-mational (cognitive) influence to conform. McDavid noted that the difficulty of an item and the degree of discrepancy between the person's position and that of the group differentially influenced conforming behavior of subjects classified on this person variable. Sistrunk found ''an interaction between manipulations of task description, private versus public response conditions, and the normative informational person variable'' (Endler & Edwards, 1978, p. 158).

Sistrunk and McDavid (1965) have noted that relationships between conform-ing behavior and achievement and affiliation motivation have been studied. However, very little thought has been given to investigating situational factors that might affect these relationships. Sistrunk and McDavid (1965) in their studies did find an interaction between achievement motivation and task difficulty.

Becker, Lerner, and Carroll (1966) have found that first-borns are more sensitive to normative cues in an influence situation, whereas later-borns are more responsive to informational cues. Rhine (1968) found that task description and birth order interact to affect conforming behavior. Moore and Krupat (1971) found that subjects low on authoritarianism conformed more to a highly positive status source than to a mildly positive status source. Persons high on authoritaria-nism did not conform differentially to the two sources.

Endler (1966), and Endler and Hoy (1967) examined the effects of reinforce-ment, a situational factor, on conforming behavior. They found that reinforce-ment had a significant effect on conforming behavior and that sex (a person factor) had a significant effect on conforming behavior in the Endler (1966) study. The situation (reinforcement) by person (sex) interactions were not signif-icant in either study. Nevertheless, situational factors were a greater source of conforming behavior than personal factors.

Witkin and Goodenough (1976), in their review of the literature on field dependence, contend that the relationship between field dependence, a person variable, and conforming behavior, is influenced by situational factors. Mausner and Graham (1970) found that field-independent persons were basically un-affected by prior reinforcement. However, field-dependent persons, when in-formed that they were less competent than their partner, conformed more than when they were led to believe that they were more competent. Snyder and Monson (1975) predicted that some persons are more influenced by situational and interpersonal cues about the appropriateness of their behavior (self-monitoring persons) and are therefore more variable across situations. Self-monitoring persons were affected in their conforming behavior by the situational manipulation of the subjects' audience. Low self-monitoring persons' conforming behavior was not affected by this manipulation.

Person by Situation Interactions and Anxiety

It is generally recognized that anxiety involves unpleasant subjective experiences and manifest bodily disturbances. Nevertheless, anxiety has been defined in many different ways. It has been conceptualized as a response, as a stimulus, as a trait, as a motive, and as a drive (Shedletsky & Endler, 1974). Lewis (1970) has defined anxiety as "an emotional state, with the subjectively experienced quality of fear or a closely related emotion (terror, horror, alarm, fright, panic, trepidation, dread, scare)" (p. 77). Spielberger (1966) suggests that some of the conceptual and empirical confusion about anxiety is due to a failure to distinguish between *trait* anxiety (A-Trait) and *state* anxiety (A-State).

Spielberger (1972) has defined A-State as an emotional reaction "consisting of unpleasant, consciously-perceived feelings of tension and apprehension with associated activation or arousal of the autonomic nervous system" (p. 29). A-Trait is defined as a measure of "anxiety-proneness—differences between individuals in the probability that anxiety states will be manifested under circumstances involving varying degrees of stress" (Spielberger, 1966, p. 15). Within the context of the state-trait model of anxiety, both person and situational variables are needed to induce state anxiety. The State-Trait Anxiety Inventory (STAI), developed by Spielberger, Gorsuch and Lushene (1970), measures A-State and A-Trait. Their A-Trait measure focuses on interpersonal or ego-threatening anxiety. Trait anxiety can be assessed empirically in at least two ways. First, one can ask a subject to estimate his or her own general level of anxiety reactions across situations (see Spielberger et al., 1970) or across categories of situations (see Endler, 1980). Or second, one can assess state anxiety reactions in a number of relevant situations (e.g., ambiguous situations) and sum or average across these situations (see Zuckerman, 1976). That is, Zuckerman (1976) conceptualizes trait anxiety as a summation of state anxiety in a number of specific and different situations. Ajzen (see Chapter 1, in this volume) has suggested an analogous approach to global measures of social attitudes. He believes that although we cannot and should not expect a global measure of attitude to predict a single action, nevertheless, such an index should predict a more general measure of behavior based on representative multiple acts of the domain being investigated (e.g., religion). Zuckerman's (1976) approach to measuring A-Trait seems to us very similar to Ajzen's (Chapter 1, in this volume) approach to measuring attitudes. It should be pointed out, however, that most of the empirical research on A-Trait has assessed A-Trait in terms of assessment of *general* levels of anxiety (see Spielberger et al., 1970; Endler, 1980), rather than on summing or averaging A-State in specific situations (see Zuckerman, 1976).

Spielberger and his colleagues have empirically demonstrated the usefulness of the A-State versus A-Trait distinction. Auerbach (1973a), Hodges (1968), O'Neil, Spielberger, and Hansen (1969), and Rappaport and Katkin (1972) have all demonstrated that high A-Trait persons in *ego-threatening situations* or *conditions* manifest greater changes in A-State levels than do low A-Trait persons. In neutral (non-threatening) situations the level of A-State arousal does not differ appreciably between high and low A-Trait persons. Nevertheless, for *physical danger* situations, e.g., the threat of electric shock, high A-Trait individuals do not manifest greater increases in A-State arousal than do low A-Trait persons (e.g., Auerbach, 1973b; Hodges, 1968; Hodges & Spielberger, 1966; Katkin, 1965; Spielberger, Gorsuch, & Lushene, 1970).

The evidence suggest that a predicted person (A-Trait) by situation (experimental condition) interaction for A-State exists when A-Trait is measured by a general trait measure such as the STAI A-Trait Scale, and the stressful situation involves ego or interpersonal threat but not other dimensions of stress such as physical danger. It should be noted that the STAI A-Trait assesses primarily the ego-threatening facet of A-Trait.

The Multidimensionality of Anxiety.   Endler (1975b; 1980) has proposed a multdimensional interaction model of anxiety. Endler et al. (1962), in their factor analysis of situations of the S-R Inventory Auxiousness, originally found three situational factors: interpersonal threat, physical danger and ambiguous. Endler and Okada (1975) developed the S-R Inventory of General Trait Anxiousness (S-R GTA), which assesses the above three facets of A-Trait, plus a daily routine or innocuous facet. Recently, social evaluation threat was differentiated from the more global interpersonal scale and included as a separate A-Trait scale. Social evaluation refers to situations where persons are being evaluated or observed by other individuals. Rosenberg's (1965) "evaluation apprehension," which refers to a subject's behavior in an experiment and which he defines as "anxiety-toned concern that he win a positive evaluation from the experimenter, or at least that he provide no sound grounds for a negative one" (p. 29), is probably a subset of social evaluation anxiety. In all probability, the Crowne and Marlowe (1964) notion of need for approval may be a basis for social evaluation anxiety. The S-R GTA was developed with the aim of maximizing the effects of individual differences and minimizing the effects of situations. Endler and Magnusson (1976a) and Endler, Magnusson, Ekehammar, and Okada (1976) have provided empirical support for the multidimensionality of A-Trait.

Endler's (1975b; 1980) Multidimensional Interaction Model of Anxiety.   One assumption of this model is that both A-Trait and A-State are multidimensional. This model makes explicit predictions for person by situation interactions. Therefore another assumption of this model is that in order for a person (facet of A-Trait) by situation (Stress condition) interaction to be effective in inducing A-State changes, it is necessary for the threatening situation to be congruent to the facet of A-Trait under consideration. Interpersonal ego threat A-Trait would be expected to interact with an ego-threatening situation in inducing A-State changes; but not to interact with an ambigious or a physical danger situation. Analogously, physical danger A-Trait would be expected to interact with a physical danger threat situation, but not with interpersonal threat.

A number of laboratory and field studies have provided empirical support for the multidimensional interaction model of anxiety. Endler and Okada (1974) examined the joint effects of physical danger A-Trait and a physically threatening situation on A-State. They conducted a laboratory experiment with 70 female and 62 male college students, in which the physical danger situation was the threat of shock. For females, they found that there was a greater change in A-State for women high on physical danger A-Trait, as compared to women low on physical danger A-Trait. That is, there was an interaction between the physical threat situation and the congruent physical danger A-Trait facet in inducing changes in A-State. This interaction did not occur when the A-Trait classification was based on the noncongruent (with physical threat situation) interpersonal A-Trait. There was also no interaction between physical danger A-Trait and the physical threat situation for males.

Endler and Magnusson (1977) evaluated the interaction model of anxiety in a real-life examination situation. The 42 male and 14 female Swedish college students were administered the Endler and Okada (1975) S-R GTA prior to an important psychology exam, and state anxiety was measured by the self-report Behavioral Reactions Questionnaire (BRQ) (Hoy & Endler, 1969; Endler & Okada, 1975), and by pulse rate, just before the examination (Stress, Trail 1), and again 2 weeks later (Non-Stress, Trial 2). For the pulse-rate measure of A-State, the interaction between interpersonal A-Trait and the examination situation was significant at the $p < .01$ level, and for the BRQ measure of A-State, the interaction was significant at the $p < .086$ level. That is, high interpersonal A-Trait subjects showed greater changes in A-State than low interpersonal A-Trait subjects (excluding the interaction between physical danger A-Trait and the examination situation, $p < .05$ for BRQ scores, none of the remaining six interactions were significant).

Endler, King, Kuczynski, and Edwards (1980) used 25 Canadian High School students to evaluate the interaction model of anxiety in a classroom situation. The S-R GTA was used to assess A-Trait; and the Present Affect Reactions Questionnaire (PARQ) was used to assess A-State. The PARQ consists of 10 autonomic-emotional items, 10 cognitive-worry items, and in the present version (PARQ III), six buffer items (Endler, 1980). The congruent classroom situation by social evaluation A-Trait interaction was significant in effecting changes in A-State arousal, as measured by the PARQ. The noncongruent trait (person) by situation interactions were not significant. Phillips and Endler (1982) found similar results with Canadian College students (79 females, 28 males). The Endler and Magnusson (1977) study, with Swedish college students, the Endler et al. (1980) study with Canadian high school students, and the Phillips and Endler (1980) study with Canadian college students all support the differential predictions of the interaction model of anxiety and provide evidence for the multidimensionality of A-Trait.

Endler, Edwards and McGuire (1979) studied anxiety in stage actors, in metropolitan Toronto, both during a rehearsal and prior to an important stage performance. There was a definite trend toward an interaction between social evaluation A-Trait and the congruent situational stress of a stage performance in eliciting PARQ A-State changes. (Because of the small sample size the results were not statistically significant.)

Diveky and Endler (1977) studied middle-management male bankers in both nonstressful "off the job" situations and stressful "on the job" situations (as reported by the bankers themselves). The social evaluation A-Trait by the congruent social evaluation situational job stress interaction was statistically significant in producing PARQ A-State arousal.

Flood and Endler (1980) examined the interaction model of anxiety in a real-life track meet, an athletic competition situation. Forty-one male athletes aged 15 to 39, competing in long, middle, and short distance track events, completed the BRQ measure of A-State and the S-R GTA measure of A-Trait 2 weeks prior to an important track meet. They then completed the BRQ again just before the major track competition (the stress condition), which they perceived as a social evaluation situation. The interaction between the stressful track meet (social evaluation) situation and the social evaluation facet of A-Trait was significant in affecting A-State. That is, high social evaluation A-Trait athletes reported greater increases in A-State between the non-Stress and stress situation than did low A-Trait athletes. There were no significant interactions between the track and field situation and the noncongruent facets of A-Trait. This field study by Flood and Endler (1980) supports the differential hypothesis and the interaction model of anxiety.

King and Endler (1982) studied 30 women ranging from 19 to 55 years of age who were required to have either a dilation and curettage (D and C) or a laparoscopy. The women completed the S-R GTA and PARQ just prior to the medical intervention procedure and again a few days later when they were home from the hospital. King and Endler found significant interactions (in the predicted direction) between the medical intervention procedure situation and the ambiguous, physical danger, and social evaluation facets of A-Trait with respect to A-State. This stressful medical situation was perceived primarily as ambiguous. Since situations like traits are mutlidimensional, they can be reacted to in a multifaceted manner.

In all of the above studies (excluding the ones by Endler & Magnusson, 1977, and Endler & Okada, 1974) we assessed the subjects' perception of the stressful situation. In all cases (except for the Endler et al., 1980 exam study and the King & Endler, 1980 study) the situation was perceived as a social evaluation situation. It is essential to assess persons' perceptions of the situation because the message that the experimenter is sending (or thinks he is sending) may not be the one that the subject is receiving. For example, in a study with 10-year-old hockey goalies at York University, we were originally quite certain that being a hockey goalie would be perceived as a physically threatening situation. Surprise! Surprise! It was perceived primarily as an ego-threatening, social evaluation situation. These 10-year-old boys were much more concerned with "letting the team down" than with the potential physical danger of being hit by a hockey puck. Analogously, in a study that I conducted in Sweden with public school students going to the dentist, it was assumed (by me) that this would be perceived as a physical threat situation. Instead, the students were much more concerned with how the dentist would perceive and evaluate them, than they were by the potential physical pain of the dentist's drill. For the most part, the results of the studies reported above support the interaction model of anxiety.

Kendall (1978) conducted a study in which he compared the Spielberger (1972) state-trait anxiety model with the Endler (1975b; 1980) interaction model of anxiety. A car accident film was used as a physical danger situation, and failure on an intellectual task was used as a social evaluation stressor situation. The results of Kendall's study supported the interaction model of anxiety, in that interactions occurred only when A-Trait facets were congruent with situational stressors.

INTERACTIONISM NOW AND IN THE FUTURE

Interactionism has come of age. What contributions has it made? What contributions can it make in the future? We know that interactions exist, we can describe them, and we know that they have an effect upon behavior. Sarason, Smith, and Diener (1975) have noted that the typical variance components studies on interaction are descriptive, but not predictive. They tell us *what* occurs (i.e., there are interactions), but they do not tell us *why* interactions are important; neither do they tell us *how* situations and persons interact in eliciting behavior. The variance components studies describe interactions; they do not explain them. Person by treatment (situation) experiments designed within the context of an interactional psychology of personality, enable us to predict the nature of mechanistic interactions (e.g., the differential hypotheses of the multidimensional interaction model of anxiety).

Proposals for the Present and Future.   Initially, the most suitable research strategy for studying interactions should emphasize mechanistic interaction or the structure of interactions. This would enable us to better understand the effective and predictive (independent) variables, and the functional relationships between antecedent conditions (independent variables) and the behavior (dependent variables) that they influence. The experiments and field studies on locus of control, conformity, and anxiety reviewed and discussed above, denote a useful start for an understanding of person by situation interactions. Granted that the ultimate goal is an understanding of dynamic interactions, additional research is still needed on how situations and individuals interact (mechanistic interaction) in modifying, effecting, and influencing behavior. Mechanistic interaction research has been conducted for a number of variables such as anxiety and hostility (e.g., Endler & Hunt, 1968, 1969), and social behavior of children (e.g., Raush, 1965). As indicated above, a number of these studies have used the variance components approach and have emphasized description. It is necessary to examine experimentally the joint effects of persons and situations on behavior, and then to examine the effects of behavior on persons and situations. This person by treatment (situation) design has to be done within the context of a theory. The anxiety studies have done this.

The research reviewed on locus of control, conformity, and anxiety has demonstrated that useful starts have been made towards predicting how persons and situations interact. Basically, the person by treatment (situation) experimental designs do not examine the dynamic multidirectional process conceptualizations of interaction. Nevertheless, this mechanistic interaction research may serve as the basis for formulating an interactional psychology of personality, the ultimate goal being an understanding of the process of interaction (dynamic interaction).

In much of the research that we conduct, we take a subsample of behavior, in a static and arbitrary manner, and infrequently investigate the chain of events. Persons are influenced by situations, but they actively and often intentionally seek out the persons and situations with whom they interact. This involves an interaction process and means conceptualizing the person as an active intentional organism seeking stimulation, instead of a passive victim of situations and events. It is necessary to obtain random and representative samplings of situations, rather than selecting our situations arbitrarily. The distinction between tbe perception of and the reaction to situations is an important one, as is the distinction between objective versus subjective (psychological) situations.

As noted earlier, it is necessary to differentiate between the specific elements within the situation and the situation as a whole, where one compares two or more global situations. For the most part, the mechanistic interaction studies (e.g., the studies on locus of control, conformity, anxiety) have examined the macro-facets of situations, and have been concerned with differences between situations, rather than studying the process of the different elements (e.g., specific contributions of different persons at a cocktail party) within a specified situation (see Magnusson & Endler, 1977). Research should now be directed towards investigating the multidirectional and multicausal elements within the situation under consideration. Within situations analyses should include person by situation interactions and person by person interactions. Every individual acts as a situational cue for every other person with whom he or she is interacting, and is simultaneously influenced by these other persons.

It is essential that we emphasize rules and strategies rather than emphasize the content of events. Perhaps we have been looking in the wrong place for the wrong thing. Argyle (1977), for example, has noted that we should investigate and analyze the generative rules of social interaction rather than attempt to make predictions about content. There are a number of methods and strategies that researchers have recently started to use that have relevance for dynamic interaction (e.g., Block, 1977 on longitudinal studies; Raush, 1977 on Markov chains; Pervin, 1977 on methods for having subjects generate their own situations; White, 1976 on intensive case studies; Argyle, 1977, on investigating rules for social interaction; and Mischel, 1973, 1977 on encoding and decoding strategies). Hopefully this will lead to progress.

SUMMARY AND CONCLUSIONS

The theorizing and research in the field of personality, during the past few years, suggest that interactionism is an idea whose time has come. Although the concept of interactionism is not a new one, but dates back at least to the time of Aristotle, it was only in the 1920s, 1930s, and 1940s that there was an discussion on the theoretical aspects of an interactional psychology of personality, and it was only in the 1960s and 1970s that there was any empirical research on the issues of interactional psychology. It was pointed out that research and theorizing are influenced by sociopolitical factors and by personal factors, and the effects of these factors on interactional psychology were discussed.

Some of the problems with respect to personality research were discussed as well as the four basic models of personality (trait, psychodynamics, situationism, interactionism) and the issues related to these models. These issues included a discussion of personality theories and their measurement models, the relationship between mediating and reaction variables, persons versus situations, and trans-situational consistency versus situational specificity.

The nature of situations in personality research was discussed, and the relationships among stimuli, situations, and environments were described. A distinction was made between situations that are selected and those that are imposed. The necessity of having a differential psychology of situations was proposed. The relationship between the perception of situations and the reaction to situations was presented, as well as the relationship between elements within a situation and situations as wholes.

The last major section of this chapter was concerned with person by situation interactions, and we discussed the relationship between mechanistic interaction and dynamic interaction. Research from three content areas (locus of control, conformity, and anxiety) was presented in order to evaluate person by situation interactions within the context of mechanistic interaction. Endler's (1975b; 1980) interaction model of anxiety was presented and the multidimensionality of anxiety was discussed.

The present and future status of an interactional psychology of personality was discussed, and the necessity for investigating dynamic or process-oriented interactionism was presented. It was suggested that it might be advisable to focus on rules and strategies of interaction rather than on content. Perhaps we should investigate the encoding and decoding strategies that persons use. There is an intricate and interdependent relationship between the subject matter (content) that one studies and the methodology or research strategy that one uses. Perhaps interactionism will not make great strides until we develop the appropriate methodologies for studying dynamic processes. Interactionism has arrived in 1980. In fact, the current automobile license plates in Ontario start with the letters PXS (followed by a 3-digit number).

ACKNOWLEDGMENTS

This chapter is based on a paper presented at *The Ontario Symposium on Variability and Consistency in Social Behavior* held at the University of Waterloo on October 20 and 21, 1979. It was written while the author was on sabbatical, and was partially supported by a SSHRC Leave Fellowship (No. 451-790497). The comments of Mark P. Zanna and Icek Ajzen are appreciated.

REFERENCES

Allport, G. W. *Personality: A psychological interpretation*. New York: Holt, Rinehart & Winston, 1937.

Allport, G. W. *Pattern and growth in personality*. New York: Holt, Rinehart & Winston, 1961.

Allport, G. W. Traits revisited. *American Psychologist*, 1966, *21*, 1–10.

Angyal, A. *Foundations for a science of personality*. Cambridge: Harvard University Press, 1941.

Argyle, M. Predictive and generative rules models of P × S interaction. In D. Magnusson & N. S. Endler (Eds.), *Personality at the crossroads: Current issues in interactional psychology*. Hillsdale, N.J.: Lawrence Erlbaum Associates, 1977.

Argyle, M., & Little, B. R. Do personality traits apply to social behavior? *Journal for the Theory of Social Behavior*, 1972, *2*, 1–35.

Auerbach, S. M. Effects of orienting instructions, feedback information and trait anxiety on state anxiety. *Psychological Reports*, 1973, *33*, 779–786. (a)

Auerbach, S. M. Trait-state anxiety adjustment to dental surgery. *Journal of Consulting and Clinical Psychology*, 1973, *40*, 264–271. (b)

Bandura, A. (Ed.). *Psychological modeling: Conflicting theories*. New York: Aldine-Atherton, 1971.

Barker, R. G. Explorations in ecological psychology. *American Psychologist*, 1965, *20*, 1–14.

Baron, R. M., Cowan, G., Ganz, R. L., & McDonald, M. Interaction of locus of control and type of performance feedback. Considerations of external validity. *Journal of Personality and Social Psychology*, 1974, *30*, 285–292.

Baron, R. M., & Ganz, R. L. Effects of locus of control and type of feedback on the task performance of lower-class black children. *Journal of Personality and Social Psychology,* 1972, *21,* 124–130.

Becker, S. W., Lerner, M. J., & Carroll, J. Conformity as a function of birth order and type of group pressure. *Journal of Personality and Social Psychology,* 1966, *3,* 242–244.

Berkowitz, L. Situational and personal conditions governing reaction to aggressive cues. In D. Magnusson & N. S. Endler (Eds.), *Personality at the crossroads: current issues in interactional psychology.* Hillsdale, N.J.: Lawrence Erlbaum Associates, 1977.

Blake, R. R., & Mouton, J. S. Conformity, resistance, and conversion. In I. A. Berg & B. M. Bass (Eds.), *Conformity and deviation.* New York: Harper, 1961.

Block, J. *Lives through time.* Berkeley, California: Bancroft, 1971.

Block, J. Advancing the psychology of personality: Paradigmatic shift or improving the quality of research. In D. Magnusson & N. S. Endler (Eds.), *Personality at the crossroads: current issues in interactional psychology.* Hillsdale, N.J.: Lawrence Erlbaum Associates, 1977.

Bowers, K. S. Situationism in psychology: An analysis and a critique. *Psychological Review,* 1973, *80,* 307–336.

Bridgwater, W., & Kurtz, S. *Columbia Encyclopedia* (3rd Ed.). New York: Columbia University Press, 1963.

Brunswik, E. *The conceptual framework of psychology.* Chicago: University of Chicago Press, 1952.

Brunswik, E. *Perception and the representative design of psychological experiments.* Berkeley: University of California Press, 1956.

Buss, A. R. Emerging field of the sociology of psychological knowledge. *American Psychologist,* 1975, *30,* 988–1002.

Carlson, R. Where is the person in personality research? *Psychological Bulletin,* 1971, *75,* 203–219.

Cattell, R. B. *The description and measurement of personality.* New York, World Book, 1946.

Cattell, R. B. *Personality and motivation structure and measurement.* Yonkers-on-Hudson, N.Y.: World Book, 1957.

Cooley, C. H. *Human nature and the social order.* New York: Scribner's, 1902.

Craik, K. H. Environmental psychology. *Annual Review of Psychology,* 1973, *24,* 403–422.

Crowne, D. P., & Marlowe, D. *The approval motive: studies in evaluative dependence.* New York: John Wiley & Sons, 1964.

Davis, W. L., & Davis, D. E. Internal-external control and attribution of responsibility for success and failure. *Journal of Personality,* 1972, *40,* 123–136.

Davis, W. L., & Phares, E. J. Internal-external control as a determinant of information seeking in a social influence situation. *Journal of Personality,* 1967, *35,* 547–561.

Dewey, J., & Bentley, A. F. *Knowing and the known.* Boston: Beacon, 1949.

Dewey, R., & Humber, W. J. *The development of human behavior.* New York: Macmillan, 1951.

Diveky, S., & Endler, N. S. *The interaction model of anxiety: State and trait anxiety for banking executives in normal working environments.* Unpublished manuscript, York University, Toronto, 1977.

Dollard, J., & Miller, N. E. *Personality and psychotherapy: An analysis in terms of learning, thinking and culture.* New York: McGraw-Hill, 1950.

Ekehammar, B. Interactionism in personality from a historical perspective. *Psychological Bulletin,* 1974, *81,* 1026–1048.

Ekehammar, B., & Magnusson, D. A method to study stressful situations. *Journal of Personality and Social Psychology,* 1973, *27,* 176–179.

Ekehammar, B., Magnusson, D., & Ricklander, L. An interactionist approach to the study of anxiety: An analysis of an S-R Inventory applied to an adolescent sample. *Scandinavian Journal of Psychology,* 1974, *15,* 4–14.

Ekehammar, B., Shalling, D., & Magnusson, D. Dimensions of stressful situations: A comparison between a response analytical and a stimulus analytical approach. *Multivariate Behavioral Research*, 1975, *10*, 155–164.

Endler, N. S. Conformity as a function of different reinforcement schedules. *Journal of Personality and Social Psychology*, 1966, *4*, 175–180.

Endler, N. S. The person versus the situation—A pseudo issue? A response to Alker. *Journal of Personality*, 1973, *41*, 287–303.

Endler, N. S. The case for person-situation interactions. *Canadian Psychological Review*, 1975, *16*, 12–21. (a)

Endler, N. S. A person-situation interaction model of anxiety. In C. D. Spielberger & I. G. Sarason (Eds.), *Stress and anxiety* (Vol. 1). Washington, D.C.: Hemisphere Publishing Corporation (J. Wiley), 1975. (b)

Endler, N. S. Grand illusions: Traits or interactions? *Canadian Psychological Review*, 1976, *17*, 174–181.

Endler, N. S. The role of person by situation interactions in personality theory. In I. C. Uzgiris & F. Weizmann (Eds.), *The Structuring of experience*. New York: Plenum Press, 1977.

Endler, N. S. The interaction model of anxiety: Some possible implications. In D. M. Landers & R. W. Christina (Eds.), *Psychology of motor behavior and sport—1977*. Champaign, Ill.: Human Kinetics, 1978.

Endler, N. S. Anxiety and the person by situation interaction model. In I. L. Kutash & L. B. Schlesinger (Eds.), *Handbook on stress and anxiety: Contemporary knowledge, theory and treatment*. San Francisco, California: Jossey Bass, 1980.

Endler, N. S. Situational aspects of interactional psychology. In D. Magnusson (Ed.), *Toward a psychology of situations: An interactional perspective*. Hillsdale, N.J.: Lawrence Erlbaum Associates, 1981.

Endler, N. S., & Edwards, J. Person by treatment interactions in personality research. In L. A. Pervin and M. Lewis (Eds.), *Perspectives in interactional psychology*. New York: Plenum Press, 1978.

Endler, N. S., Edwards, J., & McGuire, A. *The interaction model of anxiety: An empirical test in a theatrical performance situation*. Unpublished manuscript, York University, Toronto, 1979.

Endler, N. S., & Hoy, E. Conformity as related to reinforcement and social pressure. *Journal of Personality and Social Psychology*, 1967, *7*, 197–202.

Endler, N. S., & Hunt, J. McV. Sources of behavioral variance as measured by the S-R Inventory of Anxiousness. *Psychological Bulletin*, 1966, *65*, 336–346.

Endler, N. S., & Hunt, J. McV. S-R Inventories of hostility and comparisons of the proportions of variance from persons, responses, and situations for hostility and anxiousness. *Journal of Personality and Social Psychology*, 1968, *9*, 309–315.

Endler, N. S., & Hunt, J. McV. Generalizability of contributions from sources of variance in the S-R Inventories of Anxiousness. *Journal of Personality*, 1969, *37*, 1–24.

Endler, N. S., Hunt, J. McV., & Rosenstein, A. J. An S-R Inventory of Anxiousness. *Psychological Monographs*, 1962, *76*, no. 17 (whole no. 536), 1–33.

Endler, N. S., King P. R., Kuczynski, M., & Edwards, J. *Examination induced anxiety: An empirical test of the interaction model*. Unpublished manuscript, York University, Toronto, 1980.

Endler, N. S., & Magnusson, D. Multidimensional aspects of state and trait anxiety: A cross-cultural study of Canadian and Swedish college students. In C. D. Spielberger & R. Diaz-Guerrero (Eds.), *Cross-cultural anxiety*. Washington, D.C.: Hemisphere Publishing Corporation (Wiley), 1976. (a)

Endler, N. S., & Magnusson, D. Personality and person by situation interactions. In N. S. Endler & D. Magnusson (Eds.), *Interactional psychology and personality*. Washington, D.C.: Hemisphere Publishing Corporation (Wiley), 1976. (b)

Endler, N. S., & Magnusson, D. Toward an interactional psychology of personality. *Psychological Bulletin*, 1976, *83*, 956–974. (c)

Endler, N. S. & Magnusson, D. The interaction model of anxiety: An empirical test in an examination situation. *Canadian Journal of Behavioural Science,* 1977, *9,* 101–107.

Endler, N. S., & Magnusson, D. But interactionists do believe in people! Response to Krauskopf. *Psychological Bulletin,* 1978, *85,* 590–592.

Endler, N. S., Magnusson, D., Ekehammar, B., & Okada, M. The multidimensionality of state and trait anxiety. *Scandinavian Journal of Psychology,* 1976, *17,* 81–93.

Endler, N. S., & Okada, Marilyn. An S-R inventory of general trait anxiousness. *Department of Psychology Reports,* York University, Toronto, 1974, No. 1.

Endler, N. S., & Okada, M. A multidimensional measure of trait anxiety: The S-R inventory of general trait anxiousness. *Journal of Consulting and Clinical Psychology,* 1975, *43,* 319–329.

Erikson, E. *Childhood and Society* (2nd ed.). New York: Norton, 1963.

Feshbach, S. The environment of personality. *American Psychologist,* 1978, *33,* 447–455.

Fiedler, F. E. Validation and extension of the contingency model of leadership effectiveness: A review of empirical findings. *Psychological Bulletin,* 1971, *76,* 128–148.

Fiedler, F. E. What triggers the person situation interaction in leadership? In D. Magnusson & N. S. Endler (Eds.), *Personality at the crossroads: Current issues in interactional psychology.* Hillsdale, N.J.: Lawrence Erlbaum Associates, Inc., 1977.

Flood, M., & Endler, N. S. The interaction model of anxiety: An empirical test in an athletic competition situation. *Journal of Research in Personality,* 1980, *14,* 329–339.

Frederiksen, N. Toward a taxonomy of situations. *American Psychologist* 1972, *27,* 114–123.

Freud, S. *Collected papers.* Volumes I-V. New York: Basic Books, 1959.

Fromm, E. *The sane society.* New York: Rinehart, 1955.

Gibson, J. J. The concept of the stimulus in psychology. *American Psychologist,* 1960, *15,* 694–703.

Gilmor, T. M., & Minton, H. L. Internal versus external attribution of task performance as a function of locus of control, initial confidence and success-failure outcome. *Journal of Personality,* 1974, *42,* 159–174.

Guilford, J. P. *Personality.* New York: McGraw-Hill, 1959.

Hodges, W. F. Effects of ego threat and threat of pain on state anxiety. *Journal of Personality and Social Psychology,* 1968, *8,* 364–372.

Hodges, W. F., & Spielberger, C. D. The effects of threat of shock on heart rate for subjects who differ in manifest anxiety and fear of shock. *Psychophysiology,* 1966, *2,* 287–294.

Horney, K. *Our inner conflicts.* New York: W. W. Norton & Co., 1945.

Houston, B. K. Control over stress, locus of control, and response to stress. *Journal of Personality and Social Psychology,* 1972, *21,* 249–255.

Hoy, E., & Endler, N. S. Reported anxiousness and two types of stimulus incongruity. *Canadian Journal of Behavioural Science,* 1969, *1,* 207–214.

Hunt, J. McV. Traditional personality theory in the light of recent evidence. *American Scientist,* 1965, *53,* 80–96.

Ichheiser, G. Misinterpretations of personality in everyday life and the psychologist's frame of reference. *Character and Personality,* 1943, *12,* 145–160.

Jessor, R. Phenomenological personality theories and the data language of psychology. *Psychological Review,* 1956, *63,* 173–180.

Jessor, R. The problem of reductionism in psychology. *Psychological Review,* 1958, *65,* 170–178.

Kantor, J. R. *Principles of psychology* (Vol. 1). Bloomington, Ill.: Principia Press, 1924.

Kantor, J. R. *Principles of Psychology* (Vol. 2). Bloomington, Ill.: Principia Press, 1926.

Kantor, J. R. *Interbehavioral psychology.* Bloomington, Ill.: Principia Press, 1959.

Kantor, J. R. *The scientific evolution of psychology* (Vol. 2). Chicago: Principia Press, 1969.

Katkin, E. S. The relationship between manifest anxiety and two indices of autonomic response to stress. *Journal of Personality and Social Psychology,* 1965, *2,* 324–333.

Kendall, P. C. Anxiety: States, traits—situations? *Journal of Consulting and Clinical Psychology,* 1978, *46,* 280–287.

King, P. R., & Endler, N. S. Medical intervention and the interaction model of anxiety. *Canadian Journal of Behavioural Science,* 1982, *14,* in press.

Koffka, K. *Principles of Gestalt psychology.* New York: Harcourt, 1935.

Lefcourt, H. M. *Locus of control: Current trends in theory and research.* New Jersey: Lawrence Erlbaum Associates, 1976.

Lefcourt, H. M., Lewis, L., & Silverman, I. W. Internal vs external control of reinforcement and attention in a decision making task. *Journal of Personality,* 1968, *36,* 663–682.

Levinson, D. J. *The seasons of a man's life.* New York: Alfred A. Knopf, 1978.

Lewin, K. *A dynamic theory of personality. Selected papers.* New York: McGraw-Hill, 1935.

Lewin, K. *Principles of topological psychology.* New York: McGraw-Hill, 1936.

Lewin, K. Problems of research in social psychology. In D. Cartwright (Ed.), *Field theory in social science.* London: Tavistock Publications, 1952.

Lewis, A. The ambiguous word "anxiety". *International Journal of Psychiatry,* 1970, *9,* 62–79.

Magnusson, D. An analysis of situational dimensions. *Perceptual and Motor Skills,* 1971, *32,* 851–967.

Magnusson, D. The person and the situation in the traditional measurement model. *Reports from the Psychological Laboratories.* University of Stockholm, 1974, No. 426.

Magnusson, D. The person and the situation in an interactional model of behavior. *Scandinavian Journal of Psychology,* 1976, *17,* 253–271.

Magnusson, D. On the psychological situation. *Reports from the Department of Psychology,* University of Stockholm, 1978, No. 544.

Magnusson, D. Personality in an interactional paradigm of research. *Zeitschrift fur Differentielle und Diagnostiche Psychologie,* 1980, *1,* 17–34.

Magnusson, D., & Ekehammar, B. An analysis of situational dimensions: A replication. *Multivariate Behavioral Research,* 1973, *8,* 331–339.

Magnusson, D., & Ekehammar, B. Perceptions of and reactions to stressful situations. *Journal of Personality and Social Psychology,* 1975, *31,* 1147–1154.

Magnusson, D., & Ekehammar, B. Similar situations—similar behaviors? *Journal of Research in Personality,* 1978, *12,* 41–48.

Magnusson, D., & Endler, N. S. Interactional psychology: present status and future prospects. In D. Magnusson & N. S. Endler (Eds.), *Personality at the crossroads: Current issues in interactional psychology.* Hillsdale, N.J.: Lawrence Erlbaum Associates, 1977.

Magnusson, D., Gerzén, M., & Nyman, B. The generality of behavioral data: I. Generalization from observations on one occasion. *Multivariate Behavioral Research,* 1968, *3,* 295–320.

Magnusson, D., & Heffler, B. The generality of behavioral data: III. Generalization potential as a function of the number of observation instances. *Multivariate Behavioral Research,* 1969, *4,* 29–42.

Magnusson, D., Heffler, B., & Nyman, B. The generality of behavioral data: II. Replication of an experiment on generalization from observation on one occasion. *Multivariate Behavioral Research,* 1968, *3,* 415–422.

Mausner, B., & Graham, J. Field dependence and prior reinforcement as determinants of social interaction in judgment. *Journal of Personality and Social Psychology,* 1970, *16,* 486–493.

McDavid, J. W. Personality and situational determinants of conformity. *Journal of Abnormal and Social Psychology,* 1959, *58,* 241–246.

Mead, G. H. *Mind, self and society.* Chicago: University of Chicago Press, 1934.

Mehrabain, A., & Russell, J. A. *An approach to environmental psychology.* Cambridge, Mass.: MIT Press, 1974.

Mischel, W. *Personality and assessment.* New York: Wiley, 1968.

Mischel, W. Continuity and change in personality. *American Psychologist,* 1969, *24,* 1012–1018.

Mischel, W. Toward a cognitive social learning reconceptualization of personality. *Psychological Review,* 1973, *80,* 252–283.

Mischel, W. *Introduction to personality* (2nd ed.). New York: Holt, Rinehart & Winston, 1976.

Mischel, W. The interaction of person and situation. In D. Magnusson & N. S. Endler (Eds.), *Personality at the crossroads: Current issues in interactional psychology*. Hillsdale, N.J.: Lawrence Erlbaum Associates, 1977.

Moore, J. C., & Krupat, E. Relationships between source status, authoritarianism, and conformity in a social influence setting. *Sociometry*, 1971, *34*, 122–134.

Moos, R. H. Conceptualizations of human environments. *American Psychologist*, 1973, *28*, 652–665.

Murphy, G. *Personality: A biosocial approach to origins and structure*. New York: Harper, 1947.

Murray, H. A. *Explorations in personality*. New York: Oxford University Press, 1938.

Olweus, D. A critical analysis of the modern interactionist position. In D. Magnusson & N. S. Endler (Eds.), *Personality at the crossroads: Current issues in interactional psychology*. Hillsdale, N.J.: Lawrence Erlbaum Associates, 1977.

O'Neil, J. F., Spielberger, C. D., & Hansen, D. N. The effects of state anxiety and task difficulty on computer-assisted learning. *Journal of Educational Psychology*, 1969, *60*, 343–350.

OSS Assessment Staff. *Assessment of men*. New York: Rinehart, 1948.

Overton, W. F., & Reese, H. W. Models of development: Methodological implications. In J. R. Nesselroade & H. W. Reese (Eds.), *Life span developmental psychology: Methodological issues*. New York: Academic Press, 1973, 65–86.

Patterson, G. R., & Moore, D. R. Interactive patterns as units. In S. J. Suomi, M. E. Lamb, & G. R. Stevenson (Eds.), *The study of social interaction: Methodological issues*. Madison, Wisconsin: University of Wisconsin Press, 1978.

Pervin, L. A. Performance and satisfaction as a function of individual-environment fit. *Psychological Bulletin*, 1968, *69*, 56–68.

Pervin, L. A. The representative design of person-situation research. In D. Magnusson & N. S. Endler (Eds.), *Personality at the crossroads: Current issues in interactional psychology*. Hillsdale, N.J.: Lawrence Erlbaum Associates, 1977.

Pervin, L. A. *Current controversies and issues in personality*. New York: Wiley, 1978. (a)

Pervin, L. A. Definitions, measurements, and classifications of stimuli, situations, and environments. *Human Ecology*, 1978, *6*, 71–105. (b)

Phares, E. J. *Locus of control in personality*. Morristown, N.J.: General Learning Press, 1976.

Phillips, J. B., & Endler, N. S. Academic examinations and anxiety: The interaction model empirically tested. *Journal of Research in Personality*, 1982, *16*, in press.

Rapaport, D., Gill, M., & Schafer, R. *Diagnostic psychological testing*. Chicago: New Book, 1945, 2 vols.

Rappaport, H., & Katkin, E. S. Relationships among manifest anxiety, response to stress, and the perception of autonomic activity. *Journal of Consulting and Clinical Psychology*, 1972, *38*, 219–224.

Raush, H. L. Interaction sequences. *Journal of Personality and Social Psychology*, 1965, *2*, 487–499.

Raush, H. L. Paradox, levels and junctures in person-situation systems. In D. Magnusson & N. S. Endler (Eds.), *Personality at the crossroads: Current issues in interactional psychology*. Hillsdale, N.J.: Lawrence Erlbaum Associates, 1977.

Raush, H. L., Dittmann, A. T., & Taylor, T. J. The interpersonal behavior of children in residential treatment. *Journal of Abnormal and Social Psychology*, 1959, *58*, 9–26. (a)

Raush, H. L., Dittmann, A. T., & Taylor, T. J. Person, setting and change in social interaction. *Human Relations*, 1959, 12, 361–378. (b)

Reid, D. W., & Ware, E. E. Multidimensionality of internal-external control: Implications for past and future research. *Canadian Journal of Behavioural Science*, 1973, *5*, 264–270.

Rhine, W. R. Birth order differences in conformity and level of achievement arousal. *Child Development*, 1968, *39*, 987–996.

Rosenberg, M. J. When dissonance fails: on eliminating evaluation apprehension from attitude measurement. *Journal of Personality and Social psychology*, 1965, *1*, 28–42.

Rotter, J. B. *Social learning and clinical psychology*. Englewood Cliffs, N.J.: Prentice-Hall, 1954.

Rotter, J. B. The role of the psychological situation in determining the direction of human behavior. In M. R. Jones (Ed.), *Nebraska Symposium on Motivation*. University of Nebraska Press, Lincoln, 1955, 245–268.

Rotter, J. B. Generalized expectancies for internal versus external control of reinforcement. *Psychological Monographs*, 1966, *80*, (1, Whole No. 609).

Rotter, J. B. Some problems and misconceptions related to the construct of internal versus external control of reinforcement. *Journal of Consulting and Clinical Psychology*, 1975, *43*, 56–67.

Runyan, W. M. The life course as a theoretical orientation: Sequences of person-situation interaction. *Journal of Personality*, 1978, *46*, 569–593.

Rushton, J. P., & Endler, N. S. Person by situation interactions in academic achievement. *Journal of Personality*, 1977, *45*, 297–309.

Sarason, I. G., Smith, R. E., & Diener, E. Personality research: Components of variance attributable to the person and the situation. *Journal of Personality and Social Psychology*, 1975, *32*, 199–204.

Sechrest, L. Personality. *Annual Review of Psychology*, 1976, *27*, 1–28.

Sells, S. B. (Ed.), *Stimulus determinants of behavior*. New York: The Ronald Press Company, 1963.

Shedletsky, R., & Endler, N. S. Anxiety: The state-trait model and the interaction model. *Journal of Personality*, 1974, *42*, 511–527.

Sherman, S. J. Internal-external locus of control and its relationship to attitude change under different influence techniques. *Journal of Personality and Social Psychology*, 1973, *26*, 23–29.

Shute, C. Aristotle's interactionism and its transformations by some 20th century writers. *Psychological Record*, 1973, *23*, 283–293.

Sistrunk, F. Two processes of conformity demonstrated by interactions of commitment, situation and personality. *Journal of Social Psychology*, 1973, *89*, 63-72.

Sistrunk, F., & McDavid, J. W. Achievement motivation, affiliation motivation, and task difficulty as determinants of social conformity. *The Journal of Social Psychology*, 1965, *66*, 41–50.

Skinner, B. F. *The behavior of organisms*. New York: Appleton-Century Crofts, 1938.

Snyder, M., & Monson, T. C. Persons, situations, and the control of social behavior. *Journal of Personality and Social Psychology*, 1975, *32*, 637–644.

Spielberger, C. D. Theory and research on anxiety. In C. D. Speilberger (Ed.), *Anxiety and behavior*. New York: Academic Press, 1966.

Spielberger, C. D. Anxiety as an emotional state. In C. D. Spielberger (Ed.), *Anxiety: Current trends in theory and research* (VOl. 1). New York: Academic Press, 1972.

Spielberger, C. D., Gorsuch, R. L., & Lushene R. E. *Manual for the State-Trait Anxiety Inventory*. Palo Alto, California: Consulting Psychologist Press, 1970.

Stolorow, R. D., & Atwood, G. E. *Faces in a cloud: Subjectivity in personality theory*. New York: Jason Aaronson, 1979.

Sullivan, H. S. *The interpersonal theory of psychiatry*. New York: Norton, 1953.

Tolman, E. C. Psychology versus immediate experience. In E. C. Tolman, *Collected papers in psychology*. Berkeley: University of California Press, 1951. (Reprinted from *Philosophy of Science*, 1935, *2*, 356–380.)

White, R. W. *Lives in progress* (2nd ed.). New York: Holt, Rinehart & Winston, 1966.

White, R. W. *The enterprise of living: A view of personal growth* (2nd ed.). New York: Holt, Rinebart & Winston, 1976.

Wiesenthal, D. L., Edwards, J., Endler, N. S., Koza, P., Walton, A., & Emmott, S. Trends in conformity research. *Canadian Psycbological Review*, 1978, *19*, 41–58.

Witkin, H. A., & Goodenough, D. R. Field dependence and interpersonal behavior. *Research Bulletin of the Educational Testing Service*. Princeton, N.J., 1976.

Zuckerman, M. General and situation-specific traits and states: new approaches to assessment of anxiety and other constructs. In M. Zuckerman & C. D. Spielberger (Eds.), *Emotions and anxiety: New concepts, methods, and applications*. Hillsdale, N.J.: Lawrence Erlbaum Associates, 1976.

11 Some Preconditions for Valid Person Perception

Douglas N. Jackson
University of Western Ontario

In this paper I address the question of whether or not a person's behavior can be predicted from information about that person from the perspective of one who has considered this issue as a measurement problem. I firmly believe that there is an unfortunate schism between personality measurement and quantitative approaches to person perception, on the one hand, and personality and social psychology considered from an experimental perspective, on the other. I believe that each approach has much to learn from the other. Rather than defining procedures and knowledge developed from one perspective as irrelevant to the other, I submit, as have others, that progress will be substantially facilitated by amalgamating these two perspectives into a single tradition, one which takes cognizance both of reliability theory and the effects of situations. If some of what I say appears alien to some experimental social psychologists, I beg their indulgence and hope that at least the message will be clear. (I also beg the indulgence of any others who might feel that it belabors the obvious to discuss the relevance of, for example, reliability to the prediction of behavior). Where studies employing techniques borrowed from personality measurement are introduced, such as those concerned with the multivariate classification of personality, I hope that I will succeed in suggesting the possible relevance of such procedures to achieving a perspective on the central theme of this Symposium, the predictability of behavior.

There has evolved a widespread sentiment among personality researchers that there is little, if any, basis for a belief that valid predictions of future behavior can be derived from judgments based on impressions of past behavior, whether the past behavior was in response to psychological tests or other situations. These reviews have been taken to reflect not only available empirical data but also an interpretation about the nature of human judgment, in which its susceptibility to bias, distortion, stereotypy, and error has been highlighted over its potentialities for interpretation and prediction. This situation is similar to the status of flying at the turn of the century. A review of efforts to fly in a heavier-than-air device 80 years ago would have recounted the deaths in previous attempts, the variety of devices unsuccessfully employed, and the lack of a suitable body of theory. It is perhaps understandable, if not logically compelling, that many people of that era believed that flying was impossible and that ''if God had intended that people fly, He would have provided them with wings.''

My aim in this paper is to outline some of the prior conditions necessary for accurate clinical judgment and reliable and valid person perception and behavioral prediction. Such conditions are rarely, if ever, met in studies providing the bases for the aforementioned influential reviews. I shall also illustrate with empirical data how studies may be designed to incorporate some of these prerequisites. By incorporating in the design of studies principles derived from classical test theory and from knowledge of personality structure and multivariate classification, I shall attempt to demonstrate that it is indeed possible to show substantial degrees of relationship between personality characteristics judged to be present in a target person and the person's behavior.

I would like to suggest seven preconditions for accurate person perception and behavioral prediction. *First,* it is necessary to state explicitly which constructs, behavioral dimensions, or traits are of interest. *Second,* the information given to the judge and the behavior to be predicted should bear a theoretical, as well as an empirical interrelation. These constructs should show evidence of construct validity. Accuracy will be higher when the theoretical connection between the information given and the behavior to be predicted is a strong one. *Third,* substantive and empirical criteria should be employed to insure that the behavior being predicted or inferred, as well as that observed by or presented to the judge, comprises a representative sample of the behavioral dimension embodied in the construct. *Fourth,* the behavior being predicted should possess adequate levels of reliability. This problem can be conceptualized as the need to incorporate a sufficient number of behavioral exemplars of some broader class, as well as the need to identify relevant behavior across specific situations and modes of response and to insure that the behavior being predicted is sufficiently reliable to be amenable to prediction. *Fifth,* accuracy of predictions depends on processes of valid trait inference. Accuracy is possible only when an opportunity is provided judges to utilize such implicit processes of trait and behavioral inference. For example, a prediction of behavior relevant to planfulness of a target person is possible when information is given regarding the person's behavior related to orderliness because of the shared implicit (and valid) link between the two classes of behavior. *Sixth,* it is necessary to consider the probabilities or base rates of behavior, as well as the evaluative interpretation or social desirability of the behavior being predicted. These sources of information, far from representing mere bias, are an integral part of accurate behavioral prediction, logically distinct from personality constructs *per se,* but nevertheless providing additional sources of valid information. Finally, *seventh,* a variety of media for the appraisal of the validity of interpersonal judgment should be sought, including nonverbal, as well as verbal.

Let me take up each of these preconditions in turn.

THE ROLE OF CONSTRUCTS

It is important to state explicitly the particular traits or constructs of interest. If person cognition is anything like other kinds of cognition, some categorization is inevitable. But in person cognition there are two distinct sets of constructs of interest (a) those derived from implicit or lay personality theory; and (b) those derived from psychological theorizing. It should be obvious that little, if any, predictive accuracy could occur in the absence of some implicit constructs being formed by the judge about the target. Thus, a judge after observing a person kicking a dog might infer that that person would be likely to argue with other people. Such an inference is probably based on the implicit invocation of a trait or dimension such as aggression, linked to each specific behavioral exemplar. In spite of the importance of such inferences, few studies of clinical prediction are explicitly concerned with the processes underlying the clinical judgment (Holt, 1958). For example, some studies have instructed judges to view a short film strip of a target person's behavior in a particular situation and then asked the judge to predict the occurrence of quite different behavior in a different situation. It is not surprising that judges perform relatively poorly in tasks such as this in which there is no specification of the constructs by which the two behavioral samples might be linked. Indeed, one can hardly imagine how any differential predictions about behavior could be made in the absence of *some* construct about the behavior given, although the nature of the constructs and their degree of explicitness could possibly vary widely.

There is little controversy about the tendency of judges to employ implicit constructs; the controversy is about whether or not the constructs are useful abstractions of behavior, and whether or not they bear a meaningful relation to behavioral regularities as they might be observed independently. Indeed, there are personality theorists (Bandura, 1969; Mischel, 1968; Mulaik, 1964; Schneider, 1973; Shweder, 1975) who argue that much of perceived behavioral consistency is illusory, and that perceivers impose consistencies in terms of broad trait-dispositions by forcing disparate, situationally-specific observed behaviors into apparently logical perceived categories which in fact have little or no predictive utility. Mirels (1976) in a paper entitled "Implicit Personality Theory and Inferential Illusions" provided laboratory evidence apparently in support of this position by purportedly demonstrating that judgments of the joint occurrence of a "true" response to pairs of Personality Research Form (PRF) items bore little or no relation to what amounted to empirical conditional probabilities. But when more appropriate indices of association—namely, product moment correlation coefficients—were employed in a re-analysis by Jackson, Chan and Stricker (1979) the data yielded a strikingly different interpretation for both Mirel's data and new data: an appreciable and highly significant association between judgments of behavioral co-occurrence and empirical coendorsement. These findings support previous results regarding the inability of judges to employ conditional probabilities with accuracy (Kahneman & Tversky, 1973) such as those used in the Mirels study, as contrasted with the accurate use of psychological distances and correlations in a number of studies. Thus, congruences have been found between the spontaneous categories arising for example, in judges' clustering or multidimensional scaling of behavioral referrents and those arising empirically, in, for example, studies of Lay and Jackson (1969) using normal personality materials, or of Chan and Jackson (1979) in the area of psychopathology, and of Stricker, Jacobs, and Kogan (1974), who found that high school students spontaneously identified categories conforming to those identified in factor analyses of the MMPI Pd scale.

Even if one accepts the evidence that there is substantial correspondence between implicit conceptions of personality held by lay persons and regularities observed to exist in the real world, it might not immediately follow that such conceptions represent the most useful ones for predicting or understanding behavior. Meehl (1945), for example, warned a generation of personality assessors that because personality theory was not sufficiently advanced, we had little basis for attempting to improve over purely empirical methods for scale construction. It was suggested that the finding, for example, that a sample of patients diagnosed as psychopathic personality significantly answered "false" to the item: "I have been quite independent and free from family rule" could not be interpreted with the knowledge of personality then existing, and few researchers in this tradition were encouraged to explore the relation between item content and behavior. I (Jackson, 1971) published an interpretation of the above and similar findings, namely, that they are due to measurement error, an interpretation supported by findings by Goldberg and Slovic (1967) that the only items showing substantial tendencies to hold up under cross-validation were those with a judged substantive relation between item content and the criterion. I was so confident about the utility of specifying definitionally the construct that a challenge was issued (Jackson, 1971) to pit the most elaborate methods of empirical item selection using an external criterion against the efforts of a few novice item writers working for a few minutes each but who have been provided with—and this is important—a definition of the construct of concern. Figure 11.1 presents results from my analysis: the efforts from the average student far exceeded those from similar-length scales from the California Psychological Inventory in ac-

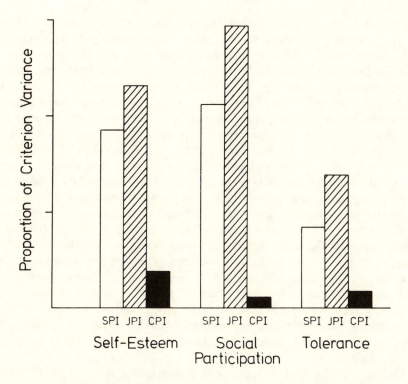

FIG. 11.1 Proportion of criterion peer rating variance accounted for by three personality scale construction strategies: Student Personality Inventory (SPI); Jackson Personality Inventory (JPI); and California Psychological Inventory (CPI).

counting for roommate-rating criterion variance, and approached the validity of scales from the much more elaborately constructed Jackson Personality Inventory. These results have been independently confirmed by Ashton and Goldberg (1973) using different scales and a slightly different procedure.

Characteristics of Dispositional Variables

Jane Loevinger (1957) once observed that traits exist in people while constructs, representing something constructed, an artifice, exist only in the minds and magazines of psychologists. The task for the personality psychologist in Loevinger's terms is therefore to attempt to derive valid, useful constructs through observations of trait-related behaviors. This for Loevinger took the form of empirically-oriented attempts to cluster personality test and attitude items so as to permit inductive generalizations. I see no such distinctions between traits and constructs nor do I have a great deal of faith in inductive correlational attempts to find psychological structure and meaning. Rather, both the actor and the psychologist are confronted with, to borrow Einstein's phrasing, a chaotic diversity of sensory experience. Both try to interpret this diversity. Both develop techniques to confirm or disconfirm observed regularities. Contrary to the position of psychologists who suggest that we are likely to be led astray by seeking to employ constructs related to lay personality theory, my position is that we should capitalize upon opportunities to employ it. The evidence, as it has unfolded, reveals in the collective wisdom of a group consensus an enormous degree of agreement, much subtlety, and surprising levels of accuracy.

There has been considerable controversy over the utility and nature of personality constructs as they might be applied to assessment and to clinical judgment. Many psychologists are uncomfortable using inferred entities whose specific behavioral referents are broader than those based on a single measure. There has been a suggestion that because studies of trait inference and person perception usually employ verbal materials, that inferential processes are entirely dependent upon the arbitrary semantic structuring of the words which symbolize underlying processes and that these semantic associations are simply not relevant to the understanding of judgmental processes and person perception. There is also controvery about whether personality constructs should be relatively broad or rather narrow. And there remains the question alluded to earlier about the body of evidence seemingly bearing on the lack of validity associated with constructs employed by judges.

The fact that some psychologists remain uncomfortable by the invocation of inferred entities or abstractions is unfortunate, as I see little or no alternative. Although the strict interpretations of operationism developed a following some 35 years ago, it is noteworthy that throughout the history of science concepts are typically clarified through a triangulation of operations and that the strongest case for the verification of constructs is usually made for those which yield multiple evidence derived from a variety of methods of measurement and formal operations. I might note parenthetically that I am in thorough agreement with Campbell and Fiske (1959), who view observed behavior as being a function of a trait-method composite, in which the method of measurement and indeed situational determinants are interwoven with observations determined by a variety of person variables. Person variables do not operate with equal strength in any given situation. It is therefore the responsibility of the research worker to devise situations which highlight the particular dispositions of interest and which provide evidence of these dispositions' trans-method and trans-situational generality. Since situational and method variance is always present in some degree, studies involving regularities and consistencies in behavior must almost inevitably become multivariate ones, both in terms of independent and dependent variables, in which the various sources of trait, method, and situational variance need to be extricated and isolated by more powerful procedures than those usually possible in experimental studies of mean effects.

Is Personality Inference Purely Semantic?

Later I'll present evidence bearing on the question of whether or not semantic associations provided explicitly by the experimenter are a necessary and sufficient basis for accounting for observed regularities and predictions about the behavior of people in studies of person perception. At this point I would just like to suggest that this hypothesis has been put forward in a manner that does not readily lend itself to conceptual or empirical scrutiny. A number of authors have merely asserted that the findings in studies employing trait ratings are due to a process of "semantic overlap" or some similar notion without attempting to spell out how this might have occurred. Since the proponents of such purported processes rarely spell out in other than vague terms their nature and implications, perhaps we should make this attempt here. An analysis of the possible role of language actually yields a variety of possible interpretations. First of all there is what Paunonen and Jackson (1979) termed the strong version of the semantic overlap hypothesis, namely that the predictions about behavior or the perceived relation between the trait terms representing different dispositions were entirely due to the lexicographical similarities between the words, and that if the information were provided the judge in other than verbal terms, then the regularities observed in studies using verbal ratings would disappear or take a different form. My interpretation of what such a putative lexicographical interpretation of person perception would involve is that persons consult a dictionary when judging another person. That is, if a person is presented with information that an individual is, for example, "reliable," this target would be rated also as "orderly" because part of the semantic meaning of reliable involves orderliness. I have seen no explicit treatment of how this position could account for more strictly inferential leaps, as when a person who is considered to be *talkative* is also seen as *dishonest* (Walters & Jackson, 1966). Surely there is no known dictionary which includes dishonesty as synonymous with talkativeness. When one presents individuals with a variety of disparate trait terms, there is no published dictionary that would permit a reliable basis for linking these in terms of their lexicographical characteristics. Even if such a dictionary did exist, there would be the further question of how such a meaning network arose. The hypothetical possibility of such a dictionary would in any case not invalidate or make trivial the presence of trait and behavioral personality inference unless it could be demonstrated that semantic meaning relationships created inaccuracies and distortions which would not have existed in the absence of the semantic medium.

A further problem with the semantic overlap position is that the rules for linking abstract trait terms with concrete behaviors would be enormously complicated, even if they could be spelled out. The tendency, for example, to be somewhat lacking in *planfulness* might be inferred from an item like "I can never get my check book to balance," but the purely semantic rules for linking the two would be difficult if not impossible to determine or codify. The potential exemplars for a dispositional trait like *planfulness* are virtually infinite. Since there is no dictionary of infinite size, I find it difficult to understand how the use of purely semantic associations would account for inferences of this type. The situation is even more complicated when one infers the probability of one concrete behavior from another. For example, by what semantic rule would one infer a negative probability of a joint occurrence for the item "I like to check on the weather before deciding what to wear on a particular day" and the item "I would enjoy wandering freely from country to country."? One could generate an almost endless array of such concrete behavioral exemplars so as to overwhelm any simple semantic dictionary. Indeed, apart from simple trait names it is doubtful that any of the components of a semantic overlap hypothesis has provided any serious basis for identifying correspondences of a lexicographical nature.

Another version of semantic hypotheses about person perception concerns connotative properties of concepts, such as the familiar evaluation, potency, and activity dimensions proposed by Osgood and others. There are two important observations about such interpretations. First of all there is substantial evidence that evaluation is ubiquitous in judging the behavior of other people, whether the information is presented verbally or nonverbally. I submit that the undesirable connotative attributes of the concept of murder extend beyond the scale value of the word, and that the direct observation of a murderous act would elicit such a connotative "meaning" quite apart from any verbal communication. Secondly, there is now overwhelming evidence that one can distinguish, using multivariate judgment or response methods, the denotative content of verbal and nonverbal messages about behavior from their connotative attributes, and that both connotative and denotative content messages have distinct, highly predictable, stable judgmental characteristics (Peabody, 1970).

Is Behavior Understandable in Terms of Broad Dispositions?

With regard to the question of whether dispositional variables are best considered as relatively broad or relatively narrow, there are two major considerations: one aesthetic and the other empirical. In general, there has been a long tradition in psychology for seeking a parsimonious interpretation of behavior in terms of concepts summarizing situational influences and those describing consistencies attributable to the person. Some theorists have suggested person variables need to be considered specifically and distinctly in terms of each type of situation. In most scientific enterprise, the simpler interpretation is to be preferred, other things being equal, as both an aesthetic preference and one dictated by conceptual and pragmatic convenience. In this connection, I refer to the paradox (or irony) of Tristam Shandy, who spent several years describing the first few days of his life. I am concerned about formulations that would require that we generate a vast array of highly specific dispositional variables having little cross-situational generality. The other criterion on which to base a decision about the breadth of the one's constructs relates to their utility, utility for understanding how judges operate in their impressions of other people, and in terms of how such variables of personality are useful in aiding judges to make valid predictions of the behavior of other people. I shall present evidence which cannot readily be accounted for except by positing the use of a broad-based personality constructs by judges, whose judgments yield substantial evidence of validity in predicting the behavior of respondents.

INFORMATIONAL VALIDITY AND PREDICTABILITY OF BEHAVIOR

Turning now to the requirement that the information provided judges should bear evidence of both construct and empirical validity with respect to behavior being predicted, let me illustrate this requirement with an illustrative study, more or less typical of the many studies invoked in support of the idea that the clinical judgment has little or no predictive validity. Goldberg (1959) selected three types of judges varying in experience in clinical psychology, ranging from Ph.D. staff members, to psychology trainees, to secretaries. The task given a Bender-Gestalt test protocol was to decide whether or not each of 30 patients had been independently diagnosed as having organic pathology associated with a central neurological brain damage. The results of the study indicated no statistically significant differences between the groups, although there was some tendency for secretaries and psychology trainees to do better than the more experienced psychologists. Only a minority of judges exceeded chance expectancy in their diagnoses of patients, with a highest proportion of nonchance results attributable to the group of secretaries. These results, while not wholly negative, are typical of the findings leading reviewers to the conclusion that there is little validity in clinical judgment. Wiggins (1973), for example, uses the Goldberg and other studies as a basis for concluding "The argument that the clinicians' presumed expertise is based on his professional training and experience has found little empirical support in studies to date." Similarly, Mischel (1968) in reviewing 20 years of research concluded that "studies of clinical inference has led to almost uniformly negative conclusions. Clinical inferences have little or no predictive validity . . ."

I submit that the data on which such conclusions have been based do not bear directly upon the issue at hand, namely, the accuracy of clinical prediction. Rarely, if ever, do investigators of clinical judgmental accuracy proffer evidence of the substantive or empirical validity of the information provided judges. Consider Figure 11.2, which graphically portrays a clinical prediction paradigm

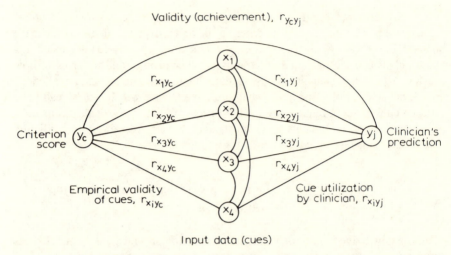

FIG. 11.2.   Clinical prediction paradigm schematized by Brunswik's lens model. (After Hammond, Hursch, and Todd, 1964). Reprinted from J. S. Wiggins (1973) with the permission of Addison-Wesley Publishing Company.

schematized by Brunswik's lens model. We see that the validity of a clinician's prediction is mediated by his or her use of cues, that each cue has an associated empirical validity, and that the degree to which each cue is effective is further mediated by the proper utilization of the cue on the part of the clinician. If evidence of the empirical validity of cues is not available in a clinical judgment study, no meaningful conclusion can be drawn about the general ability of clinicians to draw valid interpretations or predictions.[1] It is quite obvious that if the cues lack empirical validity, it is beyond the bounds of reasonableness to expect that a clinician is capable of divining silk purses out of the sows' ears of zero validity coefficients. I submit that the studies generated over the 20 year span of Mischel's review represent a classic confounding of the influence of information of dubious (or nonexistent) validity with the accuracy of clinical judgment and thus fail to provide necessary and sufficient conditions for the conclusion that clinical judgment lacks validity.

---

[1]The above observations refer to the necessity of employing valid cues to appraise the validity of clinical judgments in a scientific or ideal sense. They are not intended to bear on the normative accuracy of clinical judgments made by practicing clinical psychologists. Goldberg (1959) presumably chose the Bender-Gestalt test because it is (or was) widely used by practitioners, and was widely believed by practitioners to elicit valid data concerning organic brain damage. Goldberg's results certainly raise doubts about the wisdom of these practices and beliefs, but, until positive evidence of the validity of the cues contained in the Bender-Gestalt test becomes available, his results are insufficient for concluding that *clinical judgment* lacks validity when valid cues are present.

SAMPLING THE DOMAIN OF A CONSTRUCT

There is a long-established requirement in psychological testing that has relevance to personality measurement and person perception research—measures should be representative of the domain they are supposed to reflect. A general vocabulary test does not contain only medical terms, a measure of general quantitative aptitude is not properly represented by a test containing only number series. Similarly, a measure of assertiveness is not reflected adequately by a single specific item. Much has been written about this requirement in test theory in the last three decades under headings such as "content validity," the "substantive component of validity," "generalizability theory" and "domain sampling."

What is intuitively obvious in psychological testing is often overlooked in personality research. A single dependent measure or a biased sample is taken as representative of a broad construct like achievement or dominance. Formal procedures are necessary for examining the adequacy of measures from a substantive and domain sampling perspective. This is particularly true in person perception where there is the risk that both the sampling of cues and of outcome predictions will limit validity.

THE RELATION OF RELIABILITY TO VALIDITY

It is one of the cornerstones of classical test theory that reliability is a function of the number of items on a test (Brown, 1910; Spearman, 1910) and that consistency may be assessed by presenting a variety of items and aggregating responses. But when discussing personality, some theorists act as if such formalizations have little applicability outside of a testing situation, and that a response to an isolated situation can be regarded as an indicant of trait consistency, regardless of its reliability. Evidence regarding modest correlations between situations eliciting honest or dishonest behavior (Hartshorne & May, 1928) has thus been interpreted as evidence favoring the specificity of honesty and other alleged personality traits. Most people believe that there is some consistency across situations in the honest or dishonest behavior of persons with whom they come into contact, but are advised by distinguished personality researchers that there is not. But it would be of some interest to apply the theory of Spearman and Brown to this problem. We (Jackson & Paunonen, 1980) had occasion to take the seven-by-seven correlation matrix of honesty behavior in different situations published by Hartshorne and May (1928) and compute the reliability, in particular the Bentler theta reliability coefficient. This was approximately .80. But if we interpret this as a test, we recognize that it contains only seven items. Estimating the reliability of a test of more usual length, namely one of 50 items, the resulting reliability coefficient would be .97. This would imply that the broad personality dimension of honesty is at least as reliable as, for example, the score for intelligence as it has traditionally been estimated by psychological tests.

The same kind of reasoning might be applied to the validity of judgments of personality. Frequently, the behavior being predicted is itself quite unreliable, although this matter is usually overlooked. Mischel (1968) has suggested, for example, that rarely do trait measures correlate with specific behavioral criteria to a degree in excess of .30. The key to Mischel's observation is the term "specific behavioral criteria," which rarely possess reliabilities greater than .30. This can be illustrated by examining the relation between scale and item reliability. The 16-item Order scale on the Personality Research Form has a reliability of .85 as measured by the lower-bound coefficient alpha. But when the average item reliability is estimated by the Spearman-Brown formula, the result is a mere

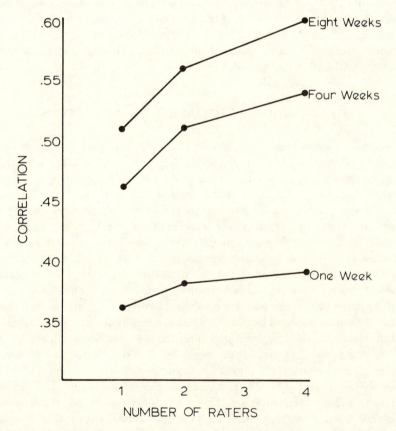

FIG. 11.3.   Validity of dominance ratings as a function of number of raters and weeks of observation (Moskowitz & Schwarz, 1979).

.26. A similar situation obtains when specific behavioral instances are assumed to be reflections of underlying traits. Since it is well known that a validity coefficient cannot exceed the geometric mean of the test and criterion reliability, it is indeed not surprising that most highly specific criteria based on particular behavioral acts cannot be predicted by any means with a validity exceeding .30. However, the situation is quite different when one refers to aggregates. Figure 11.3 contains the results from a study by Moskowitz and Schwarz (1979), who systematically varied the amount of exposure of target individuals over one or more raters and over one or more occasions in terms of the raters' prediction of behavior counts of dominant behaviors. The findings are clear. Validity increases linearly and substantially as the number of raters increases and as the numbers of groups of observations increase. Under these conditions validity coefficients are considerably in excess of .30 and operate in a manner consistent with expectations from classical reliability theory. In light of these observations it seems to me essential in studies of person perception and clinical judgment to estimate reliability or generalizability over their domains of interest. These domains usually involve behavioral exemplars reflecting traits as they are generalizable across samples of behavior, situational contexts or over occasions. In the absence of such data conclusions about the validity or lack of validity of judgments about personality are virtually meaningless. Furthermore, it is entirely appropriate in forming impressions about the validity of clinical judgment to correct for attenuation, and in particular to estimate the degree to which validities would increase if more stable criterion behavior samples had been obtained.

IMPLICIT NOMOLOGICAL NETWORKS AND TRAIT COVARIATION

To Cronbach's distinction between the various components of accuracy, such as stereotype accuracy or differential accuracy, I would like to add the concept of inferential accuracy. What I am suggesting is the use of inferential networks of the perceived joint covariation of psychological traits as a basis of predicting what an individual will or will not do in a given situation. But in order to explicate this process in person perception, it is first necessary to clarify the nature of inferential networks, the manner in which they operate, and the organization of personality to which they are related. We have undertaken a number of studies involving the multivariate classification of personality employing a technique known as modal profile analysis (Jackson & Williams, 1975; Skinner, 1977; Skinner, Jackson, & Hoffmann, 1974) which involves a classification of persons in terms of their profile shapes into a number of discrete bipolar sets. The range of these different types is contained in Figures 11.4 and 11.5 describing respectively the salient scales on Personality Research Form modal profile 2 and the salient scales obtained for the Differential Personality Inventory as represented in eight modal profiles or 16 types. Figure 11.4 depicts a bipolar profile representing two opposite types. The positive pole is characterized by high scores on PRF scales for Affiliation, Exhibition, Impulsivity, Nurturance, and Play, and low scores for Cognitive Structure, Defendence, Harmavoidance, and Order. The negative pole of the modal profile represents the mirror image of the positive pole, with high scores for Cognitive Structure, Defendence, Harmavoi-

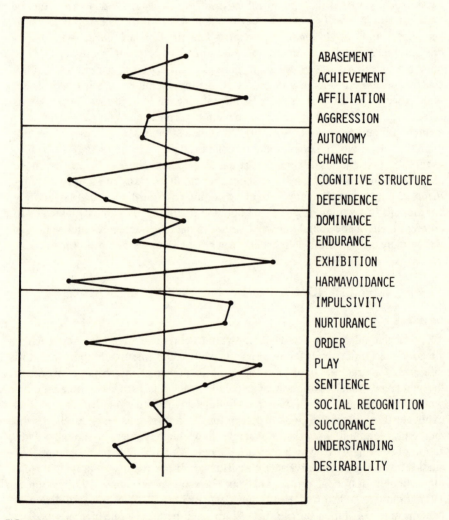

FIG. 11.4. Personality Research Form modal profile number 2, based on 796 male respondents. (Reprinted with permission from an article by S. V. Paunonen and D. N. Jackson published in the *Journal of Personality and Social Psychology,* 1979, 1645–1649. Copyrighted by the American Psychological Association, 1979.)

Profile	Negative pole	Positive pole
I	Defensiveness, repression, shallow affect	Irritability, panic reaction, mood fluctuation
II	Health concern, hypochondriasis, somatic complaints	Rebelliousness, socially deviant attitudes, impulsivity, desocialization
III	Self-depreciation, cynicism, depression, health concern	Perceptual distortion, headache proneness, hostility, irritability
IV	Health concern, sadism, broodiness, ideas of persecution, hostility, familial discord, cynicism	Insomnia, self-depreciation, neurotic disorganization, defensiveness
V	Depression, rebelliousness, familial discord	Insomnia, sadism, health concern, neurotic disorganization
VI	Health concern, impulsivity, mood fluctuation, perceptual distortion	Hostility, sadism, familial discord, desocialization, insomnia
VII	Cynicism, disorganization of thinking, perceptual distortion, rebelliousness	Insomnia, familial discord, health concern, mood fluctuation
VIII	Repression, irritability, cynicism, ideas of persecution, insomnia	Sadism, impulsivity, socially deviant attitudes, somatic complaints, hypochondriasis

FIG. 11.5.   Salient scales for eight Differential Personality Inventory Profiles.

dance, and Order, and low scores for Affiliation, etc. Similarly, Figure 11.5 presents bipolar typal dimensions of psychopathology based on responses to the Differential Personality Inventory. There are eight modal profiles depicted in Figure 11.5 representing 16 types, since a given person might resemble either pole of the bipolar dimension.

Once such modal profiles have been established, it is possible to determine the extent to which any individual resembles each of the types represented by respective poles of each modal profile. Thus, a person whose profile of 28 scales from the Differential Personality Inventory correlates +.90 with a particular modal profile is considered to resemble that type strongly. Classification proceeds by assigning a person to a type based on his or her highest correlation with a modal profile, with an absolute value of .50 as a lower bound for classification. We typically find that from 60–80% of profiles can be classified in a cross replication sample. What is interesting about this analysis is that it is possible to specify, given knowledge of an individual's typal membership, his or her probability of responding in terms of any one of the sets of behaviors constituting exemplars of the traits represented in the profile. That is, given the information that a particular respondent is represented on the positive pole of PRF modal type 2, we can specify that the probability of behaviors relevant to succorance, harmavoidance and abasement will be high, those related to aggression, dominance, endurance, and understanding will be low, while the others will have intermediate probabilities. The hypothesis evaluated in a variety of studies was that in the course of an individual's life he or she comes into contact with a variety of persons represented in each one of these types and becomes aware through such experience of the empirical covariation of behaviors representing different traits within each type. This implies that judges, having developed a degree of familiarity with the actual empirical probabilities between exemplars representing different traits, can generate judged probabilities for new exemplars. Note that some abstraction is required, since the number of exemplars of any particular trait is almost infinite. It is unreasonable to assume that any particular judge would have knowledge of all the possible probabilities between highly specific forms of behavior without recourse to some higher order structure.

An Illustrative Study

My associates and I have conducted a number of studies investigating the applicability of a model for inferential accuracy The essential elements of this model are obtained in Figure 11.6. The horizontal axis represents a series of behavioral outcomes scaled in terms of the likelihood that they will occur given certain limited information about the target person. Groups of individuals given

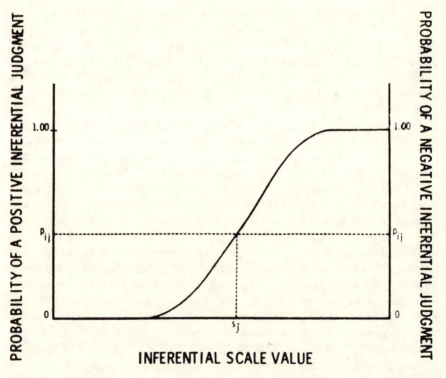

FIG. 11.6. Normal-ogive trace line for Judge I, giving the probability of a positive inferential judgment to a positively-stated item and the probability of a negative inferential judgment to the same item in reversed form at point s_j on the dimension.

certain limited relevant information about a target person would be expected to show a high degree of consensus regarding the judged likelihood that a particular behavior will occur. However, as we shall see, individual judges may vary in two important respects: (a) in terms of their readiness or threshold for attributing as likely or unlikely the range of associated behaviors; and (b) their sensitivity to the general ordering of the probabilities of behavioral relationships as these are independently determined from a group consensus judgment or from the actual correlations between observed behaviors. The first of these sets of individual judge parameters, the threshold, may be estimated by taking the intercept of the monotonically increasing function depicted in Figure 11.6, while sensitivity may be obtained simply by computing the product moment correlation between the judge's prediction that, given certain information, a particular behavioral outcome will occur with a certain likelihood and the observed probability that the behavior will occur under these conditions. Data have been accumulated from a variety of sources indicating that the two parameters for threshold and sensitivity are reliable across targets for individual judges. Of equal interest is the substantial degree of consensus identified for judgments of the likelihood of behavior given limited information about a target.

Reed and Jackson (1975), for example, presented judges with a number of brief personality sketches such as the following:

> Jack Cole has been arrested several times for theft. Usually his crimes have been poorly planned and rather reckless. He says that he does not feel guilty about his behavior and often explains his stealing something by simply saying he wanted it.

The behaviors represented in this brief description were selected to be characteristic of persons high in personality dimensions of *desocialization, impulsivity, rebelliousness* and *socially deviant attitudes*. Other targets included in the study were those constituting clinical depression, preparanoid processes, and a normal target. It is noteworthy that two of the three psychopathological targets are of common types within this population, while a third is a rarer type as determined by studies of multivariate clustering of profiles derived from the 28 scales of the Differential Personality Inventory. Two randomly divided sets of judges separately judged the probability that each of the four targets would endorse a set of 52 personality statements representing two exemplars of each of the 28 DPI scales ranging from Broodiness to Self Depreciation. These statements cover a considerably broader range of psychopathologically-relevant behavior than was contained in the brief descriptions. When the group consensus reliabilities were calculated, the resulting values were .97, .99, .99, and .99 for targets 1 to 4 respectively. The extremely stable group consensus values for all targets imply that judges agree concerning which specific behaviors were associated with particular psychopathological syndromes. The slightly lower reliability (.97) was for a relatively rare type of clinical depression, highlighting processes represented by *cynicism, depression, self depreciation* and *somatic complaints*. The profiles corresponding to the patterning of judgments about the targets were congruent with the pattern for the particular targetted types. In every case the four highest scales in the judgments were the targetted scales. There was substantial evidence in this study for the generalizability of individual judged sensitivity and threshold estimates across the targets. The highest degree of consensually-based individual sensitivities was obtained for the normal target, about which judges probably had more experience, while the lowest was for the target for clinical depression.

One question about the Reed and Jackson results was the degree to which judges used what has been termed a common stereotype of a psychologically disturbed person. It was possible, for example, that judges were simply attributing undesirable characteristics in an undifferentiated fashion to all of the pathologically implicated targets. An examination of the correlations between the average judgments for each of the four targets indicated that such an hypothesis was not supported; the mean correlation among the four targets was .00, indicating the lack of a single common stereotypic judgment. The three pathological targets, although displaying differentiated patterns of predicted behaviors, all showed a slight negative correlation with judged frequency of endorsement of item content, while, of course, the normal target was substantially associated with judged frequency of endorsement of the items in the general population. Further details of results are contained in Reed and Jackson (1975).

There are a number of elements which differentiate the approach described here from that employed in previous research. Notable among these is the use of judgment scales having substantive links to the information provided judges, the evidence for the scales' convergent and discriminant validity, and the use of targets representative of known types in the clinical population. The above study illustrates how high levels of judge reliability are possible when an opportunity is provided judges to employ implicit processes of behavioral and trait inference.

When such opportunities to employ implicit inferential processes are lacking, there is, indeed, little rational basis for expecting consistency in judging personality. Of course, reliability does not necessarily imply accuracy of judgment. We quickly recognized the need for evaluating the fit between predictions by judges and responses by persons being judged.

IMPORTANCE OF BASE RATES AND DESIRABILITY IN PERSON PERCEPTION

It is well known that base rates are an important source of data in predicting the behavior of a target. If, for example, it is known that 80% of undergraduates prefer basketball to ballet, one can attain a substantial degree of accuracy simply by predicting that everyone will attend the basketball game. This, of course, formed the basis for Cronbach's (1955) statistical identification of stereotype accuracy and the invocation of Bayes theorem in clinical prediction by Meehl and Rosen (1955). Similarly, knowledge that most individuals will respond in a desirable way can be used as a basis for behavioral prediction. There is a question of the degree to which these processes are distinguishable from those based on a substantive personality relation based on broad constructs. Several authors have cautioned that it is dangerous to confuse accuracy based upon two distinct kinds of information—that based on content and that based on response frequency.

To illustrate empirically how it might be possible to distinguish substantive traits from base rate and desirability in person perception I would like to refer to a further series of studies by Reed and Jackson (1977) in which a paradigm similar to the one already described was employed with the important addition that the behavior of real target individuals was predicted. Because it was considered to be important to predict representative criterion people, target individuals were selected in such a way that they constituted a homogeneous type characterized by a similar profile shape representing either one of two types of psychopathology or one of two types of personality within the normal range. Thus, for example, seven real persons belonging to the same cluster as that represented by Jack Cole (the personality description presented earlier) were chosen empirically using modal profile analysis from the records of psychiatric patients, prison inmates, and university students. (University student records have provided us with good examples of virtually all pathological types.) Criterion profiles were thus obtained and based on a total of 28 individuals, seven comprising each of the four types. Seven target persons were used to represent each type to increase target reliability and to permit estimation of criterion response probabilities. These were further divided into two profiles for each type by basing the two profile shape estimates upon alternative halves of the items on the Personality Research Form. When divided in this way the criterion profile scale scores yielded reliabilities of .98, .90, .75 or .89, values which were not substantially changed when the population means were removed from the scale scores in the estimate of reliability. Two groups of judges were given brief descriptions of the targets and rated the likelihood of item endorsement of each of the four types. Each set of judges, however, judged different behavioral exemplars. Thus, if the behavioral dimensions reflected in the item content of set A were irrelevant to the item content comprising the behavioral dimensions of set B, there should be no relation between the judgments in the two item sets. Similarly, if Group B was applying a different set of standards in making the judgments from those used by Group A, there should be little or no relation between the two sets of judgments in response probability. Any obtained correlation between the patterning of the judgments obtained by averaging the ratings of Group A predicting responses for items in set A and the patterning of those of Group B judging item content in set B cannot be attributable to the biases of individual judges nor to the specific content of the behavior being judged. The relation between the two constitutes an indication of the reliability across both judges and items of inferential probability ratings. When reliability was estimated in this stringent way, the lowest reliability coefficient obtained was .92, indicating substantial levels of generalizability across judges and item content. These results in my view cannot be attributed to anything but the use of broad conceptual categories in the evaluation of target descriptions and prediction of behaviors.

There is a further question, however, about the accuracy of these predictions. Figure 11.7 contains the relevant data. Since desirability might be operating as a source of response bias, this was partialled out of three of the inferential-criterion correlations. For the Hall profile, one of the two normal targets, desirability comprises a relevant aspect of the target. In other words, in the multivariate classification studies it was found that this target was characterized not only by elevations on certain content scales, but by an elevated score on desirability as well. Judgments of the probability of a response based on item set A correlated with profiles of actual target persons based on item set B (and vice versa) to about the same level as did predictions employing only one set of items. In other

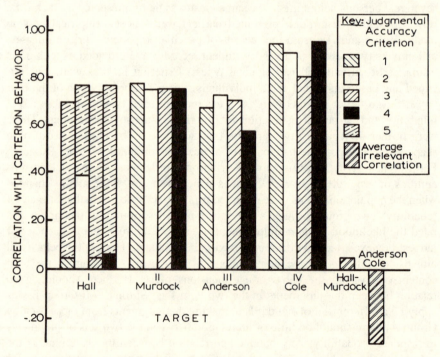

FIG. 11.7. Accuracy correlations between group consensus judgment profiles and criterion profiles: desirability partialed out. (After Reed & Jackson, 1977).

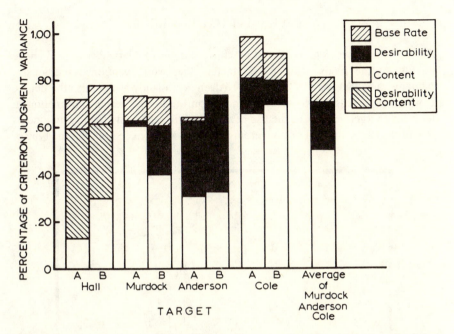

FIG. 11.8.   Percentage of inferential judgment variance attributable uniquely to each of three components, content, base rate, and desirability.

words, a broad conceptualization of behavioral consistencies, beyond the behaviors represented in particular items, would be necessary to account for the obtained results. The level of accuracy obtained was very substantial in relation to the reliabilities of the profiles being predicted. It could not be attributed to a generalized pattern of desirable-undesirable responding, nor could it be attributable to a generalized stereotype (when predictions were employed to predict an irrelevant target, the average accuracy was −.13).

One interesting further finding from the Reed and Jackson study was that it was possible to employ separate data on judged frequency of endorsement and judged desirability to determine the extent to which accuracy might be augmented by incorporating these additional data. When all three sources of information, content, base rate, and desirability, were employed, the multiple correlations for all four targets were above .80 (for the Jack Cole target it was .96) indicating that targets' responses could be accounted for to a substantial degree by the three sources of variance. Figure 11.8 indicates the degree to which each target was predictable by virtue of different sources of judgment variance. It is clear that although content accounts for a major portion of the variance in these kinds of judgments, desirability and base rate information also is important, and varies with the target.

NONVERBAL TRAIT INFERENCE

The question arises as to the extent to which findings of the type described above are due to the kinds of linguistic factors that were mentioned previously. Paunonen and Jackson (1979) therefore designed a study to appraise the degree to which such judgments were contingent on the use of verbal information in describing target persons or the use of verbal rating scales in eliciting judgments about behavior. A verbal or nonverbal format was introduced both in the type of

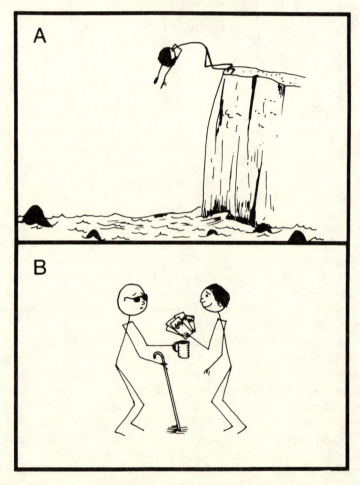

FIG. 11.9.   Sample nonverbal items used by Paunonen and Jackson (1979) depicting thrillseeking behavior (A) and nurturant behavior (B). (Reprinted with permission from an article by S. V. Paunonen and D. N. Jackson published in the *Journal of Personality and Social Psychology,* 1979, 1645–1649. Copyrighted by the American Psychological Association, 1979).

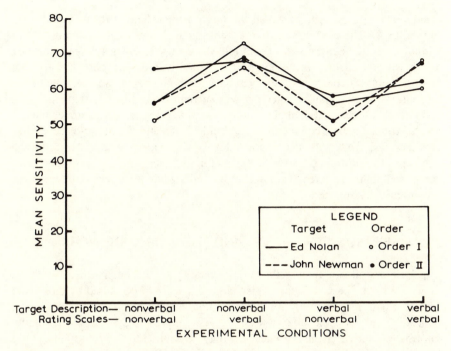

FIG. 11.10. Mean sensitivities for verbally- and nonverbally-based judgments of behavior, by condition. (Reprinted with permission from an article by S. V. Paunonen and D. N. Jackson published in the *Journal of Personality and Social Psychology*, 1979, 1645–1649. Copyrighted by the American Psychological Association, 1979.)

information provided judges about each of two targets and in the rating scales employed. Figure 9 provides an example of two of the types of nonverbal items used. These items were developed to represent each of 17 Personality Research Form scales. The two presented in the figure are those designed to depict behavior relevant to Thrillseeking (the opposite of Harmavoidance) and Nurturance. Judges obtained information about the two targets, each of which was selected to be representative of one of two personality types derived from multivariate classification studies, either in terms of a brief verbal sketch or in terms of a series of drawings presented as characteristic of the target person. In each case the four relevant salient Personality Research Form scales were highlighted. Individuals then made either verbal or nonverbal ratings. Verbal ratings were in terms of probability of endorsement, while nonverbal ratings were in terms of the probability that the individual would engage in the behavior depicted in a drawing. Results indicated very high interjudged reliability for both verbal and nonverbal ratings, ranging from .93 to .99 over the 16 combinations of target, verbal and nonverbal, and order conditions. Accuracies were computed by correlating the patterning of judges' ratings with the factor scores representing the profile characteristic of the type to which the target person belonged, as described in Figure 11.4. These accuracies were substantial, even when desirability was partialled out. Under the latter condition, the group accuracies ranged from .67 to .95 with the median in the low .80's. A multivariate analysis indicated that approximately 80 percent of the variance for both targets was attributable to content, while less than two percent was attributable to the variations in verbal and nonverbal informational and rating conditions. Figure 10 illustrates the degree of similarity between the individual judged sensitivities under these various conditions, suggesting that comparable levels of sensitivity were obtained for the two types of information and rating conditions, even though the verbal items comprised highly selected exemplars of the traits while the nonverbal items were not empirically selected.

PERSON PERCEPTION AND THE WORLD OF WORK

The lack of faith in the reliability and validity of the employment selection interview on the part of psychologists does not seem to be shared by those who are faced with responsibility for making employment decisions. Indeed, authors of leading texts on the interview (e.g., Fear, 1978) suggest how personality information derived from the interview may be applied to decision making. My hunch is that the largely discouraging negative results in studies of the employment interview are attributable to a failure on the part of researchers to undertake conceptual analyses of the links between behavior in the interview and personality constructs, and a further failure to analyze a job in a framework which would permit an evaluation of relevant personality characteristics important for job performance and satisfaction. Because I have confidence that the same processes underlying valid inferential processes in person perception generally should apply to inferences about personality in the context of hiring decisions, I have undertaken a series of studies in collaboration with Andrew Peacock, Mitchell Rothstein and others into the determinants of decisions about the probable effectiveness of persons who manifest the different personality profiles. I would like to present the results from one of these studies, in which university students played the role of employment interviewers. (In other studies [Jackson, Peacock & Smith, 1980] we have employed professional interviewers and have obtained similar results.)

In previous multivariate work the relation between Personality Research Form scales and the occupational scales of the Strong Vocational Interest Blank, Siess and Jackson (1970) identified a number of bipolar dimensions representing the convergence of personality and occupational scales. On one of these dimensions the occupations of Accountant and Office Worker were associated with salient PRF scales for Cognitive Structure and Order. At the opposite pole of this dimension were scales for Clinical Psychologist, Author-Journalist, and Advertiser together with PRF scales for Impulsivity and Change. Similarly, another dimension indicated salients for Engineer and for Physical Scientists, as well as personality scales for Understanding, Achievement, Endurance, and with opposing loadings for need for Social Recognition and Succorrance.

Assuming that the factor structure obtained for vocational interests would also reflect the personalities of persons in the occupation, Rothstein and Jackson (1980) designed a laboratory study in which judges were given the task of appraising the qualifications of candidates who presented personalities congruent with and incongruent with the occupations of Accountant and Engineer. An

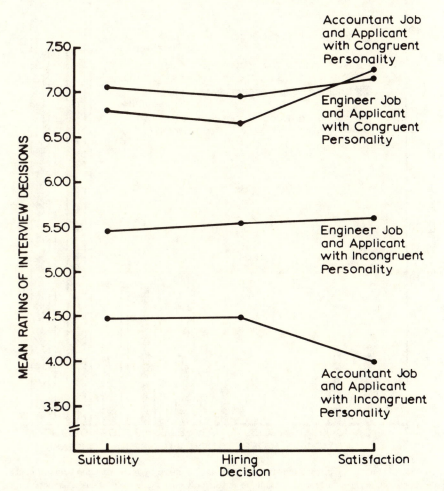

FIG. 11.11.   Mean selection decisions in the Applicant Target x Job Category interaction. (Reprinted with permission from an article by M. Rothstein and D. N. Jackson published in *Journal of Applied Psychology*, 1980, *65*. Copyrighted by the American Psychological Association, 1980.)

experienced interviewer and a university student volunteer served as the persons who helped prepare the tape recordings. Contained within the interviews were spontaneous statements by the candidate. These were actually personality statements drawn from the Personality Research Form. Thus, for the person showing the personality expected of Engineers, statements for the Achievement, Understanding, and the Endurance scales were included with negatively keyed items from the Succorrance and Social Recognition scales. The experimental design

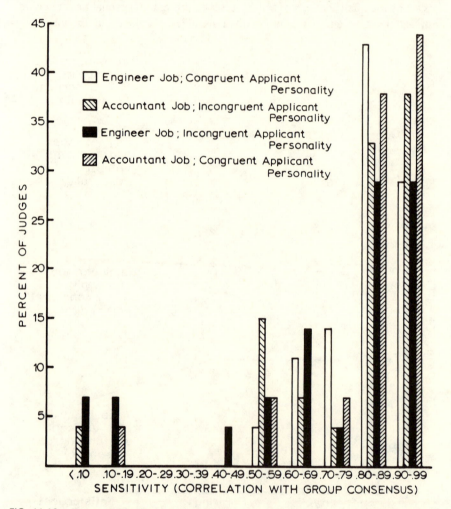

FIG. 11.12. Frequency distributions of sensitivity, as estimated by the correlation between item group consensus scale values for each condition and an individual's judgments of target likelihood of endorsement. (Reprinted with permission from an article by M. Rothstein and D. N. Jackson published in *Journal of Applied Psychology*, 1980, *65*. Copyrighted by the American Psychological Association, 1980.)

involved having judges rate a candidate for either an Engineering or Accounting job, where the candidate presented a personality similar either to an Accountant or an Engineer. In addition two levels of job information were provided raters. Some of the results are obtained in Figure 11.11. It is apparent that candidates with personality characteristics congruent with judges' conception of those required for the job were rated more highly in terms of a hiring decision, expected performance, and judged probable satisfaction.

There is another aspect to the Rothstein study, that is, judges, after listening to a brief excerpt from the employment interview, provided extremely stable aggregate estimates of the patterning of responses to a heterogeneous personality questionnaire. For both the individual with the personality congruent to that of an Accountant, and for the corresponding Engineer personality, group consensus judgments were at reliabilities of .99. However, not every judge was equally sensitive, as Figure 11.12 indicates. It will be noted that whereas the great majority of judges showed very high levels of sensitivity, a few were operating at chance levels. This implies that sensitivity to implicit nomological networks of personality characteristics are not represented equally in the population, and that in choosing clinicians or employment interviewers, selection on the basis of inferential accuracy might be appropriate.

CONCLUSIONS AND OVERVIEW

It is possible to summarize the series of studies of which the above are illustrative in terms of a set of conclusions:

1. average or consensual judgments about personality are very robust in that they generalize across both judges and items;
2. consensual judgments are accurate when assessed with respect to behavior, if the behavior to be predicted is substantively related to the information provided to judges;
3. judges are responsive to three general sources of information about the personality of a target—the *content* of traits implied by behavior, the *desirability* or evaluation of the behavior, and the *base rate* or relative frequency of the behavior. While each contributes significantly, content normally accounts for the largest share of the variance.
4. There are consistent individual differences in ability to judge personality. Such sensitivities generalize across both targets and domains of behavior.

There are converging trends in person perception research of which the above small studies sample (cf., e.g., Cantor & Mischel, 1977, 1979), indicating that cognitive processes, particularly those concerned with conceptions of trait and behavioral organization, play a crucial role. The evidence presented here represents, I hope, an indication of the possibility that conceptions of trait and behavioral organization are substantially tied to empirical probabilities of actual behaviors. Obviously much more research is required to establish the conditions under which this generalization holds, as well as the limits imposed by biases and error in judging the behavior of other people. I am confident, however, that research which attends to the important preconditions for obtaining accuracy in person perception outlined above will bear more diverse fruit than have many past efforts.

ACKNOWLEDGMENT

Supported by Research Grant No. 410-77-0320-R1 from the Social Sciences and Humanities Research Council of Canada.

REFERENCES

Ashton, S. G., & Goldberg, L. R. In response to Jackson's challenge: The comparative validity of personality scales constructed by the external (empirical) strategy and scales developed intuitively by the experts, novices, and laymen. *Journal of Research in Personality*, 1973, *7*, 1–20.

Bandura, A. *Principles of behavior modification*. New York: Holt, Rinehart & Winston, 1969.

Brown, W. Some experimental results in the correlation of mental abilities. *British Journal of Psychology*, 1910, *3*, 296–322.

Campbell, D. T., & Fiske, D. W. Convergent and discriminant validation by the multitrait-multimethod matrix. *Psychological Bulletin*, 1959, *56*, 81–105.

Cantor, N., & Mischel, W. Traits as prototypes: Effects on recognition memory. *Journal of Personality and Social Psychology*, 1977, *35*, 38–48.

Cantor, N., & Mischel, W. Prototypicality and personality: Effects on free recall and personality impressions. *Journal of Research in Personality*, 1979, *13*, 187–205.

Chan, D. W., & Jackson, D. N. Implicit theory of psychopathology. *Multivariate Behavioral Research*, 1979, *14*, 3–19.

Cronbach, L. J. Processes affecting scores on "understanding of others" and assumed similarity. *Psychological Bulletin*, 1955, *52*, 177–193.

Fear, R. A. *The evaluation interview: Predicting job performance in business and industry* (2nd ed.). New York: McGraw-Hill, 1978.

Goldberg, L. R. The effectiveness of clinicians' judgments: The diagnosis of organic brain damage from the Bender-Gestalt Test. *Journal of Consulting Psychology*, 1959, *23*, 25–33.

Goldberg, L. R., & Slovic, P. The importance of test item content: An analysis of a corollary of the deviation hypothesis. *Journal of Counseling Psychology*, 1967, *14*, 462–472.

Hartshorne, H., & May, M. A. *Studies in the nature of character: Vol. 1. Studies in deceit*. New York: Macmillan, 1928.

Holt, R. R. Clinical and statistical prediction: A reformulation and some new data. *Journal of Abnormal and Social Psychology*, 1958, *56*, 1–12.

Jackson, D. N. The dynamics of structured personality tests: 1971. *Psychological Review*, 1971, *78*, 229–248.

Jackson, D. N., Chan, D. W., & Stricker, L. J. Implicit personality theory: Is it illusory? *Journal of Personality*, 1979, *47*, 1–10.

Jackson, D. N., & Paunonen, S. V. Personality structure and assessment. *Annual Review of Psychology,* 1980, *31,* 503–551.

Jackson, D. N., Peacock, A. C., & Smith, J. P. Impressions of personality in the employment interview. *Journal of Personality and Social Psychology,* 1980, *39,* 294–307.

Jackson, D. N., & Williams, D. R. Occupational classification in terms of interest patterns. *Journal of Vocational Behavior,* 1975, *6,* 269–280.

Kahneman, D., & Tversky, A. On the psychology of prediction. *Psychological Review,* 1973, *80,* 237–251.

Lay, C. H., & Jackson, D. N. Analysis of the generality of trait-inferential relationships. *Journal of Personality and Social Psychology,* 1969, *12,* 12–21.

Loevinger, J. Objective tests as instruments of psychological theory. *Psychological Reports,* 1957, *3,* 635–694.

Meehl, P. E. The dynamics of "structured" personality tests. *Journal of Clinical Psychology,* 1945, *1,* 296–303.

Meehl, P. E., & Rosen, A. Antecedent probability and the efficiency of psychometric signs, patterns or cutting scores. *Psychological Bulletin,* 1955, *52,* 194–216.

Mirels, H. L. Implicit personality theory and inferential illusions. *Journal of Personality,* 1976, *44,* 467–487.

Mischel, W. *Personality and assessment.* New York: Wiley, 1968.

Moskowitz, D., & Schwarz, J. C. *In search of better personality measures: The validity of ratings and behavioral observations.* Paper presented at the meeting of the Eastern Psychological Association, Philadelphia, April, 1979.

Mulaik, S. A. Are personality factors raters' conceptual factors? *Journal of Consulting Psychology,* 1964, *28,* 506–511.

Paunonen, S. V., & Jackson, D. N. Nonverbal trait inference. *Journal of Personality and Social Psychology,* 1979, 1645–1649.

Peabody, D. Evaluative and descriptive aspects in personality perception: A reappraisal. *Journal of Personality and Social Psychology,* 1970, *16,* 639–646.

Reed, P., & Jackson, D. N. Clinical judgment of psychopathology: A model for inferential accuracy. *Journal of Abnormal Psychology,* 1975, *84,* 475–482.

Reed, P., & Jackson, D. N. *Personality measurement and inferential accuracy.* Research Bulletin #419, Department of Psychology, The University of Western Ontario, London, Ontario, 1977.

Rothstein, M., & Jackson, D. N. Decision making in the employment interview: An experimental approach. *Journal of Applied Psychology,* 1980, *65,* 271–283.

Schneider, D. J. Implicit personality theory: A review. *Psychological Bulletin,* 1973, *79,* 294–309.

Shweder, R. A. How relevant is an individual difference theory of personality? *Journal of Personality,* 1975, *43,* 455–484.

Siess, T. F., & Jackson, D. N. Vocational interests and personality: An empirical integration. *Journal of Counseling Psychology,* 1970, *17,* 27–35.

Skinner, H. A. "The eyes that fix you: A model for classification research." *Canadian Psychological Review,* 1977, *18,* 142–151.

Skinner, H. A., Jackson, D. N., & Hoffmann, H. Alcoholic personality types: Identification and correlates. *Joornal of Abnormal Psychology,* 1974, *83,* 658–666.

Spearman, C. Correlation calculated with faulty data. *British Journal of Psychology,* 1910, *3,* 271–295.

Stricker, L. J., Jacobs, P. I., & Kogan, N. Trait interrelations in implicit personality theories and questionnaire data. *Journal of Personality and Social Psychology,* 1974, *30,* 198–207.

Walters, H. A., & Jackson, D. N. Group and individual regularities in trait inference: A multidimensional scaling analysis. *Multivariate Behavioral Research,* 1966, *1,* 145–163.

Wiggins, J. S. *Personality and prediction: Principles of personality assessment.* Reading, Mass.: Addison-Wesley, 1973.

COMMENTARY

12 The Attitude-Behavior Relation: Moving Toward a Third Generation of Research

Mark P. Zanna
University of Waterloo

Russell H. Fazio
Indiana University

When psychologists work on a basic problem over several years, it should come as no surprise that there is a progression or pattern to the questions they ask. But how can we conceptualize this development? Although we have no particular expertise as historians of psychology, it seems to us that in social psychological research, at least, three generations of research questions emerge. The first generation question has tended to be something like: Does X affect or relate to Y? That is: Is there an effect?; or: Is there a phenomenon? We would like to call these first generation questions "Is" questions. In the realm of stereotypes, for example, one might ask: Is there a physical attractiveness stereotype? Or: Is there a stereotype for height or for clothing attire? And so on. Assuming that a particular stereotype exists, one might also ask what consequences, or effects, follow from it, which in our terminology is also an "Is" question. For example: Do teachers' social class stereotypes influence the classroom performance of their students? Does the physical attractiveness of a child influence the explanations given for his or her behavior? Or: Does the physical attractiveness of a communicator influence the impact of his or her persuasive message?

After these sorts of first generation questions have been asked (and, presumably, answered), researchers (sometimes quickly, sometimes only after several years) tend to move on to one of two sets of second generation questions. One set of second generation questions tends to ask: Under what (often social) conditions does the effect hold? Or: When, in fact, is there a relation between X and Y? These are basically questions designed to determine the boundary conditions of an effect. We would like to call them "When" questions. Returning to the example of stereotyping, a researcher working on a "When" question might ask: Under what conditions are stereotypes available in memory? Or: Under what

283

conditions do stereotypes actually influence information processing and/or overt behavior? More specifically: When do teacher expectancies actually influence student performance?

The other set of second generation questions tends to ask: What mediates the effect? Or: How can we characterize the psychological process(es) which mediate(s) the phenomenon of interest? These are basically questions of mediation, or process, which we would like to call "How" questions. For example: How do stereotypes influence information processing and/or overt behavior? Or, more specifically: How do teacher expectancies influence student performance?

Interestingly, it appears that in most areas of research both sets of questions are rarely asked simultaneously. Instead, for reasons unknown to us, in some areas only the "How" set of questions is asked in the second generation, while the "When" set, if asked at all, tends to be asked in a third generation of research. In other research domains, however, only "When" questions appear to be asked. For example, Ellsworth (1978) has noted that studies of interpersonal expectancy effects have exclusively asked: Does the phenomenon exist? and, if so, How is it mediated? After 345 studies (cf., Rosenthal & Rubin, 1978), Ellsworth reasonably argues that it is time to begin asking (in this instance) third-generation "When" questions, i.e.: Under what conditions will teachers' expectations influence the way they behave toward their pupils? Would, for example, teachers be more likely to act on their expectations when stressed or, in some other way, aroused (cf., Whitehead, Holmes & Zanna, 1978)?

The "When" and "How" questions are, of course, linked inextricably. Knowledge of the conditions under which some phenomenon occurs is potentially informative with regard to the process by which the phenomenon occurs. Likewise, understanding of the underlying process can serve both to identify the conditions under which the effect occurs and to explain why those conditions are critical determinants of the effect. Furthermore, as we shall see shortly, knowledge of the process has the potential of integrating within a single conceptual framework a "catalog" of conditions or variables that have been identified as determinants of the effect. In other words, addressing a "How" question may serve to integrate conceptually a host of previously unrelated answers to the "When" question.

Given this interpretive framework, how can we characterize the development of research on the attitude-behavior relation, its current state, and, possibly, its future direction? In our view, research on this problem began with the question: Is there a relation between attitudes and behavior? While such a relation was questioned from the beginning (e.g., LaPiere, 1934), Fazio and Zanna (1981) have recently noted that, in fact, "research has revealed everything from findings of no relation between attitudes and behavior whatsoever . . . to the nearly perfect relation observed in the context of voting behavior" (p. 164). These authors go on to recommend:

Rather than asking whether attitudes relate to behavior, we have to ask "Under what conditions do what kinds of attitudes of what kinds of individuals predict what kinds of behavior?" Instead of assessing whether a given correlation coefficient between an attitude and a behavior measure is statistically significant and/or practically substantial, we need to treat the strength of the attitude-behavior relation as we would treat virtually any other dependent variable and determine what factors affect it (p. 165).

Clearly, the suggestion is that it is more useful to begin asking, in this instance, second-generation "When" questions, i.e.: When is there a relation between attitudes and behavior? In our view, "When" questions have, in fact, dominated the recent, second generation of research in this field. For example, in their recent chapter, Fazio and Zanna (1981) reviewed a program of research which focused on the kinds of attitudes that do relate to behavior and demonstrated that attitudes based upon direct behavioral experience with the attitude object are more predictive of later behavior than are attitudes formed in more indirect ways.

Additional attitudinal qualities known to relate to the strength of the attitude-behavior relation include the confidence with which the attitude is held (Fazio & Zanna, 1978; Sample & Warland, 1973), how clear and well-defined the attitude is, as operationalized by the width of the latitude of rejection (Fazio & Zanna, 1978; Sherif, Kelly, Rodgers, Sarup, & Tittler, 1973), the temporal stability of the attitude (Schwartz, 1978) and the degree of consistency between affective and cognitive components of an attitude (Norman, 1975). Each of the cases focuses upon the "When" question in the sense that they concern the "kinds of attitudes" that will best predict later behavior.

Many of the authors represented in the present volume can also be characterized as contributing to the enterprise of determining the boundary conditions for the attitude-behavior relation. The same is true of those authors in the present volume who have focused on the personality-behavior relation. We briefly characterize this personality research and its focus upon "Is" and "When" questions. Then we consider the contributions concerned with attitudes from the same perspective. Finally, some recent research by Fazio and his associates that addresses the "How" question is presented.

The "Is" and "When" of the Personality-Behavior Relation

Several authors in the present volume have exclusively focused on the personality-behavior relation. For the most part, these authors, too, seem to be concerned primarily with the second generation question of "When." (The exception would seem to be Jackson who makes the case that if a number of preconditions pertaining to measurement are met, accurate clinical judgment as well as reliable and valid person perception and behavioral prediction are the rule.)

One main theme, proposed by interaction psychology (see Endler, this volume, for an excellent review of this field), is that both person factors and situation factors need to be considered in predicting behavior. Bem (this volume), for example, reviews a program of research that has employed variations of his so-called template-matching technique, which, in his words, is "a general tool for predicting behavior of particular persons in particular situations" (p. 173).

Mischel and Peake (this volume) also subscribe to the belief that "we need to understand why . . . obtained coherences emerge and when and why expected coherences do not" (p. 196). Nevertheless, these authors present two recent studies which suggest that neither Bem's "template-matching" solution (Bem & Funder, 1978) nor Epstein's "reliability" solution (Epstein, 1979) is sufficient to resolve the consistency debate in this area. In one study, these authors demonstrated that similar Q-sort portraits across two situations was not sufficient to yield high consistency; in the other study, they showed that while reliable measurement certainly seems to aid in establishing some coherence, "aggregating observations over occasions does not necessarily lead to high cross-situational consistency" (p. 195).

Although many issues concerning the viability of various proposals need to be resolved, it is clear that the personality field is progressing in a fashion parallel to what we noted concerning the attitude field. There exists the "Is" question, which was addressed by Mischel's early work (1968) and also by Epstein (1979). More recently, the focus has been on the "When" question as characterized, for example, by Bem's attempts to identify classes of individuals for whom traits might be predictive of behavior and by the interactional perspective described by Endler (this volume).

The "Is" and "When" of the Attitude-Behavior Relation

We have already considered somewhat the progression of research on attitude-behavior consistency from "Is" to "When" questions. Let us now turn our attention to the contributions in this volume that are relevant to this issue.

Ajzen (this volume) summarizes research that indicates that the attitude-behavior relation is enhanced by employing attitude and behavior measures of equivalent levels of specificity. For example, specific, or single-act, behaviors are best predicted by specific attitudes toward the act. In contrast, general attitudes have been found to be predictive of general behavioral patterns across multiple-acts. This improved predictability of general attitudes with multiple-act criteria may derive not only from increased reliability of the behavior measure, but increased validity as well. In Ajzen's words:

Just as "attitude toward an object" refers to a general evaluation predisposition, "behavior toward the object" stands for a general behavioral tendency. Any single action will typically be a poor representative, and hence an imperfect indicant, of this general behavioral trend (p. 5).

Thus, the attitude-behavior relation seems to be moderated by the amount of equivalence between the attitude and behavior measures. People do seem more likely to behave in accordance with their attitudes, provided one obtains appropriate measures of behavior. Ajzen also proposes (and reviews some supporting evidence) that the personality-behavior is enhanced by employing measures of equivalent levels of specificity.[1]

Interestingly, authors of three chapters in this volume present evidence which suggests that various personality or individual difference factors moderate the attitude-behavior (and/or the personality-behavior) relation. Wicklund (this volume), for example, reviews research indicating that individuals high in private self-consciousness (i.e., high in chronic self-focused attention) tend to display greater attitude-behavior consistency than individuals low in this disposition. Snyder (this volume) reviews evidence which suggests that low self-monitors (i.e., individuals who report that their behavior is guided largely by relevant inner states rather than by situational forces) behave more consistently with their attitudes than high self-monitors. Finally, Zanna and Olson (this volume) present findings from a program of research that identified two individual difference variables that moderate the critical, prior behavior-attitude link (cf., Fazio & Zanna, 1981), and hence moderate the attitude-behavior relation. In three studies these authors demonstrated that only low self-monitors (i.e., those individuals who, in general, infer attitudes from prior behavior) with relatively invariant prior behaviors toward the attitude object (i.e., those individuals for whom, in the specific instance, a clear attitudinal inference is possible) tended to behave consistently with their attitudes.[2] Each of the above three chapters can be characterized as concerned with the question of "When do attitudes predict behavior?" wherein the focus is upon classes of individuals who can be expected to display attitude-behavior consistency.

In an innovative chapter, Schlegel and DiTecco (this volume) hypothesize (and demonstrate) that attitudes based upon a great deal of experience with the attitude object, in fact, do less well in predicting behavior. This seems to be due to the fact that a single affective response to the attitude object less capably

---

[1]While we have characterized research by Ajzen and his colleagues as second generational, the heavy emphasis on issues of measurement could lead one to classify this research as first generation in nature.

[2]Interestingly, the findings reported by Zanna and Olson (this volume) would seem to qualify both Snyder's (this volume) findings for self-monitoring as well as Bem and Allen's (1974) findings for behavioral variability, at least within the attitudinal domain.

summarizes or integrates the more differentiated belief structures that result from increasing experience with the attitude object. Besides demonstrating an important boundary condition on the attitude-behavior relation, Schlegel and DiTecco have developed a potentially important methodology (and set of measures) that, in our view, ought to stimulate research on cognitive or belief structures. For example, their "paradigm" will allow researchers in the area of impression formation to begin asking the question of whether (and/or the conditions under which) our impressions of other persons are, in fact, primarily evaluative in nature.

Four authors explore the psychological connection between attitudes and behavior. Salancik (this volume), for example, argues that because "an attitude (or any behavior used to infer an attitude) has no necessary implications for behavior, at least for any particular behavior" (p. 55), one should not be surprised by the lack of consistency between an attitude and a particular behavior. Salancik then goes on to report an intriguing program of research which indicates that it is possible to create covariations between attitudes and behavior by altering the implicational context of the behavior. In one study the correlation between enjoying a course and recommending it was dramatically increased when the context was changed from a sociological project to that of practical advice, presumably because the social implications of evaluations are more salient when giving advice. Salancik summarizes his research by proposing that a person should behave consistently with his or her attitudes to the extent that "attitudes and their credible implications are made salient to a person facing a relevant choice" (p. 71).

Wicklund (this volume) and Snyder (this volume) explore the psychological connection between attitudes (and, for that matter, personality traits) and behavior from different perspectives. Wicklund reviews a program of research that suggests the psychological state of the individual is critical in moderating the attitude-behavior relation (cf., Abelson, this volume). Specifically, Wicklund reviews evidence which indicates that consistency between self-report and behavior increases when individuals are made to focus increasingly on themselves. Presumably, "only then is the person moved to steer the self-report in the direction of characteristic behavior, or analogously, to steer behavior in the direction of self-reported attitudes and values" (p. 169). So, for example, in a typical study, the consistency between self-reported sociability and how sociably subjects actually behaved in a dyadic interaction was greatly enhanced when the self-reports were completed under a self-focus-engendering situation (Pryor, Gibbons, Wicklund, Fazio & Hood, 1977).

Snyder, from a similar perspective, reviews a program of research which indicates that some social settings or interaction contexts promote a "believing means doing" orientation, and hence promote attitude-behavior consistency. In one experiment, for example, the simple act of inducing individuals "to reflect upon (their) attitudes' potential applicability to their current situation before embarking on any course of action" (p. 110) greatly enhanced the attitude-behavior relation.

Finally, Abelson (this volume) discusses the psychological relation between attitudes and behavior in three different situational contexts—individuated, scripted, and deindividuated. Generalizing from Wicklund and Snyder, among others, Abelson first proposes that the presence of individuating conditions, i.e., conditions which increase one's awareness of one's essential self-orientations, are necessary for substantial correlations between attitudes and behavior. In contrast, when one's behavior is scripted (Abelson, 1981), underlying differences between people are suppressed and the correlation between attitudes and behavior ought to be (as is often the case) minimal (cf., Wicklund, this volume). Finally, in a fascinating analysis, which is definitely worthy of future research effort, Abelson speculates that deindividuated behaviors, e.g., mass protests, rioting, are best predicted by "symbolic" attitudes, i.e., attitudes in which "the manifest issue stands in for a more 'real' issue" (p. 140; cf., Sears & McConahay, 1973).

Thus, considerable progress has been made in specifying the attitudinal qualities, personality factors, and situational variables which affect the strength of the attitude-behavior relation (see also the review by Fazio & Zanna, 1981).

The "How" Question

In our view, it is now time to turn to a third-generational question of "How." Despite what is now a voluminous literature on the attitude-behavior relation, little attention has been paid to the issue of how attitudes "guide" or "influence" behavior. Happily, some of the authors in this volume are beginning to do just that. Snyder (this volume), for example, explicitly asks what psychological processes join attitudes to behavior, and proposes two principles, the availability and the relevance principle, to account for the mediation of the attitude-behavior relation. The availability principle suggests that "only individuals who know what they believe and who know the implications of what they believe for what they do are in a position to put their beliefs into practice" (p. 113). The relevance principle suggests that "only when individuals explicitly define their attitudes as relevant and appropriate guides to action (can they) be expected to turn to their general attitudinal orientations for guidance in making their behavioral choices" (p. 114). To the extent, then, that deficits in availability and/or relevance of attitudes account for the lack of correspondence between attitudes and behavior, Snyder proposes (and presents supporting evidence) that circumstances that either increase the "availability of knowledge of one's general attitudes and the specific behavioral implications of one's viewpoints" (p. 113) or, even more importantly, increase the "relevance of attitudes as guides to action" (p. 114) promote attitude-behavior consistency.

Fazio and his colleagues have also begun to investigate the mediation of the attitude-behavior relation. It is to this more recent program of research that we now turn. The research stems from the findings described earlier that attitudes based upon direct behavioral experience with the attitude object are more predictive of later behavior than are attitudes based upon indirect nonbehavioral experience (Fazio & Zanna, 1981). In considering the issue of why this effect occurs, it became obvious that a satisfactory answer could result only from a greater understanding of the "How" question. If we understood the process by which attitudes "guide" behavior, then it would be much easier to understand why certain classes of attitudes do so more than other kinds of attitudes.

Consequently, Fazio and his colleagues have been concerned with the development of a process model of the attitude-behavior relation (Fazio, Powell & Herr, 1982). The proposed model focuses upon what has been termed the object appraisal function of attitudes. Theorists have considered one of the major functions served by attitudes to be that of organizing and structuring a rather chaotic universe of objects (Katz, 1960; Smith, Bruner, & White, 1956). An attitude is thought to provide "a ready aid in 'sizing up' objects and events in the environment" (Smith et al., 1956, p. 41).

As this object appraisal function of attitudes implies, attitudes have been shown empirically to guide information processing. In fact, supportive evidence is found in literature stemming from the "New Look" movement (Bruner, 1957; Bruner & Goodman, 1947; Lambert, Solomon & Watson, 1949), in the social perception literature (e.g., Hastorf & Cantril, 1954; Regan, Straus, & Fazio, 1974) and in the attitude literature (e.g., Lingle & Ostrom, 1980; Lord, Ross & Lepper, 1979; Proshansky, 1943). Just as Smith et al. (1956) proposed, then, attitudes appear to serve as convenient and useful summaries by which we "size up" objects in the environment.

The model proposed by Fazio et al. (1982) links this evidence regarding an attitude-perception relation with what has been in the past a needlessly separate research endeavor regarding the attitude-behavior relation. Recognition of the relevance of the object appraisal function allowed the investigators to elucidate a step-by-step process by which attitudes might "guide" behavior. The model assumes that an individual's social behavior is determined by his or her immediate perceptions of the attitude object—an assumption that seems warranted on the basis of accumulating evidence concerning social interaction that shows a perceiver's behavior toward a target person to be influenced by his or her immediate perceptions of that target person (Darley & Fazio, 1980; Snyder & Swann, 1978; Snyder, Tanke, & Berscheid, 1977; Word, Zanna, & Cooper, 1974). As a specific example, consider Kelley's (1950) classic experiment in which students were led to believe that a guest instructor was either a "warm" or "cold" person. Those students with the "warm" expectation tended to participate in the class discussion led by the guest instructor to a greater extent than did those with the "cold" expectation.

Given this assumption, the question, in terms of attitudes "guiding" behavior, centers upon the degree to which the attitude will influence these immediate perceptions. The object appraisal function and the research cited earlier concerning selective perception (i.e., the existence of an attitude-perception relation) suggest that it will, provided that the attitude has been accessed from memory upon the individual's encountering the attitude object. Attitude accessibility, then, may be an important and central factor in the attitude-to-behavior process. Accessibility simply refers to the likelihood or readiness with which a construct will be retrieved from memory (cf. Bruner, 1957; Higgins & King, 1980; Wyer & Srull, 1980). In the present case, the concern is with the likelihood that the attitude will be retrieved upon the individual's observation of the attitude object. Unless the individual does access his or her attitude and does consider the object in evaluative terms, the proposed model suggests that selective perception of the object will not occur. As a result, the individual's immediate perceptions of the object will not be based upon the attitude and will prompt behavior that is not necessarily congruent with the attitude.

To summarize, Fazio et al. (1982) propose that a process model of attitude-behavior consistency must involve the following steps. (1) Upon observation of the attitude object, one's attitude must be accessed from memory. That is, the particular evaluative categories with which one has associated the object must become salient. (2) These evaluations are apt, through a process of selective perception, to "color" one's perception of the object in the immediate situation. For example, having a negative attitude toward a target person, one is likely to closely attend to any unpleasant mannerisms exhibited by that person and to interpret ambiguous comments or behaviors in a negative manner. (3) These immediate perceptions, filtered as they are through the attitude, then influence the individual's behavioral response. Having "perceived" hostility in the person with whom one is interacting, one responds in a hostile manner. The end result is behavior consistent with the attitude that initiated and "guided" the entire process.

To date, research on this model has concentrated on the first step, accessibility of the attitude from memory. What factors might determine whether one's attitude is accessed upon observation of the attitude object? Snyder's research (this volume) suggests that activation may occur as a result of some situational cue that defines attitudes as relevant to the immediate situation. While not denying the importance of situational cues, Fazio and his colleagues have been more concerned with accessing of attitudes upon observation of the attitude object without the benefit of prompting from situational cues. From this perspective, one possible determinant of attitude accessibility, noted by Fazio, Chen, McDonel and Sherman (in press), is suggested by the very definition of attitude. Although numerous definitions have appeared in the literature, all possess one common feature. An attitude is typically considered to involve categorization of an object along an evaluative dimension. Fazio et al. (in press) suggest viewing an attitude as an association between a given object and a given evaluation and note that the strength of this object-evaluation association can vary. Furthermore, the strength of this association may determine the accessibility of the attitude from memory. If strongly associated with the object, the evaluation may be accessed easily; if only weakly associated, accessing the evaluation may be much more difficult.

In two experiments, the investigators directly manipulated the strength of the object-evaluation association. Subjects were introduced to a set of intellectual puzzles by observing a videotape of an individual working with each type of puzzle. All subjects then evaluated the interest value of each puzzle type. In order to strengthen the object-evaluation association, the experimenter, using an appropriate ruse, asked half the subjects to copy their ratings onto two additional forms. The experimenter remarked that the additional forms were for her professor and the computer keypuncher and asked the subject to help her out by copying his/her original ratings onto the forms. Since each form was distinct from the original and also involved a different ordering of the five puzzle types, the subject was forced to find a given puzzle type and its associated rating on the original and to then indicate that rating in the appropriate place on each of the other two forms. Essentially, then, these subjects were induced to repeatedly note, and express, their evaluation of each puzzle type. This simple manipulation was found to have a profound effect upon attitude accessibility. Accessibility was operationally measured by the latency with which subjects could respond to inquiries about their attitudes. Subjects were presented with a series of slides, each of which listed the name of a puzzle type followed by an evaluative adjective. The subjects' task was to press a "Yes" or a "No" control button to indicate whether the adjective was descriptive of their attitudes toward the puzzle type. Response times were significantly faster in the Repeated Expression condition than in the Single Expression condition. Hence, it appears that the strength of the object-evaluation association does determine attitude accessibility.

A second experiment employing the repeated expression manipulation revealed that the strength of the object-evaluation association exerts an impact upon attitude-behavior consistency. When provided with a "free-play" opportunity during which they could work on any of the puzzle types that they had earlier evaluated, subjects in the Repeated Expression condition were observed to have behaved more consistently with their attitudes than did subjects in the Single Expression condition. This finding is exactly what would be predicted from the notion that attitude accessibility is a central factor in the attitude-to-behavior process. Any variable that enhances attitude accessibility, as does repeated attitudinal expression, will promote attitude-behavior consistency. In sum, these two experiments provide us with some confidence concerning the utility of a conceptual framework that views attitudes as object-evaluation associations and that emphasizes the strength of this association as a key determinant of attitude accessibility.

It was mentioned earlier that one of the assets of addressing a "How" question is that it may serve to explain how and why variables that have been identified on the basis of "When" research exert their impact. In the present context, consideration of the issue of attitude accessibility may aid our understanding of why some variables determine attitude-behavior consistency. As indicated earlier, one such determinant is the manner of attitude formation. Attitudes formed through direct behavioral experience with the attitude object have been found to be more predictive of later behavior than attitudes based upon indirect, nonbehavioral experience (see Fazio & Zanna, 1981, for a review). Using the same response-time methodology described above and the standard manipulation of the manner of attitude formation, Fazio et al. (in press) found that the manner of attitude formation affected attitude accessibility. Half the subjects formed their attitudes toward a set of intellectual puzzles after being provided with an opportunity to work examples of each puzzle type (direct experience). The other subjects formed attitudes after hearing a description and seeing examples of each type (indirect experience). The response-time data revealed that subjects in the Direct Experience condition were able to respond more quickly to inquiries about their attitudes than were subjects in the Indirect Experience condition.

Fazio et al. (in press) discussed this finding of differential accessibility as a function of the manner of attitude formation in relation to Bem's self-perception theory (1972). In accord with the core assumption of that theory, the investigators speculated that individuals find behavior toward an object to be a very indicative reflection of their evaluation of the object, and hence, can develop a strong, and easily accessible, association between the object and the evaluation following direct, behavioral experience. This particular explanation is in need of further research. However, regardless of the precise mechanism by which direct behavioral experience enhances attitude accessibility, the observation that direct and indirect experience attitudes differ in their accessibility has important implications for attitude-behavior consistency. This differential accessibility would appear to explain why attitudes based upon direct versus indirect experience differ in the degree to which they prompt attitudinally consistent behavior. Direct experience appears to lead to the formation of an attitude that involves a strong object-evaluation association and hence is easily accessible. Consequently, the object is considered in evaluative terms. Following indirect experience, on the other hand, the association between the object and the evaluation may not be well-formed and the attitude, hence, is less accessible and less likely to "guide" behavior.

On the basis of this research, it appears that a process approach can be quite fruitful. Attitude accessibility appears to exert a key role in the process by which attitudes "guide" behavior. Furthermore, the research suggests that any variable that strengthens the object-evaluation association has a corresponding impact upon attitude accessibility and attitude-behavior consistency. Finally, the approach has served to suggest why one particular variable (the manner of attitude formation) moderates the attitude-behavior relation.

Despite this success, the research suffers from one serious drawback at a methodological level. In order to assess accessibility, it was necessary to have the subjects respond to inquiries about their attitudes. In effect, subjects were asked what their attitudes were. Yet in terms of the question posed earlier with regard to the process linking attitudes and behavior, the critical issue is whether individuals access their attitudes upon mere observation of the attitude object, not upon direct inquiry about the object. It appears plausible to assume, as Fazio et al. did, that latency of response to an attitudinal inquiry would covary with the likelihood of accessing the attitude upon encountering the object. That is, one would think that an individual who displays accessibility in the sense of quickly responding to an attitudinal inquiry would also be relatively likely to access the attitude without any prompting whatsoever upon mere observation of the object. In the former case, the stronger the object-evaluation association, the more quickly the person can respond to an attitudinal inquiry; in the latter case, the stronger the object-evaluation association, the more likely it may be that the evaluation ''comes to mind'' upon perceiving the attitude object. No matter how plausible, the issue of whether the strength of the object-evaluation association determines the likelihood of accessing one's attitude upon mere observation remains untested.

Consequently, Fazio et al. (1982) sought to arrive at a methodology that would permit one to draw conclusions about attitude accessibility without requiring the investigators to question the individual directly about his or her attitude. Here, a basic principle of social cognition appeared very useful. It has been demonstrated that once a category has been activated, the accessibility of that category is temporarily increased, enhancing the likelihood that the category will be applied to the interpretation of a new object (e.g., Higgins, Rholes, & Jones, 1977; Srull & Wyer, 1979). For example, Higgins et al. (1977) exposed subjects to various personality trait terms and examined whether this ''priming'' affected subsequent judgments of a target person in an ostensibly separate second experiment. Given that the primed trait terms were applicable to the description provided of the target person's behavior, they exerted an impact upon judgments of the person. Those subjects who had been primed with positive traits perceived the stimulus person as more desirable than those who had been primed with negative traits. Apparently, once the category has been primed via the exposure to the specific trait terms, the category was highly accessible and was likely to be applied to the interpretation of the target's behavior.

Fazio et al. (1982) employed this principle and methodology to examine whether at least some sorts of attitudes are accessed upon mere observation of the attitude object. It should be possible to infer from individuals' interpretation of some new information whether positive or negative categories had been activated by earlier exposure to an attitude object. If so, those interpretations should be consistent with the individual's evaluation of the attitude object. That is, if the object is positively valued and if upon mere observation of the object the individual accessed his or her attitude, then that positive category has been "primed." Hence, it should be possible to ascertain from the individual's interpretation of some newly provided, ambiguous information whether the evaluation that the individual associates with the object was activated by exposure to the object. In this case, a relatively positive interpretation would allow one to infer that the positive evaluation of the attitude object must have been activated. Obviously, the same reasoning would suggest that a relatively negative judgment would be indicative of the individual's having accessed a negative attitude toward the object upon mere observation of the object.

However, Fazio et al. (1982) predicted that such activation upon mere observation would be more likely in the case of attitudes involving a strong object-evaluation association. To be more specific, such effects should be stronger when the attitude is based upon direct experience or has been repeatedly expressed than when the attitude is based upon indirect experience and has been expressed only once. Recall that, on the basis of the latency of response to attitudinal inquiries, it appears that attitude formation through direct experience and repeated attitudinal expression enhance attitude accessibility relative to the accessibility observed following attitude formation through indirect experience.

The experimental procedure was quite complex and will only be sketched briefly here. It involved three phases, which the subject was led to believe formed three ostensibly unrelated experiments. During the initial phase of the experiment, subjects were exposed to the usual set of puzzles and three conditions were established. In the Direct Experience condition, subjects worked example puzzles and then rated the interest value of the puzzle types. In the Indirect Experience condition, subjects heard descriptions of the puzzle types and saw the very same sample puzzles with the solutions clearly indicated. These subjects then completed the interest scale. In the Repeated Expression condition, subjects again received indirect experience and completed the scale. In addition, these subjects were induced to express their attitudes repeatedly in the same manner as in the previous experiment concerning repeated expression. This design permitted the experimenters to make the usual comparison of direct to indirect experience and, in addition, to examine the effects of repeated attitudinal expression by comparing indirect experience followed by repeated expression to indirect experience followed by a single expression. Once the manipulation had been accomplished, the second phase of the experiment began, under the control of a second experimenter in a different room. This experimenter had been provided with two pieces of information by the first experimenter—the name of the puzzle type that the subject had evaluated most positively and the one that the subject had rated most negatively. The second experimenter randomly assigned the subject to a Positive or a Negative Valence condition, which determined which of the two puzzles the subject would be exposed to during the priming phase of the experiment. During this phase the subject performed the same sort of task that occurred in the Higgins et al. (1977) experiment. The subject was told that pairs of slides would be presented in a series of trials. The first slide of each pair simply presented a picture along with the name of the object depicted in the picture. The second presented a slide with a colored background and a color name printed on the background. The subject was instructed to identify the background color aloud as quickly as possible and then to recite the "memory" word that had appeared on the first slide of the pair. There were 10 such pairs of slides and the entire set was presented twice. In 9 of the pairs, the memory object was a neutral filler (e.g., umbrella, phone). For 1 of the pairs (always the 7th one), however, the memory slide presented either the most positively or the most negatively valued puzzle type. Once the trials had been completed, the subject was "debriefed," thanked, and dismissed.

However, as the subject was leaving, the experimenter stopped him/her and casually mentioned that another experimenter in the laboratory was conducting some research. Although she could not be here today, she had asked the experimenter to invite subjects to participate in her experiment. When the subject agreed to participate, as all subjects did, the experimenter simply directed the subject to the other room and then left the subject alone. In the other room, the subject found a letter from the researcher. The letter explained that she was doing some research on person perception and that frequently she described the behavior of a previous subject in the laboratory to other subjects and asked them to interpret the behavior. The letter continued by asking the subject to read the short description that appeared on a sheet on the table and then to complete the attached questionnaire. The description portrayed the behavior of a high school student named Ted, who had recently been a subject in the lab. After he had finished his experiment, he had been asked to help out with another experiment. He had agreed to participate. What was deliberately left very ambiguous was why Ted had agreed to participate. One possibility was that he was interested in the experimental task, which was not described to the subject, but had been described to Ted. Another was that he agreed simply because he had nothing to do for a half-hour before his ride home was to arrive. A third possibility was that he agreed in order to earn the promised payment of one dollar for each 10 minutes he spent working on the task.

Subjects responded in an open-ended fashion to the question "Why did Ted agree to participate in the experimental task?" Then subjects responded to three questionnaire items. "To what extent did Ted agree to participate in order to earn the extra money?" ". . . to have something to do while waiting to his ride?" ". . . because he liked and was interested in the experimental task?"

The open-ended responses were rated by two judges, blind to experimental condition, for the extent to which they implied that Ted acted out of interest in the task. These data and the responses to the questionnaire scales were combined to form a single index (standardized values of the average of the two judges'

TABLE 12.1
Mean Attribution Scores

Condition	Valence of Attitude Objects	
	Positive	Negative
Direct Experience	−.309	.285
Indirect Experience	.063	−.234
Repeated Expression	−.170	.366

Note: More positive scores indicate a stronger attribution to Ted's participating because of the money or the wait. More negative scores reflect a stronger attribution to Ted's interest in the task. Taken from Fazio, Powell, and Herr (1982).

ratings plus standardized values of the difference between the score on the "interest" scale and the average score on the "money" and "wait" scales). The data are presented in Table 12.1. The more negative the score, the stronger the attribution to Ted's interest in the task. More positive scores reflect a stronger attribution to the money or the wait.

An interactive contrast of valence condition by direct versus indirect experience revealed a statistically significant effect. Likewise, a contrast involving repeated expression versus indirect experience was significant. Within both the Direct Experience and the Repeated Expression conditions, subjects primed with a positively valued object made a significantly stronger attribution to Ted's interest in the task than did subjects primed with a negatively valued object.

The findings strongly support the proposed conceptualization. Attitudes can be accessed as a consequence of mere observation of the attitude object. However, such activation occurs only to the extent that the attitude is characterized by a relatively strong object-evaluation association. Subjects who formed their attitudes on the basis of indirect experience and who did not strengthen the associations by expressing repeatedly their attitudes failed to display any evidence of having accessed the evaluation upon exposure to the attitude object. Only when the object-evaluation association was quite strong because the person had expressed the association repeatedly or because the person had formed the attitude through direct behavioral experience with the object was there an indication that the evaluation had been accessed spontaneously upon observation of the object.

What is critical is that the evidence for subjects having accessed their attitudes was found in a situation in which the subject was merely exposed to the attitude object. The subject was never asked during the "color perception" experiment to consider his or her attitude. Nor was it to the subject's advantage to do so in the immediate situation, for the subject's task simply was to identify the background color and recite the memory word as quickly as possible. Despite the irrelevance of one's attitude to the immediate concerns, subjects who presumably possessed a strong object-evaluation association did apparently access their evaluation of the puzzle type upon exposure to the puzzle during the "color perception" task.

Obviously, much more empirical work is needed to test the proposed process model. Equally obvious, however, the process approach does show promise. The research has provided some understanding of the issue of attitude accessibility. At a conceptual level, the critical variable is apparently the strength of the object-evaluation association. Any factor that strengthens this association would seem both to decrease response latency to an attitudinal inquiry and to increase the probability of spontaneously accessing the attitude upon exposure to the object.

As indicated earlier, a process approach is not without its implications for past research that has identified determinants of attitude-behavior consistency. Research examining a process view may further suggest (as in the present case with the manner of attitude formation) how and why these variables moderate the strength of the attitude-behavior relation. As Fazio et al. (in press) note, it is conceivable that each of the attitudinal qualities that have been shown to moderate the strength of the attitude-behavior relation do so as a consequence of their effects upon the strength of the object-evaluation association and the resultant accessibility of the attitude. This speculative suggestion needs to be examined empirically, of course. Nevertheless, the implication is that it may be possible to conceptually integrate what is now a "catalog" of variables known to moderate the attitude-behavior relation.

CONCLUSIONS

Having briefly characterized three generations of research on the attitude-behavior relation, we would like to conclude by suggesting that rather than concentrating exclusively on "When" or "How" questions at any particular point in time, researchers in this (and other) areas would be better advised to ask both sorts of questions simultaneously. In doing so, it is our intuition that the negative consequences that potentially follow from pursuing one question to the exclusion of the other may be more easily avoided. By exclusively pursuing "When" questions, one is likely to achieve a more superficial understanding of the phenomenon than is otherwise possible. Understanding "process," in this case, ought to provide a "deeper" understanding. On the other hand, by exclusively pursuing the more reductionistic "How" question, one runs the risk of losing the social psychological phenomenon that generated the research interest in the first place.[3]

---

[3]Sometimes, of course, the "mediating" process of one phenomenon (e.g., interpersonal expectancy effects) can become a phenomenon in its own right (e.g., nonverbal communication).

As mentioned earlier, it is also our intuition that pursuing both questions simultaneously can lead to positive consequences. For example, knowing the process by which a phenomenon is mediated should be informative about the conditions under which it should occur, and knowing "When" a phenomenon occurs should be informative about "How" it is mediated. In any event, by asking "When" questions, researchers will have generated a body of data which researchers asking "How" questions will want to account for. The converse is true for researchers pursuing "How" questions.

ACKNOWLEDGMENTS

The preparation of this chapter was supported in part by a Social Sciences and Humanities Research Council of Canada Sabbatical Leave fellowship to Mark P. Zanna. Some of the research reported herein was supported by NIMH Grant MH 34227 and NSF Grant BNS 80–23301 to Russell H. Fazio. Correspondence can be sent to Mark P. Zanna, Department of Psychology, University of Waterloo, Waterloo, Ontario, Canada N2L 3G1.

REFERENCES

Abelson, R. P. The psychological status of the script concept. *American Psychologist,* 1981, *36,* 715–729.

Bem, D. J. Self-perception theory. In L. Berkowitz, (Ed.), *Advances in experimental social psychology* (Vol. 6). New York: Academic Press, 1972.

Bem, D. J., & Allen, A. On predicting some of the people some of the time: The search for cross-situational consistencies in behavior. *Psychological Review,* 1974, *81,* 506–520.

Bem, D. J., & Funder, D. C. Predicting more of the people more of the time: Assessing the personality of situations. *Psychological Review,* 1978, *85,* 485–501.

Bruner, J. S. On perceptual readiness. *Psychological Review,* 1957, *64,* 123–152.

Bruner, J. S., & Goodman, C. C. Value and need as organizing factors in perception. *Journal of Abnormal and Social Psychology,* 1947, *42,* 33–44.

Darley, J. M., & Fazio, R. H. Expectancy confirmation processes arising in the social interaction sequence. *American Psychologist,* 1980, *35,* 867–881.

Ellsworth, P. C. When does an experimenter bias? *Behavioral and Brain Sciences,* 1978, *1,* 392–393.

Epstein, S. The stability of behavior: I. On predicting most of the people much of the time. *Journal of Personality and Social Psychology,* 1979, *37,* 1097–1126.

Fazio, R. H., Chen, J., McDonel, E. C., & Sherman, S. J. Attitude accessibility, attitude-behavior consistency, and the strength of the object-evaluation association. *Journal of Experimental Social Psychology,* in press.

Fazio, R. H., Powell, M. C., & Herr, P. M. *Toward a process model of the attitude-behavior relation: Accessing one's attitude upon mere observation of the attitude object.* Unpublished manuscript, Indiana University, 1982.

Fazio, R. H., & Zanna, M. P. Attitudinal qualities relating to the strength of the attitude-behavior relationship. *Journal of Experimental Social Psychology,* 1978, *14,* 398–408.

Fazio, R. H., & Zanna, M. P. Direct experience and attitude-behavior consistency. In L. Berkowitz (Ed.), *Advances in experimental social psychology* (Vol. 14). New York: Academic Press, 1981.

Hastorf, A. H., & Cantril, H. They saw a game: A case study. *Journal of Abnormal and Social Psychology*, 1954, *49*, 129–134.

Higgins, E. T., & King, G. Accessibility of social constructs: Information processing consequence of individual and context variability. In N. Cantor & J. F. Kihlstrom (Eds.), *Cognition, social interaction, and personality*. Hillsdale, N.J.: Lawrence Erlbaum Associates, 1980.

Higgins, E. T., Rholes, W. S., & Jones, C. R. Category accessibility and impression formation. *Journal of Experimental Social Psychology*, 1977, *13*, 141–154.

Katz, D. The functional approach to the study of attitudes. *Public Opinion Quarterly*, 1960, *24*, 163–204.

Kelley, H. H. The warm-cold variable in first impressions of persons. *Journal of Personality*, 1950, *18*, 431–439.

Lambert, W. W., Solomon, R. L., & Watson, P. D. Reinforcement and extinction as factors in size estimation. *Journal of Experimental Psychology*, 1949, *39*, 637–641.

LaPiere, R. T. Attitudes vs. actions. *Social Forces*, 1934, *13*, 230–237.

Lingle, J. H., & Ostrom, T. M. Thematic effects of attitude on the cognitive processing of attitude relevant information. In R. E. Petty, T. M. Ostrom, & T. C. Brock (Eds.), *Cognitive responses to persuasion*. Hillsdale, N.J.: Lawrence Erlbaum Associates, 1980.

Lord, C. G., Ross, L., & Lepper, M. R. Biased assimilation and attitude polarization: The effects of prior theories on subsequently considered evidence. *Journal of Personality and Social Psychology*, 1979, *37*, 2098–2109.

Mischel, W. *Personality and assessment*. New York: Wiley, 1968.

Norman, R. Affective-cognitive consistency, attitudes, conformity, and behavior. *Journal of Personality and Social Psychology*, 1975, *32*, 83–91.

Proshansky, H. M. A projective method for the study of attitudes. *Journal of Abnormal and Social Psychology*, 1943, *38*, 393–395.

Pryor, J. B., Gibbons, F. X., Wicklund, R. A., Fazio, R. H., & Hood, R. Self-focused attention and self-report validity. *Journal of Personality*, 1977, *45*, 514–527.

Regan, D. T., Straus, E., & Fazio, R. H. Liking and the attribution process. *Journal of Experimental Social Psychology*, 1974, *10*, 385–397.

Rosenthal, R., & Rubin, D. B. Interpersonal expectancy effects: The first 345 studies. *Behavioral and Brain Sciences*, 1978, *1*, 377–386.

Sample, J., & Warland, R. Attitude and prediction of behavior. *Social Forces*, 1973, *51*, 292–304.

Schwartz, S. H. Temporal instability as a moderator of the attitude-behavior relationship. *Journal of Personality and Social Psychology*, 1978, *36*, 715–724.

Sears, D. O., & McConahay, J. *The new urban Blacks and the Watts riot*. Boston: Houghton Mifflin, 1973.

Sherif, C. W., Kelly, M., Rodgers, H. L., Sarup, G., & Tittler, B. I. Personal involvement, social judgment, and action. *Journal of Personality and Social Psychology*, 1973, *27*, 311–328.

Smith, M. B., Bruner, J. S., & White, R. W. *Opinions and Personality*. New York: John Wiley and Sons, 1956.

Snyder, M., & Swann, W. B. Hypothesis-testing processes in social interaction. *Journal of Personality and Social Psychology*, 1978, *36*, 1202–1212.

Snyder, M., Tanke, E. D., & Berscheid, E. Social perception and interpersonal behavior: On the self-fulfilling nature of social stereotypes. *Journal of Personality and Social Psychology*, 1977, *35*, 656–666.

Srull, T. K., & Wyer, R. S. The role of category accessibility in the interpretation of information about persons: Some determinants and implications. *Journal of Personality and Social Psychology*, 1979, *37*, 1660–1672.

Whitehead, L. A., Holmes, J. G., & Zanna, M. P. *The effects of arousal and expectations on interpersonal perception*. Paper presented at the annual meeting of the Canadian Psychological Association, Ottawa, June 1978.

Word, C. O., Zanna, M. P., & Cooper, J. The nonverbal mediation of self-fulfilling prophecies in interracial interaction. *Journal of Experimental Social Psychology*, 1974, *10*, 109–120.

Wyer, R. S., & Srull, T. K. The processing of social stimulus information: A conceptual integration. In R. Hastie, E. B. Ebbesen, T. M. Ostrom, R. S. Wyer, D. L. Hamilton, & D. E. Carlston (Eds.), *Person memory: Cognitive bases of social perception*. Hillsdale, N.J.: Lawrence Erlbaum Associates, 1980.

Author Index

Numbers in *italics* denote pages with bibliographic information.

Subject Index